HOW STATESMEN THINK

How Statesmen Think

The Psychology of International Politics

Robert Jervis

PRINCETON UNIVERSITY PRESS

PRINCETON AND OXFORD

Published by Princeton University Press,
41 William Street, Princeton, New Jersey 08540

In the United Kingdom: Princeton University Press,
6 Oxford Street, Woodstock, Oxfordshire OX20 1TR

press.princeton.edu

ISBN 978-0-691-17505-8

ISBN (pbk.) 978-0-691-17644-4

British Library Cataloging-in-Publication Data is available

This book has been composed in Adobe Text Pro and Gotham

10 9 8 7 6 5 4 3 2 1

For Kathe, 50 years and still going strong

CONTENTS

ACKNOWLEDGMENTS

Many authors have said that they have too many debts to fully acknowledge. Since the chapters of this book were originally published as separate essays, this is truly the case here. So at the risk of offending friends and colleagues, let me just thank the members and staff of the Arnold A. Saltzman Institute of War and Peace Studies and especially its administrator, Ingrid Gerstmann, for providing a marvelous environment in which to work and for putting up with seemingly endless requests for assistance. The errors they did not catch are mine alone.

These articles originally appeared in the sources listed below. Permission from the publishers to reprint them is gratefully acknowledged.

1. "Understanding Beliefs," *Political Psychology* 27 (October 2006): 641–63. Republished by permission of John Wiley & Sons.
2. "The Drunkard's Search," in Shanto Iyengar and William McGuire, eds., *Explorations in Political Psychology* (Durham: Duke University Press, 1993), pp. 338–60. All rights reserved. Republished by permission of the publisher.
3. "Representativeness in Foreign Policy Judgments," *Political Psychology* 7 (September 1986): 483–505. Republished by permission of John Wiley & Sons.
4. "Political Implications of Loss Aversion," *Political Psychology* 13, Special Issue: Prospect Theory and Political Psychology (June 1992): 187–204. Republished by permission of John Wiley & Sons.
5. "Signaling and Perception: Drawing Inferences and Projecting Images" in Kristen Renwick Monroe, ed., *Political Psychology* (Mahwah, N.J.: Lawrence Erlbaum, 2002), pp. 293–313. Reproduced by permission of Taylor and Francis Group, LLC, a division of Informa PLC.
6. "Bridges, Barriers, and Gaps: Research and Policy," *Political Psychology* 29 (August 2008): 571–92. Republished by permission of John Wiley & Sons.

7. "Why Intelligence and Policymakers Clash," *Political Science Quarterly* 125 (Summer 2010): 185–204. Reprinted by permission of the Academy of Political Science.

8. "Identity and the Cold War," in Melvyn Leffler and Odd Arne Westad, eds., *The Cambridge History of the Cold War*, vol. II, (Cambridge: Cambridge University Press, 2010), pp. 22–43. Republished by permission of Cambridge University Press.

9. "Deterrence and Perception," *International Security* 7 (Winter 1982–83): 3–30. Republished by permission of MIT Press.

10. "Psychology and Crisis Stability," in Andrew Goldberg, Debra Van Opstal, and James Barkley, eds., *Avoiding the Brink* (London: Brassey's (UK) Ltd., 1990), pp. 17–42.

11. "Domino Beliefs and Strategic Behavior" in Robert Jervis and Jack Snyder, eds., *Dominoes and Bandwagons: Strategic Beliefs and Great Power Competition in the Eurasian Rimland* (New York: Oxford University Press, 1991), pp. 20–36. Republished by permission of Oxford University Press.

12. "Perception, Misperception, and the End of the Cold War" in William C. Wohlforth, ed., *Witnesses to the End of the Cold War* (Baltimore: The Johns Hopkins University Press, 1996), pp. 220–39. © 1996 The Johns Hopkins University Press. Reprinted with permission of Johns Hopkins University Press.

HOW STATESMEN THINK

Introduction

Just as my path to writing *Perception and Misperception in International Politics*[1] was not straightforward, so the way I came to write these essays was haphazard. In almost all cases the precipitating factor was an invitation to contribute to a journal or an edited book, and while these may have been distractions from larger projects on which I was working, they also enabled me to pull together ideas and research that I had been accumulating in files and in my head. It might have made sense for me to continue concentrating on political psychology after writing *Perception and Misperception*, but I was drawn into other topics including the Cold War, the role of nuclear weapons on world politics, debates about appropriate American nuclear strategy, and the mechanisms by which systems work. Political psychology retained its hold on me, however, and while I could not keep up with all the literature, I continued to believe that this approach had a great deal to offer to anyone who wanted to understand how we as individuals think and act, how collectivities develop, and how states react to each other. In this I always was both attracted and repelled by parsimony. Even without close personal contact with scholars like Thomas Schelling, Glenn Snyder, and Kenneth Waltz, I would have sought explanations that involved relatively few moving parts. Not only did I find them aesthetically satisfying, but with my bad memory I could hardly operate without them. But partly because of my fascination with history and the propensity for unfolding politics to surprise me, I also saw a rich and complicated variety in human and international behavior. Political

---

1 Jervis, *Perception and Misperception in International Politics* (Princeton: Princeton University Press, 1976; 2nd ed., 2017).

psychology seemed to hold out the possibility for combining if not reconciling these conflicting impulses.

In the preface to the new edition to *Perception and Misperception* I have outlined what I see as the main developments in the field over the past forty years. Many of them are represented in the essays here, and before introducing them I just want to note a few things about the field.[2] For better and for worse, political psychology is a *they* rather than an *it*. There are many different kinds, proceeding from different assumptions, employing different methodologies, and asking different questions. Some look for commonalities, while others focus on differences among individuals or categories of them. Often there is a stress on pathologies, but parts of the field look for strengths as well. In the past decade new instruments have allowed much better understanding of how the brain works, and so neuroscience is now yielding important if contestable insights. Other studies build on the older tradition of research on cognition and look at how individuals perceive the world and seek to solve problems, while for others the better approach is a continuation of social psychology in the belief that only when we look at the social setting in which individuals are bathed and which they produce by their interactions can we gain a well-rounded appreciation for what is happening.[3]

As a perusal of the main journal in the field, *Political Psychology*, indicates, the focus of most of my colleagues has been on attitudes and voting behavior. Of course there is some overlap between this and my concerns with international politics and leaders' decisions and perceptions, but not only are the individuals involved quite different, but also politics and political choices are much more important to the people I study than they are to the general public. Nevertheless, all of them are human beings faced with a surfeit of information and multiple pressures. So I think that despite many differences, most forms of political psychology share five distinguishing characteristics.

First is the belief that to understand human behavior we have to examine how people think, interpret their environments, and reach decisions. Simple stimulus-response models rarely will do. There are a large variety of stimuli to which people can respond, and they often are quite ambiguous. To turn to international politics, theories that stress the importance of the state's external environment, although extremely useful for some purposes, leave many central questions unanswered. Even when we find common patterns of be-

2 For good surveys of political psychology as it applies to international politics, see Rose McDermott, *Political Psychology in International Relations* (Ann Arbor: University of Michigan Press, 2004), and David Houghton, *Political Psychology: Situations, Individuals, and Cases* (New York: Routledge, 2009).

3 For surveys, see Kristen Monroe, ed., *Political Psychology* (Mahwah, N.J.: Lawrence Erlbaum, 2002) and Leonie Huddy, David Sears, and Jack Levy, eds., *The Oxford Handbook of Political Psychology* 2nd ed. (New York: Oxford University Press, 2013).

havior, they are likely to be fully intelligible only when we understand how the actors see the world. Many consequential foreign policy decisions—including ones that shape the world, such as Britain's decision to fight on after the fall of France in 1940, which is touched on below[4]—are deeply contested, and knowing only the external situation does not tell us why different individuals came to different conclusions, let alone who prevailed. We need to look inside the "black box" of the state to study the goals, beliefs, and perceptions of the decision-makers.

A related way of putting this is to note that standard notions of rationality are not so much incorrect as insufficient to catch either the objectives toward which people strive or the means by which they try to reach them. This does not mean, however, that the perspectives of political psychology and rational choice theory are entirely antithetical. The form of rational choice that is most appropriate to the study of international politics is game theory, which revolves around actors' anticipations of others' behavior and of others' anticipation of their behavior. Game theory cannot put flesh on this skeleton, however, because it cannot speak to how these expectations are formed and what they will be.[5] Political psychology is essential here.

A good deal of the field examines deviations from rationality. In many instances this may not be useful, however, partly because the very notion of rationality may be indeterminate or contested. Indeed, a focus on rationality, or the lack thereof, can lead us into two traps. First, it inclines us to giving points or demerits to the decision-makers in a way that may obscure understanding. Second, we may too easily infer the rationality of decisions from the quality of the outcomes. While we might want to think that greater individual rationality and better decision-making processes lead to better policies, we should not assume that this is the case and, even if the generalization is correct, there are sure to be multiple exceptions.

A second component of political psychology is the search not only for common patterns, but for generalizations that apply only to some groups and that separate them from others, and also for individual idiosyncrasies. Much of the discussion in the subsequent chapters, like a great deal of the field, looks for patterns that, if not universal, are at least widespread. But there is a tension here between such a search and the realization that individual and group differences are important. We must be careful not to overgeneralize from Western experience or experimental subjects.[6] Even within the same

4 See "Why Intelligence and Policymakers Clash," ch 7.

5 This limitation is noted in David Kreps, *Game Theory and Economic Modelling* (New York: Cambridge University Press, 1990), p. 101.

6 Joseph Henrich, Stephen Heine, and Ara Norenzayan, "The Weirdest People in the World," *Behavioral and Brain Sciences* 33 (2010): 61–135. "Weird" here stands for Western, Educated, Industrialized, Rich, and Democratic, with the argument that the people in these societies are

culture, people differ in the ways they process information, draw inferences, and reach decisions. Furthermore, since international politics is interactive, we must also come to grips with the fact that political leaders are less prone than scholars to homogenize people and that they devote serious attention to trying to understand the goals and perceptions of those with whom they are dealing.

Third, political psychology explores the nexus between people's behavior and their self-images and identities.[7] Although much remains to be understood, it is clear that the way individuals and groups view others and the way they view themselves are reciprocally related. Thus people sometimes think badly of others in order to think well of themselves, or see another state as aggressive because they think that their own state is peaceful and therefore that the other's hostility can be explained only by its malign nature. Individuals and collectivities often define themselves as similar to those whom they admire and as different from—and usually better than—those with whom they have conflicts. The other side of this coin is important as well, as people are prone to find differences with those they dislike. The substance of even favorable self-images can vary, as can the importance of the role they play in national behavior. Soviet and American identities during the Cold War illustrate this nicely, which is why I have included a chapter on this subject.

In general, people want to see their own behavior as rational and consistent, which has interesting consequences in the form of self-perception. Contrary to common belief, people lack privileged access to their own motives and calculations, which means that people develop retrospective explanations for their own behavior.[8] Not only are these likely to be built on preferred self-images, but also this tendency to develop retrospective explanations is more than a curiosity because people are likely to let such explanations guide their future behavior.[9] This process can produce a form of path-dependence in

quite different from those in others. Other more fine-grained distinctions are, of course, possible, for example, between cultures that depend on rice and those that cultivate wheat: T. Talhelm, et al., "Large-Scale Psychological Differences Within China Explained by Rich versus Wheat Agriculture," *Science* 344 (May 9, 2014): 603–8.

7 Constructivism has rediscovered the importance of identities and has stressed their collective nature. For a good empirical treatment, see Ted Hopf, *Social Construction of International Politics: Identities and Foreign Policies, Moscow 1955 and 1999* (Ithaca: Cornell University Press, 2002) and *Reconstructing the Cold War: the Early Years, 1945–1958* (New York: Oxford University Press, 2012).

8 For a summary of the literature, see Timothy Wilson, *Strangers to Ourselves; Discovering the Adaptive Unconscious* (Cambridge: Harvard University Press, 2002).

9 Daryl Bem, "Self-Perception Theory," *Advances in Experimental Psychology*, vol. 6 (New York: Academic Press, 1972), pp. 1–62. For an application to international politics see Deborah Larson, *The Origins of Containment: A Psychological Explanation* (Princeton: Princeton University Press, 1985).

which the driver is not the action that the person took, but rather her later explanation for why she did it.

Fourth, as the previous paragraphs indicate, people have emotions as well as cognitions, and indeed, the two often are inextricably combined. Only in the past generation or so have political psychologists rediscovered them, however. Fear, anger, and pride—and perhaps love—are central to international politics, but have not figured prominently in our scholarship. Fear, of course, is the subject of much analysis of politics, especially international politics, but in most cases one could substitute the term "threat perception" without distorting the author's meaning because the emotional connotation of fear is drained from the analysis. Even more strikingly, hatred is rarely mentioned, as though we could understand the sources and consequences of international conflict without creating space for the impulse that is so palpable throughout history. Fortunately, political psychologists who analyze international politics are now exploring the subject, [10] and several of the essays in this book seek to rectify the omission of emotions from *Perception and Misperception*.

The final essential element of political psychology is an appreciation of the limits of a priori reasoning and a deep commitment to empirical research. Abstract theorizing is crucial, but looking with care at cases and making relevant comparisons is needed not only to probe our generalizations and theories and to elucidate causal processes, but also to develop ideas that we can bring to other cases and sources of evidence. While many approaches to the study of politics take for granted actors' preferences and ideas about how to reach them, these are often the most important parts of the explanation for behavior, and it is doubtful that we can understand them without employing political psychology.[11] Although political psychology should not be confused with clinical psychology, it does tell us that we have to observe and listen to people.

---

10 For an overview, see Rose McDermott, "The Feeling of Rationality," *Perspectives on Politics* 2 (December 2004): 691–706. Also see my preface to the new edition of *Perception and Misperception* (2017); Neta Crawford, "The Passion of World Politics: Propositions on Emotion and Emotional Relationships," *International Security* 24 (Spring 2000): 116–56; Jonathan Mercer, "Emotional Beliefs," *International Organization* 64 (Winter 2010): 1–31; Mercer, "Emotion and Strategy in the Korean War," *International Organization* 67 (Spring 2013): 221–52. For good discussions of emotions by historians, see Barbara Keys, "Kissinger, the Emotional Statesman," *Diplomatic History* 35 (Summer 2011): 587–609; Frank Costigliola, "'I React Intensely to Everything': Russia and the Frustrated Emotions of George F. Kennan, 1933–1958," *Journal of American History* 102 (March 2016): 1075–101.

11 See, for example, Christopher Achen and Duncan Snidal, "Rational Deterrence Theory and Comparative Case Studies," *World Politics* 41 (January 1989): 143–69, and my reply, "Rational Deterrence: Theory and Evidence," *World Politics* 41 (January 1989): 143–207

When political psychology is applied to international politics, as it is here, and especially when we explore misperception, we must realize that there is an almost inescapable tendency to look at cases of conflict, surprise, and error. When things go wrong, they not only attract the actors' attention, they also attract ours. How many studies of American policy toward Vietnam would there have been if the United States had decided not to fight there (and if this had not led to disasters elsewhere)? The tendency to look mainly at cases where things go wrong makes the analysis of causation difficult as we lack comparisons to cases with better results and may attribute the failure to decision-making factors that are constants rather than variables. These factors, of course, can be important to understanding how people behave, but may not discriminate between good decisions and bad ones. So we have to be careful to distinguish when we are arguing that certain perceptual processes are common and when we are claiming that they are likely to lead actors astray. The other side of this coin is that concentrating on errors and conflict (and of course the two are not the same) can give us an unbalanced picture of world politics and the skill of leaders. Many if not most of the cases I and others in the field draw upon are ones where errors are made, the states do not communicate well, and each participant sees the situations differently (what I call the "*Rashomon* effect" after the famous Japanese short story and movie). But we need to know about more successes, such as the way in which during the Vietnam War the United States and China accurately communicated their "red lines" and correctly interpreted each other's signals.[12]

Plan of the Book

The twelve essays are divided into four sections. The first presents a broad overview of key concepts and arguments in political psychology, the second discusses two of the important heuristics and biases that have received a great deal of attention: representativeness and Prospect Theory. The next section zeros in on applications to international politics, and the closing part looks in more detail at beliefs and perceptions of particular relevance to issues of national security. The lines between these topics are blurry and alternative categorizations are possible, but I think this grouping is relatively coherent.

All the essays have been lightly edited to reduce repetitions, to remove inessential material to keep this collection to a reasonable length, to change the verb tense of sentences to take account for the fact that the Cold War is over, and in a few places to add some new material and update references.

---

12 James Hershberg and Chen Jian, "Reading and Warning the Likely Enemy: China's Signals to the United States about Vietnam in 1965," *International History Review* 27 (March 2005): 47–84.

"Prospect Theory: The Political Implications of Loss Aversion," includes some material from my "The Implications of Prospect Theory for Human Nature."[13] "Political Psychology Research and Theory: Bridges and Barriers" has had more material deleted. In its original form,[14] it was written in honor of Alexander George, a leading student of political psychology and international politics. While I have retained a focus on George's scholarship, I have directed the discussion to the general issues and arguments rather than his specific contributions.

"Psychology and Crisis Stability" and "Domino Beliefs" focus on the Cold War, and I have added some material to the former to show the continuing relevance of the problem and have deleted some material on problems of Soviet-American postures. I also deleted material from the latter essay that evaluated the validity of the domino theory and the circumstances under which it was most likely to apply, because this analysis is less relevant to political psychology. "Perception, Misperception, and the End of the Cold War" was written for the proceedings of a conference of Soviet and American officials who participated in these events, and although I have retained the focus on the contributions of these people, I have removed some material that made sense only within the context of what was said there.

It may be helpful to say a little more about each of the essays.

"Understanding Beliefs," which begins the collection, presents some of the arguments that are applied in the later chapters. Drawing on a classic book in political psychology, *Opinions and Personality* by M. Brewster Smith, Jerome Bruner, and Robert White,[15] I argue that expectations on the one hand and personal and political needs on the other are the two main sources of political beliefs and perceptions. As psychologists discuss them, the former is cold, cognitive, and unmotivated and the latter is hot and motivated. "The Drunkard's Search" discusses how both kinds of biases lead to looking at information that is most readily available, easiest to process, and most understandable rather than to probing more deeply for what is more illuminating and diagnostic. Although the story about the drunkard looking for his keys under the lamp post because the light is better there is a joke, we find it funny because it is all too true.

One of the short-cuts or heuristics that psychologists have isolated is the tendency for people to make judgments on the basis of representativeness, which is the extent to which an instance or case resembles a stereotype while

13 "The Implications of Prospect Theory for Human Nature," *Political Psychology* 25 (April 2004): 163–76

14 "Bridges, Barriers, and Gaps: Research and Policy," *Political Psychology* 29 (2008): 571–92.

15 M. Brewster Smith, Jerome Bruner, Robert White, *Opinions and Personality* (New York: Wiley, 1956).

downplaying if not ignoring the frequency with which the stereotype is present within the relevant population (what is known as the base rate). When you hear hoof beats, think of horses, not zebras, medical students are told when learning about diagnosis. Good advice, and the reason it is given is that without special reminders people will ignore the importance of bearing in mind the actual frequency of phenomena. In "Representativeness, Foreign Policy Judgments, and Theory-Driven Perceptions,"[16] I argue that while representativeness sometimes characterizes perceptions of politics, when the base rate is seen by the person as part of a causal account of why things happen as they do, it is overweighted rather than underweighted because it establishes expectations that influence the way new information is interpreted.

Probably the best known and intriguing psychological theory that has been developed since the publication of *Perception and Misperception* is Prospect Theory. Like the representativeness heuristic and many other insights that I and others have drawn upon, it was developed by Daniel Kahneman and Amos Tversky, and the former received the Nobel Prize in economics for it (Tversky having died before the award was made). In brief, the theory argues that while people are generally risk-averse when it comes to the possibility of making gains, they will accept risks to avoid losses, and that their behavior is influenced by whether the situation is framed in terms of a possibility of making gains or the converse probability of avoiding losses. "Prospect Theory: The Political Implications of Loss Aversion" asks what this theory leads us to expect about political behavior. Economists have been challenged and tantalized because Prospect Theory argues that people violate standard postulates of rationality; for students of international politics it opens up important lines of inquiry about when and why states engage in risky behavior. Among other things, it indicates that when each of two opposing states believes itself to be in the realm of losses war is especially likely.

Political psychology speaks to important issues of the theory—or theories—of international politics. In "Signaling and Perception" I bring together two strands of literature that have been kept separate, but actually depend on each other. My first book, *The Logic of Images in International Relations*,[17] developed and applied abstract theories of signaling, separating signals from indices, explaining how actors used them to project desired images, and analyzing the logical status of kinds of actions for distinguishing between honest and deceptive behaviors. Building on this work, Michael Spence developed related concepts that have had great influence on economics (earning him the Nobel

---

16 The essay was originally titled "Representativeness in Foreign Policy Judgments"; the one I use here gives a better sense of the argument.

17 *The Logic of Images in International Relations* (Princeton: Princeton University Press, 1970; 2nd ed, New York: Columbia University Press, 1989).

Prize) and political science.[18] But neither Spence nor I paid a great deal of attention to how various categories of verbal and nonverbal behavior actually were perceived. In this essay, I stress the need to do so and to unify theories of signaling and theories of perception, although here I only begin the task.

Political psychology not only seeks to help build theory, in many formulations it also shares with the discipline of social psychology out of which it grew the desire to make this a more just and peaceful world. Building on the path-breaking work of Alexander George, "Political Psychology Research and Theory: Bridges and Barriers" explores the tensions as well as the synergies between these two objectives, notes the psychological and political barriers inhibiting the application of psychological research to foreign policy decision making, and outlines some areas in which our findings might have a receptive audience.

Some of these themes are approached from a different angle in the next essay, "Why Intelligence and Policymakers Clash." This research grew out of the postmortems I did for the CIA on the intelligence failures surrounding the Iranian Revolution of 1978–79 and the assessment that Iraq had active programs to develop weapons of mass destruction before the 2003 invasion.[19] The main tasks and dominant needs of policymakers differ from those of intelligence organizations. Most centrally, the former have to act. For both political and psychological reasons, they must have confidence, benefit from being able to present multiple reasons for pursuing a course of action, and need to believe that they can succeed. At its best, intelligence brings out alternative interpretations and highlights the ways in which policies can go wrong. Even with the best will in the world, this is a difficult mix. Examining it helps us understand the ways in which security policies are formed and how foreign policy outcomes are the product of contested ways in which information is processed, inferences about the state's external environment are developed, and policies are formulated, sustained, and altered.

A great deal of work in the past decade has stressed the importance of national identity. Neither the psychological underpinnings nor the empirical manifestations have been sufficiently explored, however. In "Identity and the Cold War" I look at how Soviet and American identities affected their relations, especially in seeing the other side as inevitably hostile. But the symmetry is not perfect here as Soviet identity was more deeply tied to beliefs about the danger posed by the capitalist world than American identity was in its perception of the threat posed by communism, which was one reason why the

18 Michael Spence, *Market Signaling: Informational Transfer in Hiring and Related Screening Processes* (Cambridge: Harvard University Press, 1974).

19 *Why Intelligence Fails: Lessons from the Iranian Revolution and the Iraq War* (Ithaca: Cornell University Press, 2013).

United States was able to capitalize on the Sino-Soviet split and why the end of the Cold War reinforced rather than threatened the American image of itself.

The final set of four essays narrows the focus to the intersection of political psychology and national security issues. Most of the analysis draws its examples from the 1930s and the Cold War, but the arguments apply more generally. Deterrence theory comes in many variants and often baroque elaborations. One obvious point is generally given short shrift, however: that the effect of policies designed to deter others depends on how the others would perceive them. It is all well and good to talk about credibility, punishment, and reward in the abstract, but as they work out in the real world they depend on what the targets value, believe, and think about the state's behavior. To take just one example, in the fall of 1969, Richard Nixon tried to frighten the Soviet Union into putting pressure on North Vietnam by staging a nuclear alert. Unfortunately for him, however, the Soviets hardly noticed.[20] In "Deterrence and Perception" I explore many of the ways threats can be less potent or more potent than a priori reasoning would lead us to expect, drawing most heavily on British beliefs on the damage that German bombers could inflict in a war. For a variety of reasons, including German deception, not only the British public but British political leaders of all political persuasions overestimated the threat and so increased German coercive capabilities. Perceptions, not the reality, mattered.

Deterrence stresses the importance of credible threats in keeping the peace. But, as Schelling pointed out as he develops this theory but others have sometimes neglected, this endeavor simultaneously requires states to make credible promises not to strike if the other side reciprocally does not attack. There was a real danger, Schelling realized, that "the reciprocal fear of surprise attack" could produce instability in a crisis and a war that no one wanted.[21] Dealing with this problem became a cornerstone of American defense policy and underpinned arms control negotiations[22] but little attention was paid to the impact on stability of how people process information, draw inferences on what others are likely to do, and analyze their own alternatives. This is the subject of the next essay, "Psychology and Crisis Stability." If the end of the Cold War has reduced the saliency of inadvertent war, it has not eliminated it, either between the United States and Russia or between other nuclear-armed rivals, especially India and Pakistan.

---

20 William Burr and Jeffrey Kimball, *Nixon's Nuclear Specter: The Secret Alert of 1969, Madman Diplomacy, and the Vietnam War* (Lawrence: University of Kansas Press, 2015).

21 Thomas Schelling, *The Strategy of Conflict* (Cambridge: Harvard University Press, 1960), ch. 9.

22 I have discussed this in "Arms Control, Stability, and the Causes of War," *Daedalus* 120 (Winter 1991).

If crisis instability was one of the main American fears during the Cold War, another was that minor defeats would ramify throughout the entire system, just as one falling domino could knock over many others. The Munich analogy was central to American policy and remains important today, as much of the current debate between those who urge strategic restraint and those who advocate deeper security involvement turns on whether local defeats and instabilities will ramify or remain contained. In "Domino Beliefs" I explore the characteristics and workings of the belief that this kind of positive feedback is relevant in world politics.

It is perhaps fitting to end this collection with an essay that brings psychology to bear on how the Cold War ended. Many of us who lived through it doubted that this conflict would ever come to an end, and the fear that if it did it would do so through all-out war was a dominating feature of this era. Images of the other side as deeply hostile and beliefs that concessions, rather than being reciprocated, would lead to perceptions of weakness seemed unlikely to disappear. "Perception, Misperception, and the End of the Cold War," explores how the momentous change took place. This returns us to the basic argument of this volume that a full understanding of politics requires us to probe how people perceive their environments, draw inferences about what others are like and how they will respond to alternative actions the state could take, and reach judgments. The Cold War has ended, but not only theorizing but also the analytical and policy problems we continue to face call for the application and further development of political psychology.

PART I

Political Psychology

1

Understanding Beliefs

The question with which M. Brewster Smith, Jerome Bruner, and Robert White began their classic *Opinions and Personality* fifty years ago is still appropriate today, albeit with more linguistic sensitivity toward gender: "Of what use to man are his opinions?"[1] I think their answer was essentially correct as well: People adopt opinions not only to understand the world, but also to meet the psychological and social needs to live with themselves and others. I want to use this basic insight to examine some of the puzzles in what people believe. Since I specialize in international politics, I will draw most of my examples from that realm but do not think that our findings are limited to this arena.[2]

1 Brewster Smith, Jerome Bruner, and Robert White, *Opinions and Personality* (New York: Wiley, 1956), p.1; also see Alice Eagly and Shelly Chaiken, "Attitude Structure and Function," pp. 269–322 in Daniel Gilbert, Susan Fiske, and Gardner Lindzey, eds., *The Handbook of Social Psychology* (New York: Oxford University Press, 1998), pp. 303–9; Alexander George. Comment on "Opinions, Personality, and Political Behavior," *American Political Science Review* 52 (March 1958): 18–26; Kenneth Hammond, *Human Judgment and Social Policy* (New York: Oxford University Press, 1996), ch. 11; Daniel Katz, "The Functional Approach to the Study of Attitudes," *Public Opinion Quarterly* 24 (Winter 1960): 163–204; Irving Sarnoff and Daniel Katz, "The Motivational Bases of Attitude Change," *Journal of Abnormal and Social Psychology* 49 (January 1954): 115–24; Phillip Tetlock, "Social-Functionalist Metaphors for Judgment and Choice: The Politician, Theologian and Prosecutor," *Psychological Review* 109 (July 2002): 451–72.

2 My concern is with beliefs that matter a greater deal to the individual and so I will put aside discussion of non-attitudes and the stability of political beliefs in the general public. For more information on this latter topic, see Phillip Converse, "The Nature of Belief Systems in Mass Publics," pp. 206–26 in David Apter, ed., *Ideology and Discontent* (New York: Free Press, 1964); John Zaller, *The Nature and Origins of Mass Opinion* (New York: Cambridge University Press, 1992).

Beliefs and Related Concepts

There are terminological and conceptual thickets surrounding the words we use here. I will focus on beliefs partly about facts but more about cause-and-effect relationships. How do things work? Why do others act as they do? What will be the consequences of my own behavior? Definitions of related terms differ, and the notions of beliefs, opinions, attitudes, ideas, and even policy preferences overlap and interweave. Attitudes and opinions involve a strong evaluative component. Indeed, this dimension often dominates, as when people say they have a negative attitude toward radical Islam even if they know little about it. But when an attitude is different from a purely subjective taste, it also involves causal claims. For example, I abhor radical Islam because I think it produces oppression and violence toward other religions.

OVERTONES OF BELIEFS

Although my focus is on beliefs in the sense of what people think about causes and effects, it is noteworthy that the term is used in other senses as well, and I think this tells us that equating beliefs with scientific or social scientific knowledge would be limiting. Although political psychologists rarely deal with statements like the following, they are important to people's lives: "I believe in God." "I believe I am falling in love." "I believe that it is vital to win the war in Iraq." Even this abbreviated list illustrates three things. First, beliefs can refer to inner states as well as outer realities. We often interpret our feelings and seek to understand exactly what it is that we believe. Second, beliefs and statements about beliefs can be exhortatory. To say "I believe we must do this" is to urge others—and ourselves— on. Statements like "I believe my views will prevail" combine these two elements.

The third and perhaps most important point is that many beliefs have a strong element of commitment and faith, even when religion is not involved. Scientists say that they believe in their theories or findings, and this often means not only that they have confidence in their validity, but that their claims are important to them and that it is important that others accept them as well. When people talk about "beliefs to live by," moral and empirical considerations are fused. When people say that they believe that democracy can be brought to the Middle East and that doing so will make this a better world, they are combining how they see the evidence and what their values and desires lead them to think should and must be true. In the early 1950s CBS's lead commentator, Edward R. Murrow, broadcast a series of five-minute episodes entitled *This I Believe* in which famous and everyday people explained their outlooks and personal philosophies in an attempt to solidify American faith in their country in the face of the dual challenges of communism and McCarthyism. The other side of this coin is revealed by a doctor's response to his critics' rejection of his findings that a controversial treatment helped many heart attack victims: he said his detractors suffered from "emotional disbelief."[3]

One can argue that this shows only that the word "belief" has multiple meanings and that we would be better off separating them and attaching different labels to each. I suspect, however, that the common term may be pointing to something deeper, which is the inextricable role of emotion in sensible thought. Over the past decade or so, psychologists and political psychologists have come to see (or to "believe"?) that a sharp separation between cognition and affect is impossible and that a person who embodied pure rationality, undisturbed by emotion, would be a monster if she were not an impossibility.[4]

Investigating Beliefs

We want to understand why people believe what they do, whether these beliefs are warranted by the available evidence, and whether they are correct. Although these tasks are different, we often fuse them. Thus we often think that correct beliefs require no explanation, implicitly assuming that they are self-evident and follow directly from commonly available evidence. But we often believe as much in the face of evidence as because of it, and in some of these cases we turn out to be correct. In other cases, correct beliefs may be adopted to smooth our relations with others or to increase our psychological comfort.

INCORRECT BELIEFS MAY BE SINCERE AND SENSIBLE

It is then tempting, but a mistake, to seek to explain correct beliefs in a way fundamentally different from the way we explain incorrect ones.[5] Nevertheless, people are prone to associate faulty reasoning processes with incorrect

---

3 Quoted in Nicholas Wade, "The Uncertain Science of Growing Heart Cells," *New York Times*, March 14, 2005.

4 For good summaries, see Rose McDermott, "The Feeling of Rationality: The Meaning of Neuroscientific Advances for Political Science," *Perspectives on Politics* 2 (December 2004): 691–706; George Marcus, "Emotions in Politics," *Annual Review of Political Science* 3 (June 2000): 221–50; George Marcus, "The Psychology of Emotion and Politics," pp. 182–221 in David Sears, Leone Huddy, and Robert Jervis, eds., *Oxford Handbook of Political Psychology* (New York: Oxford University Press, 2003); Robert Zajonc. "Emotions," pp. 591–634 in Daniel Gilbert, Susan Fiske, and Gartner Lindzey, eds., *The Handbook of Social Psychology* (Boston: McGraw-Hill, 1998); my own views can be found in the preface to the second edition of *Perception and Misperception in International Politics*, 2nd ed. (Princeton: Princeton University Press, 2017; originally published 1976).

5 Larry Laudan, *Progress and Its Problems: Toward a Theory of Scientific Growth* (Berkeley: University of California Press, 1977).

beliefs even when more careful analysis would indicate that this comforting association does not hold. Given the complexity and ambiguity of our world, it is unfortunately true that beliefs for which a good deal of evidence can be mustered often turn out to be mistaken.[6]

In parallel, we often have difficulty taking seriously beliefs with which we disagree. This is not only a mistake, it is also disrespectful of the people we are trying to understand. When someone believes something that we cannot, we often ask whether she is a fool or a knave. This is obviously most likely to be the case with beliefs that are now unpopular. Thus because most academics believe that it was a mistake for the United States to have fought in Vietnam, they cannot believe that a sensible person could have accepted the validity of the domino theory.[7] Rather than explore what evidence the people who held these beliefs pointed to, what theories of politics were implicitly evoked, and why a more complacent view did not seem compelling, these academics seek hidden motives and psychological pressures. These may indeed have been present, but the fact that most of us now find the domino theory disastrously incorrect should not lead us to conclude it was not central to decision-makers.

Grasping others' incorrect beliefs also poses severe difficulties for contemporary observers. Thus it was very hard for American leaders to believe that Japan would attack Pearl Harbor, even though they (partly) expected an attack against the Philippines. Knowing that Japan could not win this war made the Japanese beliefs inaccessible. During the run-up to the war in Iraq it was similarly impossible for outsiders to see that Saddam Hussein was more afraid of his generals, his people, and Iran than he was of the United States, with the result that everyone, even opponents of the war, concluded that his refusal to fully cooperate with the UN showed that he was developing weapons of mass destruction (WMD).

It is especially hard to appreciate the beliefs that upheld views that are now morally unacceptable, for example, those supporting slavery. It is then very tempting to attribute the beliefs to economic interests, which spares us the difficulty and the pain of reconstructing a worldview in which slavery appeared appropriate, effective, and beneficial for all. The line between understanding and approving is too thin to make this a comfortable task.

AMBIVALENCE AND UNAWARENESS

It may be hard to tell what a person believes because she is ambivalent, confused, or contradictory. We sometimes say that a person does not know her

---

6 For an application to intelligence, see Jervis, "Why Intelligence and Policymakers Clash," in this volume.

7 For further discussion, see Jervis, "Domino Beliefs," in this volume.

own mind, and we often half believe something, or simultaneously believe it and do not. I think this was the case with whether Richard Nixon and Henry Kissinger believed that the peace agreement with North Vietnam could be sustained. They were under no illusions that the North had given up its commitment to take over the South. With its troops already in the South and a large army on its own territory, the North could be restrained only by the fear that blatantly breaking the agreement would call up an American military response, most obviously a resumption of bombing. When the agreement was signed, Nixon and Kissinger told themselves, each other, and the South Vietnamese that this threat was credible enough to prevent major North Vietnamese violations, and that if did not avert aggression from the North, the Americans would carry it out. While it is impossible to be certain whether Nixon and Kissinger believed what they were saying, my guess is that what they were expressing was something between a hope and an expectation. They partly believed it, or believed it on some days but not others, or believed it with some probability but less than certainty. A related way of thinking was revealed by the diary entry of a top Foreign Office official after Hitler seized the non-German parts of Czechoslovakia: "I always said that, as long as Hitler *could pretend* he was incorporating Germans in the Reich, we *could pretend* that he had a case."[8]

Further problems are created by the fact that the driving beliefs may be so widely shared they need never be expressed, at least not in a way that is connected with specific actions. Because they are rarely analyzed by the person, we often call these beliefs "assumptions," and we need to excavate them, as James Joll did in his essay "1914: The Unspoken Assumptions," in which he argues that specific beliefs say less about the origins of World War I than does the prevailing intellectual climate that was built on Social Darwinism, honor, and other ideas that the leaders had absorbed in school.[9] In other cases, the driving beliefs may not be voiced because they are disreputable or illegitimate. Thus a search of even confidential or private documents will rarely reveal an American decision-maker saying that he favored overthrowing a Third World regime in order to benefit American corporations or further his own domestic political interests. Although the person will not express these views, here he or she perhaps is aware of them.

In a third category of cases even this is not true (and one might therefore question whether the ideas that motivate us should be called beliefs at all). It is not only those schooled in psychoanalysis who argue that we do not

8 David Dilks, *The Diaries of Sir Alexander Cadogan* (New York: G. P. Putnam, 1972). p. 161, emphasis added.

9 James Joll, "1914: The Unspoken Assumptions," pp. 307–28 in H. W. Koch, ed., *The Origins of the First World War* (London: Macmillan, 1972).

understand how we reach many of our conclusions because much cognitive processing is beyond the reach of conscious thought.[10] The reasons we give for many of our beliefs are sincere in that we do believe them, but these are stories we tell ourselves as well as others because we understand as little about what is driving our beliefs as we do about what is driving others. To extend the previous example, someone who was in fact moved to favor military intervention because of economic of political interests might not be aware of this because of the strong societal norms of putting national security interests first. All we can do is infer operative beliefs from behavior, often by arguing that the explicit reasons given are implausible. As I noted earlier, this is how many scholars explain the U.S. policy in Vietnam. It is not surprising that arguments in this vein will be particularly contentious. Those who use ego-dynamics may look for Freudian slips, and Marxists will look for benefits accruing to large corporations, but it is hard to get evidence that will carry weight with people who approach these questions from different perspectives. Skepticism here, like that called up by the concept of false consciousness, is warranted but does not do away with the problem that people's self-knowledge is sharply limited.

Understand Beliefs

Understanding beliefs means trying to fathom what caused them and what consequences they had. We are interested in whether beliefs are powerful in the sense of producing behavior and autonomous in the sense of not directly following from other factors. To return to the Smith, Bruner, and White formulation, this means trying to determine the relative weights of reality appraisal, personal needs, and social adjustment. The latter two are similar in that they serve purposes other than seeking an accurate view of the world, and we can refer to them together as a functional explanation because they explain the person's beliefs by the social and psychological functions that they serve. This is not to say that the line between appraisal and functionality is always clear or to deny that many of the ways in which we try to make sense of our world combine these approaches. Susan Clancy's fascinating and empathetic but not credulous study of why people come to believe that they have been abducted by space aliens shows how this belief not only renders

---

10 Richard Nisbett, and Timothy Wilson, "Telling More Than We Can Know: Verbal Reports on Mental Processes," *Psychological Review* 84 (March 1977): 231–59; Timothy Wilson, *Strangers to Ourselves* (Cambridge: Harvard University Press, 2002). Arguments that people's attitudes toward political issues and candidates develop through "online processing" in which the sources of the beliefs quickly become lost to the person fit with these findings: see, for example, Kathleen McGraw, Milton Lodge, and Patrick Stroh, "An Impression-Driven Model of Candidate Evaluation," *American Political Science Review* 83 (June 1989): 309–26.

coherent what was previously confused, but also provides an explanation that, while disturbing on one level, gives a meaning that restores a form of integrity to the person's life.[11] One chapter is titled "Why Would I Want to Believe It?" which indicates both that people ward off attacks on their beliefs by claiming there could be no ulterior (or interior) motive and that there can be quite different but reinforcing reasons for holding beliefs.

CONSISTENCY AND EXCESS REASONS

It is often hard to tell what beliefs are causal, not only in separating statements the person knows are false from what she "really" believes, but in the sense of determining which of a plethora of justifications played the largest role in guiding behavior. In examining the beliefs that precede action, we often find claims that contradict or are in some tension with one another and see people generating more arguments for the conclusions than would be necessary to produce them. While these two phenomena are in one sense opposites, the first revealing inconsistencies and the second displaying excess reasons or belief overkill, they have common psychological roots in the conflicting needs of reality appraisal and serving psychological, social, and political functions. In the end, definitive conclusions are often beyond reach, but the exploration of why this is so is itself illuminating, as we can see in the beliefs leading to World War I.

The story, especially on the German side, at first seems straightforward. The war was essentially a preventive one. German leaders felt that an eventual war was inevitable, that Germany could win it at a relatively low price if it were fought in 1914, and that growing Russian military strength meant that Germany would lose or at least greatly suffer if the war was postponed. At bottom there remains much to this argument; indeed, I do not think there is a better one-sentence explanation of the war. But there are problems.[12]

We find forms of troubling inconsistency. One is temporal: these beliefs were quite long-lasting yet did not produce war prior to 1914. Part of the reason for the different effect is that events in the preceding years deepened the beliefs and created a sense of urgency, compounded by the fact that the assassination of Archduke Franz Ferdinand allowed Germany to mobilize both its Austro-Hungarian ally and its own domestic opinion. But I do not think this entirely disposes of the problem since the basic German geostrategic problem was not new.

11 Susan Clancy, *Abducted: How People Come to Believe They Were Kidnapped by Aliens* (Cambridge: Harvard University Press, 2005).

12 A good summary is Holger Herwig, "Germany," pp. 150–87 in Richard Hamilton and Holger Herwig, eds., *The Origins of World War I* (Cambridge: Cambridge University Press, 2003).

There are other forms of inconsistency as well. German policy in July 1914 had as its preferred outcome not war with Russia, but the Russian abandonment of its Serbian client, perhaps because Russia itself feared being deserted by Britain and France if it fought. The problem is not so much that such a Russian retreat was unlikely (German leaders recognized this) as it is that this "solution" would not have dealt with the fundamental threat of growing Russian strength. Indeed, if Russia had been forced to back down it probably would have stepped up its rearmament, and even if the bonds between Russia, Britain, and France were severed, there was no reason to believe that this would have been permanent. At best, Germany's nightmare would be postponed, not eliminated. This means that it is hard to square German hopes for peace with the beliefs that are posited to be central for the decision to go to war. Another inconsistency appears in the beliefs themselves. Although many statements support the position that the decision-makers thought that the war would be short, there were discordant notes. The Russian defense minister realized that signing the mobilization orders might be sentencing his country to death; the British Foreign Secretary famously said at dawn of the day Britain went to war, "The lamps are going out all over Europe; we shall not see them lit again in our life-time"; and the Chief of the German General Staff declared that war "would destroy the culture of almost the whole of Europe for decades to come."[13] Furthermore, Germany respected Holland's neutrality in order to permit the entry of supplies from neutrals, and most German leaders were deeply disturbed when Great Britain joined the war. These responses would not make sense if the war was expected to end quickly.

In casting doubt on what the decision-makers believed, these inconsistencies open up four lines of inquiry. First, it can be extremely difficult to determine what people really believe. We might want to rule this a metaphysical question that we should not ask. But then we would have to abandon much of the notion of beliefs.

The second point shows why it would be a mistake to put aside the question of what was believed: knowing whether German leaders thought the war would be long or short points us toward very different explanations of their behavior. If they thought a war would be short and victorious, it would be seen as relatively cheap, which means that any number of impulses could have produced war. But if the war was expected to be long (and therefore very costly), only the strongest motivation would have been sufficient to overcome the obvious reasons not to fight. In the same way, the initial scholarship on the Vietnam War assumed that American decision-makers believed that they could win quite quickly. This focused people on why the officials were so

13 Quoted in Annika Mombauer, *Helmuth von Moltke and the Origins of the First World War* (New York: Cambridge University Press, 2001), p. 202; also see p. 206.

wrong (the "quagmire theory"), with less attention paid to the motives to fight because the decision seemed relatively easy if the price tag was believed to be low. But when the *Pentagon Papers* revealed that the leaders had fairly accurate perceptions of the costs and risks, the question to be answered was not why they so misperceived the likely course of the war, but what goals and beliefs were so pressing as to make them fight in the face of such daunting prospects.

A third line of inquiry is whether we can explain the contradiction among the beliefs in 1914 by reality appraisal or whether they were strongly functional. I will discuss this general topic in more detail later, but the obvious point is that holding to discrepant beliefs allowed decision-makers to keep in touch with the possibility that turned out to be the case without having to abandon the belligerent policy that they felt was necessary. They *had* to believe that the war would be short. To have believed otherwise would have put them in an intolerable position, because if they could *not* fight, they would have had to alter many of their policies, beliefs, and values. The historian Elie Halevy argues that the diplomatic and strategic interconnections linking the European states were so tight and obvious that "everyone knew, *who chose to know*" that an Austrian attack on Serbia would bring in all the other continental powers.[14] But the phrase I have italicized is a telling one—people can indeed choose not to pursue knowledge when they think that knowing certain things would generate terrible pressures.

A final question in this series is about the consistency of people's beliefs. Scholars greatly value consistency. Consistency to them means rigor, logic, and rationality; its lack implies error if not moral weakness. As I will discuss below, although decision-makers do feel pressures for consistency on some occasions, they do not appear to put it among their highest values. Perhaps because they are not trained to seek great rigor, perhaps because they see life as full of contradictions, and perhaps because they appreciate the extent to which seeming inconsistencies can bring political success, they do contradictory things and hold contradictory beliefs. When Franklin D. Roosevelt famously said, "I am a juggler, and I never let my right hand know what my left hand does,"[15] he was only being more explicit than most politicians. So when we look at his policy toward Japan before Pearl Harbor it may not be surprising that in November 1941 he seemed to believe the following: the United States should enter the war as soon as possible; Germany not Japan was the main enemy; the United States was so much stronger than Japan that the latter

14 Élie Halévy, *The Era of Tyrannies* (New York: New York University Press, 1966), pp. 232–33.

15 Quoted in Warren Kimball, *The Juggler: Franklin Roosevelt as Wartime Statesman* (Princeton: Princeton University Press, 1991), p. 7.

would not dare attack; economic sanctions against Japan might not force that country to comply with American demands; Japan was likely to attack the Philippines (an American possession) in the belief that the United States would otherwise use it as a base to interdict Japanese attacks on British Malaya and the Dutch East Indies; but Japan would not attack Pearl Harbor.[16]

At times, inconsistencies can be used to uncover the beliefs that are driving a person's stance. This is especially true when people claim to be following a principled belief but change their conclusions depending on the principle's substantive implications. For example, at first glance it would seem that American conservatives uphold the principles of decentralization, Federalism, and states' rights, and that liberals want to give more power to the central government. But each group has no difficulty endorsing the "wrong" position when it leads to the "right" outcome. Thus conservatives favor taking class-action suits out of the hands of state courts, pass legislation that removes much of the state and local control over education, and prevent states from permitting assisted suicide or the medicinal use of marijuana. Liberals, being no more consistent, shamelessly call for states' rights in these instances. Conservatives generally see genes as playing a large role in human behavior, but make an exception for sexual orientation, which liberals, who usually stress the role of the environment, see as fixed. In the foreign policy area, beliefs about whether a policy of "engagement" will be efficacious are almost always driven not by general beliefs about cause-and-effect relationships, but rather by how deeply the person abhors the regime in question. During the Cold War liberals urged engagement with Eastern Europe but isolation for South Africa, while conservatives took the opposite position.

If it is sometimes difficult to analyze the causal role of beliefs because they are inconsistent, in other cases people adduce more beliefs than are necessary to produce the behavior. The war in Iraq provides a nice example. George W. Bush and his colleagues apparently believed these key points: Saddam had a large and growing WMD program; there were close links between his regime and al Qaeda; the war would be quick; political reconstruction would be relatively easy; and liberation would light the path for the rest of the Middle East. This is odd. If a nuclear-armed Iraq could not have been deterred from coercing its neighbors, then this menace to American interests was sufficient to have triggered war. If Saddam was harboring al Qaeda, this by itself could have led to an invasion, as it did in Afghanistan. Had the prospects for establishing democracy in Iraq been great and likely to trigger positive domino effects throughout the region, then overthrowing Saddam would have been a great opportunity even if there were no pressing danger. It is the excess rather

16 For a different view, see Marc Trachtenberg, *The Craft of International History* (Princeton: Princeton University Press, 2006), ch. 4.

than the paucity of reasons that confuses analysts. This is probably why Richard Haass, who was head of the State Department Policy Planning Staff during the run-up to the war and personally heard all of these beliefs expressed, replied to the question of why the administration went to war by declaring: "I will go to my grave not knowing that. I can't answer it."[17]

To disentangle excess beliefs and determine which of them were primarily responsible for the policy, we can try to see which was most compatible with what the person believed over a prolonged period as well as fitting with other actions she had taken.[18] Although this assumes a degree of consistency that, as I have noted, may be problematic, it is noteworthy that Bush and his colleagues consistently held a healthy—or unhealthy—respect for the utility of American force in world politics. Although this approach still leaves us with the question of the sources of these beliefs (and there is no logical stopping place once we start down that road, important as it is to explore),[19] it at least will tell us that the claim that force would work was not developed to justify the war.

A second long-standing belief was that while force is efficacious, deterrence is flawed. This position was taken by leaders of the Bush administration during the Cold War when they (except for Bush, who was not deeply involved in these questions) strongly favored nuclear counterforce and missile defense. Their belief that an Iraq armed with nuclear weapons could not be deterred from coercing its neighbors fit with this outlook, even if it was badly flawed.[20]

It is harder to find roots for the belief that there were serious links between al Qaeda and Saddam, even putting aside the lack of evidence and plausibility for the claim. No one reached this conclusion before they contemplated invading Iraq, and the speed and avidity with which Bush and his colleagues searched for Saddam's connections to terrorism suggest a conclusion in need of justification. So I think it would be reasonable to doubt that this belief was an independent pillar of the behavior.

The final set of beliefs supporting the war concerned democracy: democracies are peaceful and share interests with each other; democracy could readily be established in Iraq once Saddam was overthrown; and the example of

17 Quoted in Nolan Lemann, "Remember the Alamo," *New Yorker*, October 18, 2004, p. 157.

18 For a similar demonstration that the positions taken by American leaders on what emerged as the Monroe Doctrine can only be explained by their maneuvering for domestic advantage, see Ernest May, *The Making of the Monroe Doctrine* (Cambridge: Harvard University Press, 1975).

19 For a good study of the sources of beliefs in historical explanations, see Clayton Roberts, *The Logic of Historical Explanation* (University Park: Pennsylvania State University Press, 1996), ch. 10.

20 Robert Jervis, *American Foreign Policy in a New Era* (New York: Routledge, 2005), ch. 3.

Iraq would encourage democratic movements throughout the region. Were these beliefs a foundation of the policy? Bush and the advisors he most relied on did not have a history of propounding these beliefs and had not hesitated to cooperate with tyrannical regimes in the past. Furthermore, although September 11, 2001, changed a great deal, there is no reason why it should have led anyone to have greater faith in democracy as the antidote to world problems. Indeed the value of democracy and the possibility of spreading it was not stressed during the run-up to the war but became salient only in the wake of the failure to find WMD. So here too the causal role of the beliefs is questionable.

Reality Appraisal

The difficulty of determining whether and how particular beliefs affect behavior stems in part from the fact that they can form for quite different reasons. Further exploration then requires us to return to the categories used by Smith, Bruner, and White.

Many of our beliefs are dominated by the need to understand our environments, and almost all of them embody an element of this objective. It is impossible here to summarize how reality appraisal operates, but central is the fact that the world is so complex and our information processing capabilities so limited that in significant measure people must be theory driven. Beliefs are hard won from our world, and so it is not only ego that leads us to be quite attached to them. Although this model of people as "cognitive misers"[21] needs to be modified by the findings that people will deploy more cognitive resources in areas that are most important to them, that people vary in the extent to which they are theory driven, and that people who are more open to discrepant evidence tend to make more accurate predictions,[22] there remains much to the basic argument that to make sense of their surroundings people usually have to rely more heavily on what they have come to believe than on actual facts.

Four implications follow for how beliefs operate. First, people are strongly influenced by their expectations: people tend to see what they expect to see. In international politics perhaps the most striking examples come from cases

21 See, e.g., Susan Fiske and Shelly Taylor, *Social Cognition* (New York: McGraw-Hill, 1991).

22 See, e.g., Shelly Chaiken, "Heuristic Versus Systematic Information Processing and the Use of Source Versus Message Cues in Persuasion," *Journal of Personality and Social Psychology* 39 (November 1980): 752–66; Philip Tetlock, *Expert Political Judgment: How Good Is It? How Can We Know?* (Princeton: Princeton University Press, 2005); Daniel Kahneman, *Thinking Fast and Thinking Slow:* (New York: Farrar, Straus, and Giroux, 2011).

of surprise attack.[23] The Israelis were certain that Egypt lacked the military strength to attack in 1973 and so misinterpreted what in hindsight were obvious tip-offs that an attack was coming;[24] in April 1940 the British and Norwegians were so sure that Germany would not expose its forces to British naval superiority that they were unmoved by their sinking a transport containing German soldiers who told them that they were on their way to invade Norway; when Secretary of War Stimson was told of the Japanese attack on Pearl Harbor, he said "My God, this can't be true. This [message] must mean the Philippines," where he had expected the attack; when a Soviet front-line unit reported coming under German artillery fire as the latter country attacked, it received the reply, "You must be insane. And why is your signal not in code?"[25]

Of course these cases are selected on the dependent variable because we are looking only at instances of surprise. This makes it impossible for us to say that this cognitive bias is a central cause of error. Indeed most correct inferences are also strongly influenced by expectations, leading to the second implication of the role of theory-driven beliefs, which is that a proposition is most likely to be accepted when it is seen as plausible—in other words, when it fits with more general beliefs. This is why almost everyone interpreted the scattered and ambiguous evidence as showing that Saddam Hussein had vigorous WMD programs.[26] This inference made a great deal of sense, as the regime had used gas against Iran and its own Kurds, pursued nuclear weapons before the Gulf War, initially tried to maintain these programs despite UN sanctions, and engaged in a great deal of denial and deception. Without this background, the intelligence reports would have been read very differently.

The third general proposition is that judgments of plausibility can be self-reinforcing as ambiguous evidence is taken not only to be consistent with preexisting beliefs but also to confirm them. Logically, the latter is the case only when the evidence both fits with the belief and does not fit with competing ones. But people rarely probe the latter possibility as carefully as they should, assuming it instead.

23 The literature is very large: key works include Richard Betts, *Surprise Attack* (Washington, D.C.: Brookings Institution, 1982); Barton Whaley, *Codeword Barbarossa* (Cambridge: MIT Press, 1973); Roberta Wohlstetter, *Pearl Harbor: Warning and Decision* (Stanford: Stanford University Press, 1962); also see Jervis, *Perception and Misperception* (1976, 2017), ch. 4.

24 A reexamination of the Israeli case stresses not general cognitive processes but the rigid views and personality of the head of Israeli intelligence: Uri Bar-Joseph and Arie Kruglanski, "Intelligence Failures and Need for Cognitive Closure: On the Psychology of the Yom Kippur Surprise," *Political Psychology* 24 (March 2003): 75–99.

25 Quoted in Harry Howe Ransom, *Central Intelligence and National Security* (Cambridge: Harvard University Press, 1958), p. 54; quoted in John Erickson, *The Soviet High Command* (London: Macmillan, 1962), p. 587.

26 Jervis, *Perception and Misperception* (1976, 2017).

The fourth implication of theory-driven processing is that the model of Bayesian up-dating not only does not but cannot fully apply.[27] The basic point of Bayesianism is that people should and do modify their beliefs according to the likelihood that observed new events or information should occur if the prior beliefs are correct. The difficulty is that people who hold different beliefs will see the new event or information in different ways, and there is no objective arbiter to which we can appeal. This is not a problem when we are trying to adjust our estimate of whether a jar has more blue balls than red ones as they are drawn out at random. The evidence of a ball's color is clear enough so that people can agree on it irrespective of their priors. This is sometimes true in politics, but often is not. For example, supporters of the Bush administration argued that the events in countries like Lebanon and Egypt in the months following the Iraqi elections in January 2005 showed how American policy was reshaping the Middle East. Those who disagreed not only argued that their beliefs need not be fundamentally changed because they are underpinned by so much other evidence, but also disputed the interpretation of these events themselves, seeing them as either superficial or as products of internal politics. In other words, the inevitable impact of priors on the understanding of new "facts" undercuts the thrust of a significant part of the Bayesian model.[28]

Although—and because—we need theories, strong beliefs, and expectations in order to make any sense of our complex and contradictory world, reality appraisal can lead us astray. But, more importantly, this is not the only impulse shaping our beliefs, as Smith, Bruner, and White so clearly show.

Functions of Beliefs

Functional explanations of beliefs cast doubt on their causal role. A full understanding of how beliefs operate requires backward as well as forward linkages; we need to look for the causes as well as the consequences of the beliefs to see whether the connection between beliefs and behavior is spurious with both being driven by a common third factor. Beliefs may be rationalizations for policies as well as rationales for them. When social, political, and personal needs are strong, the results can be summarized by the saying, "If you want something really bad, you will get it really bad." The explanation for why a policy is adopted and why it was carried out so incompetently often are linked, in the same way that the need to see that a policy can succeed will diminish

27 For a good review, see Alan Gerber and Donald Green, "Bias," *Annual Review of Political Science* 2 (June 1999): 189–210.

28 For a further discussion, see the preface in the second edition of Jervis, *Perception and Misperception* (2017).

reality appraisal and draw the actor into a conceptual and perceptual world that, while comfortable, cannot provide good guidance for behavior.

If the discussion of reality appraisal and how it goes wrong is linked to cognitive biases, the functions of beliefs are linked to motivated ones.[29] People's needs to work with others, further their political goals, and live with themselves tap into their emotions and drive them to certain beliefs. A classic demonstration is the study by Albert Hastorf and Hadley Cantril, "They Saw a Game."[30] Purely cognitive biases cannot explain why students at Dartmouth and Princeton who viewed films of a penalty-filled game between their two football teams saw the other side as at fault. When we look at elite beliefs and decision-making, we see four overlapping areas in which motivated biases are at work and beliefs are highly functional. These are the hesitancy to recognize painful value trade-offs, the psychological and political need for people to see that their policies will work, the impact on beliefs of goals and feelings of which people are unaware, and the propensity of people to infer their own beliefs from how they behave.

One can reply that these sorts of functional pressures are unlikely because they imply knowledge of the very cognitions that people are trying to ward off, if not the conclusions to which they are being steered. At times, the line between awareness and lack of it is very thin. People often say things like "I don't think that this is something I want to hear about," or "That is a subject we are better off not analyzing."[31] But beyond this borderline a great deal of

29 On the difficulties and possibilities of separating kinds of biases, see Chaim Kaufmann, "Out of the Lab and into the Archives: A Method for Testing Psychological Explanations of Political Decision Making," *International Studies Quarterly* 38 (December 1994): 557–86; Philip Tetlock and Ariel Levi, "Attribution Bias: On the Inconclusiveness of the Cognition-Motivation Debate," *Journal of Experimental Social Psychology* 18 (January 1982): 68–88. For a general discussion of motivated processing, see Steven Spencer, Steven Fein, Mark Zanna, and James Olson, eds., *Motivated Social Perception: The Ontario Symposium, Volume 9* (Mahwah, N.J.: Erlbaum, 2003).

30 Albert Hastorf and Hadley Cantril, "They Saw a Game," *Journal of Abnormal and Social Psychology* 49 (January 1954): 129–34.

31 The importance of preconscious processing helps explain why many decisions, including ones that prove to be very successful, are made quickly and intuitively rather than on the basis prolonged calculation: Malcolm Gladwell, *Blink: The Power of Thinking Without Thinking* (New York: Little Brown, 2005); Deborah Larson, "Truman and the Berlin Blockade: The Role of Intuition and Experience in Good Foreign Policy Judgment," in Deborah Larson and Stanley Renshon, eds., *Good Judgment in Foreign Policy: Theory and Application* (Lanham, Md.: Rowman and Littlefield, 2003), 127–52. This also means that the person's sense that there are no viable alternatives to his policy that triggers the functional pressures may be incorrect and that a fuller and less biased search could have led to a better outcome, as we will discuss below. Under U.S. law, being willfully blind to facts or the likely consequences of one's actions can make the person legally culpable and the "ostrich" defense is of questionable value: Jeremy Baker and Rebecca Young, "False Statements and False Claims," *American Criminal Law Review* 42 (Spring 2005):

cognitive processing is preconscious, and the understanding that a certain position *must* be affirmed can affect the person's thinking without her being aware of it. One does not have to accept Freudian notions of the unconscious and repression to conclude that we can be strongly influenced by impulses of which we are unaware. The requirement for bolstering beliefs can be triggered by the implicit realization that the decision is a hard one and that more thorough analysis could lead to high conflict. When people lack good choices, they are likely to imagine that the one they select is better than it is.

Varied forms of self-deception are then common in politics, but they are not unique to this realm, as novels make clear. Scientists also feel the same social and psychological pressures, and Richard Feynman famously said to his fellow-scientists, "The first principle is that you must not fool yourself— and you are the easiest person to fool."[32] This is one reason why errors in science are often detected by people not involved in the original discoveries and why the scientific community cannot be trusted to make unbiased judgments about the danger of experiments and technologies in which it has a large stake.

AVOIDING PAINFUL TRADE-OFFS

In difficult political and psychological situations, reality appraisal, far from pointing the way out, can be a menace to the person if the reality it points to is too painful to contemplate. My first discussion of the tendency to avoid value trade-offs treated it as cognitive,[33] but this was a mistake, because its roots are primarily motivated or functional. Although people often have to make trade-offs—budgets, for example, force them on us—avoidance is often possible and necessary.[34] People are especially prone to shy away from trade-offs when dealing with incommensurable realms and moral choices,[35] which

---

427–62; William Simon, "Wrongs of Ignorance and Ambiguity: Lawyer Responsibility for Collective Misconduct," *Columbia Public Law & Legal Theory Working Paper,* No. 0480, October 7, 2004.

32 Richard Feynman, "The Cargo Cult Science," this was in turn adapted from his 1974 Caltech commencement address, which was published in *Engineering and Science* 37 (June 1974): 10–13.

33 Jervis, *Perception and Misperception* (1976), 128–42.

34 For strongly political interpretations that argue that leaders sometimes can succeed in avoiding trade-offs, see Barbara Farnham, *Roosevelt and the Munch Crisis: A Study of Political Decision-Making* (Princeton: Princeton University Press, 1977); Richard Neustadt, "Presidents, Politics and Analysis," presented at Graduate School of Public Affairs, University of Washington, Seattle, 1986. Although there are obvious political reasons why people would want to downplay the costs of their preferred policies even if they were aware of them, the beliefs discussed here seem to have been sincere and were expressed in private as well as in public.

35 Alan Fiske and Philip Tetlock, "Taboo Trade-Offs: Reactions to Transactions that Transgress the Spheres of Justice," *Political Psychology* 18 (June 1997): 255–97

explains why those who oppose the use of torture on moral grounds resist the argument that its use might save lives.[36] I would similarly expect that if Bush and his colleagues had decided that the prospect of Iranian nuclear weapons was truly intolerable, they would have come to see the negative consequences of an air strike as quite small.

The desire to avoid trade-offs is clear in the discussion of Iraq. As a soldier's mother put it, "I know my son's there for a reason. And whatever might happen, that's the way it's supposed to be. And if I took it any other way, I'd be in a funny farm."[37] Elites do not put it this revealingly, but their beliefs often serve the same functions. As I discussed above, proponents of the war had more reasons than they needed, and opponents differed on all these points. If reality testing were shaping the beliefs, then one should have found quite a few people who believed that while the war was necessary, it would be very costly, or who thought that while threat was present, opportunity was not (or vice versa), or that the war would be cheap but was not necessary. But these positions are uncomfortable, and so it is not surprising that we do not find people taking them. For political leaders, as well as for the mother quoted earlier, if they took it any other way, they'd be in a funny farm.

POLICIES CALL UP SUPPORTING BELIEFS

The second and relating functional source of foreign policy beliefs is the pressure generated by policies. One reason why political leaders are slow to see that their policies are failing is that good reality appraisal would force them to acknowledge the high costs and risks they are facing. Thus building on the psychological work on defensive avoidance, Richard Ned Lebow and others have shown that if the actor is committed to proceeding, even highly credible threats by the adversary are likely to be missed, misinterpreted, or ignored.[38] This is one reason why attempts to explain wars as the product of rational choices on both sides will often fail, just as the policies themselves fail.

One of the hallmarks of the functional source of beliefs is that planning on the surface looks meticulous, but in fact is terribly deficient because it is built

36 For a critique of the Senate Select Committee on Intelligence's report on the torturing of suspected terrorists on the grounds that it conveniently found that these techniques were not only unacceptable, but also were ineffective and had never been understood by the administration or the Congressional committees, see Robert Jervis, "The Torture Blame Game," *Foreign Affairs* 94 (May/June 2015): 120–27.

37 Quoted in Sasha Abramsky, "Supporting the Troops, Doubting the War," *The Nation,* October 4, 2004, p. 11.

38 Irving Janis and Leon Mann, *Decision Making: A Psychological Analysis of Conflict, Choice, and Commitment* (New York: Free Press, 1977); Robert Jervis, Richard Ned Lebow, and Janice Stein, *Psychology and Deterrence* (Baltimore: Johns Hopkins University Press, 1985); also see Jervis, "Deterrence and Perception," in this volume.

on unrealistic and unexamined assumptions. As Isabel Hull notes in regard to Germany thinking about colonial warfare in the early twentieth century, "Realistic planning would have revealed the impossibility of the grand goals; rather than giving these up, planning itself was truncated."[39] Indeed, when a part of the organization does engage in effective reality appraisal, it may be neutered, as was the case with a planning division in the Japanese army in the 1930s.[40] It is tempting to dismiss this as the product of military culture, but the U.S. Forest Service, committed to stamping out all forest fires, disbanded its research arm when it showed that healthy forests required periodic burning.[41]

British planning for the bombardment of Germany throughout the 1930s illustrates the ways in which beliefs supporting the efficacy of a policy can be shielded from reality appraisal. The incredible costs of fighting World War I not only contributed to the subsequent appeasement policy, but also convinced the British that if war were to come, they could not fight it as they had done before. A way out was strategic bombardment that could deter devastating German air attacks on Britain and win the war without having to suffer the horrendous losses of ground warfare. It then *had* to be true that an effective bomber force could be developed, and supporting beliefs were called up to meet this demand. So it is not surprising that British planners convinced themselves that the bomb loads their planes could carry would be sufficient to do grave damage to German industries and cities, that British bombers could fly without protection from fighter escorts, that the aircraft could readily find their targets, and that bombing would be accurate. Although many plans were cranked out, these central assumptions were never scrutinized. In fact, even rudimentary questioning and military exercises would have revealed that German cities were obscured by clouds much of the year, that navigation systems were not adequate to direct planes to them, that bombs would miss their targets, and that even direct hits would rarely put factories out of action for long.[42] A history of Bomber Command notes that "seldom in the history of warfare has a force been so sure of the end it sought—fulfillment of the Trenchard doctrine [of strategic bombing]—and yet so ignorant of how this might be achieved as the RAF between the wars."[43] In fact, the certainty

39 Isabel Hull, *Absolute Destruction: Military Culture and the Practices of War in Imperial Germany* (Ithaca: Cornell University Press, 2005), p. 143; see Holger Herwig. "Germany," in Richard Hamilton and Holger Herwig, eds., *The Origins of World War I* (Cambridge: Cambridge University Press, 2003), p. 155, for a similar discussion of German planning for World War I.

40 Michael Barnhart, *Japan Prepares for Total War* (Ithaca: Cornell University Press, 1987), pp. 200–202, 240, 258.

41 Ashley Schiff, *Fire and Water: Scientific Heresy in the Forest Service* (Cambridge: Harvard University Press, 1962), pp. 169–73.

42 John Carter, *Airpower and the Cult of the Offensive* (Maxwell Air Force Base, Ala.: Air University Press, 1998); Jervis, "Deterrence and Perception," in this volume.

43 Macdonald Hastings, *Bomber Command* (New York: Dial Press, 1979), p. 44.

with which the ends were held and the ignorance about means were closely linked. Reality appraisal was unacceptable because it would have called the highly valued goals into question.

The same pressures for beliefs to support policy explain many of the deficiencies in American planning for the aftermath of the overthrow of Saddam. Reality appraisal would have been politically and psychologically painful; to have recognized that reconstruction was likely to be long, costly, and uncertain would have been to give ammunition to the war's critics. When confronted with the Army Chief of Staff's estimate that it would take several hundred thousand troops to garrison Iraq, Deputy Secretary of Defense Paul Wolfowitz told Congress that "it's hard to conceive that it would take more forces to provide stability in post-Saddam Iraq than it would take to conduct the war itself.... Hard to imagine."[44] This was indeed a failure of imagination, but under these circumstances imagination could not have been allowed free rein. It is hard to ask important questions and conduct unbiased analysis when the answers may be unacceptable.

BELIEFS SUPPORTING THE ESTABLISHED ORDER

The third function of beliefs is much broader, consisting of people's conceptions of the political and social structures that gratify them. In his pioneering study, Lippmann argued that stereotypes form not only because they permit "economy of effort," but also because they "may be the core of our personal tradition, the defenses of our position in society."[45] Marxists—and apolitical cynics— analyze the beliefs of the ruling classes in this way. During the Cold War, members of the political and economic elite who incorrectly said that the establishment of revolutionary regimes anywhere in the world would menace American security interests were not lying. Rather, the knowledge that such regimes would adversely affect their economic interests led them to believe that American national security was at stake as well. People in the upper income brackets can cite many reasons why cutting their taxes would benefit the entire economy and pull others out of poverty. These beliefs, which can involve somewhat complicated economics, are not insincere, but they nevertheless derive from personal interest.

Beliefs about what is right and just may have similar roots. E. H. Carr famously showed how the morality espoused by status quo states nicely justified the prevailing arrangements that suited them so well;[46] most Americans

44 Quoted in Peter Slevin and Dana Priest, "Wolfowitz Concedes Iraq Errors," *Washington Post*, July 24, 2003.

45 Walter Lippmann, *Public Opinion* (New York: Macmillan, 1992), p. 95.

46 Edward Hallett Carr, *The Twenty Years' Crisis: 1919–1939* (New York: Harper Torchbooks, 1946).

joined president Bush in believing that the vigorous exercise of American power abroad is in the world's interest. Looking within U.S. society, trial lawyers believe that unimpeded access to the courts for liability and class action suits is the best way to control rapacious companies; police officers believe that the establishment of civilian oversight boards will encourage criminals to produce false claims and defy the police; professors believe that government support for universities in general and their specializations in particular will produce a stronger and better society (but that government direction of research harms these goals). Some or all of these beliefs may be correct, but they are remarkably convenient.

BELIEFS PRODUCED BY ACTIONS

In contrast to the usual method of explaining actions by the beliefs that we think generated them, the previous pages have discussed how beliefs form to provide rationalizations for actions. In the final category of cases, not only do actions produce beliefs, but also, once formed, these new beliefs influence later actions. The theory was developed years ago by Daryl Bem, and the basic point is related to the one noted above that people often do not know why they act as they do. They then implicitly analyze their own behavior in the same way they analyze that of others and ask what beliefs and motives could have been responsible for it.[47] Answers like inadvertence, fleeting impulses, the desire to do something and get on with it, all seem inappropriate if not frivolous and, although often correct, are rejected. Instead, the person looks for more serious and lasting beliefs and motives, and then attributes her behavior to them. This would be no more than a psychological curiosity if the effects stopped there. But, once formed, these explanations guide future behavior. If I think that I gave money on one occasion because I am a generous person, I will give more in the future; if as a national leader I ordered the use of force to free hostages, I must believe that this instrument is efficacious and therefore should respond similarly in other situations; if as president I gave a stiff response to another country, it must be because that state is deeply hostile and that deterrence if not force is required to meet it. The last example is not hypothetical but is the foundation for Larson's fascinating analysis of the psychological origins of American Cold War policy.[48] Most scholars have seen Truman's containment policy as growing out of his steady response to

47 Daryl Bem, "Self-Perception Theory," in Leonard Berkowitz, ed., *Advances in Experimental Social Psychology, Volume 6* (New York: Academic Press, 1972), pp. 1–62; also see Eldar Shafir, Itamar Simonson, and Amos Tversky, "Reason-Based Choice," *Cognition* 49 (October–November 1993): 11–36.

48 Deborah Larson, *Origins of Containment* (Princeton: Princeton University Press, 1985).

increasing Soviet provocations. Revisionist scholars disagree, seeing the impulse as being generated by the need to keep the world open to capitalist penetration, but they too explain Truman's actions as following from his beliefs, albeit ones that were formed by the functional process noted previously. Larson argues that both these views fail to see that Truman was at first unsure of himself and inconsistent and that his position hardened only after he came to interpret his hesitant steps as implying that the Soviet Union was aggressive and could be countered only by firmness. Having attributed these beliefs to himself, Truman then acted on them more consistently.

Beliefs: Powerful and Autonomous

Kenneth Boulding's intriguing article on learning and reality testing begins with these words: "The Aztecs apparently believed that the corn on which their civilization depended would not grow unless there were human sacrifices. What seems to us an absurd belief caused thousands of people to be sacrificed each year."[49] This brings us back to the question of whether beliefs are powerful and autonomous. Boulding claims that here they were. They were powerful in that they drove human sacrifices and the wars that were necessary to procure them, and they were autonomous in the sense of not being a direct product of the Aztecs' objective situation. It is easier to demonstrate the former than the latter. The Aztecs did indeed act on their belief in the potency of human sacrifices. Such a correspondence is not automatic. A classic study in the 1930s showed that many people who said that they would discriminate against nonwhites in fact did not do so.[50] Overall, the relationship between expressed attitudes and behavior is mediated and complex, but we often do find beliefs to be linked to behavior. One important example is that Ronald Reagan's readiness to deal with Mikhail Gorbachev (on American terms, to be sure) can in part be explained by his image of the Soviet Union, which despite being highly skeptical and critical, involved more openness to change than was true of the beliefs of his hardline advisors.[51] But beliefs are not unmoved movers. Although an explanation of behavior in terms of beliefs does not have to trace all their roots, it does have to rule out spurious correlation by meeting the objection that they were formed to meet social, political, or psychological needs and that, relatedly, they merely reflect self-interest.

49 Kenneth Boulding, "The Learning and Reality-Testing Process in the International System," *Journal of International Affairs* 21, no. 1 (1967): 1.

50 Richard LaPiere, "Attitudes Versus Actions," *Social Forces* 13 (December 1934): 230–37; for a review of the literature see Howard Schuman and Michel Johnson, "Attitudes and Behavior," *Annual Review of Sociology* 2 (August 1976): 167–207.

51 Kith Shimko, *Images and Arms Control* (Ann Arbor: University of Michigan Press, 1991).

Upton Sinclair put it crudely but correctly: "It is difficult to get a man to understand something when his salary depends on his not understanding it."[52] In cases like these, we can explain both the beliefs and the behavior by some underlying factor, and we need to scrutinize statements like Boulding's in this light. Without claiming any expertise on this case, I doubt that the Aztec practices of human sacrifices are best explained by their beliefs, or, at the very least, we cannot leave it at that but need to ask how and why those beliefs formed. This would not be a problem if there were reasonable grounds for the conviction that corn would not grow without human blood, but it probably developed because it was highly functional for the maintenance of Aztec society, justifying as it did constant warfare, the prominence of warriors and warrior values, and hierarchical control.[53]

While ideas can indeed have consequences, in this case I doubt if we should make them the center of our attention. It is similarly doubtful that we can explain President Bill Clinton's initial refusal to intervene in the former Yugoslavia by his reading Robert Kaplan's *Balkan Ghosts* and being convinced that the conflict was generated by "ancient hatreds."[54] Instead, it is likely that he was attracted to the book's claim because of his need for reasons not to intervene. In much the same way, when in a private note Vice President Dick Cheney characterized as "a junket" Ambassador Joseph Wilson's trip to Niger to investigate the reports that Saddam had sought uranium from that barren country,[55] it is hard to avoid the conclusion that he saw it in this way in order to discredit Wilson's motives in his own mind. By contrast, Reagan's image of the Soviet Union, flawed as it may have been, was relatively autonomous. The perception that change was possible predated Gorbachev's rise to power and does not seem to be a rationalization for anything else.

The relationship between interests and ideas (and of course neither concept is unproblematic) is one of the oldest in social science and if Marx, Mannheim, and Weber could not settle it, I certainly cannot. The extremes are easy enough to rule out. Even if we believe in the existence of objective interests,

52 Upton Sinclair, *I, Candidate for Governor, and How I Got Licked* (Berkeley: University of California Press, 1994), p. 109.

53 For a general discussion of the functional nature of beliefs in societies, see Marvin Harris, *Cultural Materialism: The Struggle for a Science of Culture* (New York: Random House, 1979). The methodological weaknesses in his arguments are more disturbing than their rejection by most of his fellow anthropologists, which is not surprising as they cut against the core precepts of the discipline.

54 Robert Kaplan, *Balkan Ghosts: A Journey through History* (New York: St. Martin's Press, 1993).

55 Quoted in David Johnston, "Notes Are Said to Reveal Close Cheney Interest in a Critic of Iraq Policy," *New York Times*, May 14, 2006.

they do not dictate all beliefs. Not only do some wealthy people think that tax cuts for the rich are ethically wrong, they believe that such policies are bad for the economy (but note that those who think that such cuts violate our obligations to follow citizens usually also think they will reduce overall economic growth).

Reality appraisal and the functional role of beliefs conflict and combine in complex ways. While few of us can accept Richard Nixon's claims that national security required harassing Vietnam dissenters, punishing his political adversaries, and covering up the Watergate break-in, this was not a conscious rationalization. Nixon made these arguments in private, and I am sure that he could have passed a lie-detector test. Furthermore, one can defend his conclusions. The North Vietnamese were looking for signs about what the American public would support, and Soviet leaders may have looked to Nixon's handling of domestic opponents for clues as to whether he would back down in a crisis. Nevertheless, the coincidence between these beliefs and Nixon's strong impulses to quash his opponents to gratify his psychological needs and maintain his domestic power invites suspicion, and no leader likes to recognize that he is more concerned about his own future than with the good of the country.

Others displayed similar patterns. One of Reagan's associates reported that he had the capacity to "convince himself that the truth is what he wants it to be. Most politicians are unable to do this, but they would give their eye teeth if they could."[56] Thus Reagan was able to make himself believe that he was not trading arms for hostages in Iran, although later had enough self-insight to realize that this is in fact what he had done. But he was not unique in creating self-justifying rationalizations. Nixon not only thought his version of Watergate was accurate, but also earlier told his top assistant that "PR [public relations] is right if it emphasizes the truth. It's wrong, at least for us, if it isn't true."[57] An associate of Slobodan Milosevic made a similar report: "He decides first what is expedient for him to believe, then he believes it."[58] Clinton convinced himself that the donors he invited for overnight stays at the White House were his friends,[59] and Harry Truman noted in his diary that "I have told Sec. of War, Mr. Stimson, to use [the atomic bomb] so that

56 Lyn Nofziger, *Nofziger* (Washington, D.C.: Regnery, 1992), p. 45; also see p. 285.

57 Harry Robbins Haldeman, *The Haldeman Diaries: Inside the Nixon White House* (New York: G. P. Putnam, 1994), p. 287, also see p. 521.

58 John Burns, "Serbia's Enigma: An Aloof Leader Who Stoked Fires of Nationalist Passion," *New York Times*, December 22, 1992.

59 Howard Kurtz, *Spin Cycle: How the White House and the Media Manipulate the News* (New York: Simon and Schuster, 1998), pp. 138–39.

military objectives and soldiers and sailors are the target and not women and children."[60]

The capacity for self-deception bordering on delusion enables people to work their way through difficult situations.[61] Before World War I, British leaders were able to pursue a policy of containing Germany without building a large army by convincing themselves that the intervention of its small one would be decisive. When the war started, Woodrow Wilson was able to reconcile his preference for a British victory with his desire that the United States remain neutral by believing in the face of clear facts that Britain was abiding by international law and respecting the rights of neutral trade.[62]

But as these and other cases show, self-deception often eventually brings political and personal grief. It was initially very convenient for Nixon to believe that his actions were required by the imperatives of national security, but in the end his beliefs served neither the country nor his own interests. What he did was extremely risky, and he was unable to make an accurate cost-benefit calculation in terms of his own political stakes in part because he had convinced himself that the national interest required these unacceptable tactics. He and the country would have been better off if he had been more of a hypocrite. Had he realized that while his own and the national interest were both legitimate they were not identical, he might have seen the world more clearly and sought a better way to deal with the conflicts between them. Wilson might have been able to develop an effective strategy to preserve neutral rights, restrain both Britain and Germany, and put the United States in a position to end the war sooner had he not quickly avoided the trade-offs but instead carefully thought about them.[63] A fuller if more painful search might similarly have revealed better ways for Germany to deal with its dilemmas before 1914.[64]

Beliefs are filled with puzzles and ironies like this, and I think they deserve more attention. A scientist starts his book on the brain by declaring that

60 Robert Ferrell, *Off the Record: The Private Papers of Harry S. Truman* (New York: Harper and Row, 1980), p. 55. I believe that Truman later understood what he had done and while he claimed never to have had second thoughts about dropping the bomb, in fact he did doubt its morality in ways that affected his later attitudes toward nuclear weapons. As Robert Trivers, *Natural Selection and Social Theory* (New York: Oxford University Press, 2002), pp. 55–93, argues, self-deception may also be functional because it facilitates the actor's deception of others.

61 On more limited and often healthy forms of self-deception, see Shelly Taylor, *Positive Illusions: Creative Self-Deception and the Healthy Mind* (New York: Basic Books, 1989); Daniel Gilbert, *Stumbling on Happiness* (New York: Knopf, 2006).

62 John Coogan, *The End of Neutrality: The United States, Britain, and Maritime Rights, 1899–1915* (Ithaca: Cornell University Press, 1981).

63 Ibid., 217–19.

64 Jack Snyder, *The Ideology of the Offensive: Military Decision Making and the Disasters of 1914* (Ithaca: Cornell University Press, 1984).

"Believing is what we humans do best."[65] We certainly are quick to form beliefs, but how and how well we do so is another question. According to Bob Woodward, on his deathbed CIA Director William Casey gave a deceptively simple answer to the question of why he had engaged in a series of arguably illegal covert actions: "I believed."[66]

65 Michael Gazzaniga, *The Social Brain: Discovering the Networks of the Mind* (New York: Basic Books, 1985), p. 3.

66 Bob Woodward, *Veil: The Secret Wars of the CIA 1981–1987* (New York: Simon and Schuster, 1987), p. 507.

2

The Drunkard's Search

Just like the drunk who looked for his keys not where he dropped them, but under the lamppost, where the light was better, people often seek inadequate information that is readily available, use misleading measures because they are simple, and employ methods of calculation whose main virtue is ease.[1] For example, in 1949 when Sen. Joseph O'Mahoney tried to convince his colleagues not to cut the Air Force budget, he argued, "We do not need details here. All we need to know is that this ... is a reduction from a 58-group air force to a 48-group air force. In my judgement, a 58-group air force would be too little."[2] This argument is straightforward and makes minimal demands on one's ability to find and process information. But it is not satisfactory. Even a person who believed that the air force should be larger than 58 groups still should want to know the costs and effectiveness of smaller forces. If a much larger force was beyond reach, one could prefer a force of 48 groups to one that was ten groups larger if the gap in effectiveness was relatively slight and the cost difference very great. Furthermore, the most important consideration might not be the size of the force, but its composition, training, state of readiness, and supplies. It is also possible that expansion might profitably be delayed a few years if changes in technology were in the offing.

1 For previous uses of this metaphor, see Abraham Kaplan, *The Conduct of Inquiry: Methodology for Behavioral Science* (New Brunswick, N.J.: Transaction Publishers, 1964), and Richard Betts, "Conventional Strategy: New Critics, Old Choices," *International Security* 7 (Spring 1983): 140–62.

2 Warner Schilling, "The Politics of National Defense: Fiscal 1950," in Warner Schilling, Paul Hammond, and Glenn Snyder, eds., *Strategy, Politics and Defense Budgets* (New York: Columbia University Press, 1962), p. 129.

Of course, information and decision costs must be considered when judging the desirability of a decision-making procedure, and methods that seem irrational when these factors are ignored can become rational once they are weighed. But there is more to it than this. In many cases, searching further or looking at less obvious criteria could significantly increase the chance of a better decision at a manageable cost. Without being able to specify exactly how much effort would be optimal, it seems likely that people seize on easier ways of processing and calculating information than they would if they were fully aware of what they were doing.[3]

Ways of Decreasing the Burden of Cognition

SIMPLE MODELS AND DECISION RULES

The propensity to conserve cognitive resources in seeking and processing information manifests itself in several forms. First, people prefer simple decision rules and unitary causal accounts to ones that posit a multiplicity of factors and causal paths. In areas in which they are expert, people may reject an explanation as too simple, but even here there may be more lip service than actual avoidance of simplicity. In some contexts, simplicity is valued for well thought-out reasons: parsimony is a criteria for a good scientific theory not only because it increases the theory's power (i.e., the ability to explain a lot with relatively few independent variables), but also because at least some scientists believe that the phenomena they are trying to capture are themselves parsimonious. But finding parsimony at the end of data collection and analysis is one thing; assuming it from the start is another.

Two linked manifestations of the preference for seeing a minimum of causal factors are the propensity of people to believe conspiracy theories and the hesitancy of even sophisticated observers to give full credit to the role of accidents and confusion. Conspiracies are complicated in the sense of involving a large number of activities that may seem bewildering, but the underlying causation is simple: everything is knit together into a coherent plan. The drive to see conspiracies varies across personalities and cultures, but a

---

3 People, then, are "cognitive misers," but the results may be a greater degradation in the quality of the decision making than is often realized. (The phrase "cognitive misers" comes from Susan Fiske and Shelley Taylor, *Social Cognition: From Brains to Culture* (New York: McGraw Hill, 1991); this concept, as they acknowledge, comes from Herbert Simon, *Models of Man: Social and Rational* (New York: Wiley, 1957). Also see David Braybrooke and Charles Lindblom, *A Strategy of Decision: Policy Evaluation as a Social Process* (New York: Free Press, 1963); Charles Lindblom, "The Science of Muddling Through," *Public Administration Review* 19 (Spring 1959): 74–88.

general cognitive bias also is important.[4] Even those who reject one or another of these theories often sense the attractiveness of an explanation that ties so many odd bits of behavior together. It sometimes takes a great deal of training and experience to produce a reaction against this kind of explanation as being "too neat to be true."

If the belief in conspiracies is common, the resistance to accepting a large role for chance is almost universal. People see order even in random data and seek parsimony even when it is not present. Thus, they are slow to explain the policies of states in terms of a multiplicity of bureaucratic factors or a multiplicity of changing motives; other states are seen as coordinated and Machiavellian when in fact they may be blundering and incoherent.[5] People who know how uncoordinated their own government is rarely explain the behavior of others in this way.

A similar pattern is displayed when people are asked to report how many kinds of evidence they used to arrive at a decision (e.g., which stocks to buy, what disease a patient has, whether to admit an applicant to graduate school). People claim to use a large number of cues, but statistical analysis of the pattern of their choices indicates that they rely on only very few. People also report that they look for complex interactive patterns (i.e., they would buy a stock if indicator A were high and B were low or if B were low and A were high, but not if both were either high or low) when in fact they treat the same variables in a simple additive manner.[6] In the same way, when people search for the solution to puzzles in experimental settings, they focus on rules with only one element. They are slow to explore the possibility that the required answer is conjunctive (i.e., the presence of two or more elements) and even slower to think of possibilities that are disjunctive (i.e., one element present but another absent). This was a clear result of Jerome Bruner, Jacqueline Goodnow, and George Austin's *A Study of Thinking*, in which subjects were asked to reconstruct the rule by which an item was determined to belong to a category established by the experimenter.[7] The task was relatively easy if having an attribute was both a necessity and sufficient cause for inclusion in the category; it was more difficult if having such an attribute was necessary but not

---

4 For a good discussion of the sources of the propensity to perceive conspiracies in the United States, see Joseph Uscinski and Joseph Parent, *American Conspiracy Theories* (New York: Oxford University Press, 2014).

5 Robert Jervis, *Perception and Misperception in International Politics* (Princeton: Princeton University Press, 1976; 2nd ed., 2017).

6 See Robyn Dawes and Bernard Corrigan, "Linear Models in Decision Making," *Psychological Bulletin* 81 (February 1974): 95–106.

7 Jerome S. Bruner, Jacqueline J. Goodnow, and George A. Austin, *A Study of Thinking* (New York: Wiley, 1956).

sufficient; it was beyond most people's reach when there were several sufficient conditions.[8]

CERTAINTY

The preference for simple calculations also is revealed by people's tendency to think in terms of certainties and, when they must employ probabilities, to use round numbers, especially 50 percent. Cognitive resources are conserved by declaring that many alternatives are simply impossible. Sometimes a more sophisticated formulation is called up: "The chance that X will occur is so unlikely that it is not worth thinking about." But conditions can change that increase the likelihood of X without triggering further consideration for it. The preference for absolutes also is found in experiments: people who are shown statements of the form "Some X are Y" and "All (or No) X are Y" are more likely to remember the former as being the latter than vice versa.[9]

A related device is for the person to refuse to consider complicating factors. Thus, during the Cold War it seems that the U.S. intelligence community paid little attention to the possibility of extensive deception and that analysts who raised this problem were not taken seriously.[10] Because this stance was not limited to those with a benign view of the USSR, the best explanation for the avoidance of complicating factors is the need to keep one's task manageable. It was hard enough to try to estimate Soviet capabilities and intentions; to constantly have had to doubt much of the information that one was using would have made the problem intolerable. All of one's time and intellectual energy would have been taken up by trying to tell what information was deceptive, and very little time would have been left for the main job. The Germans in World War II similarly failed to grasp any of the innumerable clues that their spy network in England had been "turned" and taken over by the British. Although the British blatantly used the network to deceive the Germans

8 Similarly, when people are asked to determine the rule that generates a string of numbers or letters, they almost always stop after having found a way of producing positive cases; they do not see if cases that the rule says should be negative in fact are so.

9 Robyn Dawes, "Memory and Distortion of Meaningful Written Material," *British Journal of Psychology* 57 (May 1966): 77–86; for an interesting population discussion of when and why people feel certain, see Robert Burton, *On Being Certain: Believing You Are Right Even When You're Not* (New York: St. Martin's Press, 2008).

10 Unfortunately, at least some of those within the U.S. government who have worried about deception have developed such exaggerated claims and fears that the whole enterprise had been somewhat discredited. Examples are James Angleton, who was in charge of counterintelligence for the CIA, and David Sullivan, a former CIA analyst who has published his arguments in "Evaluating U.S. Intelligence Estimates," in Roy Goodson, ed., *Intelligence Requirements for the 1980s: Analysis and Estimates* (Washington, D.C.: National Strategy Information Center, 1979), pp. 49–73.

on the location of the invasion of the Continent, even after D-Day the Germans continued to take the reports from their "agents" at face value, much to the amazement of the British.

BENCHMARKS AND ANALOGIES

The burdens of calculation are further reduced by the use of benchmarks to guide decisions. Round numbers often serve this function. Herbert York explained that the Atlas missile was designed to be able to carry a one-megaton warhead in large part because, having ten fingers, we built our number system on the base of ten.[11] Similarly, although considerations of both strategy and domestic politics were important in determine the rough number of Minuteman missiles President John Kennedy decided to procure in the early 1960s, the advantage of the figure 1,000 as compared to, say, 875 or 1,163 was that it was a round number. The other side of this coin is that when a person wants others to believe that a figure she has selected was the result of complex and detailed calculations, she will pick a number that is *not* round.

Benchmarks also can be provided by other people's behavior. States often compare their performance with other states, even when this comparison is not fully appropriate.[12] Or an actor will copy another actor believing (or acting as though he believes) that the two of them are in such similar positions and have such similar interests that they can save themselves a lot of cognitive work simply by following the other's lead. It would be hard to otherwise explain the call for an American Fractional Orbiting Bombardment System after the Soviets had tested one, or NATO's drive to match the Soviet's SS-20. There were other more reasonable arguments for the deployment of new missiles in Europe, but they were rarely publicized, and even if many people used the SS-20s only as an excuse, the fact that they believed that other audiences would find this excuse persuasive needs to be explained.

When people try to determine whether a policy has succeeded, they often use two related measuring rods. First, if the situation is competitive, they ask who won and who lost. This is appropriate if the situation is zero-sum, but it will be misleading if both sides could be better off (or worse off) than they would have been had alternative courses of action been followed. Even when misleading, the question often is asked because it is easier to answer than a more complex one would be. Under some circumstances, actors ask whether they are gaining (or losing) more than another, and doing so is sensible when

11 Herbert York, *Race to Oblivion: A Participant's View of the Arms Race* (New York: Simon and Schuster, 1970), pp. 89–90.

12 For a related discussion, see Martha Finnemore, *National Interests in International Society* (Ithaca: Cornell University Press, 1996).

the nature of the interaction makes relative position or standing crucial, as is often the case when power or status are involved. But use of this measure does not seem to be restricted to situations where it fits.[13]

The second benchmark is to compare the result of the interaction to the result of previous ones. Doing better than before is equated with winning, which in turn is equated with success. A good example is provided by the way that observers—at least American observers—judged American policy in 1986 after the Soviets arrested Nicholas Daniloff and the United States gained the reporter's freedom by a complex trade of suspected spies and a dissident. Politicians and reporters alike compared this exchange to similar cases in the past, often arguing that the United States "lost" because it had previously kept Soviet spies in jail longer and more dissidents had been released in similar trades. Setting aside the difficulties in deciding whether the circumstances of earlier cases really were the same, what is crucial here is that many people jumped from the judgment that the Soviets did better this time to the conclusion that the Soviets "won" and "set a precedent that would make Western governments think twice about arresting Soviet spy suspects."[14] But even if this trade was more palatable to the Soviets than earlier ones, it may not have been so attractive as to tempt them to repeat the adventure. By the same token, the terms of the trade could have been worse than in previous cases without being excessively costly. But the baseline of the past establishes our expectation, and so we concentrate on deviations from it, even if logically they do not carry much meaning.

Other benchmarks are more ad hoc, rising out of the prominent features of the environment. For example, when President Lyndon Johnson "began to search for the elusive point at which the costs of Vietnam would become unacceptable to the American people, he always settled upon mobilization, the point at which reserves would have to be called up to support a war that was becoming increasingly distasteful to the American public."[15] Although Johnson's view may have been correct, he neither sought a way around the ceiling nor considered whether a shorter war with mobilization might have been more acceptable than a longer and inconclusive one fought with fewer men. Instead, the ceiling was taken as an absolute prohibition. In the same way, when a person is considering a major purchase, she may well set an upper limit on what she is willing to spend and not consider going higher even for something of greater value. As these examples show, benchmarks can be used by

13 For a good discussion of when and why victory is perceived, see Dominic Johnson and Dominic Tierney, *Failing to Win: Perceptions of Victory and Defeat in International Politics* (Cambridge: Harvard University Press, 2006).

14 Serge Schemann, "A Limited Success for Gorbachev," *New York Times*, October 1, 1986.

15 Herbert Schandler, *Lyndon Johnson and Vietnam: The Unmaking of a President* (Princeton: Princeton University Press, 1977), p. 56.

the actor to restrain himself. In moments of calm, he can construct barriers that are difficult for him to break through under circumstances of temptation. Furthermore, as Thomas Schelling has shown, benchmarks can be particularly useful when several people are involved by providing a way for people to coordinate their behavior and can guide bargaining.[16] But these functions also depend in part on the fact that benchmarks are artificially attractive.

USING COMMON DIMENSIONS

People also can ease their burden of calculation by comparing alternatives only on the dimension that they have in common. This is fully rational if that dimension is by far the most important one, but the method will be employed whether or not this is the case, as is brought out by an experiment in which subjects are asked to compare pairs of students. For each student there were scores on two dimensions, of which one was common to both of them and another that was different. For example, one student might have scores for English skills and psychological stamina, while the other would have scores on English skills and aptitude for quantitative analysis. In their evaluations, subjects weighed the common dimensions more heavily: the student with the higher English skills was likely to be rated as superior overall, even if the gap on this dimension was slight and the student who lagged here did extremely well on the unique dimension. Neither cautioning subjects about the effect nor giving them feedback as to the correct approach changed their method, and when the subjects were questioned after the experiment, they denied that they had given extra weight to the common dimension. This discredits one obvious explanation, which undermines the possibility that people are giving extra weight to any dimension that was held in common on the not unreasonable grounds that the very fact that it is common indicates that it was important.[17]

Few foreign policy cases are as clear as this experiment, although the way in which states compare each other's military strength (discussed below) fits this pattern. In other cases as well, it seems at least plausible that a policy that is believed to be superior to the alternatives on the one dimension that is shared by all will have a major advantage. Although the noncognitive explanation of the importance of the common dimension cannot be dismissed— any policy proposal will have to speak to the concern that is most deeply felt—ease of comparison is still likely to play a role.

16 Thomas Schelling, *The Strategy of Conflict* (Cambridge: Harvard University Press, 1960), ch. 3.

17 Paul Slovic, "Choice between Equally Valued Alternatives," *Journal of Experimental Psychology: Human Perception and Performance* 1: 280–87; Paul Slovic and Douglas MacPhillmay, "Dimensional Commensurability and Cue Utilization in Comparative Judgment," *Organizational Behavior and Human Performance* 11 (March 1974): 172–94.

USING ONLY THE MOST READILY AVAILABLE INFORMATION

To ease calculations, people concentrate on questions about which they have a good deal of information, pay most attention to the factors on which they are best informed, and attribute the causes to variables with which they are familiar. Of course, outside the laboratory it is hard to tell which way causality runs (and it may be reciprocal) as people seek information about factors they believe are important. But this is not the entire story, as Tversky and Kahnneman's research on availability shows. They have found that ease of recall strongly influences judgments in ways that cannot be explained by the rational seeking and using of information. For example, if a person is asked whether the number of words beginning with a particular letter is greater than the number of words in which the letter appears third, he is likely to answer in the affirmative because it is easier to recall the first letters of words. But this ease of recall is not a good measure of frequency. The fact that it is hard for us to call to mind words with a given third letter does not mean that such words are uncommon.[18]

As with the other effects we have discussed, the impact of readily available information often is not perceptible. Thus, experiments have shown that if the salience of a factor is increased, people will treat that factor as of greater importance, even though they do not understand the manipulation and probably would deny that it had any effect on them.[19] For example, while actors usually attribute their own behavior to the stimuli they confront and observers attribute the behavior to the actor's internal characteristics, if videotapes are used to change the actors' and observers' perspectives, the attributions change correspondingly.[20] Differences in interpretation of events often can be traced to differences in the information that is salient, with each person attributing greater importance to the factors with which he is most familiar.

In foreign policy as well, the degree to which a factor is seen as influential depends in part on the amount of information that the decision-maker has about it. What the decision-maker is most likely to know are his own worries and plans, thus contributing to the egocentric nature of inference. This bias is not necessarily a self-serving one—the actor does not always see himself in a favorable light. Rather, people place themselves at the center of others' attention, believing that others are reacting to them or trying to affect them. Since

18 Daniel Kahneman and Amos Tversky, "On the Psychology of Prediction," *Psychological Review* 80 (July 1973): 237–51.

19 Fiske and Taylor, *Social Cognition*.

20 See Robert Arkin and Shelley Duval, "Focus of Attention and Causal Attributions of Actors and Observers," *Journal of Experimental Psychology* 11 (September 1975): 427–38; Dennis Regan and Judith Toten, "Empathy and Attribution: Turning Observers Into Actors," *Journal of Personality and Social Psychology* 32 (November 1975): 850–56; Michael Storms, "Videotape and the Attribution Process: Reversing Actors' and Observers' Points of View," *Journal of Personality and Social Psychology* 27 (August 1973): 165–75.

the decision-maker knows about her state's policy in great detail, it will be relatively easy for her to find some element in it that could have been the cause or the object of the other state's actions. By contrast, many of the other possible causes of the other state's behavior are seen only in dim outline.

It was to correct this propensity and to better understand Soviet behavior in the Strategic Arms Limitation Treaty (SALT) negotiations that Marshall Shulman, as Secretary of State Cyrus Vance's assistant, kept a chart of what he called "correlated activities,"[21] which showed all the events that were likely to be affecting the Soviets, not only those that were of primary interest to the United States. Of course, people can draw inferences only when they have some information to work with. But rarely are they aware of the degree to which hidden factors could be more powerful than those about which they are informed. They implicitly assume that factors not in their purview are unimportant.[22]

It is also easier to see how a new technology fits into one's own plans than it is to see how an adversary might use it. The difficult task of discerning the implications of new developments can be made easier by using a framework that the person already understands well, which usually is his nation's capacities and intentions. He will have much less information on how the other side might employ the new device and so will pay less attention to this problem or, when he studies it, will implicitly assume that the other side will see it as he does. This was the pattern in many of the Royal Navy's attempts to grasp the implications of new technologies before World War I. When trying to understand how the torpedo boat would change warfare, both those who urged its adoption and those who denied its importance paid most attention to how it could be used in the blockade that the Royal Navy planned to institute in the event of war. Little thought was given to how England's enemies might use torpedo boats to thwart the blockade, a mission that they could in fact perform well.[23] Similarly, most of the discussion of submarines was in terms of their utility to the British, which was slight. Only a few people shared Lord Balfour's insight: "The question that really troubles me is not whether *our* submarines could render the enemy's position intolerable, but whether *their* submarines could render our position untenable."[24] Some of this effect

21 Strobe Talbott, *Endgame: The Inside Story of SALT II* (New York: Harper and Row, 1979), pp. 80, 120, 146.

22 Thus, telling someone about a possible factor is likely to increase the weight he will give to it. See Baruch Fischoff, Paul Slovic, and Sarah Lichtenstein, "Fault Trees: Sensitivity of Estimated Failure of Probabilities to Problem Representation," *Journal of Experimental Psychology: Human Perception and Performance* 4 (May 1978): 330–44.

23 Alan Cowpe, "The Royal Navy and the Whitehead Torpedo," pp. 23–36 in Bryan Ranft, ed., *Technical Change and British Naval Policy: 1960–1939* (New York: Holmes and Meier, 1977).

24 Paul Kennedy, "Fisher and Tirpitz Compared," in Gerald Jordan, ed., *Naval Warfare in the 20th Century* (London: Croom Helm, 1977), pp. 109–26. An exception was the British analysis of airships. By 1911 they had come to see this weapon as Germany's and had concentrated on

may be explained by the tendency of military commanders to think in terms of taking the initiative rather than having to react to what the adversary is doing. But probably at least as important is the fact that they can make the problem of judging new weapons less intractable by concentrating on how they could use them rather than trying to guess how the other side might do so, a question about which there is less information and whose answer requires the use of a less familiar mental framework.

In a variant of this pattern, states assume that other states will use their weapons in the same way that the state is planning. This makes some sense because a great deal of thought presumably went into developing the state's own plans, and if the problems and outlook of other states are similar they are likely to come up with similar answers. But even if these conditions do not hold, the simplifications that are permitted by assuming that they do hold exert such a strong attraction that decision-makers are not likely to abandon them. Thus, in the 1930s the British believed that the Germans planned to use air power in the same way that the British did, which was in strategic attacks on the adversary's homeland. There was little in German military doctrine to lead to this conclusion and German airplanes were not suited to this mission, but those factors were not sufficient to destroy the illusion of symmetry.[25] Until shortly before the outbreak of World War II, the British Air Ministry used the same assumption when estimating the size of the German air force. It thought that "the best criteria for judging Germany's rate of expansion were those which governed the rate at which the RAF could itself form efficient units."[26]

Consequences

INERTIA

The first consequence of the need to simplify calculations is that incrementalism is encouraged. Decision making is made much easier if the person searches only for alternatives when the current policy is failing badly, limits the search to policies that are only marginally different from the current one, concentrates on the particular value dimension that is causing trouble, evaluates only a few alternatives, and adopts the first alternative that puts the decision-maker above an acceptable level of satisfaction. Furthermore, some of these processes operate at the perceptual level as well as at later and more conscious levels of deliberation. Thus, people engage in "perceptual satisficing"—in other

---

how to defeat them, not on how to use them for their own purposes. See also Robin Higham, "The Peripheral Weapon in Wartime: A Case Study," in Jordan, ed., *Naval Warfare in the 20th Century*, pp. 90–104.

25 See Jervis, "Deterrence and Perception," in this volume.

26 F. Hinsley, E. Thomas, C. Ransome, and R. Knight, *British Intelligence in the Second World War* (New York: Cambridge University Press, 1979), p. 299.

words, rather than waiting, collecting more information, and comparing several accounts, each of which is at least minimally satisfactory, they accept the
first image or belief that makes minimal sense out of the data available.

Linked to this characteristic is the tendency for a policy to continue even
as the rationales for it shift. Some of the forces stem from bureaucratic, domestic, and international politics as vested internal interests often support
continuity, and their policies constitute commitments that are hard to break.
But this phenomenon has a cognitive component as well. Once a person has
worked through the arguments that led him to a conclusion, he is likely to
conserve his resources by not reexamining it unless he has to. As the reasons
that originally led to the policy erode, they often are gradually replaced by
new and sometimes incompatible ones. Thus, an experientially induced belief can persevere even when the person is told that the evidence that established it is false.[27] A similar process may be at work in cases—such as support
for foreign aid—that have seen a relatively constant policy supported by changing rationales.

IGNORING INTERACTION EFFECTS

A second consequence of the need to keep calculation manageably simple is
that problems that involve many interrelated elements often are analyzed as
though each element were separate.[28] While people think they are using interactive models and complex methods of calculation, in fact they implicitly
assume additivity. People are better at seeing what variables are important
than they are at combining them. This is consistent with Richard Cyert and
James March's finding that organizations deal with complexity by dividing up
problems into smaller ones and seeking separate solutions for each part of
them ("factored problems—factored solutions").[29]

The same patterns appear in political decision making. Interactive models place enormous strain on our cognitive abilities and, even when we know
they are appropriate, we shy away from using them. Thus, the flaw in the Royal

27 See Jervis, *Perception and Misperception* (1976, 2017); Lee Ross, Mark Lepper, and Michael Hubbard, "Perseverance in Self-Perception and Social Perception: Biased Attributional
Processes in the Debriefing Paradigm," *Journal of Personality and Social Psychology* 32 (November 1975): 880–92.

28 Robyn Dawes, "A Case Study of Graduate Admissions: Applications of Three Principles
of Human Decision Making," *American Psychologist* 26 (February 1971): 180–88; Robyn Dawes
and Bernard Corrigan, "Linear Models in Decision Making," *Psychological Bulletin* 81 (February
1974): 95–106; Hillel Einhorn, "Expert Measurement and Mechanical Combination," *Organizational Behavior and Human Performance* 7 (February 1972): 86–106; Robert Jervis, *System Effects:
Complexity in Political and Social Life* (Princeton: Princeton University Press, 1997), chs. 1, 7.

29 Richard Cyert and James March, *A Behavioral Theory of the Firm* (Englewood Cliffs, N.J.:
Prentice-Hall, 1963).

Navy's analysis of the threat posed by air power to battleships in the interwar period: "Although specific problems ... such as the effect of underwater explosives were occasionally analyzed in depth, there was little continuing research into the ... problem as a whole."[30] Taken one at a time, the problems might be manageable, but when combined the threat could be overwhelming. The German analysis in late 1916 and early 1917 employed the same shortcut and similarly produced erroneous results. In deciding whether to adopt unrestricted submarine warfare, the Germans estimated the amount of goods that Britain needed to maintain her position and the numbers of ships that the Germans thought they could sink. The conclusion was that they could quickly reduce the flow of material coming into Britain to below the minimum level and that Britain therefore would sue for peace before the impact of U.S. entry into the war could be felt. While the specific calculations were accurate, the influence of one of the factors on the others was neglected. That is, once the United States entered the war, the British were willing to suffer what earlier would have been intolerable loss of shipping because they realized that if they held on a bit longer the tide would turn.[31]

The pattern of dividing up problems and examining each solution in isolation contributes to the propensity for states to follow policies that embody conflicting elements. To say that the right hand does not know what the left hand is doing is not quite accurate: rather the right hand does not pay any attention to the implications of the left hand's activities. Thus, in the interwar period Japan acted as though its policies toward China would not influence the prospects for relations with the West.[32] Similarly, in 1918 the French ministry of war supported Japanese intervention in Siberia but "tended to ignore the obvious consequences of this policy on [French] relations with the Bolsheviks, or preferred to treat European Russia and Siberia as two separate theaters of action."[33]

Net Assessment

The Drunkard's search is illustrated by the way that the British judged German air power in the 1930s and how American analysts compared Soviet and American nuclear strengths throughout the Cold War. In both cases, the

---

30 Geoffrey Till, "Airpower and the Battleship in the 1920s," in Ranft, ed., *Technical Change and British Naval Policy*, 119.

31 The German error may well have been a motivated one growing out of the intractable dilemma it faced. Fred Iklé, *Every War Must End* (New York: Columbia University Press, 1971).

32 Akira Iriye, *After Imperialism: The Search for a New Order in the Far East, 1921–1931* (New York: Atheneum, 1969).

33 Michael Carley, "The Origins of the French Intervention in the Russian Civil War, January–May 1918: A Reappraisal," *Journal of Modern History* 48 (September 1976): 432.

basic question asked was "Who is ahead?" not "Do we have sufficient military force to support our foreign policy?" A glance at almost any article on what is called nuclear or strategic balance shows a preoccupation with the question of whether or not the United States trailed the Soviet Union. Carrying this approach to its absurd end, Secretary of Defense Caspar Weinberger argued that the United States had to spend as much as the Soviets did. But this general error was not committed only by hawks. While doves used different indicators and argued that the situation was one of parity or U.S. superiority, they framed the question in the same way. Similarly, in the interwar period both Neville Chamberlain and Winston Churchill focused on the question of whether the United Kingdom had what they called "air parity" with Germany.

But this approach, while simple, is highly misleading. Most obviously, the United States and the USSR could have had equal numbers of strategic forces, but the weapons could have been configured in such ways that both sides had first-strike capability, thus creating tremendous instability. While everyone knew of this danger, it sometimes was lost sight of in comparing the size of the two side's forces. Less frequently recognized was the fact that depending on the task and context, a state could have more military power than its adversary and still not have enough or that it could be inferior and still have more than it needed. In the interwar period, air parity might have been sufficient to deter a German direct attack on England, but not enough for "extended deterrence" against German expansion to the east. Similarly, the analysis of many hawks during the Cold War implied that a significant margin of superiority—perhaps what Herman Kahn called a "not-incredible first strike capability" —was needed if the American commitment to NATO was to be credible.[34] The implications of the arguments of many doves was that significantly less than parity was needed to protect the United States and probably to protect vital European interests as well. But the logic of both positions was abandoned when much of the debate focused on the question of who was ahead, which is a much more manageable question than estimating how much was enough to deter the Soviets and how various configurations of forces could have contributed to terminating a war in the least possible unfavorable way.

In general, it is very difficult to estimate what would happen in the event of a war—the "outputs" of the weapons—because the interaction of what each side will do is terribly complex. It is much easier to measure the "inputs"— what weapons each side has—even though the relationship between these and the outputs is tenuous. So, just as the drunk looks under the lamppost, so it is that analysts use inputs to judge military balance.

34 Herman Kahn, *On Thermonuclear War* (Princeton: Princeton University Press, 1960).

During the interwar period, little attention was paid to the composition of the forces on both sides, and numbers of planes often were compared without separating fighters from bombers. On some occasions, the British fighter force was compared to the German one and the bombers were compared to those of the adversary. But even this was not sensible because while fighters would sometimes meet in an air battle, bombers never would. What was really needed was some way of judging how many German bombers could penetrate British defenses on a sustained basis and how much damage they could do.[35] Similarly, one wanted to know how much the British bombers could damage German targets. So comparing each side's bombers with the other's fighters and anti-aircraft guns would have made some sense. Even this, however, would have omitted many crucial factors, such as the ability of defenders to disperse or hide and the ability of the attackers to navigate across hostile terrain in good weather and in bad—in the first year of the war, few British bombers could find the way to their targets. But at least such measures would have been closer to what would affect the outcome of a war than the simple comparison that was used.

Furthermore, in looking at inputs, people have preference for absolutes, for examining what is most easily quantified, and for stressing what they have most information on. Thus in the 1930s the British judged comparative air strength by counting the number of planes each side had. Sometimes they distinguished the total number from what they called "first-line" aircraft (planes of the most modern design) but even this degree of complexity was often dropped.[36] This was not because the British treated the whole question of the comparison casually. There were long debates over how to calculate first-line strength,[37] but the attempts to push beyond this measure were few and desultory.

Quality of the aircraft was omitted from most calculations. For example, the British official history notes that in looking at the effectiveness of a planned expansion of their bombers, the British took "no account of the fact that paper plans were ... actively being made within the Air Ministry to incorporate the new heavy four-engined machines into the bomber force."[38] While those who favored a stronger bombers component had an interest in underestimating British strength, strategic misrepresentation cannot explain why those who

35 The British estimates of how much damage would be done by each ton of bombs that landed was also highly inaccurate. For a discussion, see Paul Bracken, "Unintended Consequences of Strategic Gaming," *Simulation and Games* 8 (September 1977): 283–318. But this error was not entirely cognitive.

36 Martin Gilbert, *Churchill: A Life* (Englewood Cliffs, N.J.: Prentice-Hall, 1967).

37 Ibid.

38 Norman Gibbs, *Grand Strategy: Rearmament Policy* (London: Her Majesty's Stationer's Office, 1976), p. 569.

opposed the air ministry's plans ignored the question of quality. Government critics like Churchill who called for a rapid expansion of the RAF also generally ignored the linked questions of what aircraft were ready for production and whether it would have been better to postpone increased procurement until a new generation of planes was available.

Quality of personnel likewise was given short shrift. Although the Germans suffered from the "teething problems" associated with a young and expanding force, questions of training, morale, and maintenance were generally ignored. Similarly, emphasis on numbers of planes usually excluded consideration of each side's production capacity, which was vital for sustaining and increasing its force in wartime. A country might be better off with a somewhat smaller standing air force supported by large and flexible production facilities than it would be with a larger force what would not be maintained in the face of wartime losses. But production facilities remained marginal to the British estimate of the military balance.[39]

This pattern of assessment was not limited to air power. In judging their naval strength before World War I the British also relied exclusively on numerical comparisons without consideration of quality. As the battles showed, strength of armor, accuracy of fire, ship design, and the effectiveness of shells were extremely important, and the German superiority in the latter two categories cost the British dearly. The impact of factors such as these also shows up in ground combat. In 1940, French tanks were superior to German tanks in numbers and roughly equal in quality. Tactics, training, morale, coordination, and political will made all the difference. But even had planners been aware of their importance, it is doubtful whether they could have developed sufficient understanding of them to have usefully employed these factors in their analysis.

In summary, British decision-makers concentrated on what was relatively easy to measure at the expense of trying to develop more complex, but more revealing, measures of relative strength. By implicitly assuming that both sides were planning to use their airplanes in the same way, which they could have learned was not correct, they were able to concentrate on only one dimension, just as the experimental subjects did. The yardstick they employed was distinguished only by the extent to which it facilitated comparisons and decisions. It gave them manageable simplicity, summary numbers they could hold in their minds and easily use.

The same pattern was apparent during the Cold War. Heavy reliance was placed on "static indicators" such as numbers of missiles and warheads, the amount of throw-weight, and the extent of the damage that each side could

---

39 For exceptions, see Gilbert, *Churchill*, 631–35, 650, 671–72; also see John Slessor, *Central Blue: The Autobiography of Sir John Slessor* (London: Cassell, 1956).

do to the other. (The indicators of the latter capability were themselves derived from highly oversimplified calculations.)[40] Although there was some discussion of "counter-balancing asymmetries," arguments often were couched in terms of which side was ahead on any of these dimensions. For example, in the fall of 1981 many officials in the United States were disturbed by reports that Soviet missiles had become more accurate than American missiles, just as in other periods there was fear that the Soviets were developing better bombers than what the United States possessed. Calculations are facilitated by such comparisons, but this conservation of cognitive resources is purchased at the price of answering questions that make no sense. The accuracy of each side's missiles and the quality of its bombers were significant, but the direct comparison of these factors was not. Each weapons system should have been evaluated in terms of its ability to carry out its mission; an increase in, say, the quality of Soviet bombers may have had important implications for U.S. air defense, but it said nothing about the utility of American bombers. There may have been reasons to be disturbed if Soviet missiles were extremely accurate, but comparison with the accuracy of American missiles says nothing about the ability of either side's forces to carry out their missions.

At first glance, numbers of bombers and missiles (or their destructive capabilities) would seem to make more sense. But they do not. As noted earlier, whether the state is ahead or behind its adversary in strategic weaponry says little about the question of whether the state's military force is adequate for its foreign policy. Furthermore, in a counterforce war in which strategic forces are to be attacked, what is crucial is the match between the numbers and characteristics of the weapons (particularly accuracy) on the one hand and the numbers and characteristics of the targets (particularly how protected they are) on the other.[41] This complex matter is not illuminated by comparing the two sides' weapon systems themselves. One side could have more weapons, warheads, throw-weight, or even hard-target kill capability than the other, yet be less able to wage a counterforce war than the adversary because the latter's forces are more protected than the former's. To come closer to what

40 For good discussions of the technique of net assessment, see Paul Baugh, *Politics of Nuclear Balance: Ambiguity and Continuity in Strategic Policies* (New York: Longman, 1984); George Seiler, *Strategic Nuclear Force Requirements and Issues* (Maxwell Airforce Base, Ala.: Air University Press, 1983); and Peter Pry, *The Strategic Nuclear Balance: And Why it Matters* (New York: Crane Russak, 1990). Pry purports to link the present dynamic analyses that could shed light on how a nuclear war might end but in fact commits many of the errors described here. Lynn Eden shows that when calculating the effects of nuclear bombs, American analysts focused on the blast effects of the weapons and ignored the impact of the devastating fires that would be triggered: Lynn Eden, *Whole World on Fire: Organizations, Knowledge, and Nuclear Weapons Devastation* (Ithaca: Cornell University Press, 2004).

41 This assumes that the targets are protected by being difficult to destroy, not by being difficult to find.

we want to know, we need to consider the state's ability to locate the adversary's forces and communicate with its own, but here again knowing or estimating which side is "ahead" in this regard does not tell us which side's forces, if either, could complete its required missions.

Arms control negotiations show the same concern with equality of static indicators, especially numbers of missiles and warheads. Indeed, the Jackson amendment passed in the wake of SALT I agreements required that future treaties should "not limit the United States to levels of intercontinental strategic forces inferior to the limits provided for the Soviet Union."[42] In the months that followed its passage, this somewhat vague prescription hardened into a mandate for a force of the same size as that of the USSR, and Secretary of State Henry Kissinger's attempts to gain agreement within the administration on proposals embodying "offsetting asymmetries" failed because opponents were able to rally forces in and outside of government to the misleading standard of numerical equality. Furthermore, even more sophisticated analysts, who saw that there was no magic in equality, generally argued that lower numbers of weapons would make the world safer and paid surprisingly little attention to the goal of stability that arms control was initially designed to reach and whose relationship to reduced numbers was only problematical.[43]

Similar intellectual shortcuts are revealed by the tendency to compare how well American forces would have done in a first strike with how well the USSR would have done if it struck first. In fact, while both of these estimates were significant, it does not matter who was "ahead" in this regard. Both sides cannot simultaneously strike first, and these capabilities can never be matched against each other. The degree of first-strike capability that the United Stated needed was not a function of the damage that the Soviets could have done if they had struck first.

When output is measured in terms of civilian rather than military damage, a parallel flaw often appears. One of Richard Nixon's criteria for "essential equivalence" was that the Soviet Union not be able to do more damage to the United States than the United States could do to it.[44] Winston Churchill made the same point on 1934: "I believe that if we maintain at all times in the future

42 Thomas Wolfe, *The SALT Experience* (Cambridge: Ballinger, 1979), p. 301.

43 Thomas Schilling, "What Went Wrong With Arms Control?" *Foreign Affairs* 86 (Winter 1985). Elsewhere I have argued that the emphasis on numbers makes sense in terms of the symbolic nature of arms control, Robert Jervis, *The Meaning of the Nuclear Revolution: Statecraft and the Prospect of Armageddon* (Ithaca: Cornell University Press, 1989), pp. 221–25.

44 See, for example, Secretary of Defense Melvin Laird's testimony in House of Representatives, Subcommittee on the Department of Defense, Appropriations for the FY 1973 Defense Budget and FY 1973-77 Program, 92nd Congress, 2nd Session, February 22, 1972. For further discussion, see Robert Jervis, *Meaning of the Nuclear Revolution: Statecraft and the Prospect of Armageddon* (Ithaca: Cornell University Press, 1989), pp. 16–19.

an air power sufficient to enable us to inflict as much damage upon the most probable assailant, upon the most likely potential aggressor, as he can inflict upon us, we may shield our people effectually in our times for all those horrors that I have ventured to describe."[45] But in neither case was such a simple yardstick appropriate. States do not decide to go to war on the basis of comparison between how much they will suffer and much harm will come to their adversaries. If decision-makers are even minimally rational, they compare their estimates of the probable gains and losses of going to war with what the state expects the situation to be if it does not attack. An aggressor would be deterred even if it thought that it could inflict more damage than it would receive or, in other circumstances, could attack even if it thought this balance was reversed. Such assessments of damage also fit the drunkard's search metaphor in their omission of many factors whose importance is matched only by the difficulty of measuring them, such as long-term casualties and environmental effects of nuclear war.

There is little dispute on these points: all analysts agree that it is better to use "dynamic indicators" that attempt to capture the likely courses of wars fought under various conditions. But such measures are much more expensive in terms of time and cognitive resources and do not yield simple and straightforward summary numbers. Because they involve a large number of variables of widely different kinds and are highly sensitive to conditions and context, they do not lend themselves to easy comparison over time or between two adversaries. Thus it is not surprising that static indicators remain popular; for all their inadequacies, they are relatively easy to develop and use.

Even dynamic indicators pay little attention to factors that, while crucial, are particularly difficult to capture, such as command, control, and communications. The survival and efficiency of these systems would have had an enormous impact on the way that any war could have been fought and terminated—indeed a significant advantage on this dimension would more than outweigh a major disadvantage in numbers of missiles. But decision-makers knew so little about how these systems would function in wartime that they did not figure in most assessments.

In the same way, political factors that would have influenced the outcome of a limited war were left out of most analyses of the strategic balance. We hardly need to be reminded that the victor in Vietnam was incomparably weaker than its adversary on all standard military indicators. The outcome of any war that ends through negotiations will be strongly influenced by the stakes each side has in the conflict, each side's willingness to bear pain, each side's fear that the war will continue and grow even more destructive, and

45 Gilbert, *Churchill*, 574.

each side's perception of how the other side stands on these dimensions.[46] But since these factors, which may be highly situation-specific, are so hard to estimate and complicate analysis enormously, they too are neglected.

Most attempts to assess the strategic balance also conformed to our model in that they pretended to greater certainty than the information actually permitted. They did not deal adequately with the large number of unknowns that characterized the complex weapons systems that had never been used. Would missiles have been as accurate when fired over the North Pole as they were on test ranges? Could a large number of missiles have been fired simultaneously? How vulnerable were various targets? (We could not have been certain about the hardness of our own missile silos, let alone those of the Soviets). How would nuclear explosions have affected communications systems? What would be the environmental effects of war? This list could be readily expanded even if we ignored questions about human behavior. Indeed, there may be crucial questions that we do not even know enough to ask—only in the last decade of the Cold War did people think about the effects of explosions on world climate.

These uncertainties are so enormous that they present insurmountable obstacles to a complete and thorough analysis. But what is striking from the standpoint of common sense, but expected by the model of the drunkard's search, is that few discussions contained any sensitivity analysis. That is, they did not explain how the results would have differed if the assumptions on which they were based were altered. Instead, most analyses of the effects of various strikes presented misleadingly firm conclusions about the expected consequences of nuclear war. One used to read, for example, that a Soviet first strike would probably destroy all but fifty U.S. ICBMs. But while this claim might have been based on the best estimate, what was generally ignored was that the number of ICBMs might have been much higher or lower. This number represented some sort of average of the uncertainties and concealed the extent to which the results could have been wildly different if any of the assumptions were incorrect. It matters a great deal how likely it is that an outcome will be radically different from the best estimate, and only occasionally did one get some of this information in the form of a range of 50 percent, 75 percent, or 90 percent within which the analysts were certain that the outcome would fall. In the overwhelming majority of cases, the prediction came in the form of a misleadingly precise estimate of the likely outcome rather than in a presentation of the range of outcomes within which the actual result was likely to occur. It will often turn out that if one wants 90 percent certainty, the range will be so wide that the analysis is extremely difficult to

---

46 For further discussion, see Robert Jervis, *The Illogic of American Nuclear Strategy* (Ithaca: Cornell University Press, 1984).

use.[47] At bottom is the problem that to dwell on the unknowns could render the calculations unmanageable, as perhaps the problems themselves are.

In both the 1930s and the Cold War, one can argue that it made sense for the actors to use illogical but simple measures because others whom the actors wanted to influence considered them accurate measures of strategic power. A self-fulfilling prophecy was then at work. For example, the British were under pressure to build a "shop window" force (one that had no reserves) because the Germans would count only these planes, and so deterrence would be maximized. The minutes of a British cabinet meeting paraphrased the Secretary of State for Air's explanation as follows:

[O]f his proposed bomber expansion program, he pointed to the crux of the matter, that military considerations as such really had little to do with the issues; ... arguing that "the policy now being considered was designed largely as a gesture to check Hitler's continual demands...." The program that resulted [from these deliberations] had no function other than to produce the same size front line as Germany was expected to have in April 1937. No notion of wartime use of such a force [or of the fact that Britain was more vulnerable than Germany and had more alliance commitments] ... entered into the considerations.[48]

Similarly, during the Cold War the United States had to be concerned with the throw-weight balance or the warhead balance because the Soviets, NATO allies, and neutrals believed that the side that was ahead on these dimensions was more likely to stand firm and prevail in disputes. A full discussion of this question would take us off track,[49] but it should be noted that this consideration cannot be the entire explanation for the phenomenon. Not only is there no direct evidence to support the claim that the other side actually did see the strategic military balance in this way—the Germans did not in the 1930s, and the Soviets probably did not during the Cold War—but purely military analyses that are not concerned with the second-order political implications display the same pattern of using only easily available information. What is in control, I think, is the pressure to simplify in order to conserve our time, energy, and cognitive resources.

47 Furthermore, even this approach assumes that it is legitimate to apply statistical analysis to estimating an event that has never occurred and that can occur only once. This is not to claim that any other kind of method could be used, but only to remind us of the inherent difficult of dealing with this question.

48 Malcolm Smith, *British Air Strategy between the Wars* (Oxford: Clarendon Press, 1986), pp. 156–57.

49 For further discussion, see Robert Jervis, "Rational Deterrence: Theory and Evidence," *World Politics* 41 (January 1989): 183–207.

Conclusion

We find the story of the drunkard's search humorous because we recognize that it is not entirely fictitious: people do look where the light is brightest. Nor is it entirely foolish: the costs of gathering and processing information need to be taken into account by any intelligent decision-maker. But the pattern cannot be entirely explained by the rational search for and use of information. The data that analysts and decision-makers use are often more distinguished by their ready availability than by their relation to the questions being asked. Like people in their everyday lives, leaders tend to see a minimum of causal factors at work, minimize uncertainty, use simple benchmarks and analogies, and make comparisons that are manageable but inappropriate. Intellectual resources are conserved, but at a high price.

PART II

Heuristics and Biases

3

Representativeness, Foreign Policy Judgments, and Theory-Driven Perceptions

A great deal of research in psychology deals with the propensity for people to rely on representativeness in making judgments. Representativeness means determining whether object or event A belongs to or was produced by B according to the degree to which A resembles B. A nice illustration is provided by an experiment by Daniel Kahneman and Amos Tversky, the two psychologists who pioneered this line of research. People are asked the following question: "In a metropolitan area, a sociologist surveyed all the families with six children. He found exactly 72 families in which the birth order of boys (B) and girls (G) was BGGBGB. How many six-child families do you think there were in which the precise birth order was GBBBBB?" Most people reply with a number around 20. But the correct answer is 72 since no one specific order of boys and girls is less likely than any other. What is going on here is that people see regularity in the latter string and randomness in the former and since they know that the birth order should be random, they think the latter is much less probable than the former. To put it a bit differently, BGGBGB represents or resembles the process which is thought to generate the outcome.[1]

---

1 Daniel Kahneman and Amos Tversky, "Subjective Probability: A Judgment of Representativeness," *Cognitive Psychology* 3 (July 1972): 430–54; also see Maya Bar-Hillel and Baruch Fischhoff, "When Do Base Rates Affect Predictions?" *Journal of Personal and Social Psychology* 41 (October 1974): 671–80. For a good summary of this literature, see Richard Nisbett and Lee Ross, *Human Inference* (Englewood Cliffs, N.J.: Prentice-Hall, 1980); for further discussion of

The same thought process is at work when people are asked to make series of guesses about which card, an A or a B, will be turned up in a deck containing 70 percent A's and 30 percent B's. Most will guess A 70 percent of the time and B 30 percent. Since A is always more likely to turn up than B, it would actually make more sense to guess A each time, but most people use the strategy of "event matching" and produce guesses whose distribution matches the characteristics of the sample.

Several preliminary points should be made about this inference process. First, what often is being revealed is that people lack an intuitive grasp of many of the principles of statistics. Some of these principles are quite arbitrary (e.g., the ordinary least-squares rule in regression analysis), so in some cases this does not mean that these judgments will be less accurate than those derived from alternative normative models. Even when the statistical principles are not arbitrary, as they are not in the examples given above, when they are arcane it is not surprising that untrained people fail to use them. But in these cases, judgements will be less accurate than they could be.

Second, if some people are ignorant of the relevant aspects of statistics, others explicitly and consciously reject them. This is true, for example, of the "gambler's fallacy," which is linked to the strategy of event matching. This fallacy denies the independence of events that are in fact independent, and instead sees certain random events as "overdue." Thus, if heads come up in three successive tosses of a coin, many people will be willing to give odds that tails will appear next. My grandfather was one such person. He could never be convinced that chance was not directed, that things did not have to even out in the end. So this error will not automatically be corrected if it is pointed out to the person.

Third, the question of how resemblance is determined is not self- evident. For the purposes of the discussion here, we can use the obvious definition of perceived similarity on important dimensions even though it comes perilously close to circulatory.[2] Fourth, the point is not that representativeness lacks all validity as a cue to the nature of the object under consideration, but that under some conditions people tend to rely on it excessively.

---

the meaning of representativeness, see Amos Tversky and Daniel Kahneman, "Judgments of and by Representativeness," pp. 84–98 in David Kahneman, Paul Slovic, and Amos Tversky, eds., *Judgment under Uncertainty: Heuristics and Biases* (New York: Cambridge University Press, 1982), pp. 85–87.

2 For thorough discussions, see Maya Bar-Hillel, "What Features Make Samples Seem Representative?" *Journal of Experimental Psychology, Human Perception, and Performance* 6 (August 1980): 578–89; Amos Tversky, "Features of Similarity," *Psychological Review* 84 (July 1977): 327–52.

Forms of Representativeness

Many of our beliefs about the world are implicitly based on representativeness. Thus one series of investigations showed that both naive subjects and trained clinicians mistakenly see patterns in the Draw-a-Person and Rorschach tests that would be present if the symptoms and pathologies resembled each other. People incorrectly report that patients who are suspicious are likely to draw figures with distorted eyes and those who are dependent will emphasize mouths. Similarly, homosexuals were incorrectly reported to find more anuses, genitalia, and humans with confused or uncertain gender in Rorschach pictures than did heterosexuals.[3] These "illusory correlations" are seen because people expect that the symptoms will resemble the underlying condition that they believe generates them.

For many years, scientists held analogous beliefs about the forces that formed the major features of the earth. Because high mountains and deep canyons are large and dramatic, it seemed that they could only have been generated by matching processes. This view, called catastrophism, was not unscientific, but it may have gained plausibility from the fact that it tapped representativeness and thus seemed to make sense to experts and lay people alike. Some of the resistance to the idea that the earth had been shaped gradually may have come from the discrepancy between slow and steady causes and effects that were anything but smooth and even.

To take a case from political analysis, many historians have remarked on people's propensity to associate large effects with large causes. Thus most explanations of World War I rely on social and political forces roughly commensurate with the size of the impact of the conflict. Some theories point to imperialism, others to broad trends in European domestic politics, still others to the configuration of the internal systems. The assassination of the Archduke is, of course, not ignored, but it is usually seen as only the spark that set off the conflagration with the implication that if it had not occurred, any number of other events could have served the same function. This may be true, but I think that the belief owes some of its plausibility to the fact that a small cause could in no way resemble the major reordering of the world that the war brought about. If the war had been short and limited in its consequences, attributing its causes to broad factors like the social dislocation that

---

3 Loren Chapman and Jean Chapman, "Genesis of Popular but Erroneous Psycho-Diagnostic Observations," *Journal of Abnormal Psychology* 72 (June 1967): 193–204; Loren Chapman and Jean Chapman, "Illusory Correlation as an Obstacle to the Use of Vital Psycho-Diagnostic Signs," *Journal of Abnormal Psychology* 74 (June 1969): 271–80.

accompanied political and economic development or the division of the previously unoccupied parts of the globe would have seemed less attractive.

Some explanations of the causes of late-nineteenth-century imperialism also are supported by representativeness. Again without implying that the explanations are incorrect, accounts that saw internal dynamism and upheaval as producing similar effects abroad drew on representativeness. It seems natural to argue that societies that were rapidly growing at home would spread their control over the globe. In the same way, arguments that saw imperialism as motivated primarily by the search for profits usually saw the domestic societies of the imperialist states as driven by avarice.

Of course, it makes some sense to expect the same kinds of motives to be displayed in the state's foreign policy that are present in its domestic arrangements, but there is no necessary connection here, as Schumpeter pointed out.[4] His argument that those who sought the maximization of profits at home would seek peace, not conquest, may have met resistance in part because it violated representativeness. Similarly, arguments that attribute imperialism not to any domestic feature of the state but rather to the anarchic nature of the international system[5] may face psychological difficulties because they give a cause which has no resemblance to the effect.

Representativeness can also contribute to the propensity for people to see the causes of national behavior as lying within the characteristics of individual decision-makers. Of course in some cases this is correct, but in most formulations such an account has the psychological advantage of seeing cause and effects as similar. One interesting example is the reaction of British leaders to the analytic problem posed by the fall of France in June 1940. They needed to assess whether the French government would continue the fight from North Africa and, if it did not, whether it would keep the fleet out of German hands. For a considerable period of time, they framed the question as, "Can we trust Pétain?" They sought a correspondence between a personal attribute and national behavior: if the statesman is trustworthy, the acts he undertakes in the name of his state will be honorable. This overlooked not only the substance of Pétain's views, which were defeatist, but also the highly constraining objective situation that France was in. After a week of looking at the matter in this light, Churchill and his colleagues shifted their approach to a more rational one that did focus on these factors. But the fact that their initial response was to draw inferences in terms of representativeness may indicate that people instinctively reason this way.

---

4 Joseph Schumpeter, *Imperialism and Social Classes* (Cleveland, Ohio: World, 1968).

5 Kenneth Waltz, *Theory of International Politics* (Reading, N.J.: Addison-Wesley, 1979).

Representativeness and Base Rates

The cases of representativeness discussed so far have been those in which outcome A is seen as being produced by B because of the resemblance between them. More striking are the cases in which A is seen as an example of B because of their similarity. It is not an error to see resemblance as an important bit of evidence as in whether A is a B, but experiments have shown that under many circumstances people give too much weight to this kind of evidence and concomitantly ignore another kind, known as base rate data. This is the prior probability that A is a B, which is determined by the proportion of B and non-B in the population from which A is drawn. The base rate is then the probability that A is or will be a B that exists prior to receiving any information about A. If A resembles B but B's are rare, a rational person will not jump to the conclusion that A is a B but will dilute the evidence of similarity by considerations of the base rate.[6] It should take more and better evidence to convince me that a rare event is about to occur than that a common one is in the offing.

The major point made by Kahneman, Tversky, and those who have followed their lead is that in most circumstances people rely too heavily on representativeness and pay insufficient attention to the base rate. The result is that they make interferences that are not optimal. Thus, in one of the demonstrations that piqued interest in the effect, subjects received the following instructions:

A panel of psychologists has interviewed and administered personality tests to 30 engineers and 70 lawyers, all successful in their respective fields. On the basis of this information, thumbnail descriptions of the 30 engineers and 70 lawyers have been written. You will find on your forms five descriptions, chosen at random from the 100 available descriptions. For each description, please indicate your probability that the person described is an engineer, on a scale from 0 to 100.

One of the descriptions read as follows:

Jack is a 45-year-old man. He is married and has four children. He is generally conservative, careful, and ambitious. He shows no interest in political

6 The exact way to combine the two factors is given by Bayesian statistics. The controversies in this area discussed by Duncan Hunter, *Political Military Applications of Bayesian Analysis: Methodological Issues* (Boulder, Colo.: Westview, 1984), and Isaac Levi, *Decisions and Revisions: Philosophical Essays on Knowledge and Value* (New York, Cambridge University Press, 1984), do not bear on the argument here. For further discussion of the difficulties with using Bayesianism in foreign policy judgments, see my preface to the new edition of Robert Jervis, *Perception and Misperception in International Politics*, 2nd ed. (Princeton: Princeton University Press, 2017; originally published in 1976).

and social issues and spends most of his free time on his many hobbies, which include home carpentry, sailing, and mathematical puzzles.

Most subjects said that the likelihood of Jack being an engineer was at least 50 percent even though, before they read the sketch, they would have said (and did say under conditions in the control group) that the chance that he was an engineer was only 30 percent. In other words, the base rate information did not have great impact.[7]

This is further shown by the fact that the estimate of the person's occupation is not sensitive to changes in the base rate. That is, the people's estimates do not vary with the information they are given about the percentages of lawyers and engineers in the population from which the sketch is selected. Whether they are told that the population contains 80 percent engineers, 50 percent, or 20 percent does not matter. Short of extreme base rates they are solely influenced by the inferences they draw from the sketch itself.[8]

This sort of demonstration strikes many people as very odd and some may be tempted to insist that the subjects are rational. After all, one may argue, the sketch should tell you the person's profession. But this claim would be true, and the base rate should be ignored, only if two conditions are met: (a) you have a stereotype of an engineer that is valid 100 percent of the time, and (b) there is a perfect match between the sketch and the stereotype. This is not to argue what when these conditions are not met representativeness is irrelevant, but as long as it is not definitive, the prior probabilities should not be neglected. In the experiment above the evidence from the sketch obviously is not definitive. Even if the stereotype it evokes fits engineers more than it does lawyers, few of us would argue that it fits almost all of the latter and almost none of the former. Yet people act as though this were the case.

Regression toward the Mean

A related way of describing this effect is that people neglect or underestimate the role of chance and so do not pay sufficient attention to the distribution of the characteristics of events within the population from which a particular

7 Daniel Kahneman and Amos Tversky, "On the Psychology of Prediction," *Psychological Review* 80 (July 1973): 237–51.

8 Ibid.; also see Garry Wells and John Harvey, "Do People Use Consensus Information in Making Causal Attributions?" *Journal of Personal and Social Psychology* 35 (May 1977): 279–93; Malvin Manis, Ismel Dovalina, Nancy Avis, and Steven Cardoze, "Base Rates Can Affect Individual Predictions," *Journal of Personal and Social Psychology* 38 (February 1980): 231–40; Bar-Hillel and Fischhoff, "When Do Base Rates Affect Predictions?" 671–80. For a good review of the literature, see Michael Birnbaum, "Base Rates in Bayesian Inference," in Rüdiger Pohl, ed., *Cognitive Illusions: a Handbook on Fallacies and Biases in Thinking, Judgment, and Memory* (New York: Psychology Press, 2004), pp. 43–60.

event is drawn. Some of the time when an event or bit of behavior is quite extreme, this will be only an accident, not a trend. But people are likely to expect trends and so think that one extreme value will be followed by others. They neglect the possibility that it may have been an accident, in which case one should expect later events or behavior to return to values closer to the average—what is called regression toward the mean.

Thus, most of us are puzzled by those students who do very well on the midterm but fall back on the final. We may think of several alternative explanations: the student is having emotional difficulties, other courses are taking too much of her time, or the student is too lazy to keep up with the work. Any of these may be true, of course, but we usually overlook the possibility that the good performance was the product of chance. With over a hundred students in the class, one should expect a few of them to do much better on the midterm than they usually will do. A lower grade on the final will then not call for a special explanation; it will rather be the student's norm.

Kahneman and Tversky provide a nice anecdote that illustrates both the phenomenon and the traps one can fall into by ignoring it. Israeli Air Force flight instructors noted a pattern: When a student made a particularly good landing, they would praise him only to find that the next landing was not nearly as good; when the student made a poor landing the instructor would give strong criticism and the next attempt would show improvement. The instructors drew the obvious inference that praise went to the students' heads and adversely affected their performance whereas criticism had the intended impact. But what probably was at work was regression toward the mean. Extreme performances, either good or bad, are exceptions, and, by the laws of chance, the events that follow them will usually be closer to the average. The instructors' comments may not have had any impact.[9]

Only when people believe that chance is playing a role will they expect regression.[10] But decision-makers generally underestimate the importance of accidents and random processes.[11] Even though they acknowledge that international affairs are uncertain and pay lip service to Machiavelli's Fortuna, the common ethos that calls for action probably encourages them to underestimate the importance of accidents. Many decision-makers would then deny the relevance of the statistical principle of regression if it were explained to them and may not be sufficiently sensitive to the possibility that one or two sharp and extreme events will be followed, not by more of the same, but by behavior closer to the mean.

9 Kahneman and Tversky, "On the Psychology of Prediction," 250–251.

10 Richard Nisbett, David Krantz, Christopher Jepson, and Ziva Kunda, "The Use of Statistical Heuristics in Everyday Inductive Reasoning," *Psychological Review* 90 (October 1983): 339–63.

11 Jervis, *Perception and Misperception* (1976, 2017).

One American official in Vietnam said that one of the axioms of the war is that "things are never as good as they seem when they are good, or as bad as they seem when they are bad,"[12] which shows both an awareness of regression and that not everyone understood it. Similarly, observers are likely to draw far-reaching inferences from a state's extreme actions. For example, one of the arguments in favor of using force to try to free the crew of the Mayaguez was that anything less would have led the Cambodians to repeat this kind of impudence. While this belief may have been true—and the interactive nature of international politics in which each side responds to the other's behavior makes it more likely—it is interesting that no one gave any thought to the possibility that this was an aberration, which, even if not thwarted, would not have started a trend.

Explaining the Biases

How are these biases to be explained? There are several plausible reasons, some difficult to tease apart from each other. First, people either do not understand or have no faith in statistics. General knowledge of statistics, let alone one of the more arcane principles, is not widely held. Furthermore, many of the experiments may confuse the subjects. That people may not understand the basic situation is indicated by some variants of the engineer-lawyer experiment presented above. If people are given only the base rate and no sketch, they estimate the probability that the person is an engineer at the percentage given by the base rate. But if they are given a sketch that contains no useful information, they ignore the priors and put the chance at 50-50.[13] Ignorance is not the only explanation, however. Psychologists who are trained in statistics commit errors like those we have discussed.[14] The other side of this coin is that, as we will discuss below, people without knowledge of statistics do use base rates under conditions in which they seem clearly relevant.

A second and related explanation is that base rate data are underutilized because they are pallid, given in dry percentages, whereas information about the particular case is vivid since it is given in the form of a more lifelike sketch.[15] But it is hard to develop a definition of vividness that is not circular,

12 Quoted in Peter Braestrup, *Big Story* (Garden City, N.Y.: Doubleday, 1978), p. 501

13 Kahneman and Tversky, "On the Psychology of Prediction," 237–251. For somewhat different findings see Zvi Ginosar and Yaacov Trope, "The Effects of Base Rates and Individuating Information on Judgments about Another Person," *Journal of Experimental Social Psychology* 16 (May 1980): 228–42.

14 Amos Tversky and Daniel Kahneman, "Belief in the Law of Small Numbers," *Psychological Bulletin* 76 (August 1971): 105–10.

15 Richard Nisbett and Eugene Borgida, "Attribution and the Psychology of Prediction," *Journal of Personal and Social Psychology* 32 (November 1975): 923–43; also see Richard Nisbett,

and other experiments have shown that even when base rates seem to be vivid, they may still be underutilized.[16]

A third contributing factor may be the excessive confidence that people have in their own cognitive abilities.[17] If people think that they can draw accurate inferences from the material about the particular case before them, they will pay little attention to the prior probabilities. To return to the example of the engineer and lawyer, if a person thinks that he knows which kind of people join either profession and thinks that he can match the sketch with his image, he will behave as the experimental subjects do. This probably is part of the explanation, and perhaps a large part, when we are dealing with decision-makers who are particularly self-confident.

A final explanation is that people downplay base rate data because they do not see it as being related to the task at hand. Thus, in the first example given above, most people would see the base rate as influencing whether a sketch of a lawyer or of an engineer would be drawn from the pile, but as irrelevant to the question of whether the person described was a lawyer or an engineer. This explanation implies that base rates will be used if and when they are believed to be relevant to the task of judging individual cases. This is borne out by findings that, in contrast to the results reported so far, priors will be heeded if they can be interpreted as part of the analysis of the causes of the outcome of the case being considered. In other words, problems with exactly the same solution will be answered very differently depending on whether the base rate seems intuitively relevant. For example, consider these two problems:

1 A cab was involved in a hit-and-run accident at night. Two cab companies, the Green and the Blue, operate in that city. You are given the following data:
   (i) 85 percent of the cabs in the city are Green and 15 percent are Blue.
   (ii) A witness identified the cab as a Blue cab. The court tested his ability to identify cabs under the appropriate visibility conditions.

Eugene Borgida, Rick Crandall, and Harvey Reed, "Popular Induction: Information Is Not Necessarily Informative," in John Carroll and John Payne, eds., *Cognition and Social Behavior* (Hillsdale, N.J.: Erlbaum, 1976); Eugene Borgida and Richard Nisbett, "The Differential Impact of Abstract vs. Concrete Information on Decisions," *Journal of Applied Psychology* 7 (September 1977): 258–71; Shelly Taylor and Susan Fiske, "Salience, Attention, and Attribution: Top of the Head Phenomena," in Leonard Berkowitz, ed., *Advances in Experimental Social Psychology*, vol. 11 (New York: Academic Press, 1978).

16 See the summary in Eugene Borgida and Nancy Brekke, "The Base-Rate Fallacy in Attribution and Prediction," pp. 63–95 in John Harvey, William Ickes, and Robert Kidd, eds., *New Directions in Attribution Research*, vol. 3 (Hillsdale, N.J.: Erlbaum, 1981).

17 Hillel Einhorn and Robin Hogarth, "Confidence in Judgment: Persistence of the Illusion of Validity," *Psychological Review* 85 (September 1978): 395–416.

When presented with a sample of the cabs (half of which were Blue and half of which were Green) the witness made correct identifications in 80 percent of the cases and erred in 20 percent of the cases.

(iii) Question: What is the probability that the cab involved in the accident was Blue rather than Green?

2 A cab was involved in a hit-and-run accident at night. Two cab companies, the Green and the Blue, operate in the city. You are given the following data:

(i) Although the two companies are roughly equal in size, 85 percent of cab accidents in the city involve Green cabs, and 15 percent involve Blue cabs.

(ii) Question: What is the probability that the cab involved in the accident was Blue rather than Green?[18]

The problems are formally identical since, if no further information is given, it is justifiable to assume that with 85 percent of the cabs being Blue, then 85 percent of the accidents will involve Blue cabs. The first problem then becomes the second one. But people treat the two very differently: they pay much more attention to the base rate in the second case than they do in the first. Knowledge of statistics and vividness of the information are constant between the two problems. What is different is that the number of Blue and Green cabs in the city does not seem relevant because it is hard to build this factor into a causal chain leading to the particular accident under consideration. The fact that Blue cabs are much more often involved in crashes than are Green, on the other hand, can more easily be fit into a causal account (e.g., Blue cars are badly maintained, the Blue company hires bad drivers, the company puts pressure on its drivers to do a lot of business and so the drivers are reckless, etc.). Thus, in his discussion of the importance of perceived causality, Icek Ajzen notes the following in reference to the original Kahneman and Tversky experiment: "Clearly, the proportion of engineers and lawyers in the original sample did not cause any member of the sample to become an engineer or a lawyer, nor did it provide information about any other factor that might be viewed as having causal effect on a person's professional choice."[19] This is not entirely unrelated to the resistance to utilizing statistical data. To someone at ease with statistics, the fact that 80 percent of the people are lawyers can be seen as a cause—to use the term in a loose sense—of the chances that any sketch will be that of a lawyer. This formulation, however, shifts the

18 Kahneman and Tversky, "On the Psychology of Prediction," 237–51; also see Bar-Hillel, "What Features Make Samples Seem Representative?"

19 Icek Ajzen, "Intuitive Theories of Events and the Effects of Base-Rate Information on Prediction," *Journal of Personality and Social Psychology* 35 (May 1977): 304.

focus from the causes of why a particular person ends up in a given profession to the cause whereby the person and his sketch were selected. The latter focus is not common in the tasks of our everyday lives and so is not one we easily adopt.

By contrast, data about the individual can usually be interpreted causally. Indeed, this is one reason why people draw inference from sketches that actually provide little diagnostic information. We can easily construct an account that ties the person's characteristics to his profession even if the account is incorrect. Thus, what may be crucial is not that some of the information deals with prior probabilities and other information concerns the particular case, but rather the perceived relevance of the data, which are often seen in terms of causality. This emphasis on perceived relevance fits nicely with arguments that perceptions are driven by expectations and beliefs,[20] and, as we will show, can also explain how base rates readily enter into foreign policy judgments.

Applications to Foreign Policy Judgments

How do these arguments and findings help elucidate foreign policy decision-making? Unfortunately, the problems are clearer than the applications.

To start with, in politics the base rate information is not objective or provided to the person by an authority. This means that both decision-makers and analysts have to determine what the base rate is. This problem has two parts, one theoretical, the other empirical. The theoretical problem is that while the concept of the base rate as the distribution of the characteristic in the population is unambiguous in the experiments, this is not true in international politics. Scholars and decision-makers have to make difficult judgments about both the numerator and the denominator of this fraction. For example, consider the crucial question facing statesmen of determining whether another state is hostile. To estimate the numerator, contemporary decision-makers or scholars later evaluating the choice would have to decide exactly what past behavior should be included in the category of hostility. Is the statesman concerned only with armed aggression? With demonstrations that involve the implicit use of force? With attempts to thwart his state by political and diplomatic means? With a general disposition to harm his state? More difficult still are questions about what constitutes the denominator. What is the relevant population? An obvious answer would be all states since the beginning of the state system. We will call this the general base rate. But if hostility is not equally distributed across this population, a base rate keyed to all states would be

20 Jervis, *Perception and Misperception* (1976), 143–216; Jervis, "Understanding Beliefs," in this volume.

misleading. Several more specific denominators are possible: the past behavior of the particular state under scrutiny, the behavior of all states in the
objective situation that the other is in, the behavior of all states with a given
domestic configuration, or the behavior of states led by people whose personalities match that of the other state's leader.[21]

The list could be extended, but this brief version should suffice both to
note the difficulty and point to a further complication: the choice of the base
rate depends in part on the person's beliefs about international politics. Again,
the problems with the numerator are less severe than those plaguing the selection of the relevant population, but they are not insignificant. Someone
who believes that diffuse hostility often turns to more specific and damaging
acts will want to count all cases of general ill-will. Others would disagree and
want to count only those cases in which hostile intentions blossomed into
expansionist behavior.

The choice of the denominator is even more clearly theory driven. A person who believes that nuclear weapons have transformed international politics would ignore all cases since 1945. The belief that great powers behave
differently from small states implies that one has to divide the population of
states along these lines. Those who stress the domestic sources of foreign policy would want to look at the population of states that share the important
domestic characteristics with the country being examined. Statesmen who
think that tradition and national character are crucial would look at the previous history of the country.

Not only are there no objective answers as to which theories are correct
and therefore as to which populations are relevant, but also the choices partly
depend on the statesman's view of the other state, thus introducing a note
of circularity into the analysis. For example, in judging Soviet intentions in
the 1980s, a dove would have sought data on stagnant underdeveloped states
facing two enemies, one much more powerful than itself. A hawk would have
said that the base rate should be the behavior of unstable totalitarian states
with messianic ideologies. Or a hawk might have called for data on states that
have been prone to break their treaty obligations.

As this line of inquiry indicates, many of the "facts" that would be useful
in determining the appropriate base rate are not objective. The matter of
whether the Soviets had broken many treaties is an obvious example. Furthermore, if one seeks a base rate that is deemed particularly relevant to the
case at hand, the distinction between the prior activity and the evidence about
the particular instance begins to break down. To say that one wants base rate

---

21 For an application to intelligence analysis, see Robert Jervis, *Why Intelligence Fails: Lessons from the Iranian Revolution and the Iraq War* (Ithaca: Cornell University Press, 2013),
pp. 193–95.

information that incorporates what you know about the other state's previous behavior requires judging this behavior along dimensions that are related to those called for in the final inference. Thus the argument about whether the proper base rate to use in connection with Soviet behavior is that of treaty-breakers is obviously linked to arguments about whether the USSR was aggressive.

These theoretical obstacles in determining the base rate should not blind us to the less interesting empirical difficulties. Even after we decided which base rate was relevant, we would need to do the research necessary to compute it. In some cases, this is quite easy: often there are data on the number of wars a state has participated in. But if either scholars or decision-makers wanted to know the base rate for armed conflict by, say, states undergoing rapid industrialization or states led by oligarchies, they would not find the data rapidly available. Furthermore, subjective judgments as well as extensive research would be necessary. Deciding which cases count as examples of rapid industrialization is not easy.

More difficulties would arise if one wanted data not on participation in wars but on aggressiveness. And yet this is what statesmen are likely to be most concerned with. Not only does this mean we must judge how many states were aggressors, but also we must count the cases in which a country's expansionist proclivities were checked before they could lead to fighting.

There are two related implications of these difficulties. First, it would be hard for decision-makers to use precise base rates if they wanted to. Second, it is difficult to determine whether statesmen in fact do use base rate information. So many priors could be employed and the data would be so approximate that it is hard to specify inferences that would be incompatible with the use of base rates. Rapid shifts of belief with each new bit of information about the other state would be quite good evidence that priors were not being given much weight, but this rarely occurs.

An alternative approach would be to simply ask statesmen if they paid any attention to base rates. Of course they might not know what information influenced them,[22] but it would not be entirely without significance if they replied—as I think they would—that such considerations are irrelevant and that all that matters is the information about the case at hand. As we will see later, they probably smuggle base rates in through the back door, but I think they would defend judgments of representativeness.

22 See Richard Nisbett and Timothy Wilson, "Telling More than We Can Know: Verbal Reports on Mental Processes," *Psychological Review* 84 (March 1977): 231–59; Eliot Smith and Frederick Miller, "Limits on Perception of Cognitive Processes: A Reply to Richard Nisbett and Timothy Wilson," *Psychological Review* 85 (July 1978): 355–62; Andres Ericsson and Herb Simon, "Verbal Reports as Data," *Psychological Review* 87 (May 1980): 215–51.

One explanation for why decision-makers would ignore base rates is their belief that the other state's behavior is unambiguous. Indeed, as I noted earlier, if the stereotypes are completely valid and the information about the case is sufficient to tell which category the other state fits into, then disregarding the base rate is appropriate. For example, if all states that reject reasonable settlements of disputes are aggressive, and if one can determine that the offer the other state rejected is reasonable, then one can conclude that the other state is aggressive without weighing the prior probabilities. Since people often underestimate ambiguity and overestimate their cognitive abilities, it is likely that statesmen think that they can draw more accurate inferences from what the other state is doing than in fact they can. But I also suspect that even when statesmen admit that the information about the other does not permit a firm conclusion, they would be hesitant to admit the value of general base rates. For them, as for the subjects in the experiments, this information would not seem relevant to judging the case at hand.

Why Laboratory and Natural Setting Produce Different Results

But I think that statesmen use, and would acknowledge using, specific base rates of the kind discussed earlier—that is, the propensities of particular kinds of states and of states in particular kinds of situations. The reasons for this parallel the arguments of Ajzen and of Tversky and Kahneman.[23] These base rates can be interpreted in causal terms and fit with statesmen's beliefs about international politics. For example, if decision-makers believe that domestic instability is often linked to external expansion, then when they look at the ambiguous actions of a state undergoing internal turmoil they will be more likely to perceive aggressiveness than they would if the actions had been taken by a stable state. The prior probabilities are part of the leader's theory of when and why states are likely to be aggressive and so influence her expectations and through them her perceptions of specific cases.

To say that the decision-maker combines two independent factors—base rate data and information about the particular case—does not quite catch what is happening. Rather the person's beliefs about the relevant base rate often influences the way she interprets the information about specific instances of the other's behavior and both are influenced by other beliefs. Here the laboratory experiments are a misleading guide to the way people process

23 Icek Ajzen, "Intuitive Theories of Events and the Effects of Base-Rate Information on Prediction," *Journal of Personality and Social Psychology* 35 (May 1977): 303–14; Amos Tversky and Daniel Kahneman, "Causal Schemata in Judgments under Uncertainty," in Martin Fishbein, ed., *Progress in Social Psychology* (Hillsdale, N.J.: Erlbaum, 1980).

information in most natural situations. In the experiments people are given fairly objective information about not only the base rate but also the particular case—for example, the ability of the person to see whether a cab is Blue or Green or the sketch of the person who is either a lawyer or an engineer. In most natural situations, by contrast, the information about the event cannot be described in terms that all people, irrespective of their general beliefs, would agree to. Take the Russian invasion of Afghanistan. To call it an invasion is to accept a certain version of the events. Some would call it self-defense; others might agree with the Russians that it was fraternal assistance; many would label it unprovoked aggression; still others might say it was provoked aggression. The characterization of Russian behavior is influenced by one's views of general Soviet behavior.

One can reply that this problem can be avoided by taking information about the case at a much more specific and concrete level. The model could be what international relations scholars who have tried to objectively label the degree of conflict and hostility in behavior by focusing not on a general assessment but on the details of the acts. Thus, one might not characterize what the Soviets did in Afghanistan at all, but merely use data involving troop movements. Sometimes this will be appropriate, as it probably was with the CIA exercise in which analysts were asked to revise their estimates of the course of Sino-Soviet relations on the basis of specific incidents on the frontier dividing the two countries.[24] But quite often behavior is uninterpretable when torn from its context. The fine-grain specifics make no sense when viewed in isolation—or rather they could make very different kinds of sense depending on the surrounding events. It is then not clear that the task people are asked to perform in the experiment captures the cognitive dynamics that are dominant in most real-life situations.

What is most important in many cases is the theory-driven nature of perception and interpretation. Beliefs and images of other countries, once established, are very slow to change. While people notice new information and think they are being guided by it, in fact their interpretations are strongly affected by what they already believe and expect. People are then very conservative in the sense of not changing much on the basis of new data.

But the psychological experiments and explanations concerning base rates imply that people are not conservative enough—that they are too readily swayed by the evidence they receive that bears directly on the particular case and neglect the important trends in the general population from which the evidence is drawn. This view parallels the advice offered by Carl von Clausewitz when he argued, "Only those general principles and attitudes that

24 Richards Heuer, "A Problem Solving Perspective on the Role of Methodology in Governmental Foreign Affairs Analysis," Washington, D. C. 1978 (mimeo).

result from clear and deep understanding can provide a comprehensive guide to action. It is to these that opinions on specific problems should be anchored. The difficulty is to hold fast to these results of contemplation in the torrent of events and new opinions.... A strong faith in the overriding truth of tested principles is needed; the vividness of transient impressions must not make us forget that such truth as they contain is of lesser stamp."[25] But without arguing that this is never a problem, I think the emphasis is misplaced. More often than giving up their established opinions too easily, people maintain them in the face of large amounts of discrepant information that would be convincing to someone who did not have preexisting beliefs to the contrary.

A few examples will help to show how the theory-driven nature of perceptions is relevant to the question of when people use base rates. A statesman who believes that communist countries tend to be aggressive is likely to see expansionist motives behind past Soviet, Chinese, or Cuban behavior even if that behavior did not resemble the acts of other aggressors. As Ole Holsti showed in his classic study,[26] John Foster Dulles saw the reduction of the Soviet army in the mid-1950s not as evidence that his beliefs about Russia were incorrect, but as showing that their economy was in trouble and that they were conserving their resources to be better able to menace the United States later. Similarly, someone who believed that democratic states are rarely aggressive would be very slow to conclude that any such country was a threat to the status quo even if it behaved in ways that other observers would call menacing. An obvious objection to this line of argument is that by interpreting the concept of base rate information as people's beliefs about how various categories of actors have behaved in the past, I am coming perilously close to merging this concept with that of representativeness. Could one not say that, in my formulation, a communist state is representative of the category of aggressors? Although this is a problem, the two concepts remain fairly distinct because one can separate the aspects of the state's foreign policy being scrutinized from the category of states in which it is placed.

Perceptual thresholds also shift with the kind of situation the decision-maker believes he is facing. This too shows the use of base rates, although few decision-makers would put it in these terms. If a statesman is in a situation in which he believes threats to his country are common—for example, his country has suddenly been weakened, wars are occurring elsewhere, a worldwide depression has broken out—his sensitivity to threats will increase. Others' be-

25 Carl von Clausewitz, *On War,* edited and translated by Michael Howard and Peter Paret (Princeton: Princeton University Press, 1976), p.143

26 Ole Holsti, "Cognitive Dynamics and Images of the Enemy: Dulles and Russia," in David Finlay, Ole Holsti, and Richard Fagen, eds., *Enemies in Politics* (Chicago: Rand McNally, 1967).

havior that otherwise would not have been alarming will be seen as menacing. Decision-makers may not be completely aware of this process and it would not be entirely accurate to say that they are combining base rate data with information on the particular case. Rather the priors strongly influence the perception of the information about the case. But the impact is similar in that changes in the base rate will change the inferences that are drawn.

The same impact of prior probabilities is shown when evidence about a specific incident is rejected because it is implausible—i.e., does not fit with what people believe the nature of these incidents should be. This way of thinking characterizes much of everyday life, international politics, and scientific investigation. If I think my friend is in town, it will take much less of a resemblance between a stranger and him for me to "see" him than it will if I know that he is in another part of the country. The reason most Americans felt that Japan would refrain from attacking the United States in 1941, although Japan's behavior closely resembled that of an uncontrolled expansionist, was that they believed that states rarely seek a war with a much stronger adversary.

Sometimes more specific base rates are used. Less than two months before the Japanese attacked, the chief of army intelligence at Pearl Harbor noted five possible Japanese moves in order of their likelihood. Listed last was what Japan actually intended. His reason for thinking that a simultaneous attack on United States, Britain, and the Netherlands East Indies was so improbable was that this action would violate the Axis principle of "defeating one opponent at a time."[27]

As I have discussed at length elsewhere,[28] the same pattern holds in scientific investigations. As one scientist put it,

> The process of explaining away deviations is in fact quite indispensable to the daily routine of research. In my laboratory I find the laws of nature formally contradicted at every hour, but I explain this away by the assumption of experimental error. I know that this may cause me one day to explain away a fundamentally new phenomenon and to miss a great discovery. Such things have often happened in the history of science. Yet I shall continue to explain away my odd results, for if every anomaly observed in my laboratory were taken at its face value, research would instantly degenerate into a wild-goose chase after imaginary fundamental novelties.[29]

27 Quoted in Gordon Prange, *At Dawn We Slept* (New York: McGraw-Hill, 1981), p. 289.

28 Jervis, *Perception and Misperception* (1976), 156–72.

29 Michael Polanyi, "The Unaccountable Element in Science," in Marjorie Grene, ed., *Knowing and Being: Essays by Michael Polanyi* (London: Rutledge and Kegan Paul, 1969), p. 114.

In these instances, the evidence about the particular case is rich, memorable, and vivid, and the beliefs that formed the base rate estimates are dry and pallid. Yet, witnessing the Japanese invasions of its neighbors and observing startling results in the laboratory make little dent in expectations established by prior probabilities.

An additional example brings this point out particularly clearly. The day before the Egyptian attack in 1973, Israeli intelligence concluded that "[t]hough the actual taking up of emergency positions on the Canal appears to contain indications testifying to an offensive initiative, according to our best evaluation no change has occurred in the Egyptian assessment of the balance of power between their forces and the IDF [Israeli Defense Force]. Therefore, the probability that the Egyptians intend to resume hostilities is low."[30] The Egyptian activities were detailed and vivid and closely fit the stereotype of preparations to attack. But the inference drawn gave little weight to representativeness because the analysts felt they understood why this response was unlikely.

In many situations the relevant base rates help form the expectations about how others will behave and so have great impact. Indeed, the most important determinant of a state's interpretation of another's specific actions usually is the preexisting image of the other. This image constitutes the most relevant base rate; the population of concern is the other's perceived past behavior.[31] The parallel to the one hundred slips of paper containing the sketches of engineers and lawyers is the actions that the other has taken. The estimated prior probability is then seen as clearly relevant to the inference about the other's current behavior. If the other state has been hostile in the past, it is likely to be hostile in the future. Connections of causation link the base rate and the inference about the individual, as they did in the Tversky and Kahneman experiment when the taxis had specified accident histories.

Because our beliefs resist discrepant information, people will usually give the prior probabilities too much weight, rather than too little as do subjects in most experiments. Thus the point of making the CIA analysts separate priors and inferences about specific incidents in the exercise mentioned above was to make them see that some incidents were inconsistent with their beliefs and to force to the surface the question of whether the beliefs should be al-

30 Agranat Report, "A Partial Report of the Commission of Enquiry of the Government of Israel" (Jerusalem: Government Printing Office, 1974), p. 5.

31 An objection similar to that noted earlier can be raised by arguing that treating the image of the other as a base rate blurs the distinction between information about the particular case and estimates of the prior probability. In reply I would argue, first, that my approach is similar to that used by Tversky and Kahneman in the taxi experiment and, second, that one can analytically distinguish between data and beliefs about the other's previous behavior that set the most relevant base rate and inferences about a new act that the other has taken.

tered.[32] Similarly, other discussions of ways to minimize misperception have sought to make people understand the degree to which their expectations influence their perceptions, to see that they are often wrong to infer that the new information provides independent confirmation of their beliefs, and have encouraged them to consider alternative explanations in the light of which the data would appear to be different.[33]

What accounts for the great difference between the downplaying of the base rate and overuse of representativeness in laboratory settings and the opposite phenomena in many foreign policy inferences? It is not, I think, the subject matter. If we replicated the original Tversky and Kahneman experiment and gave subjects a description of some behavior said to have been taken at random from a pool of actions of seventy aggressive and thirty peaceful states, there is no reason to doubt that we would get the same results.

Most of the explanation lies, I think, in the factor stressed by Tversky and Kahneman and by Ajzen.[34] Their evidence indicates the importance of whether the prior probabilities can easily be perceived as relevant, especially through a causal chain. As we have seen, they usually can be when we are dealing with inferences about other nations. The established beliefs about the state or kind of state that the statesman is dealing with are clearly relevant to the likely meaning of the specific acts it undertakes.

A second explanation is that the base rates in most natural situations have been developed by the person through experience and analysis. That the estimates of the priors so produced are often incorrect is important but not relevant here. What is significant is that the person has faith in their validity, they seem reasonable, and they are the object of some thought and so are fairly salient. This argument is supported by the finding that doctors use base rates when they are developed out of their own practices.[35] Thus, it is quite possible

32 Heuer, "A Problem Solving Perspective on the Role of Methodology in Governmental Foreign Affairs Analysis"; also see Zeev Maoz, "Scientific Logic and Intuition in Intelligence Forecasts," in David Singerand and Richard Stoll, eds., *Quantitative Indicators in World Politics* (New York: Praeger, 1984).

33 Jervis, *Perception and Misperception* (1976), 409–18; Robert Jervis, *Why Intelligence Fails: Lessons from the Iranian Revolution and the Iraq War* (Ithaca: Cornell University Press, 2013); Alexander George, *Presidential Decision-Making in Foreign Policy: The Effective Use of Information and Advice* (Boulder, Colo.: Westview, 1980), pp. 169–208.

34 Tversky and Kahneman, "Causal Schemata in Judgments under Uncertainty;" Ajzen, "Intuitive Theories of Events and the Effects of Base-Rate Information on Prediction."

35 Jay Christensen-Szalanski and James Bushyhead, "Physicians' Use of Information in a Real Clinical Setting," *Journal of Experimental Psychology: Human Perception and Performance* 7 (August 1981): 928–35; also see Jay Christensen-Szalanski and Lee Beach, "Experience and the Base-Rate Fallacy," *Organizational Behavior and Human Performance* 29 (April 1982): 270–78; Jay Christensen-Szalanski and Lee Beach, "Believing Is not the Same as Testing: A Reply to Ruth Beyth-Marom and Headly Arkes," *Organizational Behavior and Human Performance* 3 (April

that people will ignore base rate information that comes in the form of data presented to them out of the blue, but will use it, often excessively, when it is evidence about regularities in their environment that they have developed through experience.[36]

Foreign Policy Cases that Resemble the Laboratory Findings

The crucial distinction then is not between laboratory settings on the one hand and natural settings on the other, but rather between situations in which the prior probabilities seem arbitrary and are not linked to the person's beliefs about the specific case, and situations in which the priors are a product of the person's analysis and are an important part of the ideas she brings to bear on new information.

Most foreign policy cases fall into the latter category, but not all. When the cases fit into the former category I would expect the same downplaying of the base rate that is so striking in most experiments. This may be the case, for example, in the crucial and not well-understood processes whereby decision-makers form their images of states or situations they are confronting for the first time. Here there are no preexisting beliefs of what the other is like or how the situation will develop. It is not clear what the appropriate base rate would be and none is likely to be salient. It is probable that in this kind of a context the decision-maker looks at the resemblance between the country's behavior and others with which he is familiar and does not think about the relative frequency with which these alternative models arise.

Indeed, in these circumstances decision-makers would probably reject the relevance of base rate data. Like the subjects in most of the experiments, they would argue that the information directly bearing on the case being examined provides the only germane evidence. This is especially likely to the extent that they underestimate the ambiguity of this evidence and overestimate their cognitive abilities. The result will be that they will give representa-

1983): 258–61; Ruth Beyth-Marom and Hadley Arkes "Being Accurate but Not Necessarily Bayesian: Comments on Christensen Szalanski and Beach," *Organizational Behavior and Human Performance* 31 (April 1983): 255–57.

36 For other discussions of the conditions under which people use base rates, see Icek Ajzen and Martin Fishbein, "Relevance and Availability in the Attribution Process," pp. 63–89 in Jos Jaspers, Frank Fincham, and Miles Hewstone, eds, *Attribution Theory and Research: Conceptual Development and Social Dimensions* (New York: Academic Press, 1983); Borgida and Brekke, "The Base-Rate Fallacy in Attribution and Prediction," 63–95; Sussan Kassin, "Consensus Information, Prediction, and Causal Attribution: A Review of the Literature and Issues," *Journal of Personal and Social Psychology* 37 (November 1979): 1966–81; Nisbett, Krantz, Jepson, and Kunda, "The Use of Statistical Heuristics in Everyday Inductive Reasoning," 339–63.

tiveness excessive weight; statesman will decide the equivalent of whether the person is an engineer or a lawyer entirely on the basis of a short sketch without noting the prior likelihoods.

If this argument is correct, rare events and kinds of actors will be perceived more frequently than they actually occur and, conversely, more common ones will not be seen as often as they are present. When an event or actor resembles a model with which decision-makers are familiar, they will not dilute their confidence that the case fits this category by consideration of how often examples of this kind occur. Decision-makers will not think, "Much of the other's behavior indicates that he is seeking an ambitious objective, but such a goal is very rare and so maybe he actually has other intentions."

Thus, when people meet a new situation or first form their images of another actor, they may err in seeing it as an example of an unusual type. Successful guerilla wars, for example, are infrequent. Yet even a low level of fighting in a country is often sufficient to trigger the expectation that the guerillas have a good chance of winning because the country resembles Cuba or Vietnam. Perhaps the most important example would be the tendency to conclude, on the basis of ambiguous evidence, that another state has extremely hostile intentions. Few states make serious efforts to conquer much of the world: Hitlers are very rare. But they are perceived more frequently, and I think the weight given to representativeness is part of the explanation. The same processes could lead to instances of great friendship, another rare intention, to be perceived more often than it occurs. But while this error may be committed, it will be corrected relatively quickly by the other's subsequent behavior.

Representativeness, however, will not dominate in all cases in which the statesman has no strong preexisting beliefs about the actor he is judging. The priors will exert a very powerful influence if he thinks there are good reasons why the rare event will not take place. This was true, for example, of most observers' perceptions of Iran in the year before the revolution. The year 1978 saw extensive rioting, vacillating leadership, and little rallying to the regime. An inference based on representativeness would have predicted revolution. That most people did not draw it can partly be explained by the fact that they knew why revolutions in a situation like that prevailing in Iran are very rare — that is, when unarmed protesters try to overthrow a regime that has the support of large and unimpaired security forces, the ruler at some point uses massive strength and the crowd breaks.[37] Thus, as long as people have salient beliefs about the reasons underlying the frequency distribution of events, actors, or situations, representativeness is not likely to dominate.

---

37 This is the major reason for the U.S. intelligence failure in this case: Jervis, *Why Intelligence Fails*, ch. 2.

Conclusion

Laboratory demonstrations show a striking tendency for people to pay little attention to base rate data and to draw conclusions largely on the basis of the extent to which the case under consideration resembles others. But this way of thinking characterizes the way statesmen draw inferences only in exceptional circumstances. The first problem is that while in the experiments it is clear what the base rates are, this is rarely the case in naturally occurring situations. Many base rates could be constructed, and the decision on which is most relevant is often linked to judgments about the instance under consideration.

But what is most significant is that statesmen usually give the prior probabilities heavy, not light, weight, although they do not realize this. Far from being carried away by the information about the specific event and not being sufficiently conservative in their treatment of the evidence, statesman usually see the event in terms of their estimate of the priors and are unwilling to credit representativeness when the particular case resembles a model that they do not believe is likely to apply.

There are several reasons for this divergence between the laboratory results and those that seem to hold in the outside world. First, as other scholars who have worked in this area have argued, base rates are utilized when they are seen as relevant, which is usually the case when they can be casually linked to the outcome of the incident under consideration. Base rates in international politics generally are of this type because they are the perceived probabilities that a state of a certain kind will behave in a given way. Thus the base rate is incorporated into the statesman's beliefs about the other country and into his expectations of how it is likely to behave in the future. When this is true, the theory-driven nature of perception means that evidence about the particular case will carry relatively little independent weight.

Second, for the decision-maker base rates are built up from her continuing interactions with her environment. They encapsulate her best estimates about what the world is like. They are important to her; she has good reasons why she thinks they are correct (even if they are not); they are salient to her and usually are linked to many other beliefs. None of this is true for the experimental studies in which the priors are given to the subjects.

The laboratory studies are fascinating, the experimental manipulations ingenious, and many of the important variables seem to have been correctly identified. But the striking finding that base rates are often given insufficient weight is not the dominant pattern in naturally occurring situations. Indeed, because of the way prior probabilities are developed and interact with judgments of particular cases, the opposite is more usually true.

4

Prospect Theory

THE POLITICAL IMPLICATIONS
OF LOSS AVERSION

Being central to Daniel Kahneman's Nobel Prize in economics, Prospect Theory is probably the best-known theory in political psychology. Is it valid? If
so, what are the implications for political decision making, international politics, and social life in general? I do not have full answers, but this sketch may
prove a useful stimulant to further research.

In summary, the theory argues that people tend to be risk-averse for gains
(this was generally known before) but simultaneously to be risk-acceptant for
losses (this was the surprise).[1] People are loss-averse not only in the obvious

---

1 The basic article is Amos Tversky and Daniel Kahneman, "Rational Choice and the Fram-
ing of Decisions," *Journal of Business* 59 (October 1986): 251–78; also see George Quattrone and
Amos Tversky, "Contrasting Rational and Psychological Analyses of Political Choice," *American
Political Science Review* 82 (September 1988): 719–36. For some applications to politics, see
Nancy Kanwisher, "Cognitive Heuristics and American Security Policy," *Journal of Conflict Res-
olution* 33 (December 1989): 652–75.; Steven Peterson and Robert Lawson, "Risky Business:
Prospect Theory and Politics," *Political Psychology* 10 (June 1989): 325–40; Rose McDermott,
Risk-Taking in International Politics: Prospect Theory in American Foreign Policy (Ann Arbor:
University of Michigan Press, 1998); William Boettcher, *Presidential Risk Behavior in Foreign
Policy* (New York: Palgrave Macmillan, 2005); Jeffrey Taliaferro, *Balancing Risks: Great Power
Intervention in the Periphery* (Ithaca: Cornell University Press, 2004); David Welch, *Painful
Choices: A Theory of Foreign Policy Change* (Princeton: Princeton University Press, 2005); Jack
Levy, "Declining Power and the Preventive Motivation for War," *World Politics* 40 (October
1987): 82–107; Rose McDermott, "Prospect Theory in Political Science Gains and Losses From
the First Decade," *Political Psychology* 25 (April 2005): 289–312.

sense of trying to avoid losses, but also in losses looming larger than equal gains. Losing ten dollars, for example, annoys us more than gaining ten dollars gratifies us. What is peculiar about this is that, contrary to most versions of expected utility theory, the reference point—usually the status quo—is crucial. More than the hope of gains, the specter of losses activates, energizes, and drives actors, producing great (and often misguided) efforts that risk—and frequently lead to—greater losses. Although a setback might be quite minor when compared to the person's total value holdings, he will see it in terms of where he was shortly before and so may take the gamble of an even greater loss in order to gain a chance of reestablishing his position. Furthermore, the choice between alternatives will be influenced by the way in which the question is framed. People will choose the risky alternative when the choice is posed in terms of avoiding losses when, in the exact same case, they would take the less risky course of action if the frame of reference is the possibility of improving the situation.

The evidence as to the theory's validity is suggestive but not conclusive. The bulk of it comes from the answers people give to questionnaires asking them to choose between alternatives of different risks and payoffs. The results could be a hothouse artifact of the laboratory,[2] as I suspect is in part the case for the supposed tendency of people to pay insufficient attention to base rate information.[3] Perhaps the main reason for thinking that the effect is real is that the tendency for people to be risk-acceptant for losses resonates with personal experience. I doubt that I am alone in having been willing to tolerate an unusually high risk of significant losses in return for the chance of paying no penalty at all, or in having been willing to invest significant additional resources in a venture in the hope, if not the expectation, of recouping a recent loss. It is not an accident that people are warned against throwing good money after bad—they often do. Similarly, economists tell us that it is not rational to be influenced by "sunk costs" because having put a lot into a venture is not a good reason to continue with it. But the fact that these are valid prescriptions does not mean that the behavior is not common. Indeed, the popularity of these admonitions indicates that unless special steps are taken the contrary behavior will be likely.

It is noteworthy when leaders do cut their losses. Here, as in many areas, there is a strong selection bias as our attention is drawn to cases when states

2 Donald Wittman, "Contrasting Economic and Psychological Analyses of Political Choice: An Economist's Perspective on Why Cognitive Psychology Does not Explain Democratic Politics," in Kristen Monroe, ed., *The Economic Approach to Politics* (New York: Harper Collins, 1991), pp. 405–32; Vernon Smith, "Rational Choice: The Contrast between Economics and Psychology," *Journal of Political Economy* 99 (August 1991): 877–97.

3 Jervis, "Representativeness, Foreign Policy Judgments, and Theory-Driven Perceptions," in this volume.

continue in a failing effort because these lead to large and dramatic failures. If the state pulls back, the policy is likely to attract less attention. Occasionally it does, however, and a clear example is President Kennedy's decision not to use American air power to try to rescue the invasion at the Bay of Pigs. He knew that the result of not doing so would be the certain loss of the invasion force, but he believed that the probability of success through air power was slight enough not to merit the additional losses in world opinion that open American involvement would entail. Most historians view the president's decision as not only correct but also courageous, which I think indicates an implicit acknowledgment of the power of loss aversion. Furthermore, the invasion planners at the CIA were confident that Kennedy would escalate rather than see the invasion smashed, which indicates an understanding that it is hard for people to resist the impulse to commit further rather than accept a certain loss.[4]

The explanation for loss aversion in political life may not be entirely psychological. Both domestic and international politics could account for the pattern. A leader who accepts even a limited defeat is likely to be punished at the polls. Gambling by accepting a chance of a greater loss in return for a chance of no loss (or even a victory) might be irrational from the standpoint of the national interest, but rational from the standpoint of the power-seeking politician. The difference between smaller and larger national losses may not translate into a similar difference in the loss of political power: a small loss might be sufficient to lose the politician the next election and a larger loss might even rally support to him.[5] Similarly, Dennis Ross argues that during the Cold War Soviet leaders would run high risks to avoid losses because retreating would significantly damage the ruling domestic coalition.[6]

Losses may not scale in their international impact either. That is, it is possible that in terms of reputation and credibility a small loss would cost the country not much less than a significantly larger one. (This effect would not hold for more concrete kinds of losses, such as territory and economic strength, however). Indeed, decision-makers seem to believe that small losses will multiply via the domino effect.[7] Gains are not expected to have such consequences.

4 For a study of personality characteristics that may be relevant here, see James David Barber, *The Presidential Character: Predicting Performance in the White House* (Englewood Cliffs, N.J.: Prentice-Hall, 1972); for a strong critique, see Alexander George, "Assessing Presidential Character," *World Politics* 26 (January 1974): 234–82.

5 George Downs and David Rocke, *Optimal Imperfection? Domestic Uncertainty and Institutions in International Relations* (Princeton: Princeton University Press, 1995), ch. 3.

6 Dennis Ross, "Risk Aversion in Soviet Decision-Making," pp. 237–51 in Jiri Valenta and William Potter, eds., *Soviet Decision-Making for National Security* (Boston: Allen and Unwin, 1984).

7 Jervis, "Domino Beliefs," in this volume; for the argument that this way of seeing things is peculiarly American, see Patrick Morgan, "Saving Face for the Sake of Deterrence," in Robert

So a rational statesman would not be willing to run high risks to secure a moderate gain but would accept much higher risks to avoid a short-run loss of the same magnitude because it would lead to greater losses over a longer period of time.

To say that the explanation for this odd behavior is political rather than psychological is misleading, however. While we may not need Prospect Theory to explain statesmen's choices if we can show that they are based on an analysis of how others will reward or punish them, the theory may tell us how others are reaching their judgments. Thus if it is true that the political costs that leaders incur from losses are not proportional to the magnitude of the loss, the reason may be that domestic opinion operates according to Prospect Theory in finding even small losses so painful that it prefers high risks to accepting them and will punish any leader who permits them to occur. Prospect Theory may also help account for the belief in domino effects because it indicates that people will focus more on losses than on gains. Thus in the late 1970s the United States was deeply concerned that the loss of influence in Ethiopia would have widespread repercussions but paid little attention to the simultaneous gain of influence in Somalia. Similarly, earlier in the Cold War the United States was preoccupied with what it saw as losses that might lead to further dominoes falling but paid little attention to the reversal of Soviet fortunes in Egypt, the Central African Republic, Ghana, or even China, events that constituted major gains for American power and interests that one might think would have dwarfed the defeats that loomed so large in American eyes. But the very fact that this was not understood was crucial to American behavior and can be explained at least in part by the psychological processes discussed here. Before proceeding further, however, I should note that neither the psychologists nor I have a good explanation for the phenomenon. That is, we cannot root it in a broader theory of why people think and decide as they do. This situation is not intellectually satisfying, but nevertheless, loss aversion appears to be pervasive and powerful.

General Effects of Loss Aversion

There seem to be many instances where people and organizations are risk-acceptant for losses. One nice example is that betting is said to be particularly heavy on the last horse race. People who have lost money throughout the afternoon place heavy bets on the final race; they are willing to risk more money to gain a chance of recouping their earlier losses. Again, the problem is more

---

Jervis, Richard Ned Lebow, and Janice Stein, *Psychology and Deterrence* (Baltimore: Johns Hopkins University Press, 1985), pp. 125–52.

complicated than those in the standard pencil-and-paper tests. A husband or wife who returns home having lost a part of his or her paycheck is likely to experience suffering that is relatively insensitive to the amount of the loss. Even without the spouse's disapproval, the cost to the person's ego may be significant and again much more sensitive to the fact of a gain or loss than to the magnitude of the gain or loss. But this fact, far from undermining Prospect Theory, may constitute one of the reasons why it operates.

Perhaps the best generic example of the willingness to take great risks to avoid any loss is the frequency of cover-ups. If a person has committed a nontrivial transgression, she may devote significant resources to trying to cover it up, even though doing so exposes her to much greater penalties if the activities are later discovered. Knowledge of the Watergate break-in would not have cost Nixon his presidency; even his sponsorship of it might not have. It was the cover-up that destroyed him. Of course, the objective odds cannot be known and so a standard expected-utility model could be built to account for Nixon's behavior, although it is far from clear that such a model would be consistent with the rest of his life. Furthermore, there could be large numbers of cases in which people admit to their transgressions, but since these do not give rise to major political scandals, we tend to overlook them. But although firm evidence is lacking, I suspect that cover-ups are more frequent than they would be if people acted on unbiased estimates of costs and probabilities instead of being driven by the need to get off without paying any penalty at all.

More generally, Prospect Theory leads us to expect people to persevere in losing ventures much longer than standard rationality indicates. Vietnam is an obvious case. American leaders were continually willing to escalate even though they knew that the prospects of eventual victory were far from certain and that their actions would greatly increase the domestic and international costs they would pay in the event of failure, and sunk costs loomed large in the secret deliberations. As usual, alternative explanations are possible. First, a person believing in the domino theory would pay high costs to avoid a limited defeat. Second, instances of long, losing wars are a sample of cases biased in the same way that cover-ups are. Instances in which actors cut their losses are less dramatic and so may be lost sight of. Third, continuing along a difficult or costly path sometimes pays off in the long run. Loss aversion may then contribute to useful perseverance. Albert Hirschman speaks of the "hiding hand."[8] That is, sometimes we embark on a program without much sense of the many obstacles. Were we aware of them at the start, we would never have begun. But if we see the obstacles only after we have put in a great deal of time

---

8 Albert Hirschman, *Development Projects Observed* (Washington, D.C.: Brookings Institution, 1976).

and effort, we will be reluctant to write off our investment and so will continue, and perhaps succeed.[9] The refusal to accept a loss then can be functional, even though the difference in the stance toward losses than toward gains still needs to be explained. These arguments cannot be definitively refuted, but neither do they deny that Vietnam fits what Prospect Theory leads us to expect.

In other wars as well, statesmen lose all sense of proportion about the magnitude of losses when some loss appears certain. Thus Fred Iklé points out that in February 1918 the Germans objected to the Austrian suggestion that they shift their war objectives and agree that "their two countries were obliged to fight for the prewar possessions of Germany. But Ludendorff granted this concession only after vehement opposition: "If Germany makes peace without profit, then Germany has lost the war." What curious inability to distinguish between loss of some territories and loss of the nation!"[10] Cutting losses after the expenditure of blood and treasure is perhaps the most difficult act a statesman can take; the lure of the gamble that persevering will recoup the losses is often too great to resist. Furthermore, and what is crucial to the claim that this behavior cannot be explained by a normal expected-utility approach, the same people who gamble in this way are cautious when faced with choices that involve gains: they will take much greater risks to try to return to where they were than they will to make major improvements in the status quo.[11]

Effects on Bargaining, Deterrence, and Causes of War

The proposition that actors react very differently to the prospect of losses than to the chance of making gains has important implications for international bargaining and conflict. If loss aversion is widespread, states defending the status quo should have a big bargaining advantage. That is, a state will be willing to pay a higher price and run higher risks if it is facing losses than if it is seeking to make gains. A related proposition that is consistent with the literature[12] is that coercion can more easily maintain the status quo than alter

---

9 For further discussion, see the preface to the new edition of Robert Jervis, *Perception and Misperception in International Politics*, 2nd ed. (Princeton: Princeton University Press, 2017; originally published 1976).

10 Fred Iklé, *Every War Must End* (New York: Columbia University Press, 1971), p.82.

11 For an application of this argument to World War I with a stress on the impact of differences in regime type, see Hein Goemens, *War and Punishment: The Causes of War Termination in the First World War* (Princeton: Princeton University Press, 2000).

12 Thomas Schelling, *Arms and Influence* (New Haven: Yale University Press, 1966); Robert Jervis, *The Meaning of the Nuclear Revolution: Statecraft and the Prospect of Armageddon* (Ithaca: Cornell University Press 1989).

it—deterrence is usually easier than what Schelling calls compellence. These arguments, however, assume that it is clear to the actors which of them is the defender and which is the challenger. Sometimes this is true, but often it is not.

This yields a third implication: conflicts and wars are more likely when each side believes it is defending the status quo. Since the reason why the perceived status quo will be vehemently defended is that states will run high risks rather than suffer even a small but certain loss, the proposition can be broadened to argue that conflicts and wars are most likely when each side believes it will suffer significant losses if it does not fight. As James Fearon notes, wars can be rational if both sides are risk-acceptant.[13] Perceptual biases compound the problem. When states overestimate others' hostility, as they frequently do, they will expect losses unless they take strong if not aggressive action. Both sides can readily come to believe this. Not only will each accept high risks to avoid a bad outcome, but each is likely to think that the other side is merely striving for gains and so is likely to be willing to back down.

A fourth implication is that during the Cold War a superpower's impulse to intervene in a local conflict was greater the more its local client was suffering. This was exemplified twice in the 1973 war, first increasing the pressure on the US to resupply Israel when it was losing, and then increasing the credibility of a Soviet move when the tide of battle shifted against Egypt. Superpowers are less prone to intervene, and their threats to do so are less credible, when such actions would bring gains to the client. Again, the danger is that both sides will fear losses (and will not understand either the other's perspective or the chances of success), thereby generating not only conflicts but undesired and unforeseen ones. But to the extent that perceptions are shared, loss aversion should stabilize local conflicts by making it unlikely that either side can "win big." If the local clients realize this, they will have to moderate their demands and actions.

More generally, by giving a bargaining advantage to the side that fears or suffers losses, loss aversion supports stability. This affects day-to-day diplomacy as well as crisis bargaining. For example, loss aversion and the resulting caution probably is part of the explanation for why neither the United States nor the Soviet Union was anxious to gamble on a reunited Germany in the early years of the Cold War. The result might have been to greatly improve either side's position, but it would have meant foregoing the sure and current advantage of controlling part of that country. To call the results stability, however, is to miss the other half of the story: because actors place a higher valuation on what they have than on what they might gain, they will refuse

13 James Fearon, "Rationalist Explanations for War," *International Organization* 49 (Summer 1995): 37–414.

to accept bargains that a third party would judge to make them better off. The general level of trading within and among countries will then be lower than most theories would lead one to expect.

War-Peace Decisions

Prospect Theory produces inferences about both the short- and the long-run causes of wars. If it is correct, we would expect that wars and other conflicts would be more strongly and more commonly motivated by the desire to avoid losses than by the hope of making gains. States should be more often pushed into war by the fear that the alternative to fighting is a serious deterioration in their position than pulled in by the belief that war can improve a situation that is already satisfactory. As I will note below, sometimes the status quo itself is unsatisfactory. But more often, even if it leaves a great deal to be desired, the status quo is at least tolerable in the sense that the state is willing to live with it rather than running a significant risk of suffering the greater losses than a war might bring. Fear is usually a more potent motivator than the desire for expansion. A statesman will run a significant risk of destruction of his own power and his regime and devastation of his country if he thinks the alternative will lead to a certain and significant deterioration in his power and security, but he would not be willing to run similar risks if he believed that the status quo could be maintained by diplomacy even though war, if successful, could bring great gains. Wars are then less frequently caused by aggression than by spirals of fear and insecurity.[14] The famous historian A.J.P. Taylor exaggerates as usual when he claims that "every war between Great Powers [between 1848 and 1918] started as a preventive war, not a war of conquest,"[15] but the preventive motive indeed is frequent.[16]

Loss aversion similarly implies that the restraints in a limited war are more likely to be broken by a side that fears that failing to do so will result in significant losses than by the side that believes that expansion can bring it significant gains. By contrast, approaches that give no special place to the status quo as a reference point lead us to think that states would escalate when doing so is expected to yield more utility than maintaining the restraint. Since there is no reason why states should adopt a different stance toward avoiding losses

14 Jervis, *Perception and Misperception* (1976, 2017), ch. 3.

15 A.J.P. Taylor, *The Struggle for Mastery in Europe* (New York: Oxford University Press, 1954), p. 166.

16 Jack Levy, "Declining Power and the Preventive Motivation for War," *World Politics* 40 (October 1987): 82–107; for the argument that most of the wars the United States has fought have been preventive, see John Gaddis, *Surprise, Security, and the American Experience* (Cambridge: Harvard University Press, 2005).

than toward making gains, they should be as likely to increase the level of violence to break stalemate and secure a decisive victory as to ward off a defeat. In fact, I doubt if this is actually true. The United States threatened escalation in the final stages of the Korean War to force a settlement, but it is far from clear what it would have done if the Chinese had not agreed to a truce following Stalin's death. The Chinese, in turn, intervened not in the summer of 1950, when such action might have pushed the United States off the peninsula, but in the fall when the alternative was to accept a hostile regime on its borders (that is, when it was certain that the status quo would deteriorate badly if China did not fight). The risks China was willing to run to regain Formosa— an objective of great value—were much less.

Although it is often said, especially of aggressors, that the appetite grows with the eating, this does not seem to be as true as it would be were gains and losses to be treated symmetrically. Although states sometimes do overreach themselves (as the United States did in crossing the 38th parallel in Korea), it is relatively unusual for the side with the upper hand to increase the level of violence or continue to fight to gain additional objectives, even if doing so seems militarily feasible. Thus the Chinese did not push deeper into Indian territory in 1962 when their initial attack met with great success and, contrary to what Kissinger seems to have believed, India probably would not have turned on West Pakistan in 1971 even if the United States had not tried to deter such a move. Only in the last of his wars did Bismarck yield to the temptation to make extra gains, and even in this situation he took Alsace and Lorraine only because he was convinced that even if he did not the French would be immutably hostile. Although it was Hitler who taught the world that ambitions and risk-taking increased with success, this picture actually is not accurate: Hitler's outlook and stance remained remarkably unchanged throughout his monstrous career.

This does not mean that unprovoked aggression never occurs. Hitler, to take only the most obvious example, was driven by the desire to drastically alter the status quo, not by the fear that he was encircled by hostile powers that would destroy Germany unless he took arms against them. The case of postwar Soviet foreign policy is ambiguous in this regard, and it would not be surprising if both motives were at work. Indeed, it should be stressed that Prospect Theory does not deny that actors may want to change the status quo or that the combination of the strength of the motivation to do so and the perceived possibilities of success can lead to expansion and war. Actors will take some risks to improve their situations even if they are risk-averse for gains. But, the theory argues, actors should be much more willing to run risks when they believe that failing to do so will result in certain losses. Wars will then frequently be triggered by fear of loss; fighting in order to act on an opportunity will be relatively rare.

Great methodological problems plague the attempt to develop fully convincing comparisons (see below), but it appears that when states take very high risks it is usually the case that they believe they will have to accept certain losses if they do not do so. Furthermore, this recklessness surprises other countries—both those that are attacked and neutrals—because they expect the state to be more cautious, which it usually is because the more normal context is one of facing gains rather than losses. Thus Japan attacked Great Britain and the United States in December 1941 not because its leaders had much confidence they could win, but because they saw that the alternative was a sure loss of their position in Southeast Asia and China.[17] Observers thought the choice for war was odd because it is hard to empathize with the pressures people feel when faced with losses.

This case is far from unique. Although the German motivation in 1914 was mixed, one important component was the belief that the diplomatic and military situation was deteriorating and that German security would be much lower in a few years if Germany did not fight. Its leaders knew that victory was far from certain; I find it hard to believe that they would have run this risk is they thought that the status quo could have been maintained by peaceful means and that the only reason to fight was to gain even more territory, power, and prestige. The other participants in World War I also were much more strongly driven by fears than by hopes. All were worried that their power and security were being undermined by the course of events. While they had expansionist ambitions, these were not sufficient to lead them to stake the future of their countries on a war that they all entered with great trepidation. Similarly, although Israel's 1967 war resulted in its gaining territory, the motivation, as in 1956 and in the war of attrition of 1969–70, was the belief that unless these risky actions were taken, the status quo would deteriorate badly.

The other side of this coin is harder to see because it consists of nonevents: states are slow to take advantage of opportunities to expand at some risk,[18] especially when compared with their behavior when they feel their position is under attack. We tend to take peace and even the lack of demands for change as natural. But they are not: given the postulates of power politics and expected utility, we should see states pushing to alter the status quo in their favor as often as they exert themselves to maintain it. We should see more Hitlers, at least in smaller versions of power and ruthlessness. These are not

17 For the contrary claim that Japan was in fact willing to give up these positions, see Marc Trachtenberg, *The Craft of International History* (Princeton: Princeton University Press, 2006), ch. 4.

18 Richard Ned Lebow, "Windows of Opportunity: Do States Jump Through Them?" *International Security* 9 (Summer 1984): 147–86.

absent, of course. Bismarck fought in order to expand, or really to create, his state; the dramatic weakening of a country or empire often draws others to attack; aggression occurs. But are these events as frequent as they would be if opportunity were as strong a motivation as the fear of loss?

Crisis Stability

Prospect Theory helps explain the presence or absence of crisis stability, conceived of as the danger that a crisis will lead to an all-out war despite this not being the preference of either side.[19] Because people are willing to take unusual risks to recoup recent losses, even if these setbacks are quite minor when compared with their total value holdings, a decision-maker might risk costly escalation or even world war if such a move held out the possibility of reversing a defeat. In cases in which a standard expected-utility model would predict the actor to cut his losses, he might up the ante.

The danger would be especially great if both sides were to feel that they were losing, something that could easily happen because antagonists often have different perspectives and use different baselines. The Middle East crisis of 1973 may be an example of such a situation, with the Americans feeling that they could not allow Israel to lose and the Soviets feeling that at least a limited Arab victory was necessary to regain their influence.

A second consequence of loss aversion for crisis stability is that if the decision-maker thinks that attacking provides even a chance of escaping unscathed even if it risks a much larger war, he may decide to strike even if the standard probability-utility calculus calls for restraint. Similar dynamics could operate on a smaller scale in less severe crises, such as those set off by a hostile coup in an important Third World country or the limited use of force by the adversary in a disputed area. With his attention riveted on the deterioration that will occur unless he acts strongly to reverse the situation, the decision-maker might take actions that entail an irrationally high chance of major escalation.

The powerful aversion to losses can be a force for peace, however, if restraint holds out the hope of maintaining the status quo. The decision-maker may hold back if he believes that even though striking first could be advantageous, it would lead to certain retaliation while he might be able to keep the peace if he did not fire. As long as there is any hope of avoiding total war, decision-makers are likely to recoil from the thought of starting it. Even General Curtis LeMay's successor as head of SAC, General Thomas Power, argued against preemption "so long as there is the slightest hope that we can prevent

19 For full treatment, see Jervis, "Psychology and Crisis Stability," in this volume.

a Soviet attack through diplomatic means of a strong posture of deterrence."[20] Similarly, Neville Chamberlain argued for continued appeasement on the grounds that "we were in no position to justify waging a war today in order to prevent a war hereafter."[21]

Implications for Social Efficiency and Stability

Closely related to loss aversion is the endowment effect,[22] and it also has important effects on stability. A series of striking experiments shows that the value a person attaches to an object increases substantially when he or she takes possession of it. For example, students who were given a mug would part with it only for a price much higher than they had earlier (before they received it) said it was worth. This effect cannot be explained by people getting what they value or increasing the value they place on it as they see its uses. These forces may be at work in some cases, but not in the experiments, and the effect cannot be subsumed under our normal categories of evaluation and instrumental rationality. Indeed, experiments indicate that people are not aware of the endowment effect and underestimate how much they would value the object if they were to receive it.[23]

It is not certain exactly how the effect comes about. People may identify with their possessions, and so they value something more highly once it belongs to them. Here socialization in a capitalist system may play a role, with a conflation of the value of the individual with that of his or her possessions. But some of the effects run counter to capitalism by inhibiting trades that would otherwise be efficient. If I place excessive value on a possession, I will trade it to you only at an inflated price. The same is true for you, and so we could have a situation in which the "objective value" or our pre-possession evaluation would indicate that we would both be better off swapping, but once each of us possesses the item, we will not trade. Even when this is not the case, the endowment effect links to loss aversion in that we will feel more pain by losing an object than we feel gratification upon first gaining it.

---

20 Thomas Power and Albert Arnhym, *Design for Survival* (New York: Coward-McCann, 1964), pp. 80–81.

21 Quoted in Wolfgang Mommsen, foreword to Wolfgang Mommsen and Kettenacke Lothar, eds., *The Fascist Challenge and the Policy of Appeasement* (Boston: Allen and Unwin, 1983), pp. ix–xii.

22 Daniel Kahneman, Jack Knetsch, and Richard Thaler, "Anomalies: The Endowment Effect, Loss Aversion, and Status Quo Bias," in David Kahneman and Amos Tversky, eds, *Choices, Values, and Frames* (New York: Cambridge University Press, 2000), pp. 159–70; Jack Knetsch, "The Endowment Effect and Evidence of Nonreversible Indifference Curves," in ibid., 171–79.

23 George Loewenstein and Daniel Adler, "A Bias in the Prediction of Tastes," in ibid., 726–34.

While in laboratory situations these striking effects decrease social efficiency by inhibiting trades, the implications for the real world may be quite
different. As people endow their possessions, lives, and perhaps self-images
with greater value, their level of satisfaction increases. Social stability is enhanced as an added force of inertia operates. You like what you have—be it
your territory, job, or spouse—and so are unwilling to trade it for an object
that would seem to an outsider to be of greater value. This produces considerable inefficiency, but reducing it might come at too high a price. Imagine a
world in which everyone was willing to change what he or she was doing in
the hope of making greater gains. Efficient in some sense surely; but what
would be the societal costs of constant and rapid change? What would be lost
in the sense of the stability, regularity, and solidity of social life? Furthermore, envy and jealousy would be increased if people did not place a higher
valuation on what they have than on other's possessions. Most marriages and
countries break up when things go badly; rarely are these bonds severed because one party feels that it can make more gains by alternative arrangements.
Imagine how high the divorce rate would be if even happy people were constantly looking around and asking whether they might be even happier with
another partner. Other social arrangements, from job-holding to personal
routines to the existence of countries, would be similarly at risk if people were
as willing to accept risks to make gains as they are to avoid losses. The fact
that people are less driven to change than they would be without the endowment effect raises the general level of contentment within societies and helps
make them work; the knowledge that others will fight very hard to keep what
they have increases predictability and decreases overt social conflict.

International stability may be enhanced, as many states are similarly prone
to settle for the status quo rather than undertake risky actions that could bring
gains if they succeed but lead to war if they do not. During the Cold War, each
side generally respected the other's sphere. Although each undertook some
measures of rollback, neither was willing to press these policies hard. As attractive as overthrowing or ousting the other side from an area appeared,
these gains were not sought in the face of significant risk.[24] The United States
abstained from aiding the rebels in East Germany in 1953 and Hungary in
1956; the Soviets' moves in Africa and even Vietnam and the successful American effort to overthrow the Soviet-backed regime in Afghanistan proceeded
with care and never appeared dangerous. By contrast, each side was willing
to be bolder when it was protecting what it considered to be its established
position, as the United States was during the Cuban missile crisis. Furthermore, because each side recognized these risk-taking propensities, security

---

24 Gregory Mitrovich, *Undermining the Kremlin: America's Strategy to Subvert the Soviet
Block, 1947–1956* (Ithaca: Cornell University Press, 2000).

increased even more. The challenger understood that the defender would not yield readily, thereby increasing the costs and risks of mounting a challenge; the defender believed that the challenger was likely to back down if met by a resolute response.

Loss aversion not only may render some situations particularly dangerous, but also may indicate that some policies that would otherwise be attractive should in fact be avoided because they will inflict more pain than standard analysis would imply. For example, economic policies that produce impressive average growth over time but involve cycles of gains and losses may produce less human happiness than policies that produce slower but steadier increases in wealth. The currency crisis in Southeast Asia in the late 1990s ended a period of rapid growth and drastically lowered the standard of living of millions of people. Although many of them remained better off than they had been a generation ago, the pain inflicted by the losses probably was so great that they would have felt themselves better off if they had experienced a steady upward trajectory, even if it brought them out at a point lower than the one they reached through the boom-and-bust cycle.

We may also treat gains and losses differently on a moral dimension. We are likely to see penalties levied against a person or group as more severe and less fair than rewards for the actor's competitor, even if these are functionally equivalent. As Allan Silver pointed out, the University of Michigan's affirmative action system would be less acceptable if twenty points were subtracted from the scores of white applicants rather than being added to the scores of African Americans.[25] Similarly, Secretary of Defense Donald Rumsfeld had to amend his remarks that draftees had such a short term of service after their training that they added "no value, no advantage really" to the army. After the former draftees protested, he explained that he had not meant to disparage them, but rather to argue that the volunteers could render even more service.[26]

Some international effects probably are less benign. While valuing what it has contributes to the state's sense of well-being and so counteracts the desperation that leads to many wars, negotiations are inhibited as each side feels that the cost of making a concession is greater than the gain received from the concession by the other side. For example, each side might be more pained by giving up a thousand missiles in an arms control agreement than it would be gratified and made secure by having the adversary's force reduced by the

25 Allan Silver, "Race and the Admissions Puzzle," letter to the editor, *New York Times*, January 18, 2003, p. A16.

26 David Firestone, "Threats and Responses: Opposition; Kennedy in Sweeping Attack, Faults Bush in Iraq and Taxes," *New York Times*, January 22, 2003, p. A9.

same amount. Or two countries might be better off by most measures if they would exchange some bits of territory, but the bargain would be made impossible by the high subjective evaluations each side placed on what it had.

Renormalization and Adjustment

Gains and losses take their meaning from whether one is better or worse compared to some point of reference; indeed, such a point is required to give the concepts of gain and loss their meaning. What the reference point is and how it changes then are central, but it is also in some sense arbitrary. It is usually but not always the status quo because it seems instinctive for people to measure gains and losses from where they are. Indeed, it is natural in that this is what we do without thinking about it or even being aware of it. But it is not fully rational in that the status quo is only one possible reference point among several (e.g., an absolute zero, what you aspire to, what others have). This matters because, in what Prospect Theory is best known for, people make different choices depending on the manipulation of the reference point that makes an identical situation seem different in terms of people being in the realm of gains in one and being in the realm of losses in the other.

Although the status quo is the most common reference point, two others can be salient and influence risk-taking and behavior. One is aspiration level: what actors hope to achieve, believe they deserve, and strive to reach. Shortfalls may be coded as losses, and people may be risk-acceptant for gains as measured from the status quo if the latter is below their aspiration level.

Another alternative reference point is what others have, which also can influence aspiration level. I suspect that most of us have, on occasion, estimated what we can and should get on the basis of what our peers have (of course, this raises the question of who our peers or reference groups are). Even if we are not inherently competitive, looking at others shows what is possible and provides some evidence of what we may be able to achieve. Furthermore, many goods are inherently positional, in that rewards flow not from how well an actor has done in absolute terms but from how the actor's wealth or performance compares to that of other actors.[27] Only one person can win a race; only one actor can gain a lead over all its competitors and be well positioned to make further gains; there are only a small number of houses that can be built along the beach; only a few people can visit an area that remains unspoiled. Perhaps because of these effects, we may have become accustomed

27 The classic study is Fred Hirsch, *Social Limits to Growth* (Cambridge: Harvard University Press, 1976); see also Robert Frank, *Luxury Fever: Money and Happiness in an Era of Excess* (Princeton: Princeton University Press, 1999).

to judging our own situation and well-being by comparing it to that of others even if the goods are not inherently positional.

If others are improving their lots, then we may not code a change that puts us above the status quo, but behind the progress others are making, as a gain. To put this differently, although we may use the status quo as a reference point, it will be a status quo not in absolute terms but in relative or positional terms, as we look at whether we are maintaining our position vis-a-vis others. The concern with relative rather than absolute gains that characterizes much of international politics is usually attributed to the actors' need to be able to re-sort to force in an anarchical world (in which case they need not be strong, but stronger than their adversaries). But a psychological component may also be present in the basic ways in which actors judge how well they are doing.

The belief in inevitable progress can produce a different, and steadily changing, reference point. If and when the Soviet leaders believed the com-munist ideology, they expected a steady increase in the power of communism and the number of countries that were freed from the grip of capitalism. The status quo was not only politically but psychologically arbitrary, and so stag-nation for them would have the same psychological impact as losses for oth-ers. This might explain what Western observers saw as the unusual propen-sity of the Soviet Union to take risks to increase its influence and aid leftist regimes as well as the collapse of the USSR when it became clear that the system could not advance either internally or externally.

Reference points can change over time as people adjust to new circum-stances. But the fact that this adjustment is not instantaneous is necessary for the basic phenomenon of loss aversion to occur. (Thaler's interesting discus-sion describes this phenomenon in terms of the frequency with which people "settle their accounts."[28]) If we renormalized for losses as soon as they oc-curred, we would simply adjust our reference point downward to the new status quo, and we would not be prone to accept risks in order to gain a chance at reestablishing our former position. When you have suffered a loss that you cannot immediately recoup, when does this get incorporated into your new sense of the status quo? By mid-October 1962, did the Soviets con-sider the strategic balance with missiles in Cuba as the benchmark from which gains and losses would be measured? If the blockade and associated bargain-ing had not succeeded in removing the missiles, how long would it have taken for the United States to treat the new situation as the status quo? A personal anecdote illustrates some of these questions. When I was young and foolish, I tried to body-surf an undisciplined wave and ended up crashing into the sand. For a minute or two I was paralyzed, and the thought that the paralysis

28 Richard Thaler "Mental Accounting Matters," in Daniel Kahneman and Amos Tversky, eds., *Choices, Values, and Frames* (New York: Cambridge University Press, 200), pp. 241–68.

would be permanent crossed my mind. But the paralysis passed quickly, to be replaced by nasty pain and a very unpleasant stiff neck. If the paralysis had lasted much longer, I would have treated the pain and suffering that accompanied movement as a major gain over the other outcome. But because my paralysis was so short-lived and I did not have time to assimilate it, I compared my current situation to that which existed before the injury and so was annoyed and grumpy.

We rapidly, if not effortlessly, adjust to good fortune and any improvement in our lives. Indeed, we get accustomed to it so readily that the immediate burst of pleasure produced by the change soon dissipates. Very soon after we have gained territory, influence, status, or wealth, we consider our new position to be the status quo from which we will judge future gains or losses. This is one reason why gains produce fewer lasting increments to subjective well-being than would otherwise be the case. The morning after the Berlin Wall came down, politically sophisticated Americans felt much better. Not only did they see East Germany and the rest of Eastern Europe becoming free, but America was much more secure. They soon came to take this for granted, however.

Individuals and collective actors adjust to losses with much greater difficulty. Both the delay in adjustment and its eventual occurrence are significant. Actors do generally make the best of bad circumstances. Terrible tragedies do not always ruin a person's life forever; sadness fades and subjective well-being is much less affected by absolute value position than one would intuitively expect. Most states similarly adjust to losses of power and influence and come to accept reduced status and territory. But they rarely do so quickly. At first they seek to recoup their losses, and their reference point is the earlier rather than the current status quo. This was clearly the case for Egypt after the 1967 war. That state could not accept Israeli occupation of Sinai as normal, and the 1973 war was triggered by the belief—probably correct—that although war was risky, there was no chance that peaceful diplomacy could succeed. This means that at any particular time many states are likely to feel themselves in the realm of losses because they can look back at an earlier "golden age."

The fact that both sides can have different reference points and so can simultaneously be impelled by loss aversion can render dangerous the strategy of the fait accompli. Alexander George and Richard Smoke note that deterrence can alter the status quo before the defender has time to react.[29] But unless the latter quickly adjusts to the new situation, it may be willing to run unusually high risks to regain its previous position. The other side, expecting

29 Alexander George and Richard Smoke, *Deterrence in American Foreign Policy* (New York: Columbia University Press, 1974), pp. 536–40.

the first to be rational, will be surprised by its continued resistance. Because each side will see itself as defending the status quo, it will therefore have strong incentives to stand firm and, believing the adversary sees the situation as the state does, will expect the other side to retreat. Each will be driven by a strong resistance to accept what it sees as an unfavorable change.

Concluding Observations on Methodological Difficulties

Getting good evidence for any of these effects will not be easy. The endowment effect is difficult to verify because states and people in society are not given things the way people in experiments are given mugs and candy bars at random. Furthermore, it would be difficult to specify that the added valuation comes immediately rather than as a result of the ties that are built up between the country and the territory or other value that has been gained. But it might be possible to find cases in which countries conquered or otherwise gained territory almost accidentally—areas they had not been seeking as primary goals—and then see how much they were willing to pay to keep them.

It is at least as difficult to gather firm evidence on the main inferences from Prospect Theory. Crucial is the argument that people will run much higher risks to avoid losses than to make gains. The experimenter gives the subjects the payoffs and probabilities; in real life people construct their subjective estimates of both of these elements. Similarly, the experimenter can frame the same question differently and see how people respond; in social and political life actors do their own framing. Thus while we can find cases in which different actors employ different frames,[30] correlations between differences in framing and differences in choice and preferences may be spurious: the same factors that lead an actor to frame the situation in a particular way may drive her choice. Even if we find that actors' preferences change as the way they frame the choice changes, third variables may still be at work. We generally find people taking higher risks when they consider themselves to be in the realm of losses than when they are seeking gains, but the difficulty is that the framing may be endogenous to the choice because the person both frames the question and answers it. If two individuals differ in the risks they are willing to take in the same situation, and if one frames it as avoiding losses (and acts boldly) while the other frames it as seeking gains (and is more cautious), it is extremely difficult to determine whether the framing itself is a cause or an effect, or whether the relationship is spurious. The decision to take a risk could lead a person to see the situation as one in which losses will occur if the risk is not taken. Even more likely, the same factors of personality

---

30 Rose McDermott, "The Failed Rescue Mission in Iran: An Application of Prospect Theory," *Political Psychology* 13 (June 1992): 237–63.

or context that lead to accepting or minimizing risk can also determine how the problem is framed. Ingenuity and careful research can reduce, but not completely eliminate, these difficulties.[31]

Showing that people are loss-averse obviously means demonstrating much more than that they do not like losses. Rather, what is crucial is demonstrating that differences in risk-taking propensity vary according to the direction of the expected changes from the status quo. The difficulties are formidable. First, we can rarely specify with great precision the risks that an actor perceives in various courses of action. Fifty-five years after the Cuban missile crisis we still argue about how risky Nikita Khrushchev believed his move would be. Furthermore, showing that people are more risk-acceptant for losses than for gains requires comparisons that are quite difficult because they call for a measure of the subjective utility of various outcomes. Most decisions lack an objective yardstick of lives or dollars; we cannot readily find comparisons as convincing as those which arise when people are faced with the possibility of a loss or a gain of a given amount of money or a certain number of lives. Thus even if we can show that a statesman took risks when the alternative would have been to accept a smaller but certain loss, we need also to show that in other situations he preferred continuing the status quo to accepting a similar gamble that might have resulted in an improvement equal in magnitude to the loss he found unacceptable. Without precise—or at least decent—measures of the magnitude of the gains and losses (which are of course subjective), greater risk-taking in the latter cases can be attributed to differences in the utilities in the cases. Of course, confirmation of expected-utility theories are plagued by similar difficulties of measurement, but without a set of very good comparisons there will always be a great deal of room for dispute. Nevertheless, it is clear both that Prospect Theory yields important and counterintuitive propositions and that many cases indicate that statesmen are indeed more risk-acceptant for losses than for gains. The psychological world does not appear to be symmetrical, and the implications for human and national behavior are many and important.

31 James Davis, *Threats and Promises: The Pursuit of International Influence* (Baltimore: Johns Hopkins University Press, 2000); Rose McDermott, *Risk-Taking in International Politics*.

PART III

Political Psychology and International Relations Theory

5

Signaling and Perception

PROJECTING IMAGES
AND DRAWING INFERENCES

Some essential part of the study of mixed-motive games is necessarily empirical. This is not to say just that it is an empirical question how people do actually perform in mixed-motives games, especially games too complicated for intellectual mastery. It is a stronger statement; that the principles relevant to successful play, the strategic principles, the propositions of a normative theory, cannot be derived by purely analytical means from a priori considerations.

—THOMAS SCHELLING, *THE STRATEGY OF CONFLICT*

A marriage commitment is a very personal thing. It shouldn't be used to judge someone's character.

—BARBARA COZZI, MANAGER OF A RETAIL STORE, COMMENTING ON THE
MILITARY ADULTERY SCANDALS IN THE SPRING OF 1997

Signaling and Perception

An essential problem of political and social life is how actors communicate with each other, especially in international politics.[1] In a sense, it is the topic of all the essays in this book. But for this chapter some professional autobiography is relevant. My dissertation began as a study of how countries form images of

1 Schelling's quotation comes from his book *The Strategy of Conflict* (Cambridge: Harvard University Press, 1960), 162–63; Cozzi is quoted in Carey Goldberg, "On Adultery Issue, Many Aren't Ready to Cast First Stone," *New York Times*, June 9, 1997.

others and predict what they will do, but after a bit of thought I realized that studying perception and misperception in isolation would be one-sided. Just as actors need to predict what others will do, so they also want others to make desired predictions about their own behavior; actors not only perceive others, they signal in order to project images that may be either true or false. (Indeed, when they interpret others' behavior, they realize that the others are also trying to project desired images.) At a certain point, however, the understanding that the topics of drawing inferences and projecting images were intimately related became less pressing than the realization that I could not analyze both if I were to finish my dissertation in the foreseeable future. So I split the topics apart, taking what I thought was the more manageable subject of projecting images for my thesis and returning to misperception when it was done. The dissertation turned into *The Logic of Images in International Relations* and the second study appeared as *Perception and Misperception in International Politics.* [2]

Although the two studies did touch on each other in a few places, as I wrote them they really did not represent two sides of the same coin. What makes this more than a personal anecdote is that the topics of how actors seek to influence others' perceptions of them and how they perceive others have been kept separate by most other scholars as well. One impetus for this chapter is my view that much recent work on signaling carried out by economists and those influenced by them is flawed by the failure to see that the two topics should be joined. [3] This means, of course, that this chapter should unite them, but after forty-five years I can still make only limited steps in that direction.

The Problems Actors Face

The general problem is easily enough stated. To establish their own policies, actors need to estimate what others will do and how they will react to alternative kinds of behavior on the part of the actor. [4] *Logic of Images* and the more recent economistic approaches have the same starting point: the only behaviors that are informative are those that distinguish among actors who will react differently, or, to use the term now often employed, different actor "types." If I am to figure out whether another state is bluffing or not, or

2 Robert Jervis, *The Logic of Images in International Relations* (Princeton: Princeton University Press, 1970; 2nd ed., New York: Columbia University Press, 1989); *Perception and Misperception in International Politics* (Princeton: Princeton University Press, 1976; 2nd ed., 2017).

3 Jeffrey Banks, *Signaling Games in Political Science* (New York: Gordon and Breach, 1991); James Morrow, *Game Theory for Political Scientists* (Princeton: Princeton University Press, 1994).

4 Exceptions to this generalization are not trivial, but are largely put aside here.

whether its apparent hostility is rooted in fear or expansionism, or whether a potential ally will come to my assistance if I am attacked, I should look only at behavior that discriminates between the alternative possibilities. Thus, I should pay no attention to the things that both a bluffer and a serious state would do, nor to a posture that both a fearful state and an aggressor would assume, nor to a promise that both a trustworthy and an untrustworthy ally would make.[5] The inference process is rendered especially difficult because actors who know that they are being observed and want to influence others have powerful incentives to project images that will lead perceivers to draw the desired impression whether or not it is accurate. As I stressed in *Logic of Images*, deception is common in politics as in everyday life, which means that detecting it is a crucial task.

All this seems quite obvious, but it rests on the plausible but questionable assumption that behavior is not situationally determined, or at least is not entirely so. That is, an alternative approach argues that most of actors' behavior stems from the situations they are in, not their personal characteristics and predispositions. This is linked to the level of analysis question in international politics and to the parallel question of the internal versus the external sources of behavior discussed in psychology. Students of international politics are familiar with Arnold Wolfers's argument that a significant number of cases resemble a house that is on fire, and here we don't need to know much about the individuals in it to predict that they will rush for the exits.[6] As important as these cases are, however, they may be quite rare and we should remember that the situation is something that the actors create (collectively to be sure, but not without individual choices). Furthermore, few decision-makers believe either that they completely lack freedom of action or that others are completely alike.

---

5 Implicit in the discussion so far—and an assumption for everything that follows—is that there are significant differences among actors: that they not only differ in their capabilities but also in their goals, beliefs about how to reach those goals, and willingness to pay costs to do so. This seems self-evident, just as it used to be considered self-evident that individuals had stable personalities that strongly influenced their behavior. However, it can be argued that this assumption is incorrect and that situational variables determine behavior.

6 Arnold Wolfers, *Discord and Collaboration* (Baltimore: Johns Hopkins University Press, 1962), pp. 11–15. For further discussion of perceptions and the levels of analysis question, see Jervis, *Perception and Misperception* (1976, 2017), ch. 1, and James Goldgeier and Philip Tetlock, "Psychology and International Relations Theory," *Annual Review of Political Science* 4 (2001): 67–92. Going further than Kenneth Waltz, John Mearsheimer's offensive realism rests on the assumption that the pressures of the international system are so extreme that intentions, motives, and actor types are irrelevant: *The Tragedy of Great Power Politics* (New York: Norton, 2001). That this is a minority position does not make it incorrect.

PERCEPTIONS CONTROL

The value of various kinds of behaviors for determining how the actor will behave in the future is the linchpin of signaling and perception. The former must depend on the latter because the impression conveyed by any behavior depends on how it is perceived. This is obscured by much of our discourse because we talk about how actors *should* behave in order to project a given image and the sort of information perceivers *should* pay attention to. The language is prescriptive because this theorizing is more deductive than empirical. But what if (all? some?) perceivers infer differently? Indeed, if signaling theories are arcane, perceivers who have not read the literature will draw inferences differently, which means that the theory will neither describe the thoughts of perceivers nor prescribe the signalers' behavior. A theory of signaling, then, requires a careful investigation of how signals are perceived.

As I was writing this chapter for its original publication, two news stories appeared that help explain what I mean. When the chief of the Indonesian armed forces, General Wiranto, traveled to East Timor in the wake of the militia violence that followed the referendum for independence, the capital city of Dili was calm. The Indonesians presumably wanted to show that they could keep the peace. However, the British representative to the UN thought that this "illustrates that you can never know whether these people are going to switch [the violence] on or switch it off."[7] The second story involved a murder suspect who had freely undergone a prolonged police interrogation. The police chief was suspicious: "How many innocent people do you know who will sit there and answer questions for hours?"[8] Perception is laden with interpretation and theory. Almost no inferences—perhaps none at all—are self-evident in the sense that all people under all circumstances looking at the information would draw the same conclusion. Thus, knowing how theorists read a signal does not tell us how the perceiver does.

A few more examples may make the problems clearer and flag some questions. The other evening, I was walking down Broadway and saw twelve policemen in about as many blocks. Should I have been reassured that so many policemen were there to guarantee my safety, or alarmed that the neighborhood is so dangerous as to require this force? When a university institutes a teaching award, is this a signal that it takes teaching seriously or that it did not take it seriously before? Or is it a signal that it wants others to believe that it takes teaching seriously, and, if so, how and in what direction does this cor-

---

7 Seth Mydans, "Jakarta Concedes a Loss of Control Over Timor Forces," *New York Times*, September 12, 1999, p. 8.

8 James Bennet, "His Life as a Murder Suspect," *New York Times Magazine*, September 12, 1999, pp. 48–53.

relate with taking it seriously? If a previous winner of the teaching award was just given tenure, will (should?) other assistant professors think that winning the award will boost their chances, or infer that the university, having ostentatiously rewarded one good instructor, will not feel the need to do so again in the near future? When I see a sign in a restaurant bathroom saying "Employees must wash their hands," am I reassured that the hygiene standards are appropriately high, disturbed that the people handling my food must be reminded to follow the dictates of common sense, or do I fear that they will respond to the insult by not washing?

As these examples show, most communications convey two messages: what the actor is saying and the fact that he needs to say it. For a bank to increase its reserves against possible losses strengthens its position, but the opposite effect may be produced when others learn that it has done so and infer that its solvency is in doubt. For an actor to claim that it is committed to taking a certain action will increase the costs it will pay if it behaves otherwise, and if this were the only effect, this would increase others' estimates of how likely it is to carry out this act. The fact that the actor felt the need to commit itself conveys information, however, and others may infer that only the weak need to try to bolster their resolve. In much the same way, when a state tries to reassure its ally that it will stand by it, the ally's uneasiness may increase as it infers both that the threat is greater than it had believed and that the patron feels that such reassurances are necessary.

My point is that although behavior may reveal something important about the actor, often it is not clear exactly what is being revealed, what is intended to be revealed, and what others will think is being revealed. If a husband leaves his wife and small children for another woman, should the new love infer that he is likely to remain faithful to her because he has made such a sacrifice to be with her, or should she worry that someone who has deserted one family is likely to repeat the offense? What inferences do we expect the Soviets to have drawn from the Western bombing of Dresden at the end of World War II? That, as some Western leaders thought at the time, the willingness to kill a large number of Germans and weaken their Eastern front to facilitate Soviet victories showed that they took Soviet interests into account? Or that the West was brutal and likely to try to coerce the USSR in the postwar world?

It might seem as though consistency provides the key. For example, observers should infer that the actor is "tough" (i.e., has high resolve) if it behaves strongly. In a situation resembling a game of chicken in which high conflict or war is the worst possible outcome for both sides, a strong reaction is one that runs a significant risk of an undesired clash. A belligerent response would therefore unambiguously show resolve. But this is too simple. Observers' interpretations remain crucial as they have to decide what is risky, whether the actor thought the behavior was risky, and whether the behavior is likely to be repeated. Furthermore, to the extent that resolve is inferred from actions that the observer thinks the actor believes have a significant chance of leading to war, we run into a paradox of the kind that deterrence and game theory have made familiar: what is believed to be risky is actually safe and vice versa. If the adversary believes that only a state that was willing to go further would take such a bold step, then the step would be safe because the adversary would back down in the face of such a response. But this, in turn, would mean that a state that was not willing to take much risk of additional escalation, as well as a state that was, would be willing to act in this way, thereby permitting deception and robbing the behavior of much of its meaning.[9] This twist of the argument would be true only if perceivers believed it, however, which reinforces the point that the impact of behavior depends on the perceiver's beliefs about the links between the other's present and future actions.

It is exactly the meaning of the similarity of behavior and the nature of these links that requires theorizing and so is often subject to dispute. Thus when President Clinton hired the high-powered Washington lawyer Robert Bennett to defend him against the sexual harassment charges by Paula Jones, not only did the *Washington Post* sharply increase its coverage of the story, but, in a very different arena, confidence in the dollar increased. "If Paula Jones has no case, the *Post* editors figured, how come Clinton needs a hired gun like Bennett?"[10] According to a currency trader, hiring Bennett "was really a boon for the dollar. We were starting to lose faith in him and that helped turn things."[11] These inferences overlap in seeing Clinton as taking the charges seriously but differed because the perceivers have different substantive interests, and the currency traders were looking for a character trait, a willingness to act strongly in the face of adversity rather than becoming paralyzed and indecisive, whereas the *Post* (and others) were estimating whether the charges had merit. What is central, however, is that the inferences will strike many observers as strange and that neither the existence of links nor why some people discerned them is entirely clear.

9 Robert Jervis, *System Effects: Complexity in Social and Political Life* (Princeton: Princeton University Press, 1997), pp. 255–58, 266–71.

10 Quoted in Daniel Klaidman, "Clinton versus Paula Jones," *Newsweek*, December 1, 1997, p. 31.

11 Thomas Friedman, "It's a Mad, Mad, Mad, World Money Market," *New York Times*, May 8, 1994, p. E1.

Typologies of Informative Behavior

Not all behavior is equally informative about what actors will do in the future. The distinction of intuitive appeal is between words and deeds. But, even putting aside what the philosopher J. L. Austin called performative utterances—cases in which "in saying what I do, I actually perform that action," such as naming a ship in a christening and saying "I do" in a marriage ceremony[12]—words can carry significant evidence of their validity. Indeed, if this were not so, it would be hard to explain why actors who mistrust each other bother to listen or talk at all. Many deeds, furthermore, are ambiguous or can be used for deception.

Two alternative distinctions have been proposed; neither is completely satisfactory. In *Logic of Images* I distinguished between indices and Signals (I will use the term "Signals" with a capital "S" when talking about this concept and write "signals" in the lower case for all behavior that the sender or the perceiver believes carries information). Signals (with a capital S) are like a language in that their meanings are established by agreement, implicit if not explicit. Thus words, special forms of communication like diplomatic language, and many actions have meaning only because both the signaler and the perceiver agree as to the message that the former is trying to convey. The obvious difficulty for both sides is that Signals can be used to project a false as well as a true image.

Indices, by contrast, are behaviors (either verbal or nonverbal) that the perceiver believes are inextricably linked to a characteristic that helps predict what the actor will do in the future. Observers therefore see them as reliable and not available for deception. Most attention has been focused on actors' intentions or types, but let me give an example of capabilities. Anyone can claim to be physically strong; lifting a heavy weight provides more credible evidence of that characteristic. Similarly, having a screaming fit is an index to being hot-tempered, although people in everyday life and statesmen (e.g., Hitler) have been known to put on acts for the benefit of observers. These indices can be seen as samples of the behavior of interest; others are believed to be correlates—and perhaps causes—of it, as when democracy is used as an index of the propensity to follow a peaceful foreign policy.

For behavior to be taken as an index, the perceiver must believe that the actor cannot manipulate it to project a false image, either because manipulation is impossible or excessively costly or because the actor is unaware that the perceiver is tracking it. But the meaning and indeed the existence of indices depends on the perceiver's theories about the links between the behavior and underlying characteristics. Thus, in many of the cases discussed earlier,

12 John Austin, *Philosophical Papers* (London: Oxford University Press, 1961), pp. 220–39.

behavior was interpreted differently by different observers because some of them saw a certain connection whereas others either saw none or believed that the link was quite different.

COSTLY SIGNALS AND CHEAP TALK

Economists, and political scientists who have been influenced by them, have distinguished between "costly signals" and "cheap talk." The basic argument follows from Schelling's intuition that a behavior that costs nothing can be equally well taken by an actor of any type and so provides no information.[13] Statements of intent, for example, are cheap in that both a Hitler and a statesman who really was committed to peace could equally well declaim benign goals. It follows that perceivers should focus on behavior that is costly to undertake. Such behavior cannot readily be faked: only an actor who is willing and able to behave in a certain way can have the ability and incentives to send these costly signals. Political figures often say things like what Bernie Sanders said of Hillary Clinton during the 2016 presidential campaign when, in response to his attacks, she moved at least a bit to the left in her speeches: "The question is not what she says. The question is what her record has been and what she will do if she is elected President."[14] The last sentence implies that her record (an index), is a better guide to her future behavior as president than her speeches are, a claim that is plausible but of course debatable.

Many costly signals fit within my category of indices. As I noted in *Logic of Images*, when states feel the need to impress others with their resolve, they often increase their defense spending irrespective of the increase in capability that will result, and indeed occasionally at the cost of such capability. But the distinction between cheap and costly behavior has a number of difficulties, some of which are shared with my discussion of Signals and indices. To start with, cheap talk is sometimes defined as behavior that does not cost the actor anything to undertake and sometimes as behavior that can be taken equally well by an actor of any type. These definitions overlap, but are not identical. Indeed, behavior often is highly diagnostic if it is cheap for an actor of one type but not for an actor of another kind. Thus if a state is peaceful, giving up offensive weapons will be far less of a sacrifice than if it is an expansionist, which is why such a move carries great credibility for the latter state. Some actions are not costly, but are indeed informative because they can be undertaken only by a certain type of actor. When the Mafia representative arranges to have the horse's head placed in the owner's bed in the famous scene in *The*

13 Thomas Schelling, *Arms and Influence* (New Haven: Yale University Press, 1966), p. 150.
14 Quoted in Ryan Lizza, "The Great Divide," *New Yorker*, March 21, 2016, p. 39.

Godfather, this is an index of the mob's power and ruthlessness in a way that is not well caught by the notion of a costly signal.

We must also distinguish between two different kinds of costly signals. One consists of cases in which the cost is incurred as the behavior is undertaken. For example, taking an action in the face of significant domestic opposition can be a costly signal of the decision-makers' commitment to the policy. But the term "commitment" shows a second category of costly signals: threats and promises that will be costly to break. This is the function of Signals that the state is committed to following a given policy. Here the cost comes not with the issuing of the Signal, however, but only later if the actor does not live up to it.[15]

It might seem that problems of interpretation do not arise with costly signals because costs are objective and will be seen the same way by all participants. But what the actor feels to be a cost, observers may not so categorize, or vice versa, as the example of Br'er Rabbit reminds us. Had the United States engaged in high defense spending in the late 1940s, it would have been felt as economically and politically costly by American leaders. But Stalin might not have seen it that way, because he believed that insufficient demand was the main danger facing the American economy, which therefore would have benefited from higher defense spending. Indeed, throughout the Cold War the Soviets claimed that the periodic increases in the U.S. defense budget reflected the power of arms manufacturers or the needs of the economy, in which case they would not have been taken as indications that the United States was willing to sacrifice blood in a limited war or run high risks during a crisis.

The central role of perceivers' beliefs leads to another difficulty with the notion of costly signals, one that is also brought out by the example just given. In some cases, the cost that is borne is very tightly related to the characteristic being judged, but often it is not. For example, high defense spending may be an index, but exactly what is it an index of? The perceiver must do a great deal of interpretive work to answer this question. For the Soviets, it might be an index of the power of various groups and classes in the United States, and so might yield valuable information about which sectors were dominant. Depending on other beliefs, it could lead to the judgment that the United States was aggressive, or that it would behave cautiously in a crisis because these sectors would not want to risk a conflict that might undermine their positions. Observers, Marxist or not, might also infer that the United States lacked confidence in its military might, that it was seeking to substitute arms for the

15 Schelling, *Strategy of Conflict*; Jervis, *Logic of Images*. Also see James Fearon, "Signaling Foreign Policy Interests: Tying Hands Versus Sinking Costs," *Journal of Conflict Resolution* 41 (February 1997): 68–80.

willingness to shed blood in a war, or that it hoped to impress others, which would save money in the long run. Others with different theories could draw the opposite inference: only a country that was a "tough" type would be willing to spend a lot on defense. Knowing that the behavior is costly, then, tells us little about what inferences observers will draw; it is probably fruitless to argue about what inferences they should draw.

CHANGING TYPES

Most discussions assume that the actor's type remains constant. Indeed, this assumption underpins the use of signals to predict future policy. Behavior can change as well as reveal an actor's type, however, and this is particularly true for costly measures. For example, fighting in Vietnam undermined America's containment policy because having paid a high price for one limited war, it would not do so soon again. It was the Soviet appreciation of this change in American domestic opinion, not the fact that the United States would not pay the price necessary to secure victory, that drove the (limited) Soviet perceptions of American weakness in the aftermath of the war.[16] Similarly, psychologically as much as materially, Britain and France were shattered by World War I and so were unwilling to follow the same kind of stiff policy toward Germany in the 1930s that they had adopted in the earlier period. They were no longer the same type of actors as they had been, as most perceivers—most acutely Hitler—realized. I suspect that it is generally true that paying a significant price will set off a variety of political, social, and psychological processes that can alter the actor's goals, views of the world, self-image, and other characteristics that underpin its behavior. Here, too, much depends on how the actor and observers understand the previous policy, most obviously whether they see it as a success and worth the effort.[17]

INDICES

Although the category of costly signals overlaps with the concept of indices, it does not exhaust it. The basic logic is that only an actor of a certain type would behave in this way and that the behavior is a good predictor of what the actor will do in the future. When an index approximates a sample of the behavior that is expected in the future, the belief about its significance is likely

16 Ted Hopf, *Peripheral Visions: Deterrence Theory and American Foreign Policy in the Third World, 1965–1990* (Ann Arbor: University of Michigan Press, 1994).

17 For the literature on learning, see George Breslauer and Phillip Tedock, eds., *Learning in US and Soviet Foreign Policy* (Boulder, Colo.: Westview, 1991); Russel Leng, "Crisis Learning Games," *American Political Science Review* 82 (March 1988): 179–94; Jack Levy, "Learning and Foreign Policy," *International Organization* 48 (Spring 1994): 279–312.

to be seen as self-evident. Other indices invoke much more interpretive work, as when states attribute certain foreign policy propensities to other states according to the latter's domestic regimes. But the form of the inference is the same: only an actor of type X would undertake action Y, therefore the actor is of type X (or, less informatively, actor of type X is more likely than others to undertake action Y).

These links may seem clear to an observer, but there is room for dispute and error. Thus, after the Soviets shot down the Korean airliner that strayed over their territory in August 1983, Ronald Reagan asked, "What can be the hope of legitimate and moral discourse with a state whose values permit such atrocities?"[18] And in the summer of 1959, when Khrushchev complained to Nixon about the American placement of missiles in Turkey, he asked, "If you intend to make war on us, I understand; if not, why [do this]?"[19] Similarly, in the months preceding the Japanese decision to attack Pearl Harbor, the military argued that if the Americans "do not accede to the conditions we have presented [in the negotiations], we must take the view that they harbor designs to bring Japan to its knees; thus, it is clear that if we make concessions we will soon be put to their poisoned sword."[20] The Poles reacted so strongly to the discovery of the Katyn massacre of their prisoners in 1943 not only because of its intrinsic horror, but also because they saw it as an index of the Soviet rejection of the possibility of a noncommunist Polish government after the war. The Soviet leaders, in turn, took the Polish refusal to accept the Soviet false claim that the men had been killed by the Nazis as evidence that this regime would not accommodate Soviet interests. None of these inferences were foolish, but all could be debated, either at the time or later. The connections that seemed so clear to the perceivers rested on a set of unarticulated generalizations about politics and classes of actors.

In as much as the interpretation of indices depends on theories, perceivers are likely to go astray when these are incorrect. Furthermore, actors who understand the theories and can manipulate the behavior that is being used as an index can project a desired image even if it is false. Of course, perceivers use indices because they believe that actors cannot manipulate them, but only in some cases is this correct. Even indices that seem to tap the relevant characteristic quite directly and that involve high costs can be controlled by actors who are willing to pay the price, which was the case with the behavior

18 Quoted in Michel Sherry, *In the Shadow of War: The US since the Late 1930s* (New Haven: Yale University Press, 1995), p. 403.

19 Barton Bernstein, "Reconsidering the Missile Crisis," in James Nathan, ed., *The Cuban Missile Crisis Revisited* (New York: St. Martin's Press, 1992), p. 59.

20 Quoted in James Morley, ed., *The Final Confrontation: Japan's Negotiations with the United States, 1941*, vol. 5, *Japan's Road to the Pacific War* (New York: Columbia University Press, 1994), p. 171.

of Jesús Guajardo, who was hired to infiltrate the camp of the Mexican rebel leader Emilano Zapata in order to kill him:

> Guajaredo "deserted" to Zapata with his entire unit and asked to be taken into his army. Such a development represented welcome reinforcements for Zapata, who desperately needed soldiers and, above all, arms. Nonetheless, he was skeptical, and he ordered Guajardo to attack a Carranzist garrison to prove his revolutionary commitment. Guajardo provided his "proof." He not only carried out the attack, but even executed the Carranzist soldiers he captured. After that, Zapata felt he could "trust" Guajardo and agreed to a meeting at the Chinameca hacienda. On 10 April 1919 he proceeded there with several companions. Guajardo received him with an honor guard standing at attention. When Zapata approached, a "salute of honor" was fired and Zapata was killed instantly.[21]

Signals and Reputation

Perceivers can use an index to draw inferences even—or especially—when they do not think the actor is trying to communicate anything. By contrast, Signals imply that the actor intends to communicate, and the perceiver's first task is to try to determine what the actor is trying to say. A necessary condition for the effective use of a Signal is that senders and perceivers interpret it in the same way. Thus, diplomatic language is often employed because the meanings of words and phrases have come to be precisely understood and, to note the other side of the coin, on other occasions actors take care to see that their Signals are ambiguous and so can be disavowed if need be. Even when ambiguity is not intended, however, Signals frequently fail because the perceiver does not understand what message the actor is trying to communicate.

Understanding does not mean believing, however, because deceivers as well as honest actors can send the same Signals. As noted earlier, Signals are cheap to send, but this does not mean that costs do not enter in. Signals are implicit or explicit statements of how the actor will behave in the future, and costs are incurred if and when the actor does not behave accordingly. This is one of the main reasons why perceivers pay attention to Signals and is usually discussed in terms of the importance to an actor of its reputation.

Putting aside the validity of these claims,[22] we need to distinguish reputation, which involves general beliefs about the actor's type, from Signaling reputation, which is the actor's reputation for living up to its word, for usually

---

21 Friedrich Katz, *The Secret War in Mexico: Europe, the United States, and the Mexican Revolution* (Chicago: University of Chicago Press, 1981), p. 533.

22 Hopf, *Peripheral Visions*; Jonathan Mercer, *Reputation and International Politics* (Ithaca: Cornell University Press, 1996).

doing as it says it will do. Of course, actors may not have Signaling reputations overall, but Signaling reputations in particular areas. Thus I might be
believed to be ready to carry out my promises but not my threats; to send
valid Signals about my capabilities but not about my intentions; to be willing
and able to keep my word in the economic area but not on military issues. But
more importantly, Signaling reputation needs to be distinguished from a more
general reputation. For example, most of us know of at least a few colleagues
who, while being conscientious and carrying out a large number of duties,
regularly promise to do more than they can. This contrasts with others who
do much less, but who can be counted on to live up to the few commitments
that they make. In a parallel manner, in the spring of 1997 a Cambodia expert
said that he was predisposed to accept the Khmer Rouge statements about
the split within the group, including the killing of the former second in command and the fall of Pol Pot: "They don't call people traitors who are not
traitors. They don't announce they have arrested people who are not arrested.
This is not to suggest that they are angels; just to suggest that they operate
along a fairly standard, well-known script."[23] In much the same way, referring
to himself in the third person, a Cambodian leader declared, "What Hun Sen
threatens, Hun Sen dares to do."[24] The truth of this statement says nothing
about the range of objectives for which Hun Sen will threaten and act.

Turning to international politics, a state may be known as willing to pay a
high price to protect its allies, to be a bully, or to be generally predisposed to
cooperate with international organizations irrespective of whether it has previously issued Signals to that effect. Past behavior can be used as an index to
the state's characteristics and to how it will behave in the future in a way that
does not depend on Signals.[25] For example, fighting in Korea should have
given the United States a reputation for defending countries against aggression

23   Quoted in Seth Mydans, "Cambodian Rivals Say They Will Bring Pol Pot to Justice," *New
York Times*, June 22, 1997, p. 8.

24   Quoted in Seth Mydans, "Hun Sen Says He's Enjoying Being Cambodia's Sole Ruler,"
New York Times, July 11, 1997, p. A12.

25   I think attribution theory is very useful here and have applied it in *Perception and
Misperception* (1976, 2017), ch. 2. Elsewhere ("Additional Thoughts on Political Psychology and
Rational Choice," *Political Psychology* 10 (September 1989): 513–14) I have flagged—but not
answered—the question of the extent to which reputation attaches to an individual leader, a
state, or a category of states (democracies, revolutionary regimes, etc.). It appears that the reason why the Hutu extremists killed the Belgian peacekeepers at the beginning of the Rwandan
genocide was that the American withdrawal from Somalia convinced them that other Western
democracies would pull their troops out of a peacekeeping mission if they were faced with even
a small number of casualties (Jones, personal communication, and Bruce Jones, "Military Intervention in Rwanda's Two Wars: Partisanship and Indifference," in Barbara Walter and Jack Snyder, eds., *Civil Wars, Insecurity, and Intervention* (New York: Columbia University Press, 1999),
p. 133.

even though—or perhaps partly because—it had not made a commitment to do so. The other side of this coin is that it is a concern with Signaling reputation rather than general reputation that leads actors to feel that they must live up to a promise or a threat, although if they had known this would prove necessary, they would not have issued it in the first place.

Perceptual Biases

Signals affect behavior only as they are perceived and interpreted, and the difficulty with constructing a parsimonious theory is that perceptions and their causes are quite varied. Nevertheless, several main tendencies can be detected. Although I cannot build them into a unified theory of signaling and perception, any attempt to create such a theory has to incorporate them.

In efforts to make sense of their world, people are moved by both motivated (that is, affect-driven) and unmotivated (purely cognitive) biases.[26] The former derive from the need to maintain psychological well-being and a desired self-image, the latter from the need for short-cuts to rationality in an environment characterized by complex and ambiguous information. Motivated and cognitive influences are hard to separate,[27] and I merely discuss the single most important bias of each type.

The generalization that is most powerful, in the sense of occurring most often and exercising most control over perceptions, is that information is interpreted within the framework established by preexisting beliefs.[28] Three implications are crucial here. First, images of other states are strongly influenced by the often implicit theories held by statesmen that specify the existence and meaning of indices (e.g., democracies are peaceful; countries experiencing rapid economic growth will demand an increased international role). These theories can vary from one individual or society to another and often are related to general ideas about how people and politics function. For example, if a new regime in a country suppressed democracy and civil liberties and proclaimed the superiority of the dominant racial group, many observers would predict that it would menace its neighbors. Indeed, it might be seen as a potential Nazi Germany. But it was the Nazi experience itself that made these links between domestic and international politics so salient; one reason for the appeasement policy was that in the 1930s oppressive regimes

26 For further discussion, see Jervis, "Understanding Beliefs," in this volume.

27 Chaim Kaufmann, "Out of the Lab and into the Archives: A Method for Testing Psychological Explanations of Political Decision Making," *International Studies Quarterly* 38 (December 1994): 557–86; Philip Tetlock and Ariel Levi, "Attribution Bias: On the Inconclusiveness of the Cognition Motivation Debate," *Journal of Experimental Social Psychology* 18 (January 1982): 68–88.

28 Jervis, *Perception and Misperception* (1976, 2017), ch. 4.

were not believed to be especially aggressive. A second consequence of the influence of preexisting beliefs is that images of individual states, once established, will change only in response to discrepant information that is high in quantity or low in ambiguity. This helps account for the inertia of many policies, the frequency with which states are taken by surprise, and many of the occasions on which signals are missed or misinterpreted. Third, and relatedly, observers who believe different theories or hold different images of the state will draw different inferences from its behavior. The same Signals and indices will be read very differently by observers with different beliefs about the actor.

This means that if observers—and actors—are to estimate how signals will be received, they need to understand the theories and cognitive predispositions of the perceivers. If you want to know whether an act will be seen as hostile or not, you should first inquire as to whether the observer already has an image of the actor as malign; to tell whether a promise or a threat will be viewed as credible, it is crucial to discern the perceivers' theories and beliefs about the actor. This is true irrespective of the truthfulness of the signals. The famous "Double-Cross" system that the British used during World War II to control the Nazi spy network in Britain and feed it misleading messages would not have worked had the British not cracked many German codes, thus enabling them to understand what reports the Germans would believe.

This shows the psychological naiveté of signaling theories that, although acknowledging the importance of preexisting beliefs, argue that new information is combined with old as specified by Bayesian updating of prior beliefs on the basis of new information. The model generally used is of a person who has to estimate the proportions of red and blue chips in a paper bag; increasing evidence is provided as one chip after another is drawn at random from the bag. The assumption, appropriate for this example, is that judgments of specific bits of evidence are independent of expectations. That is, whether I think the bag contains mostly red or mostly blue chips does not affect whether I see any particular chip as red or blue; the color of the chip is objective and will be perceived the same way by all people, irrespective of their prior beliefs. But this is a poor model for perceptions of actors' types: how I perceive your signal is strongly influenced by what I already think of you.[29] Even what might seem to be the clearest signals will make no impression if the perceiver's mind is made up or is focused elsewhere. It did not require the impeachment trial of President Clinton to show us that people with different beliefs and interests differ not only in their estimates of how much new evidence should change priors, but also in their evaluations of whether this evidence points in one direction or its opposite.

---

29 For further discussion, see the preface to the second edition of *Perception and Misperception* (2017).

Cold cognitive processes driven by the requirement to simplify the contradictory and complex informational environment are not the only ones at work. Affective forces or "motivated biases" also influence how signals are perceived. The most important force of this type is an aversion to facing psychologically painful value trade-offs discussed in other chapters of this book. An implication for signaling is that motivated biases often reinforce cognitive inertia. A decision-maker who has staked his or her ego and/or domestic fortunes on a line of policy will find it difficult to recognize that it is likely to fail. Perceptions will be systematically distorted to shield the person from excessively painful choices. Lebow showed this process at work in defeating the appreciation of indications that the state is heading for an undesired war unless it changes its policy.[30] Thus it is to Nehru's political and psychological commitment to his "forward policy" and not to China's lack of adequate signals that we must attribute his failure to see that the PRC would attack in the fall of 1962 if India did not make concessions. Similarly, although German secrecy and deception played a large role, much of the reason why British intelligence misread Germany in the 1930s was that the analysts did not want to draw inferences that contradicted British policy.[31]

Motivated biases also help explain faulty signaling. Actors often misunderstand how others will interpret their behavior not only because they fail to grasp others' theories and images of them, but because they view their own behavior in a biased way. Individuals and states generally think well of themselves, believe that they have benevolent motives, and see their actions as reasonable and legitimate. So it is not surprising that in some cases these views are not only rejected by those with whom they are interacting, but also are at variance with what disinterested observers see. Self-justification, if not self-righteousness, can lead actors to believe that their acts will be seen as benign when there is good reason for others to draw a very different inference. A state may thus believe that it is signaling firm but nonaggressive intentions by behavior that most reasonable perceivers would take to be hostile and threatening.

Note on Methodology

Understanding signaling and perception requires us to study them together. A theory of perception that ignores the fact that perceivers realize that actors

30 Robert Jervis, Richard Ned Lebow, and Janice Gross Stein, *Psychology and Deterrence* (Baltimore: Johns Hopkins University Press, 1985); Richard Ned Lebow, *Between Peace and War* (Baltimore: Johns Hopkins University Press, 1981); the underlying psychology is found in Irving Janis and Leo Mann, *Decision Making* (New York: Free Press, 1977).

31 Wesley Wark, *The Ultimate Enemy: British Intelligence and Nazi Germany, 1933–1939* (Ithaca: Cornell University Press, 1985).

have strategic objectives and may be trying to deceive them would be faulty; so would a theory of signaling that neglects how observers perceive and how actors think that observers perceive. What we need, then, are studies that are two-sided in looking at both the actor and perceiver (assuming for the sake of convenience only bilateral rather than multilateral cases). Scholars can then look at the image an actor is trying to project, the behaviors that it adopts to do so, and then, shifting attention to the perceiver, examine what influences the perceiver and what inferences it draws. At the next stage we can see what the perceiver thinks it must do to send the desired message in response, what it does to reach this goal, and how the actor in turn judges both the other's behavior and determines how the other perceived its behavior. I suspect that it is rare for actors, especially adversaries, to understand the situation the same way, to be able to discern how the other sees them and their behavior, or even to know what signals are taken to be most important.

Of course, the story will rarely be simple and unambiguous, and there are many obstacles to such investigations: actors may not articulate their objectives, even in internal memoranda; the links between policies adopted and objectives sought are often elusive to later observers, and perhaps to decision-makers themselves; it is difficult to track the information that is received and the inferences that are drawn; events often come thick and fast, obscuring the relative impact of each. Nevertheless, a number of studies have proceeded in this way, some more explicitly than others, and they can be both mined for insights and used as models.[32] Indeed, the end of the Cold War has provided an unusual opportunity to combine interviews and documents from several courtiers in a way that lends itself to studies of this kind.[33]

32 Raymond Garthoff, rev., ed., *Détente and Confrontation: American Soviet Relations from Nixon to Reagan* (Washington, D.C.: Brookings Institution 1994); Garthoff, *The Great Transition* (Washington, D.C.: Brookings Institution, 1994); Ole Holsti, Robert North, and Richard Brody, "Perception and Action in the 1914 Crisis," in J. David Singer, ed., *Quantitative International Politics* (New York: Free Press, 1968), pp. 123–58; Chihiro Hosoya, "Miscalculations in Deterrence Policy: Japanese-US Relations, 1938–41," *Journal of Peace Research* (June 1968): 97–15; Richard Neustadt, *Alliance Politics* (New York: Columbia University Press,1970); Neustadt, *Report to JFK: The Skybolt Crisis in Perspective* (Ithaca: Cornell University Press, 1999); Ernest May, *The World War and American Isolation, 1914–1917* (Cambridge: Harvard University Press, 1959); Wallace Theis, *When Governments Collide: Coercion and Diplomacy in the Vietnam Conflict, 1964–1968* (New Haven: Yale University Press, 1980).

33 Bruce Allyn, James Blight, and David Welch, *Back to the Brink: Proceedings of the Moscow Conference on the Cuban Missile Crisis* (Lanham, Md.: University Press of America, 1992); James Blight, Bruce Allyn, and David Welch, *Cuba on the Brink: Castro, the Missile Crisis and the Soviet Collapse* (New York: Pantheon, 1993); James Blight, Bruce Allyn, and David Welch, *Cuba on the Brink: Castro, the Missile Crisis and the Soviet Collapse* (New York: Pantheon, 1993); John Gaddis, *We Now Know: Rethinking Cold War History* (New York: Oxford University Press, 1997); Deborah Larson, *Anatomy of Mistrust: US-Soviet Relations During the Cold War* (Ithaca: Cornell

Conclusion

Politics, especially international politics, falls at the intersection of psychology and game theory. The latter is crucial because not only are outcomes the product of the interaction of separate national policies, but also each actor needs to anticipate what others will do in light of the fact that others are symmetrically trying to anticipate what the actor will do. (Although in some cases individuals and states ignore strategic interaction and act as though others are on auto-pilot and will not react to what they do, these cases are exceptional, even though they are important because they often lead to disaster.[34]) But if reactions, anticipations, and anticipations of reactions drive politics, the beliefs, perceptions, and images that give life to them cannot be understood by the use of highly simplified assumptions and stylized facts. The way Signals and indices will be read are determined by the perceivers' needs, theories, and expectations. There are powerful generalizations about international interactions, but they rest in part on how people analyze information. Furthermore, our generalizations only take us so far and need to be supplemented by an understanding of how different individuals see the world and how particular conjunctions of circumstances combine to affect perceptions. Inasmuch as signals convey meaning, peoples' interpretations must be at the center of our attention.

University Press, 1997); William Wohlforth, ed., *Witnesses to the End of the Cold War* (Baltimore: Johns Hopkins University Press, 1996).

34 Jervis, *System Effects*, 258–60.

6

Political Psychology Research and Theory

BRIDGES AND BARRIERS

Political psychology, at least as it deals with international politics, tends to be normatively inflected and reformist. Like the social psychology of the 1930s in which it has its roots, the objective, to slightly alter Marx's phrase, is not only to understand the world but also to change it. The earlier generation of social psychologists were deeply concerned with a number of social ills, especially prejudice (what we would call now racism). They wanted to understand its causes and manifestations not only because this was an important phenomenon that told us much about the interaction of individual thinking and social forces, but also because this was a deep evil that needed to be ameliorated if not extinguished.

Political psychologists dealing with international politics sought to understand the twin problems of inadequate decision making and unnecessary international conflict.[1] The two problems were seen as linked in that part of the reason why states engaged in unnecessary conflict was believed to be the propensity for suboptimal decision making, including the tendency to perceive others as more hostile than they are and, concomitantly, to underestimate the threat that your own county is posing to others, often inadvertently.

---

1 They also tended to see more international conflicts as avoidable, and I actually think that was the case, but they clearly realized that some adversaries did pose a threat that needed to be met with threats if not force: for further discussion, see Robert Jervis, *Perception and Misperception in International Politics* (Princeton: Princeton University Press, 1976; 2nd ed., 2017), ch. 3.

So it is not surprising that Alexander George, one of the leading figures in applying political psychology to international politics, also was devoted to seeking to improve American foreign policy and the processes by which it is developed. This was clearest in his final book, *Bridging the Gap: Theory and Practice in Foreign Policy*,[2] but was reflected in almost everything else he wrote as well. Due to the importance and range of the topics he analyzed, his scholarship raises many interesting questions about the relationship between research on political psychology and foreign policy practice.

As George realized, this double focus marks foreign policy analysis off from the natural sciences and even from much social science, and it presents both opportunities and difficulties. I will start with the latter and look at three ways in which the attempt to improve policy and the desire to understand it interfere with, contradict, or complicate each other. Less abstractly, following George we then examine prescriptions for better policymaking procedures. He and others developed good ideas, but this area is plagued by motivated biases because decision-makers are responding to powerful political pressures and psychological needs. This means that there are good reasons for them to reject methods that scholars advocate. By contrast, unmotivated biases are at work when decision-makers adopt inappropriate shortcuts to rationality, and here scholars' help may be more welcome. I will then show how good social science methods can help produce better decisions. But the flow of ideas is not simply one way. In the areas of coercion and cooperation, scholars and officials have much to teach each other, as I will outline in concluding.

Description and Prescription

It is not only theorists as individuals who have dual concerns. The theories they produce often are simultaneously descriptive and prescriptive: According to George, "[Hans] Morgenthau ... claimed not only that his version of political realism could explain and predict the play of international politics but also that it could and ought to guide statesmen engaged in the conduct of foreign policy."[3] Morgenthau argued that we could see from history that states generally pursue the national interest, neither bowing to the dictates of domestic pressures nor seeking supranational interests, and that, contrary to the stereotype of realists as bellicose, they tend to respect others' legitimate interests and use conciliation, law, and international organizations to minimize conflict and preserve their states' power. Furthermore, according to Morgenthau, this is how a wise statesman *should* behave. The problem here is not

---

2 Alexander George, *Bridging the Gap: Theory and Practice in Foreign Policy* (Washington, D.C.: Institute of Peace Press, 1993).

3 Ibid., 109.

whether Morgenthau is correct in either the empirical generalizations or the prescriptions, but rather the relationship between the two. The minor point is that it is not clear whether the description would hold if it applied to everyone. In the language of game theory, is the analysis of realism (or of any alternative perspective) an equilibrium solution? If all the states respect others' legitimate interests, could "rogues" exploit this behavior? Evolutionary game theorists have shown that the optimal strategy for any one player varies with the mix of strategies others are following,[4] but the shifting patterns that result can be hard to catch in most standard theories.[5]

More significantly, theories that are both prescriptive and descriptive run into difficulties when the actors do not behave as they should, where "should" means as our theory both expects them to and says is appropriate. Thus John Mearsheimer acknowledges that "any time that a state behaves in a strategically foolish fashion, it counts as a clear contradiction of my theory."[6] Morgenthau not only argued that states pursue the national interest as defined by power, but he also constantly lectured Americans on the need to do so and kept being upset—both in the sense of having his theory embarrassed and in the sense of being emotionally aroused—when the United States did foolish things like fighting in Vietnam. In the early years of the Cold War, he and other realists spent considerable energy refuting idealists who placed excessive faith in world public opinion and the UN, and paid insufficient attention to economic and military power. Realist theories not only indicated the importance of the latter, however, but also left little room for leaders to believe otherwise. I also fell into this trap when I echoed Morgenthau and others in asserting that once a country had developed secure retaliatory forces, marginal differences in the nuclear balance did not matter, without fully confronting the embarrassing fact that leaders in both the United States and USSR had adopted a quite different view.[7] The analytical problem is not that we were unable to persuade leaders of the validity of our views, but that as long as we

4 John Maynard Smith, *Evolution and the Theory of Games*, (New York: Cambridge University Press, 1982).

5 Robert Jervis, *System Effects: Complexity in Political and Social Life* (Princeton: Princeton University Press, 1997).

6 John Mearsheimer, "Conversations in International Relations: Interview with John J. Mearsheimer (Part I)," *International Relations* 20 (March 2006): 112; also see John Mearsheimer, *The Tragedy of Great Power Politics* (New York: Norton, 2001), pp. 3, 11–12, 35; Ido Oren, "The Unrealism of Contemporary Realism: The Tension between Realist Theory and Realists' Practice," *Perspectives on Politics* 7 (June 2009): 283–301; for a somewhat different and interesting analysis of the tension here, see Marc Trachtenberg, "The Question of Realism: A Historian's View," *Security Studies* 13 (Autumn 2003): 156–94.

7 Robert Jervis, *The Illogic of American Nuclear Strategy* (Ithaca: Cornell University Press, 1984) and *The Meaning of the Nuclear Revolution: Statecraft and the Prospect of Armageddon* (Ithaca: Cornell University Press, 1989).

could not our theories suffered a double empirical failure. Most obviously, the arguments could not explain why the states were seeking unnecessary nuclear weapons. Furthermore, as long as statesmen held to their benighted views, then nuclear superiority, "objectively" meaningless as it was, could continue to have political influence.

It is not only realists who confront this problem. Those who stress the importance of international institutions similarly make claims that are both normative and empirical. Countries that "misbehave" and fail to support institutions or operate contrary to them are not only acting inappropriately, but are also violating the theory. Similarly, human rights advocates simultaneously argue that the respect for human rights is now a potent force in world politics and berate leaders who do not recognize this. More generally, critics of realism run into difficulties when they argue that they can tell that realist prescriptions are incorrect by the fact that states that follow them often come to misfortune, usually by engaging in excessive conflict. The problem here is not only a misunderstanding of realism, but that to attribute many of the world's woes to states following its principles implies that realism is a good description of their behavior.

Theories of foreign policy could seek to be completely descriptive and explanatory, avoiding any claims about the goals that states should seek or the means that are best designed to reach them. But this would be difficult because by telling a decision-maker how others behave (including how they will react to his state's actions), an explanatory theory would lead to prescription. Furthermore, even if they are not advising governments or writing op-eds, most students of international politics and foreign policy do wish to make the world safer and better.

A second form of the tension between description and explanation on the one hand and prescription on the other is the inevitable way in which our values and preferences impinge on empirical analysis. Even if we can logically distinguish between facts and values, it is hard to believe that we can ever succeed in being fully objective, especially when the topics under investigation are highly charged and the evidence is ambiguous. Would we really expect a scholar who deeply believes that the American interest is best served by a liberal internationalist policy to explain events in the same way that an isolationist or a unilateralist would? To take another personal example, although I like to think that my explanation for the Bush Doctrine[8] is unaffected by my distaste for it, there are aspects of the account that are inextricably linked to my critical stance. Perhaps in a world with different human psychology this would not be the case, but it is inevitable in our world.[9]

8 Robert Jervis, *American Foreign Policy in a New Era* (New York: Routledge Press, 2005).
9 For a discussion in the context of measures of racism, see "Special Symposium on Political Psychology and Politicized Psychology," *Political Psychology* 15 (September 1994): 509–77.

Scholars' preferences may play a role even in their most abstract theories. Thus, Kenneth Waltz's theory of international politics indicates that under bipolarity the superpowers do not have to engage in costly conflicts on the peripheries of the system. This leads to the prescription that the United States did not need to fight in Vietnam. But it is not clear that Waltz arrived at the advice through his abstract theory or whether his distaste for the war came first.[10] Even more clearly, Morton Kaplan's systems theory bears the marks of his view of how the United States should conduct the struggle with the Soviet Union.[11] Political preferences I think also help explain why many psychologists who are concerned with world politics are prone to advocate policies based on conciliation. Perhaps their professional training has led them to this worldview, but the choice of disciple is itself not an unmoved mover and may be as much the result as the cause of a general orientation toward political and social life.[12]

In some areas our evaluation of political behavior and our explanation of it will logically be linked. A good example is in the seemingly apolitical analysis of political attitudes and voting behavior. While an academic would not use a title as provocative as *What's the Matter With Kansas?*[13] the explanation of why poor and middle-income people vote Republican does depend on one's view of what their "true" interests are. To most liberals—and I suspect it makes a difference to our research that most of us are liberals—it is self-defeating for so many of these people to vote Republican, and this leads to a search for explanations of why and how noneconomic considerations have risen to the fore, how the Republicans have framed issues and elections in a way that allows them to win, how the media distorts the parties' views, and how people get socialized into what Marxists would call "false consciousness." Someone who believes that the Republican policies lead to freedom and high economic growth that benefit people in all income brackets will naturally be drawn to very different explanations. Indeed, it is the belief that Republican policies cost the poor a great deal of money that makes their voting Republican a puzzle that requires an explanation. For a Republican, this is sensible behavior that provides another illustration of the tendency of people

10 Kenneth Waltz, *Theory of International Politics* (Reading, Mass.: Addison-Wesley, 1979); Waltz, "The Stability of a Bipolar World," *Daedalus* 93 (Summer 1964): 881–909; Waltz, "The Politics of Peace," *International Studies Quarterly* 11 (September 1967): 199–211.

11 Morton Kaplan, *System and Process in International Politics* (New York: Wiley, 1957).

12 For an excellent discussion of the ways in which the political orientation of an individual scholar or, even more, a scholarly community, can affect the research being done, see José Duarte, et al., "Political Diversity Will Improve Social Psychological Science," *Behavioral and Brain Sciences* 38 (January 2015): 1–13. On a personal note I might add that when I was president of the American Political Science Association in 2000–2001 I tried without success to get my colleagues to see that this was a question we needed to examine.

13 Thomas Frank, *What's the Matter with Kansas? How Conservatives Won the Heart of America* (New York: Metropolitan Books, 2005).

to do what makes them better off, and it is the Democrats' support for the poor that is against their interests and so needs a special explanation.[14]

This means that at least part of the gap between theory and practice can never be bridged impartially. In international relations (IR), those with unilateralist policy predispositions will not only prefer different foreign policies from multilateralists, but will find different patterns in the historical record and will differ in what they find odd. What one group will see as requiring a detailed explanation the other will see as the expected and indeed natural workings of international politics. We would not expect both to similarly theorize about and learn from the Marshall Plan or the Vietnam War, for example.

A third way in which theory and practice complicate each other is that scholarly analyses can constitute self-fulfilling or self-denying prophecies. Thus, social constructivists argue that the reason why realism seems to provide an accurate description of national behavior is that leaders have been tutored, figuratively if not literally, by realists. Machiavelli, after all, wrote to instruct his prince, and even scholars who have not meant to do so may have exerted influence. I suspect that this argument, taken too literally, excessively flatters us: can any instructor who has read final examinations really believe that our students have listened that carefully? But it is certainly possible that many general precepts have crept into the minds of those who make foreign policy, just as Keynes said that even economic policymakers who denigrate the value of scholarship reenact the claims of "some academic scribbler of a few years back."[15]

In recent American foreign policy the obvious example of scholarship that may be self-fulfilling is strategic thinking, epitomized by the work of Thomas Schelling.[16] Using game theory and the need for each side to anticipate what the other will do, knowing that the other is similarly anticipating how the state will act, Schelling produced a rich analysis of politics and a series of prescriptions for how to bargain in order to avoid a mutually costly breakdown while simultaneously enhancing one's interest. Most strikingly, he pointed out the advantages of the strategy of commitment, which he derived from game-theoretic analysis and familiarity with historical cases. The United States indeed did seem to behave accordingly, especially after the mid-1960s. But perhaps part of the reason for this was the power of Schelling's analysis.

Three specific examples come to mind. First, Schelling and others developed their ideas into a theory of arms control, one that stressed the value of

14 Bryan Caplan, *The Myth of the Rational Voter* (Princeton: Princeton University Press, 2007).

15 John Maynard Keynes, *General Theory of Employment, Interest, and Money* (New York: Harcourt, Brace, 1936), p. 383.

16 For example, see Thomas Schelling, *The Strategy of Conflict* (Cambridge: Harvard University Press, 1960) and *Arms and Influence* (New Haven: Yale University Press, 1966).

stability rather than lowering the level of arms. Subsequently U.S. policy shifted from its previous stress on disarmament to seeking agreements that would enhance strategic stability, especially by banning antiballistic missiles. It seems clear that a degree of education or persuasion did occur, although by the mid-1980s Schelling was decrying the fact that U.S. policy had slipped back into concentrating on reducing the levels of arms rather than enhancing stability.[17] Second, Richard Nixon probably thought he was being original in basing his Vietnam policy on what he called his "madman" theory—the attempt to coerce the North Vietnamese and Soviets by leading them to believe that they could not count on his being sensible. But in fact he was replicating Schelling's "rationality of irrationality" strategy.[18] Third, shortly after President Kennedy read a Schelling memo on the appropriate way to threaten force in the Berlin crisis,[19] he changed American policy accordingly, although of course there were multiple influences at work.

Prescriptions can be self-denying as well. A theory that says democracies are prone to be blind to threats and to engage in appeasement may, if believed by enough people, be disconfirmed by leading the state to behave differently. In quite a different way, realism could become self-denying if following its precepts led to such destruction that decision-makers later adopted a different perspective and set of policies. In vastly oversimplified form, this is Paul Schroeder's explanation for the transformation of European politics after the Napoleonic Wars.[20]

A somewhat different form of self-denying prophecy is exemplified by a perhaps apocryphal story I heard concerning Joseph Nye's interview with Central American leaders about the prospects of regional integration in the late 1960s. "Ah, Professor Nye," one of them is reported to have said, "we have learned from Professor Ernst Haas that if we start to take small steps toward economic cooperation, this will produce pressures for extensive regional integration, and because we do not want that, we will not take these limited measures." Haas's spillover theory said that European integration had progressed through a process that the leaders had not foreseen and that led to

17 Thomas Schelling, "What Went Wrong with Arms Control," *Foreign Affairs* 64 (1985/86): 219–34.

18 Ironically, Henry Kissinger was very impressed by a student of Schelling who had examined Hitler's use of the tactic, and this student was Daniel Ellsberg, who later leaked the Pentagon Papers.

19 U.S. Department of State, *Foreign Relations of the United States 1961–1963,* vol. 14: *Berlin Crisis 1961–1963* (Washington, D.C.: U.S. Government Printing Office, 1993), pp. 170–72; a longer public version is Thomas Schelling, "Nuclear Strategy in Europe," *World Politics* 14 (April 1962): 421–32.

20 Paul Schroeder, *The Transformation of European Politics, 1763–1848* (Oxford: Oxford University Press, Clarendon Press, 1994).

greater integration;[21] understanding it could indeed lead people to steering clear of the process. More broadly, theories about the occurrence of unintended consequences can be self-denying if actors anticipate those consequences, build barriers against them, or avoid the actions that set these processes in motion.

What is central here is that unlike natural science and a good deal of social science, IR scholars are theorizing about actors who not only have their own theories, but also whose theories deal with the same subjects that the scholars are exploring. This means that our explanations of their behavior can affect their behavior. Thus if leaders of democracies are persuaded by the claim that democratic states do not fight each other, they will not fear other democracies, thereby removing at least one cause of war. When the outcomes scholars are explaining are undesired by the actors, understanding can lead them to behave in a way that appears to negate our theories, for example, leaving the observed causes of mutually costly ways of resolving conflicts such as wars to be random. As Erik Gartzke puts it, "[W]ar is in the error term" of a regression equation.[22] For example, it is often argued that wars follow from "power transitions" when a rising power like Germany in the early twentieth century begins to overtake the dominant state. But if both sides understand this law of international politics, they will expect war in this situation and will seek a solution through bargaining. (This assumes, among other things, that war is considered costly rather than being seen as a positive good as in being necessary for the maintenance of order or the pursuit of glory.) Power transitions will still cause changes in the international system, but no longer will lead to wars. Here the theory, so to speak, swallows itself. Once actors have noticed the same patterns that scholars have, or once they have been convinced by the relevant scholarship, they will take this into account in a way that nullifies the theory. The gap between theory and practice is then closed, but in a way that makes the theory both powerful and invalid.

Optimal Decision-Making Processes

The general relationship between theory and policy then involves several layers of complications. They do not mean that attempts to be helpful are misguided, but only that there are limits to what can be achieved. Can we approach those limits? To explore this question, we should turn from the abstract to a specific area in which George and other psychologically informed scholars

---

21 Ernst Haas, *The Uniting of Europe: Political, Social and Economic Forces 1950–1957* (Stanford: Stanford University Press, 1958).

22 Erik Gartzke, "War Is in the Error Term," *International Organization* 53 (Summer 1999): 567–87.

have sought to offer advice, which is the policymaking process. Although the prescriptions are well grounded in research, they also bring out the differences between the perspectives, problems, and perhaps personalities of scholars on the one hand and of policymakers on the other, differences that reduce the extent to which the advice can be implemented.[23] As we will see, a number of the biases that policymakers bring to bear are motivated—that is, they involve political and psychological reasons why leaders need to structure their worlds in a certain way. This means that they will resist reforms that, while sound in the abstract, would make their lives more difficult.

There is no one best way to organize political decision making. The president (I will use this term to designate the national leader because most of our research is on the United States, but the general points should apply more broadly) needs to fashion arrangements that suit his or her purposes and style. One size does not fit all, as presidents differ along many dimensions, including willingness to delegate, reliance on formal structures, and the desire or distaste for overt conflict among advisers. Nixon notoriously froze out the Secretaries of State and Defense and ran foreign policy out of the White House. While he wanted to make the key decisions, he was uncomfortable with personal conflict (indeed, he was uncomfortable with people), and so he rarely held meetings where conflicting points of view would be vigorously debated. He also was prone to give orders that were imprudent and could afford to do so because he was surrounded by lieutenants who knew what to ignore.[24] Truman by contrast delegated enormous responsibility to his Secretary of State and in many areas it is hard to find his impact in the historical record. But he did make some key decisions, such as to stay in Berlin in the face of the Soviet blockade and to refuse to force prisoners to return to China during the Korean War. In these cases, however, he acted not on the basis of thorough studies, but, apparently, on his own intuition.[25] Dwight Eisenhower relied heavily on formal processes and extensive staff work, culminating in face-to-face arguments. His successor similarly encouraged disagreements, but dismantled much of the formal machinery. Although scholars have pointed out the problems in each of these ways of proceeding, and it can be argued

23 For further discussion, see Jervis, "Why Intelligence and Policymakers Clash," in this volume.

24 There have been scattered reports that Watergate happened because Nixon said the Democratic National Committee offices should be wiretapped, but made the mistake of saying this to an inexperienced aide who took this seriously.

25 Deborah Larson, "Truman and the Berlin Blockade: The Role of Intuition and Experience in Good Foreign Policy Judgment," pp. 127–52 in Stanley Renshon and Deborah Larson, eds., *Good Judgment in Foreign Policy: Theory and Application* (New York: Rowman and Littlefield, 2003); for further discussion, see the preface to the second edition of Jervis, *Perception and Misperception* (2017).

that decision making in each case could have been improved, the most appropriate arrangements still would have to be tailored to each individual
president.[26]

There is an unresolvable tension here. On the one hand, presidents cannot
be made into people who they are not, and the attempt to do so is likely to
make things worse. On the other hand, some styles are simply dysfunctional.[27]
They may play into the president's strengths and needs, but at the cost of
lowering the quality of the decisions. A person in a position of influence who
knows the relevant scholarship may then face a dilemma, as Condoleezza
Rice did when she was National Security Advisor. Having been a colleague
of George, she knew that the normal prescription was to bring the president
the relevant alternatives and put the needed information and questions on the
table. But she also knew that this was not her president's favored style. In the
end, she chose to facilitate a process that made Bush comfortable rather than
raise hard questions and ensure that the issues were openly debated.

Although individual differences have to be taken into account, the academic advice on policymaking procedures has important common elements,
many of them discussed by George.[28] Researchers call for leaders and their
foreign policy apparatuses to seek diverse information and views, to develop
a "level playing field" where no department or individual has an unfair advantage in convincing the president, and to try to avoid making decisions prema-
turely, before the information has been surveyed and many options developed.
Relatedly, although policies should not be changed lightly, decision-makers
should be ready to examine new information, monitor the success of their
policies, and be prepared to reconsider and change.

Underlying this advice is the need to counteract the natural propensity for
people and organizations to get locked in.[29] Individuals tend toward premature cognitive closure, coming to images, beliefs, and conclusions on the basis
of limited and fragmentary information. It is hard to keep an open mind, especially because new information is interpreted in light of the established beliefs. This means that ambiguous or even discrepant information is seen not
only as consistent with what the person believes, but also as confirming these
beliefs—that is, as being inconsistent with alternatives. Cognitive closure then
tends to be self-reinforcing. In parallel, people often exhibit a confirmation
bias in being more prone to seek information that is consistent with their

26 Alexander George, *Presidential Decisionmaking in Foreign Policy: The Effective Use of Information and Advice* (Boulder, Colo.: Westview Press, 1980), ch. 8.

27 John Burke and Fred Greenstein, *How Presidents Test Reality: Decisions on Vietnam, 1954
and 1965* (New York: Russell Sage Foundation), 1989.

28 George, *Presidential Decisionmaking in Foreign Policy.*

29 Philip Tetlock, *Expert Political Judgment: How Good Is It? How Can We Know?* (Princeton: Princeton University Press, 2005).

views than information that contradicts them. A second problem is that when it comes to making decisions, individuals tend to avoid painful value trade-offs.[30] That is, they tend to believe that the favored policy is not only best overall, but is preferred on a number of value dimensions that are logically independent of one another.

The attempt to prevent premature closure, to see that conflicting views are heard, to maintain openness to change, and to force people to confront trade-offs makes a great deal of sense, but runs into severe psychological and political obstacles.[31] Safeguards slow the decision process to allow more information to accumulate, but in some situations decisions simply cannot be postponed. When time pressures are not as great, it might make sense to retain information at lower levels of the government until a great deal of it comes in and can be processed. But nothing annoys a decision-maker more than hearing news from the media rather than from her own staff. Indeed, subordinates are rewarded for keeping their bosses on top of developments and bringing them the latest tidbits. Political pressures reinforce psychological ones: leaders suffer if it is believed that they are uninformed. Decisions sometimes can be delayed, and this may happen excessively when the options look bleak, but it is much harder to delay the formation of impressions and beliefs. In most cases pressures for closure are increased by overload—there is an enormous amount going on and except for the most important questions the leader can rarely afford to take much time with any of them. Thus it is not only crisis decisions that have to be taken very quickly.

Bringing conflicting information, options, and perspectives to bear not only takes time and effort, but also increases the burdens on the leaders, and it is not only pathology that leads them to ask their subordinates to come up with compromises. A policy that is palatable to both the State Department and the Department of Defense, for example, is likely to represent at least major elements of the national interest. Furthermore, conflict and uncertainty are annoying if not painful for most people. Scholars who urge these conditions on decision-makers probably have a higher tolerance for ambiguity than political leaders do. Although it is not unknown for researchers to jump to conclusions, their jobs afford them the luxury of not having to do so, and they often are comfortable playing with alternative understandings. In contrast, decision-makers have to act, and many like to act, or at least like to believe that they like to act, decisively. They have less patience for what academics would consider intriguing paradoxes, contradictions, or puzzles.

30 Jervis, *Perception and Misperception* (1976, 2017), ch. 4; Alan Fiske and Philip Tetlock, "Taboo Trade-offs: Reactions to Transactions that Transgress the Spheres of Justice," *Political Psychology* 18 (1997): 255–98.

31 Alexander George, *On Foreign Policy: Unfinished Business* (Boulder, Colo.: Paradigm, 2006), ch. 4.

Conflict and divisions are also likely to incur political costs. Nothing makes news more than divisions within an administration, and the news is not good. "Administration in disarray" is a typical headline under these circumstances. The president seems weak, unable to control his government. Furthermore, open conflict means that some department or faction will be defeated, and this defeat will exact a cost both within the administration and among the loser's backers in Congress and the country. There are good reasons why political leaders want the appearance of a smoothly running machine.

Even if it is true that decision-makers should be open to the possibility that their policies are failing, there are nevertheless good reasons why they are not. Reexamining takes time, and bureaucracies and their leaders rarely have much to spare. Reexamination also is politically and psychologically disruptive. These costs might well be worth paying if the deliberations could be kept secret, but if the policy is significant, this is not likely to be possible, at least not in a country like the United States. When members of Congress and the interested public, let alone foreign governments, see that the policy is up for grabs, supporters will be distressed and various groups will mobilize in a way that is likely to embarrass the government and limit its freedom of action. The very fact that a policy is under scrutiny, even if it is reaffirmed at the end, is likely to reduce support for it and to make the government appear weak.

Good decision-making processes involve planning. Even if individuals can react quickly, bureaucracies and governments cannot. They therefore need to think about how they will respond to important opportunities and dangers that may arise. This is particularly true for complex foreign policy problems that call for the integration of multiple policy instruments and coordination among multiple agencies. Few situations are likely to perfectly match those that were contemplated, but the exercise is important for getting people and units to understand others' perspectives and develop lines of communication. As Eisenhower said, "Plans are worthless but planning is everything."[32]

The advice is impeccable but may be impractical. Leaving aside the obvious point that contingencies are infinite but planning resources are limited, decision-makers confront political and psychological obstacles to setting the machinery in motion. Planning concedes that things can go wrong and therefore gives ammunition to the policy's critics and may make it harder to push the policy through. This might be less of a problem if planning could be kept secret. But this cannot be counted on, and this scuttled one of my few attempts to intervene in the policy process. In 2007 when it appeared that the United States was likely to withdraw from Iraq before even a minimal stability

---

32 *Public Papers of the Presidents of the United States: Dwight D. Eisenhower, 1957* (Washington, D.C.: Government Printing Office, 1958), p. 818.

was achieved, I urged my friends in government to plan what we would do in the face of the probable interventions by neighbors. They did not disagree with my logic, but said that I was asking the impossible because any such effort would soon leak to the media, with unfortunate domestic if not international repercussions. So the government would simply have to do the best it could without concerted planning.[33]

Psychological factors also militate against planning for unpleasant contingencies. Decision-makers do not want to dwell on what can go wrong. These thoughts are deeply disturbing, and effective policymaking and leadership require a high degree of confidence. Years ago Albert Hirschman pointed to the benign functioning of the "hiding hand," by which he meant that we embark on many difficult endeavors only because we are unable to see all the obstacles in our way and, once we have proceeded far enough to perceive them, we are too invested to turn back.[34] In some such cases, of course, we fail. But in many others we succeed, and at the end are glad we undertook the task. How many of us would have started graduate school if we had known how long, frustrating, and painful it would be? Fooling ourselves can be highly functional.

It can also lead to policy disasters, as Iraq again illustrates. The government did almost no planning for postwar Iraq.[35] The reasons seem to be essentially two-fold. First, the armed services do not like occupations, let alone dealing with insurgencies. They see their mission as defeating other armed forces and relegate the final stages to what they call "Phase IV," which has little prestige. So there were few pressures from the bottom of the organization to plan. Even more importantly, Secretary of Defense Rumsfeld refused to permit serious planning. He was committed to transforming the military and making the forces smaller, more lethal, and more agile. Proving the validity of this concept required winning the war with a small number of troops and not getting bogged down after that. Furthermore, to have admitted the possibility that reconstruction would be long and difficult would have weakened the rationale for the war. What needs to be done then cannot be done; the scholarly advice on proper procedure is correct, but it often cannot be followed.

33 "Iraq, the U.S., and the Region after an American Withdrawal," Saltzman Institute of War and Peace Working Paper No. 2, October 2007. Because it was better able to keep secrets, the intelligence community in fact did explore this question. Of course history played out differently as the "Sunni awakening," the surge of American troops, and the changed position of Muqtada el Sadr combined to postpone the day of reckoning.

34 Albert Hirschman, "The Principle of the Hiding Hand," Public Interest, no. 6 (Winter 1967): 10–24.

35 Nora Bensahel, "Mission Not Accomplished: What Went Wrong with Iraqi Reconstruction," Journal of Strategic Studies 29 (June 2006): 453–73.

Ways of Thinking

If the prospects for improving the policy process have been undercut by the politics and psychology of national decision making, the outlook may be brighter in a related area. As George has stressed, good policy usually rests on a diagnosis of the situation and the other actors.[36] In performing these tasks, the foreign policy bureaucracies, especially the intelligence services, are engaging in activities that closely resemble scholarship because they are trying to understand the world. Of course there are myriad forms of scholarly methods, and they can rarely be carried over without some modifications. Nevertheless, I think five of the ways of thinking and doing scholarship are particularly relevant. The biases that these are designed to counter are cognitive and unmotivated, unlike those discussed in the previous section. This means that there should be less resistance to corrective measures.

The first is the most mundane, but the postmortems on the Iraq WMD intelligence failure make clear its utility. This is the use of footnotes. Intelligence estimates in fact have footnotes, but they are used to register dissents from the collective judgment. Although analysts of course try to keep track of the reports that lead them to a conclusion, many of the papers that are produced do not include careful documentation. Policymakers do not need to see these references since they will not have time to look at this material, but without footnotes in the scholarly sense it is hard for analysts to remember the number and quality of the reports that support their judgments, especially after they have reached their conclusions. In the Iraq case, both the American and the British intelligence communities overestimated the number of independent sources they were drawing upon.[37] If they had been required to footnote, decision-makers might have realized that the evidence was thinner than they had thought. Footnoting sources also brings with it the habit of asking oneself what sources disagree with the judgment or provide discrepant information.

In response to recommendations of both Senate Select Committee on Intelligence (SSCI) and a confidential report that I wrote, the intelligence community adopted the policy of using footnotes in this way. While it appears that many of the results have been beneficial, the old saying "be careful what you wish for, because you may get it" applies. Lessons for the past were learned, but also over-learned. If in the case of Iraq analysts drew inferences too far removed from specific reports anchored in designated sources, then

36 George, *Bridging the Gap*.

37 Senate Select Committee on Intelligence, *Report on the U.S. Intelligence Community's Prewar Intelligence Assessments on Iraq* (Washington, D.C.: U.S. Senate, 2004); Report of the Committee of the Privy Councilor, Chairman the Rt. Hon. Lord Butler of Brockwell, *Review of Intelligence on Weapons of Mass Destruction* (London: House of Commons, 2004).

any statement must be backed up by a footnote. The problem is that this way of writing is deadening and this way of thinking inhibits analysis that is both careful and imaginative in trying to understand what the facts mean. Intelligence analysts and policymakers should be aware of the evidence that underpins the arguments being made, but the latter must be more than the former.

The second method is central to social sciences but less often used in intelligence and policy analysis. This is the use of comparisons to probe causes and explanations. While complicated due to our inability to run experiments, to differentiate between necessary and sufficient conditions, to detect possible interactions among independent variables, and to determine the prevalence of multiple sufficient causations or equifinality (to use the term that George favored), the comparative method is perhaps our most powerful tool. It does not come naturally, however, which is why we have to beat it into the heads of our graduate students. At first glance it is not obvious why in order to probe the impact of the frontier on American history we should look both at other societies that had frontiers and at countries that lacked them, for example. Nor is it obvious to most untrained people, no matter how intelligent they are, that to understand the causes of wars we should also look at cases where war did not occur, or that to fully understand deterrence failures we should also look at cases where deterrence succeeds.

So it is not surprising that a great deal of intelligence and policy analysis asserts the importance of a factor without engaging in relevant comparisons. The case of intelligence on Iraq's WMD illustrates this in two ways. First, analysts supported their conclusion that Iraq was developing WMD by noting that suspicious materials were being procured through fronts and other means of disguising that they were destined for Iraq. This inference is quite plausible, but becomes less compelling when one realizes that fronts were extensively used even when it was obvious that WMD were not involved. Similarly, the analysts drew attention to the fact that vehicles that they believed were associated with chemical munitions frequented sites that they believed might be producing or containing such weapons without checking to see whether these vehicles also appeared at sites that were clearly not WMD-related.

Intelligence analysts were not the only ones to neglect comparisons. Many of the postmortems drew conclusions that looked convincing largely because they did not use the comparative method. One of the main arguments of the SSCI was that many of the overestimates of Iraq's WMD programs were based more on underlying assumptions than they were on hard evidence and specific reports.[38] There is much to this argument, but SSCI neglected the fact that this way of thinking also characterized areas in which intelligence was

---

38 Senate Select Committee on Intelligence, *Report on the U.S. Intelligence Community's Prewar Intelligence Assessments on Iraq* (Washington, D.C.: U.S. Senate, 2004).

correct, and that on the specific issues on which the community was divided, both those who were wrong and those who were right relied heavily on their sense of what was plausible.[39] Comparisons would have shown that it was too facile to believe that the errors could have been avoided by sticking closer to the putative facts.

A more common diagnosis for the basic errors on Iraqi WMD was that the intelligence was highly politicized. CIA and other intelligence agencies knew what their political masters wanted and conformed. This is a complex issue as many kinds of subtle influences may have been at work, but the comparative method casts doubt on this account. Intelligence agencies in countries that opposed the war appear to have reached judgments similar to those of the American community, and American analysts produced undesired answers to other questions concerning Iraq, most importantly when they denied any meaningful connection between Saddam's regime and al-Qaeda and warned that the political reconstruction of Iraq would be difficult. Of course it is possible that some third variable explains why political pressure distorted only the WMD judgments, but a search for these factors can occur only after comparisons have highlighted the anomaly, and so it is not surprising that none of the claims for politicization has seen the need for this kind of endeavor. To most people, arguments for the causal impact of political pressures on WMD intelligence are to be answered by looking only in this area, not by examining cases in which intelligence assessments did not conform to policymakers' desires.

A third way of thinking is related but even more counterintuitive. This is the importance of negative evidence or "dogs that do not bark." The phrase is from the Sherlock Holmes story in which the fact that the victim's dogs did not bark during the night of the incident was ignored by the police and Watson, but seized upon by Holmes because he realized that it showed that the perpetrator was not a stranger. The point is that things that do not happen can be highly diagnostic if a leading theory indicates that they *should* have happened. Social and natural scientists use this as part of the hypothetico-deductive method when they probe a theory by asking what the world should look like if the theory is correct. They examine their theories not by (or not only by) moving from facts to inferences, but by focusing on what the theory tells us should be true. When this leads us to find facts or relationships whose existence had not been known before or are denied by alternative theories, strong evidence is provided, and when this evidence is not found, doubt is— or should be—cast on the theory.

39 Robert Jervis, "Reports, Politics and Intelligence Failures: The Case of Iraq," *Journal of Strategic Studies* 29 (August 2006): 3–52.

The trouble is that it takes training for people to think in this way and focus on the nonevents that the theory leads us to expect. Of course Rumsfeld's famous mantra "absence of evidence does not constitute evidence of absence" has much validity, especially when we are dealing with an adversary who often wants to deceive us, but in retrospect a glaring fact about the reports of Iraqi WMD is how few of them there were despite massive Western attempts to gather this information. Most strikingly, the United States launched a major effort to query Iraqi scientists and technicians around the world, and even sent people back to Iraq to talk to their relatives whom intelligence believed were involved in these programs.[40] The results of these efforts were nil—no one reported knowing anything about current programs. The lack of evidence frustrated analysts, but was not seen as significant enough to be reflected in their judgments. It should have been, however: because the people queried would have known about the programs had they existed, their denials, although of course not definitive, were important.

No more than other kinds does negative evidence speak for itself. But being alert to it at least means that observers can seek its meaning. For example, the horrific marketplace bombing in Baghdad in early February 2007 that killed more people than any previous attack was not followed by retaliation. Whether this was because the Shia militias were lying low in anticipation of the increased American presence or whether they had come to believe that the attacks were designed to provoke and that retaliation would just play into the hands of Sunni extremists (or whether there is some other explanation) is an open question, but only those who are aware that the lack of response is significant can even ask it.

Game theory is a fourth general social science tool that analysts and policymakers could make more use of. By this I mean not the intricate derivations, but the basic understanding that international politics is a game in which each actor has to decide what to do on the basis of anticipating how others will act, knowing that others are similarly anticipating its behavior. Many officials understand this quite well, but nevertheless on a striking number of occasions others neglect the extent to which others will anticipate, thwart, or adapt to their behavior. They often plan as though others will do what is convenient for the actor rather than what is best for themselves. During the Cold War, for example, American plans for ballistic missile defenses made little room for the relatively cheap ways in which the Soviets could have adapted their forces to nullify the American efforts. More generally, deterrence policies were set with insufficient attention to how adversaries might react and "design around"

40 James Risen, *State of War: The Secret History of the CIA and the Bush Administration* (New York: Free Press, 2006), ch. 4.

those roadblocks.[41] In Iraq it was clearly best for the U.S. Army to fight open battles, and this should have led the United States to think more about how the Iraqis would act, based on their knowledge that they could not stand up to the American forces. Military planners did worry that the Iraqis would fall back on Baghdad, forcing the United States to fight house-to-house, but did not think about the more extreme possibility of the army melting away and later becoming the core of an insurgency. Anticipations are also crucial in a different way, one that is even more often neglected. When the adversary takes a significant hostile step, if it has planned adequately it will expect some response from the United States and others. If the United States is to alter the adversary's course of action, it will then have to do more than what was expected, or perhaps something different from what was expected. To take only those measures that the adversary anticipated cannot compel it to retract or even deter it from going further.

Analysts are hesitant to think in game-theoretic terms in the domestic arena as well. Few proposals for campaign finance reform considered how lobbyists eager to retain their influence and politicians eager to retain access to financing would respond; calls for changes in medical reimbursement schedules rarely sufficiently consider how doctors and patients will act in the new landscape; those who ordered judging schools and teachers by the results of standardized tests in reading and math were shocked to find that art, music, and athletics were cut from the curriculum, that science was neglected, that schools discouraged low-performing students from showing up on test days, and that teachers rather than students were more prone to cheating. Excessive consideration of possible responses can lead to paralysis, but it is unfortunate that policymakers and advocates want to assume a benign environment.

The reasons that people ignore the scholarly prescriptions to think strategically are both cognitive and affective. Strategic thinking requires empathy and thinking several steps ahead. It is easier to make a straight-line projection of what others will do than to delve into the multiple choices that may be available to an actor, and commitment to a course of action provides additional mental barriers to searching for its potential defects. People often become attached to their proposals, and anyone who has participated in gaming exercises or even discussions of the likely consequences of a policy is likely to recall the suggestion of an unpleasant way in which the adversary might respond being met by one of the policy's supporters exclaiming, "They wouldn't do that!"

---

41 Alexander George and Richard Smoke, *Deterrence in American Foreign Policy: Theory and Practice* (New York: Columbia University Press, 1974).

A related way of thinking that comes out of social science research but that is insufficiently appreciated is the prevalence of complexity, especially in the form of feedbacks, interconnections among elements, and nonlinear relationships. To repeat one example I used in my study of the subject,[42] those who advocated building double hulls on oil tankers to cut down on spills did not consider that this would take place in a complex system in which many others would react. Thus with tankers more expensive, more oil would travel by pipelines, perhaps moving spills from the sea to the land rather than reducing them. Faced with higher costs, companies might stint on other safety systems, and the captains of tankers might take advantage of the extra margin of safety to cut corners. These results are not certain, and mandating double hulls may be good public policy. But because complexity is hard to analyze and may undercut favored policy prescriptions, many advocates prefer to argue and act as though the favored change could be implemented in a world in which everything else would be held constant. For example, Saddam's decision to occupy Kuwait was premised on the belief that the United States could not retake the territory even if it wanted to because Saudi Arabia would not permit Western troops to be stationed on its soil. What he neglected was that the Saudi resistance, adamant until that point, would melt in the face of the invasion. His actions were a form of a self-denying prophecy in that they changed the environment and invalidated a key assumption that had initially been correct.

Many projections similarly downplay complexity by implicitly assuming that each factor exerts an independent influence rather than interacting with others to produce nonlinear results. A good example is provided by Aaron Friedberg's analysis of the future of Sino-American relations in which he examines conflicting arguments about the likely impact of factors such as Chinese economic growth, behavior in the region, and respect for human rights.[43] Although very well done, the analysis slights the ways in which the impact of one factor can depend on how others develop. To take the most obvious example, the growth of China's economy could have a strongly positive effect on Sino-American relations if China adopts a benign policy in the East and South China Sea, but would have a negative effect if it does not. Less dramatically, the benign effect of increased Sino-American economic activity is likely to be magnified by increases in democratization within China. The latter factor does not merely add to the former, it multiplies it.

42 Jervis, *System Effects*, 3–8.
43 Aaron Friedberg, "The Future of U.S.-China Relations," *International Security* 30 (Fall 2005): 7–45.

Areas of Substantive Collaboration

It may be appropriate to try to close at least some of the gap between scholarship and policy by turning to areas of mutual interest in which government researchers could play a role. Two problems in particular would repay serious attention.

One is a subset of cases of coercive diplomacy, an area of particular interest to George.[44] Indeed, he took a failed example of coercive diplomacy as the centerpiece of *Bridging the Gap*. One of the striking things about the post–Cold War era is that there have been five cases in which American threats to use force were not efficacious and force had to be used. This was true in Panama, the Gulf War, Haiti (a marginal case because the junta eventually backed down, but only after American planes were in the air), Kosovo, and the overthrow of Saddam. In these cases, unlike many during the Cold War, the United States would not be deterred from using force by the possible response of the other superpower, a fact that George's discussion of the failure of coercive diplomacy in the run-up to the Gulf War does not fully take into account.[45] The American interests were significant, the expected costs of acting were seen as low, and the other side's refusal to make concessions would (and did) cost it and its leaders dearly. The American threats then should have been potent and credible (indeed they were believed by most observers), and most of our theories indicate that the United States should have been able to prevail without using force. It was not, which means that something is wrong with our common understanding.[46]

At minimum, what was wrong is that the United States failed to grasp the perspectives, beliefs, and images (including images of it) that were responsible for the other side's intransigence, and the other side failed to understand what the United States would do. As is often the case, the two sides lived in very different worlds. International politics more often resembles the Japanese story and movie *Rashomon*, in which each character sees the events very

---

44 George, *Bridging the Gap*; Alexander George, David Hall, and William Simons, *The Limits of Coercive Diplomacy: Laos, Cuba, Vietnam* (Boston: Little, Brown, and Company, 1971); Alexander George and William Simons, *The Limits of Coercive Diplomacy*, 2nd ed. (Boulder, Colo.: Westview Press, 1994); Robert Art and Patrick Cronin, *The United States and Coercive Diplomacy* (Washington, D.C.: United States Institute of Peace, 2003).

45 George, *Bridging the Gap*, 79–88.

46 For further discussion of these cases, see Art and Cronin, *The United States and Coercive Diplomacy*; Dianne Pfundstein Chamberlain, *Cheap Threats: Why the United States Struggles to Coerce Weak States* (Washington, D.C.: Georgetown University Press, 2016); Phil Haun, *Coercion, Survival, and War: Why Weak States Resist the United States* (Stanford: Stanford University Press, 2015).

differently, than it does the game of chess, or even of poker.[47] Although retrospective analyses have led to some understanding of how the other side saw
the world,[48] our knowledge remains limited. Of course, complete answers are
never likely, but much more could be done, especially with the information
that should be in government archives. Making progress in unraveling these
puzzles would contribute to our understanding of coercive diplomacy and
the avoidance of unnecessary wars (although it could also lead to more cases
of coercion).

A second area in which scholarship can shed light is one in which cooperative elements loom larger than they did in the cases just discussed. Here each
side is willing to compromise and reach and abide by an agreement if it thinks
that the other will. But in international politics (and in other areas in which
verification and enforcement mechanisms are deficient as well), actors cannot be sure that their adversary/partner will comply. Each fears that the other
will cheat and that it will be taken advantage of (and each side itself is also
tempted to cheat). There are several possible instruments that could be of
service here—safety nets to offer protection if the other side cheats, inspection and verification mechanisms, amplifying the extent to which the state's
reputation will be enhanced if it lives up to the agreement and sacrificed if it
does not, and, for smaller powers, promises of outside enforcement.[49] These
are good targets for research, and as in the cases of coercion discussed above,
the government can be a partner because officials who have confronted these
problems have a wealth of experience and ideas that can be inventoried and
systematized.

The difficulties posed by the timing of proposals call for particular study.
During negotiations each side fears that showing its hand too soon will put it
at a disadvantage. The other side may see any initiative as indicating that the
state is anxious for an agreement, or even worse is simply weak, and it may
hold out for a more favorable offer and respond with intransigence rather
than reciprocating. In constructing the agreement itself, each side will have
the parallel worry about the sequences of the steps, because it has to guard
against being left in the lurch if there is a breakdown before the agreement

47 For further discussion, see Jervis, "Perception, Misperception, and the End of the Cold
War," in this volume.

48 Art and Cronin, *The United States and Coercive Diplomacy*; Kevin Woods, Michael Pease,
Mark Stout, Williamson Murray, and James Lacey, *The Iraqi Perspectives Report: Saddam's Senior
Leadership on Operation Iraqi Freedom from the Official U.S. Joint Forces Command Report* (Nor-
folk, Va.: Joint Center for Operational Analysis, 2006).

49 Robert Jervis, "Cooperation under the Security Dilemma," *World Politics* 30 (January
1978): 167–214; Kenneth Oye, ed., *Cooperation under Anarchy* (Princeton: Princeton University
Press, 1986).

is completely carried out. The situation is further complicated if one side believes that recognizing or talking directly to the other is a major bargaining chip, not to be surrendered until it is clear that the other side is ready to do business.[50]

This area has not been entirely neglected by scholarship, but like the broad topic of diplomacy in which it is situated, it has not been a high priority. I suspect that further study would find some interesting arrangements that are not obvious from a priori theorizing and would uncover intelligent designs that had solved some problems that at first seemed intractable.[51] Perhaps diplomats have been so diligent and ingenious that while we could learn from them, there is little that we could teach them, as Gartzke's argument implies.[52] But my guess is that their knowledge is not complete and that systematic study would lead us to be able to see how devices employed in some situations might be used in others and even to design mechanisms and procedures that had not been used before. Of course, improving the negotiation process could lead actors to take more chances and press harder, just as double-hulled tankers might lead to less cautious behavior. Nevertheless, I think this is an area in which bringing theory and practice together could produce mutual gains.

Conclusion

Throughout his career, Alexander George was concerned not only with understanding world politics but also with improving it. He examined decision-making deficiencies,[53] the ways in which threats were badly deployed and often supplanted diplomacy,[54] and how greater cooperation could be achieved.[55] Much of this essay has pointed to the limits on how helpful scholars can be and to the methodological, political, and psychological obstacles to bridging

50 For some examples, see James Hershberg, *Marigold: The Lost Chance for Peace in Vietnam* (Washington, D.C.: Woodrow Wilson Press, 2012); William LeoGrande and Peter Kornbluth, *Back Channel to Cuba: The Hidden History of Negotiations between Washington and Havana* (Chapel Hill: University of North Carolina Press, 2014).

51 Alexander George, *Managing U.S.-Soviet Rivalry: Problems of Crisis Prevention* (Boulder, Colo.: Westview Press, 1983); Alexander George, *Avoiding War: Problems of Crisis Management* (Boulder, Colo.: Westview Press, 1991); Alexander George, Philip Farley, and Alexander Dallin, *U.S.-Soviet Security Cooperation: Achievements, Failures, Lessons* (Oxford: Oxford University Press, 1988).

52 Gartzke, "War Is in the Error Term."

53 George, *Presidential Decisionmaking in Foreign Policy*; *Bridging the Gap*; and *On Foreign Policy*.

54 George and Smoke, *Deterrence in American Foreign Policy*.

55 George, *Managing U.S.-Soviet Rivalry*: George, *Avoiding War*; George, Farley, and Dallin, *U.S.-Soviet Security Cooperation*.

the gap between scholarship and policymaking. But in many areas the task is merely difficult rather than impossible. While scholars do not have ready-made answers, let alone all the answers, at its best scholarship can contribute to more effective policies, and here as in other areas George has shown us the way.

7

Why Intelligence and Policymakers Clash

There is nothing a Government hates more than to be well-informed; for it makes the process of arriving at decisions much more complicated and difficult.

—JOHN MAYNARD KEYNES

Let me tell you about these intelligence guys. When I was growing up in Texas, we had a cow named Bessie. I'd go out early and milk her. I'd get her in the stanchion, seat myself and squeeze out a pail of fresh milk. One day I'd worked hard and gotten a full pail of milk, but I wasn't paying attention, and old Bessie swung her shit-smeared tail through the bucket of milk. Now, you know that's what these intelligence guys do. You work hard and get a good program or policy going, and they swing a shit-smeared tail through it.

—LYNDON JOHNSON

Intelligence and Policymakers

Policymakers say they need and want good intelligence. They do need it, but often they do not like it, and are prone to believe that when intelligence is not out to get them, it is incompetent.[1] Richard Nixon was only the most vocal of presidents in wondering how "those clowns out at Langley" could misunder-

1 Keynes quoted in Robert Skidelsky, *John Maynard Keynes: The Economist as Saviour, 1920–1937* (London: Macmillan, 1992), p. 630; Johnson quoted in Robert Gates, "An Opportunity Unfulfilled: The Use and Perceptions of Intelligence at the White House," *Washington Quarterly* 12 (Winter 1989): 42.

stand so much of the world and cause his administration so much trouble.[2] Unfortunately, not only will even the best intelligence services often be wrong, but even (or especially) when they are right, they are likely to bring disturbing news, and this incurs a cost. As Director of Central Intelligence (DCI) Richard Helms said shortly after he was let go in 1973, he was "the easiest man in Washington to fire. I have no political, military or industrial base."[3] Although DCI James Woolsey's view was colored by his bad relations with President Clinton, he was not far off the mark in saying that the best job description for his position was "not to be liked."[4]

For the general public, intelligence is not popular for the additional reasons that its two prime characteristics of secrecy and covert action clash, if not with American traditions, then with the American self-image, and even those who applaud the results are likely to be uncomfortable with the means. It is telling that discussions of interventions in others' internal politics, and especially attempts to overthrow their regimes, are couched in terms of the *CIA's* interventions despite the fact that the CIA acts under instructions from the president. Critics, even those on the left, shy away from the correct label, which is that it is a *U.S. government* intervention. Political leaders see little reason to encourage a better understanding.

A New York clothing store had as its slogan "An educated consumer is our best customer." Intelligence can say this as well, but its wish for an educated consumer is not likely to be granted. Many presidents and cabinet officers come to the job with little knowledge or experience with intelligence and with less time to learn once they are in power. Even presidents like Nixon who were more informed and who doubted the CIA's abilities often held unreasonable expectations about what it could produce. Kissinger sometimes knew better, as revealed by what he told his staff about the congressional complaints that the United States had failed to anticipate the coup in Portugal:

> Why? Now goddam it, I absolutely resent—anytime there's a coup you start with the assumption that the home government missed it.... Why the hell should we know better than the government that's being overthrown....

2 Quoted in Rhodri Jeffreys-Jones, *The CIA and American Democracy*, 2nd ed. (New Haven: Yale University Press, 1998), p. 177. For excellent discussions of intelligence and its role in policymaking, see Michael Herman, *Intelligence Power in Peace and War* (Cambridge: Cambridge University Press, 1966); Gregory Treverton, *Reshaping National Intelligence in an Age of Information* (New York: Cambridge University Press, 2001), ch. 6; Mark Lowenthal, "Tribal Tongues: Intelligence Producers, Intelligence Consumers," in Loch Johnson and James Wirtz, eds., *Strategic Intelligence* (Los Angeles: Roxbury Press, 2004), pp. 234–41.

3 Quoted in Trudi Osborne, "The (Really) Quiet American: Richard McGarrah Helms," *Washington Post*, May 20, 1973.

4 Quoted in Nina Easton, "The Last Hawk: James Woolsey Wants Iraq's Saddam Hussein Brought to Justice," *Washington Post*, December 27, 2001.

I mean what request is it to make of our intelligence agencies to discover coups all over the world?[5]

Although Kissinger was right, even he sometimes expected more information and better analysis than was likely to be forthcoming and displayed the familiar schizophrenic pattern of both scorning intelligence and being disappointed by it.

Decision-Makers' Needs and How Intelligence Conflicts with Them

The different needs and perspectives of decision-makers and intelligence officials guarantee conflict between them. For both political and psychological reasons, political leaders have to oversell their policies, especially in domestic systems in which power is decentralized,[6] and this will produce pressures on and distortions of intelligence. It is then not surprising that intelligence officials, especially those at the working level, tend to see political leaders as unscrupulous and careless, if not intellectually deficient, and that leaders see their intelligence services as timid, unreliable, and often out to get them.

Although it may be presumptuous for the CIA to have chiseled in its lobby "And ye shall know the truth and the truth will make you free," it can at least claim this as its objective. No decision-maker could do so, as the more honest of them realize. When Secretary of State Dean Acheson said that the goal of a major National Security Council document was to be "clearer than truth," he understood this situation very well.[7] Some of the resulting tensions came out when Porter Goss became DCI and told the members of the CIA that they should support policymakers.[8] Of course the job of intelligence is to inform policymakers and in this way to support better policy. But support can also mean providing analysis that reinforces policies and rallies others to the cause. The first kind of support fits with intelligence's preferred mission, the one that decision-makers pay lip service to. But given the political and psychological world in which they live, it is often the latter kind of support that decision-makers seek. They need confidence and political support, and honest intelligence unfortunately often diminishes rather than increases these goods by pointing to ambiguities, uncertainties, and the costs and risks of policies. In

---

5 The secretary's staff meeting, October 8, 1975, pp. 42–43, http://www.gwu.edu/~nsarchiv /NSAEBB/NSAEBB193/HAK-10-8-75.pdf.

6 The classic statement is Theodore Lowi, *The End of Liberalism* (New York: Norton, 1969), ch. 6.

7 Dean Acheson, *Present at the Creation: My Years at the State Department* (New York: Norton, 1969), p. 375.

8 Douglas Jehl, "New C.I.A. Chief Tells Workers to Back Administration Policies," *New York Times,* November 17, 2004.

many cases, there is a conflict between what intelligence at its best can produce and what decision-makers seek and need.

Because it is axiomatic that a good policy must rest on an accurate assessment of the world, in a democracy policies must be—or at least be seen as being—grounded in intelligence. Ironically, this is true only because intelligence is seen as unbiased and proficient, a perception that developed in the wake of the technologies in the 1960s, and the pressures on intelligence follow from its supposed strengths.[9] When Secretary of State Colin Powell insisted that DCI George Tenet sit right behind him when he laid out the case against Iraq before the UN Security Council, he was following this imperative in a way that was especially dramatic but not different in kind from the norm. It is the very need to claim that intelligence and policy are in close harmony that produces conflict between them.

In principle, it could be different. George W. Bush could have said something like this: "I think Saddam is a terrible menace. This is a political judgment, and I have been elected to make difficult calls. While I have listened to our intelligence services and other experts, this is my decision, not theirs." In other cases the president could announce, "The evidence is ambiguous, but on balance I believe that we must act on the likelihood that the more alarming possibilities are true." But speeches that clearly separate themselves from intelligence will seem weak and be politically unpersuasive, and it is not surprising that leaders want to use intelligence to bolster not only their arguments but also their political standing.

Conflicting Pressures

For reasons of both psychology and politics, decision-makers want not only to minimize actual value trade-offs but also to minimize their own perception of them. Leaders talk about how they make hard decisions all the time, but like the rest of us, they prefer easy ones and will try to convince themselves and others that a particular decision is in fact not so hard. Maximizing political support for a policy means arguing that it meets many goals, is supported by many considerations, and has few costs. Decision-makers, then, want to portray the world as one in which their policy is superior to the alternatives on many independent dimensions. For example, when a nuclear test ban was being debated during the Cold War, proponents argued not only that atmospheric testing was a major public health hazard but also that a test ban was good for American national security and could be verified. It would have undercut the case for the ban if its supporters had said, "We must stop atmospheric

9 Richard Immerman, "Intelligence and Strategy: Historicizing Psychology, Policy, and Politics," *Diplomatic History* 32 (January 2008): 12.

testing in order to save innocent lives even though there will be a significant cost in terms of national security."

Psychological as well as political dynamics are at work. To continue with the test ban example, proponents who were deeply concerned with public health did not like to think that they were advocating policies that would harm national security. Conversely, those who felt that inhibiting nuclear developments would disadvantage the United States came to also believe that the testing was not a health hazard. They would have been discomforted by the idea that their preferred policy purchased American security at the cost of hundreds of thousands of innocent lives. Decision-makers have to sleep at night, after all.[10]

The run-up to the war in Iraq is an unfortunately apt illustration of these processes. In its most general form, the Bush administration's case for the war was that Saddam was a great menace and that overthrowing him also was a great opportunity for changing the Middle East. Furthermore, each of these two elements had several supporting components. Saddam was a threat because he was very hard to deter, had robust WMD programs, and had ties to terrorists, whom he might provide with WMD. The opportunity was multifaceted as well: the war would be waged at low cost, the postwar reconstruction would be easy, and establishing a benign regime in Iraq would have salutary effects on the region by pushing other regimes along the road to democracy and facilitating the resolution of the Arab-Israeli dispute. Portraying the world in this way not only maximized support for the war, but it also eased the psychological burdens on decision-makers, which were surely great in ordering soldiers into combat and embarking on a bold venture. This effect was so strong that Vice President Cheney, who previously recognized that removing Saddam could throw Iraq into chaos, was able to convince himself that it would not. There was no logic that ruled out the situation having presented a threat but not an opportunity (or vice versa), or for there to have been a threat of one kind—for example, that Saddam was on the verge of getting significant WMD capability—but not of another—for example, that he had no connections to al Qaeda. Logically, Cheney's heightened urgency about overthrowing Saddam should not have changed his view on what would follow. But it did.

The contrast with the intelligence community (IC) was sharp. It did believe that Saddam had robust WMD programs, but because it did not feel the psychological need to bolster the case for war, it did not have to pull other perceptions into line, and so the IC gave little support to the administration on points where the evidence was to the contrary. And this is where the friction arose. Intelligence denied any collaboration between Saddam and al Qaeda,

---

10 For further discussion, see Jervis, "Understanding Beliefs," in this volume.

and it was very skeptical about the possibility that Saddam would turn over WMD to terrorists. So it is not surprising that here the administration put great pressure on intelligence to come to a different view and that policymakers frequently made statements that were at variance with the assessments. It is also not surprising, although obviously it was not foreordained, that the intelligence here was quite accurate.[11]

Intelligence also painted a gloomy picture of the prospects for postwar Iraq, noting the possibilities for continued resistance and the difficulties in inducing the diverse and conflicting groups in the country to cooperate with one another.[12] Because this skepticism did not receive public attention, these estimates were subject to less political pressure, although the fact that the administration not only ignored them but also frequently affirmed the opposite must have been frustrating to the analysts. Fortunately for them, however, on these points the administration was content to assert its views without claiming that they were supported by intelligence, probably because the judgments were of a broad political nature and did not rely on secret information. Later, when the postwar situation deteriorated and intelligence officials revealed that they had in fact provided warnings, the conflict heightened as the administration felt that intelligence was being disloyal and furthering its own political agenda.

It is tempting to see the browbeating and ignoring of intelligence as a particular characteristic of the George W. Bush administration, but it was not. Although available evidence does not allow anything like a full inventory, it does reveal examples from other administrations. Because Bill Clinton and his colleagues were committed to returning Haiti's Jean-Bertrand Aristide to power after he had been ousted in a coup, they resented and resisted intelligence analysis that argued that he was unstable and his governing would not be effective or democratic.[13] Neither the Eisenhower nor the Kennedy administrations, both of which favored a test ban agreement, was happy with analyses that indicated that verification would be difficult. Although on many issues liberals are more accepting of value trade-offs than are conservatives,[14]

11 Senate Select Committee on Intelligence, *Report of the Select Committee on Intelligence on Postwar Findings about Iraq's WMD Programs and Links to Terrorism and How They Compare with Prewar Assessments*, September 8, 2006.

12 Senate Select Committee on Intelligence, *Report of the Select Committee on Intelligence on Prewar Intelligence Assessments about Postwar Iraq*, May 2007.

13 Steven Holmes, "Administration Is Fighting Itself on Haiti Policy," *New York Times*, October 23, 1993. The title of this article shows the problem: intelligence is part of the administration but is committed to independent analysis. Treverton argues that given the sensitivity of the subject and the softness of the evidence, the assessment should not have been written but rather orally briefed to policymakers: *Reshaping National Intelligence*, 188–89.

14 Philip Tetlock, "Cognitive Style and Political Ideology," *Journal of Personality and Social Psychology: Personality Processes and Individual Differences* 45 (1983): 118–26; Tetlock, "A Value

and many liberals like to think of themselves as particularly willing to confront complexity, once they are in power, they too need to muster political support and live at peace with themselves.

Intelligence does not feel the same pressures. It does not carry the burden of decision making but "merely" has to figure out what the world is like. If the resulting choices are difficult, so be it. It also is not the duty of intelligence to build political support for a policy, and so even intelligence officials who do not oppose the policy will—or should—feel no compulsions to portray the world in a helpful way. In many cases, good intelligence will then point out the costs and dangers implicit in a policy. It will make it harder for policy-makers to present the policy as clearly the best one and will nurture second thoughts, doubts, and unease. It is not that intelligence usually points to policies other than those the leaders prefer, but only that it is likely to give decision-makers a more complex and contradictory view than fits their political and psychological needs. Ironically, it can do this even as it brings good news. One might think that Lyndon Johnson would have welcomed the CIA's telling him that other countries would not fall to communism even if Vietnam did, but since his policy was justified (to others and probably to himself) on the premise that the domino theory was correct, he did not.[15]

Resistance to Fallback Positions and Signs of Failure

The same factors that lead decision-makers to underestimate trade-offs make them reluctant to develop fallback plans and to resist information that their policy is failing. The latter more than the former causes conflicts with intelligence, although the two are closely linked. There are several reasons why leaders are reluctant to develop fallback plans. It is hard enough to develop one policy, and the burden of thinking through a second is often simply too great. Probably more important, if others learn of the existence of Plan B, they may give less support to Plan A. Even if they do not prefer the former, its existence will be taken as betraying the leaders' lack of faith in their policy. It may also be psychologically difficult for leaders to contemplate failure.

Examples abound. Clinton did not have a Plan B when he started bombing to induce Serbia's Slobodan Milosevic to withdraw his troops from Kosovo.

Pluralism Model of Ideological Reasoning," *Journal of Personality and Social Psychology: Personality Processes and Individual Differences* 50 (1986): 819–27.

15 "Implications of an Unfavorable Outcome in Vietnam," September 11, 1967, in *Estimative Products on Vietnam, 1948–1975* (Washington, D.C.: National Intelligence Council, 2005), pp. 394–426; Richard Helms, with William Hood, *A Look over My Shoulder: A Life in the Central Intelligence Agency* (New York: Random House, 2003), pp. 314–15; Robert McNamara, with Brian VanDeMark, *In Retrospect: The Tragedy and Lessons of Vietnam* (New York: Random House, 1995), pp. 292–93.

Administration officials thought such a plan was not needed because it was obvious that Milosevic would give in right away. In part they believed this because they thought it was the brief and minor bombing over Bosnia that had brought Milosevic to the table at Dayton, an inference that even if it had been correct would not have readily supported the conclusion that he would give up Kosovo without a fight. The result was that the administration had to scramble both militarily and politically and was fortunate to end the confrontation as well as it did. The most obvious and consequential recent case of a lack of Plan B is Iraq. Despite intelligence to the contrary, top administration officials believed that the political and economic reconstruction of Iraq would be easy and that they needed neither short-term plans to maintain order nor long-term preparations to put down an insurgency and create a stable polity.[16] Thinking about a difficult postwar situation would have been psychologically and politically costly, which is why it was not done.

Having a Plan B means little unless decision-makers are willing to shift to it if they must, which implies a need to know whether the policy is working. This, even more than the development of the plan, involves intelligence, and so here the clashes will be greater. Leaders tend to stay with their first choice for as long as possible. Lord Salisbury, the famous British statesman of the end of the nineteenth century, noted that "the commonest error in politics is sticking to the carcasses of dead policies."[17] Leaders are heavily invested in their policies. To change their basic objectives will be to incur very high costs, including, in some cases, losing their offices if not their lives. Indeed the resistance to seeing that a policy is failing is roughly proportional to the costs that are expected if it does. Iraq again provides a clear example. In early 2007 Sen. John McCain explained, "It's just so hard for me to contemplate failure that I can't make the next step," and President Bush declared that American policy in Iraq will succeed "because it has to."[18] This perseverance in what appears to be a losing cause may be rational for the leaders, if not for the country, as long as there is any chance of success and the costs of having to adopt a new policy are almost as great as those for continuing to the bitter end.[19] An obvious

16 Senate Select Committee on Intelligence, *Intelligence on Prewar Intelligence Assessments about Postwar Iraq*; Norah Bensahel, "Mission Not Accomplished: What Went Wrong with Iraqi Reconstruction," *Journal of Strategic Studies* 29 (June 2006): 453–74.

17 Lady Gwendolen Cecil, *Life of Robert, Marquis of Salisbury*, vol. 2 (London: Hodder and Stoughton, 1921), p. 145. Of course there is a selection effect at work here: if the country changes its policy, we will never know if continuing it would have yielded success.

18 Quoted in Todd Purdum, "Prisoner of Conscience," *Vanity Fair*, February 2007, p. 14; quoted in David Sanger, "Bush Adds Troops in Bid to Secure Iraq," *New York Times*, January 10, 2007.

19 George Downs and David Rocke, "Gambling for Resurrection," in *Optimal Imperfection? Domestic Uncertainty and Institutions in International Relations* (Princeton: Princeton University Press, 1995); Hein Goemans, *War and Punishment: The Causes of War Termination and the First World War* (Princeton: Princeton University Press, 2000).

example is Bush's decision to increase the number of American troops in Iraq in early 2007. The previous policy was not working and would have resulted in a major loss for the United States and for Bush, and even a failed "surge" would have cost him little more than admitting defeat and withdrawing without this renewed effort. Predictions of success or failure were not central to the decision. In most cases, however, predictions are involved, and it is hard for decision-makers to make them without bias.

Intelligence officials do not have such a stake in the established policies, and thus it is easier for them to detect signs that the policies are failing. The fact that the leaders of the Bush administration saw much more progress in Iraq than did the IC is not unusual.[20] President Johnson's sentiments quoted at the start of this chapter rest on accurate observations. He probably was thinking about Vietnam, and appropriately so. The civilian intelligence agencies were quick to doubt that bombing North Vietnam would either cut the supply lines or induce the leadership to give in; they issued pessimistic reports on the pacification campaign and gave higher estimates of the size of the adversary's forces than the military or Johnson wanted to hear.[21]

Leaders are not necessarily being foolish. The world is ambiguous, and indicators of success are likely to be elusive. If it were easy to tell who would win a political or military struggle, it would soon come to an end (or would not start at all), and Vietnam is not unique in permitting a postwar debate on the virtues of alternative policies. Although it was a pernicious myth that Germany lost World War I because of a "stab in the back," it could have gained better peace terms if the top military leaders had not lost their nerve in the late summer of 1918. Furthermore, leaders can be correct even if their reasoning is not. The classic case is that of Winston Churchill in the spring of 1940. He prevailed over strong sentiment in his cabinet for a peace agreement with Germany in the wake of the fall of France by arguing that Britain could win because the German economy was badly overstretched and could be broken by a combination of bombing and guerrilla warfare. This was a complete fantasy; his foreign secretary had reason to write in his diary that "Winston talked the most frightful rot. It drives one to despair when he works himself up into a passion of emotion when he ought to make his brain think and rea-

20 See, for example, Kim Rutenberg, "Parts of Iraq Report Grim Where Bush Was Upbeat," *New York Times*, July 15, 2007.

21 A good summary by a former high-ranking CIA official is Harold Ford, *CIA and Vietnam Policymakers: Three Episodes, 1962–1968* (Washington, D.C.: CIA Center for the Study of Intelligence, 1998); also see Thomas Ahern, Jr., "Good Questions, Wrong Answers: CIA's Estimates of Arms Traffic Through Sihanoukville, Cambodia, During the Vietnam War," February 2004, http://www.foia.cia.gov/vietnam/4_GOOD_QUESTIONS_WRONG_ANSWERS.pdf. The pattern in Iraq seems similar.

son."[22] Fortunately, Churchill's emotion and force of character carried the day, but intelligence can get no credit. But regardless of who is right, we should expect conflict between leaders and intelligence over whether Plan B is necessary.

Confidence and Perseverance

We should perhaps not underestimate the virtues of perseverance, as pig-headed as it may appear to opponents and to later observers when it fails. Not a few apparently hopeless cases end well. This may prove to be true in Iraq, and despite widespread opinion to the contrary, the mujahedeen in Afghanistan were able to force the Soviets out of the country. Similarly, two scientists spent over twenty years working on what almost everyone else believed was a misguided quest to understand the workings of the hypothalamus, producing no results until they independently made the breakthroughs that earned them Nobel Prizes.[23] Albert Hirschman points to the "hiding hand" in many human affairs. If we saw the obstacles in our path, we would not begin many difficult but ultimately successful endeavors.[24]

Confidence is necessary for perseverance and for embarking on any difficult venture. While it can be costly, it also is functional in many situations, which helps explain why people are systematically overconfident.[25] Although it might seem that we would be better off if our confidence better matched our knowledge, it turns out that the most mentally healthy people are slightly overoptimistic, overestimating their skills and ability to control their lives.[26] This is probably even more true for decision-makers, who carry heavy burdens. As Kissinger says, "Historians rarely do justice to the psychological stress

22 David Reynolds, "Churchill and the British 'Decision' to Fight on in 1940: Right Policy, Wrong Reasons," pp. 147–67 in Richard Langhorne, ed., *Diplomacy and Intelligence during the Second World War* (New York: Cambridge University Press, 1985); the quotation is from Harold Evans, "His Finest Hour," *New York Times Book Review,* November 11, 2001.

23 Nicholas Wade, *The Nobel Duel: Two Scientists' 21-Year Race to Win the World's Most Coveted Research Prize* (Garden City, N.Y.: Doubleday, 1981).

24 Albert Hirschman, "The Principle of the Hiding Hand," *Public Interest,* no. 6 (Winter 1967): 10–24.

25 For a summary of the literature, see Richard Nisbett and Lee Ross, *Human Inference: Strategies and Shortcomings of Social Judgment* (Englewood Cliffs, N.J.: Prentice-Hall, 1980), pp. 113–15, 119–20, 150–51, 292–93.

26 Shelley Taylor and J. Brown, "Illusion and Well-Being: A Social Psychological Perspective on Mental Illness," *Psychological Bulletin* 103 (March 1998): 193–210; Taylor, *Positive Illusions: Creative Self-Deception and the Healthy Mind* (New York: Basic Books, 1989). Also see Dominic Johnson, *Overconfidence and War: The Havoc and Glory of Positive Illusions* (Cambridge: Harvard University Press, 2004).

on a policy-maker."[27] A national leader who had no more confidence than an objective reading of the evidence might be paralyzed or worn down by mental anguish after each decision. Dean Acheson understood this when he told the presidential scholar Richard Neustadt, "I know your theory [that presidents need to hear conflicting views]. You think Presidents should be warned. You're wrong. Presidents should be given confidence."[28]

There is little reason to think that President Bush was being less than honest when he told Bob Woodward, "I know it is hard for you to believe, but I have not doubted what we're doing [in Iraq]." He was aware that a degree of self-manipulation if not self-deception was involved: "[A] president has got to be the calcium in the backbone. If I weaken, the whole team weakens.... If my confidence level in our ability declines, it will send ripples throughout the whole organization. I mean, it's essential that we be confident and determined and united."[29] During the air campaign phase of the Gulf War, when the CIA estimated that the damage being inflicted was well below what the air force reported and what military planners said was needed to launch the ground attack, the general in charge, Norman Schwarzkopf, demanded that CIA get out of this business. His reasoning was not that the CIA was wrong but that these estimates reduced the confidence of the men and women in uniform on which success depended.[30]

Of course there are occasions in which intelligence can supply confidence. The breaking of German codes in World War II not only gave allied military and civilian leaders an enormous amount of information that enabled them to carry out successful military operations but also provided a general confidence that they could prevail. At the height of the Cuban missile crisis in 1962, Kennedy was given confidence by the report from his leading Soviet expert that Khrushchev would be willing to remove the missiles the Soviets had installed in Cuba without an American promise of a parallel withdrawal from Turkey. In most cases, however, intelligence is likely to provide a complicated, nuanced, and ambiguous picture.

When they are not prepared to change, leaders are prone not only to reject the information but also to scorn the messenger, claiming that intelli-

27 Henry Kissinger, *White House Years* (Boston: Little, Brown, 1979), p. 483.

28 Quoted in John Steinbruner, *The Cybernetic Theory of Decision* (Princeton: Princeton University Press, 1974), p. 332.

29 Quoted in Bob Woodward, *State of Denial: Bush at War, Part III* (New York: Simon and Schuster, 2006), pp. 325–26, also see p. 371; also see Robert Draper, *Dead Certain: The Presidency of George W. Bush* (New York: Free Press, 2007). But interestingly enough, Secretary of State Powell and his deputy, Richard Armitage, believed that self-doubt was essential to doing a good job: Woodward, *State of Denial*, 325.

30 Richard Russell, "CIA's Strategic Intelligence in Iraq," *Political Science Quarterly* 117 (Summer 2002): 201–7.

gence is unhelpful (which in a real sense it is), superficial (which is sometimes the case), and disloyal (which is rare). Intelligence may lose its access or, if the case is important, much of its role. Thus in the 1930s when a unit in Japanese military intelligence showed that the China campaign, far from leading to control over needed raw materials, was draining the Japanese economy, the army responded by reorganizing and marginalizing the offending unit.[31] Something similar was attempted in Vietnam by the U.S. military, which responded to the pessimistic reporting from the Department of State's Bureau of Intelligence and Research (INR) by having Secretary of Defense Robert McNamara insist that the INR not be permitted to analyze what was happening on the battlefield.[32]

It might be comforting to believe that only rigid individuals or organizations act in this way, but what is at work is less the characteristics of the organization and the personalities of the leaders than the desire to continue the policy, the need for continuing political support, and the psychological pain of confronting failure. When the research arm of the U.S. Forest Service turned up solid evidence that the best way to manage forests was to permit if not facilitate controlled fires, the unit was abolished because the founding mission and indeed the identity of the service was to prevent forest fires.[33]

Too Early or Too Late

For intelligence to be welcomed and to have an impact, it must arrive at the right time, which is after the leaders have become seized with the problem but before they have made up their minds. This is a narrow window. One might think that early warning would be especially useful because there is time to influence events. But in many cases decision-makers will have an established policy, one that will be costly to change, and early warnings can rarely be definitive.

Intelligence about most of the world is irrelevant to leaders because they are too busy to pay attention to any but the most pressing concerns. Intelligence on matters that are not in this category may be useful for building the knowledge of the government and informing lower-level officials but will not receive a hearing at the top. This was the case with intelligence on domestic politics in Iran before the fall of 1978, when it became clear that the troubles facing the Shah were serious. Intelligence was badly flawed here, rarely going

---

31 Michael Barnhart, *Japan Prepares for Total War: The Search for Economic Security, 1919–1941* (Ithaca: Cornell University Press, 1987), pp. 170–75.

32 Thomas Hughes, "Experiencing McNamara," *Foreign Policy* 100 (Fall 1995): 154–57; Louis Sarris, "McNamara's War, and Mine," *New York Times*, September 5, 1995.

33 Ashley Schiff, *Fire and Water: Scientific Heresy in the Forest Service* (Cambridge: Harvard University Press, 1962).

beyond the inadequate reports from the field or assessing the situation in any depth.[34] But even better analysis would not have gained much attention because the president and his top assistants were preoccupied by other problems and projects, most obviously the attempt to bring peace to the Middle East that culminated in President Carter's meeting with President Sadat and Prime Minister Begin at Camp David. As one CIA official said to me, "We could not give away intelligence on Iran before the crisis." Almost as soon as the crisis hit, however, it was too late. Top officials quickly established their own preferences and views of the situation. This is not unusual. On issues that are central, decision-makers and their assistants are prone to become their own intelligence analysts.[35]

Perhaps intelligence can have most influence if it operates on questions that are important but not immediately pressing. In the run-up to the war in Iraq there was nothing that intelligence could have reasonably told President Bush that would have affected the basic decisions. But things might have been different if intelligence in the mid-1990s had been able to see that Saddam had postponed if not abandoned his ambitions for WMD. Had this been the standard view when Bush came to power, he and his colleagues might have accepted it because they were not then far down the road to war.

As a policy develops momentum, information and analyses that would have mattered if received earlier now will be ignored. This can be seen quite clearly in military operations because it is relatively easy to mark the stages of the deliberation. At the start, the focus is on whether the operation can succeed, which means paying careful attention to the status of the adversary's forces and the possibilities of gaining surprise. But as things move ahead, new information is likely to be used for tactical purposes rather than for calling the operation into question. The greater the effort required to mount it and the greater the difficulty in securing agreement to proceed, the greater the resistance will be to new information that indicates it is not likely to succeed.

A clear example is Operation Market Garden in the fall of 1944. After the leading British general, Bernard Montgomery, was rebuffed by Eisenhower in his arguments for concentrating all Allied forces behind his thrust toward Berlin, political as well as military reasons led Eisenhower to agree to a bold but more limited attack deep into German-held territory culminating at Arnhem. The need for Allied unity and conciliating Montgomery, combined with the fact that Eisenhower had been urging him to be more aggressive, meant that "once he was committed, retreat for Ike was all but impossible."[36] Shortly

34 For further discussion, see Robert Jervis, *Why Intelligence Fails: Lessons from the Iranian Revolution and the Iraq War* (Ithaca: Cornell University Press, 2013), ch. 2.

35 For a similar argument, see Treverton, *Reshaping National Intelligence*, 183–85.

36 Harold Deutsch, "Commanding Generals and the Uses of Intelligence," *Intelligence and National Security* 3 (July 1988): 245; for cases see Brian Loring Villa, *Unauthorized Action: Mount-*

before the attack was to be launched, code breaking revealed that the Germans had more and better-trained forces in the area than the allies had anticipated. Had they known this earlier, the operation would not have been approved. But once the basic decision was made, the political and psychological costs of reversing it were so high that the intelligence was disregarded, to the great cost of the soldiers parachuted into the final bridge. The refusal or inability of a leading British general to heed the intelligence indicating that the British move into Greece in 1941 would almost surely fail can be similarly explained, as can the fact that pessimistic CIA assessments about the planned American invasion of Cambodia in 1971 were not forwarded to the president when DCI Helms realized that Nixon and Kissinger had made up their minds and would only be infuriated by the reports, which turned out to be accurate.[37]

Importance of Cognitive Predispositions

Intelligence often has its own strongly held beliefs, which can operate at multiple levels of abstraction, from general theories of politics and human nature to images of adversaries to ideas about specific situations. These need not be uniform, and the IC, like the policymaking community, often is divided and usually along the same lines. During the Cold War some factions were much more worried about the USSR than were others, and the China analysts were deeply divided in their views about the role of Mao and how internal Chinese politics functioned. In these cases, analysts, like policymakers, were slow to change their views and saw most new information as confirming what they expected to see. This is true on the level of tactical intelligence as well. A striking case was the accidental shooting down of an Iranian airliner by the USS Vincennes toward the end of the Iran-Iraq War. One of the key errors was that the radar operator misread his screen as indicating that the airplane was descending toward the ship. What is relevant here is that the Vincennes's captain had trained his crew very aggressively, leading them to expect an attack and giving them a mindset that was conducive to reading—and misreading—evidence as indicating that one was under way. A destroyer that was in the

batten and the Dieppe Raid (New York: Oxford University Press, 1989), and Guy Vanderpool, "COMINT and the PRC Intervention in the Korean War," Cryptologic Quarterly 15 (Summer 1996): 1–26, declassified and available as document 21 at http://www.gwu.edu/~nsarchiv/NSAEBB/ NSAEBB278/index.htm.

37 Deutsch, "Commanding Generals and the Uses of Intelligence," 206–7; Stansfield Turner, Burn before Reading: Presidents, CIA Directors, and Secret Intelligence (New York: Hyperion, 2005), p. 128.

vicinity had not been drilled in this way, and its operator read the radar track correctly.[38]

Differing predispositions provide another reason why decision-makers so often reject intelligence. The answers to many of their most important questions are linked to their beliefs about world politics, the images of those they are dealing with, and their general ideas if not ideologies. Bush's view of Saddam rested in large measure on his beliefs about how tyrants behave, for example. If intelligence had explained that Saddam was not a major threat, being unlikely to aid terrorists or to try to dominate the region, this probably would not have been persuasive to Bush, and not only because he was particularly closed-minded. This kind of intelligence would have been derived not only from detailed analysis of how Saddam had behaved but also from broad understandings of politics and even of human nature. Here it is not only to be expected but legitimate for decision-makers to act on their views rather than those propounded by intelligence. It is often rightly said that "policy-makers are entitled to their own policies, but not to their own facts."[39] Facts do not speak for themselves, however, and crucial political judgments grow out of a stratum that lies between if not beneath policies and facts.

Although it was not appropriate for a member of the National Security Council (NSC) staff to ask whether the Baghdad station chief who produced a gloomy prognosis in November 2003 was a Democrat or Republican,[40] it would not have been illegitimate to have inquired as to the person's general political outlook, his predisposition toward optimism and pessimism, his general views about how insurgencies could be put down, and his beliefs about how difficult it would be to bring stability to a conflicted society. Not only is it comforting for decision-makers to listen to those who share their general values and outlook, but it makes real sense for them to do so. They are right to be skeptical of the analysis produced by those who see the world quite differently, because however objective the analysts are trying to be, their interpretations will inevitably be influenced by their general beliefs and theories.

38 David Evans, "USS Vincennes Case Study," http://www.owlnet.rice.edu/~nava201/VCS/vincennes.pdf. Ironically, this tragic incident helped end the war because Iranian leaders believed the United States had done this on purpose as part of its anti-Iranian campaign, and they inferred that even worse punishment would likely be forthcoming unless the war was settled.

39 See, for example, George Tenet with Bill Harlow, *At the Center of the Storm: My Years at the CIA* (New York: HarperCollins, 2007), pp. 317, 348.

40 James Risen, *State of War: The Secret History of the CIA and the Bush Administration* (New York: Free Press, 2006), p. 130. For a general discussion of the importance of analysts' worldviews, see David Muller, Jr., "Intelligence in Red and Blue," *International Journal of Intelligence and CounterIntelligence* 21 (Spring 2008): 1–12; also see Huw Dylan, "Britain and the Missile Gap: British Estimates on the Soviet Ballistic Missile Threat, 1957–61," *Intelligence and National Security* 23 (December 2008): 794–96.

It is then not surprising that people are rarely convinced in arguments about central issues. The debate about the nature of Soviet intentions went on throughout the Cold War, with few people being converted and fewer being swayed by intelligence or competing analysis. Without going so far as to say that everyone is born either a little hawk or a little dove, to paraphrase Gilbert and Sullivan, on the broadest issues of the nature and intentions of other countries and the existence and characteristics of broad historical trends, people's beliefs are determined more by their general worldviews, predispositions, and ideologies than they are by the sort of specific evidence that can be pieced together by intelligence. The reason why DCI John Mc-Cone expected the Soviets to put missiles into Cuba and his analysts did not was not that they examined different evidence or that he was more careful than they were, but that he strongly believed that the details of the nuclear balance influenced world politics and that Khrushchev would therefore be strongly motivated to improve his position. Similarly, as early as 1934, Robert Vansittart, the United Kingdom's permanent undersecretary in the foreign office and a leading opponent of appeasement, criticized the military for being slow to appreciate the rise of Nazi power: "Prophesy is largely a matter of insight. I do not think the Service Departments have enough. On the other hand they might say that I have too much. The answer is that I know the Germans better."[41] Although contemporary decision-makers might not refer to intuition, they are likely to have deeply ingrained beliefs about the way the world works and what a number of countries are like, and in this sense they will be prone to be their own intelligence analysts.

The discrepancy between the broad cognitive predispositions of the IC and those of political leaders explains why conflict has tended to be higher when Republicans are in power. With some reason, they see intelligence analysts as predominantly liberals. Their suspicions that intelligence has sought to thwart and embarrass the administration are usually false, but to the extent that the worldviews of most intelligence officers are different from those of the Republicans, the latter are justified in being skeptical of IC analysis on broad issues. For their part, intelligence analysts, like everyone else, underestimate the degree to which their own interpretations of specific bits of evidence are colored by their general predispositions and so consider the leaders' rejection of their views closed-minded and ideological. Although not all people are equally driven by their theories about the world,[42] there is a degree of

41 Quoted in Donald Cameron Watt, "British Intelligence and the Coming of the Second World War in Europe," in Ernest May, ed., *Knowing One's Enemies: Intelligence Assessment before the Two World Wars* (Princeton: Princeton University Press, 1984), p. 268.

42 For meticulous research showing that those who are less theory-driven tend to make more accurate predictions and to better adjust their views in the face of discrepant evidence, see Philip Tetlock, *Expert Political Judgment: How Good Is It? How Can We Know?* (Princeton:

legitimacy to the leaders' position that members of the IC often fail to grasp. President Reagan and his colleagues, including DCI William Casey, probably were right to believe that the IC's assessments that the Soviet Union was not supporting terrorism and was not vulnerable to economic pressures were more a product of the IC's liberal leanings than of the evidence. They therefore felt justified in ignoring the IC when they did not put pressure on it to confirm their views, which in turn led to charges of politicization, a topic to which I will now turn.

Politicization

Politicization of intelligence can take many forms, from the most blatant in which intelligence is explicitly told what conclusions it should reach to the less obvious, including demoting people who produce the "wrong" answer, putting in place personnel whose views are consistent with those of the top leaders, reducing the resources going to units whose analyses are troubling, and the operation of unconscious bias by analysts who fear that their careers will be damaged by producing undesired reports. Even more elusive may be what one analyst has called "politicization by omission": issues that are not evaluated because the results might displease superiors.[43] Also subtle are the interactions between pressures and degrees of certainty in estimates. I suspect that one reason for the excess certainty in the Iraq WMD assessments was the knowledge of what the decision-makers wanted. Conversely, analysts are most likely to politically conform when they are uncertain about their own judgments, as will often be the case on difficult and contentious questions.

Only rarely does one find a case like the one in which President Johnson told DCI Helms, "Dick, I need a paper on Vietnam, and I'll tell you what I want included in it."[44] Almost as blatant was Kissinger's response when CIA

Princeton University Press, 2005); also see Milton Rokeach, *The Open and Closed Mind: Investigations into the Nature of Belief Systems and Personality Systems* (New York: Basic Books, 1960).

43 John Gentry, *Lost Promise: How CIA Analysis Misserves the Nation* (Lanham, Md..: University Press of America, 1993), pp. 35–37. The best general analysis of varieties of politicization is Joshua Rovner, *Fixing the Facts: National Security and the Politics of Intelligence* (Ithaca: Cornell University Press, 2011).

44 Quoted in Ralph Weber, ed., *Spymaster: Ten CIA Officers in Their Own Words* (Wilmington, Del.: Scholarly Resources Books, 1999), p. 251. It is not clear, however, whether Johnson was dictating the subjects to be covered or the conclusions to be reached. There also is some ambiguity in the incident Helms described in *A Look over My Shoulder*, 339–40. For his discussion of political pressures in the later controversy over estimating the size of enemy forces in Vietnam, see pp. 324–29. For DCI Tenet's views of the pressures by policymakers to conclude that there were significant links between al Qaeda and Iraq, see *At the Center of the Storm*, 349–50. For the claim that analysts at the World Bank are required to produce papers that support bank policy and specific projects, see Michael Goldman, *Imperial Nature: The World Bank and*

experts told Congress that intelligence did not believe that the new Soviet missile with multiple warheads could menace the American retaliatory force, contrary to what policymakers had said. He ordered the reports to be revised, and when they still did not conform, told Helms to remove the offending paragraph on the grounds that it was not "hard" intelligence but merely speculation on Soviet intentions, a subject on which intelligence lacked special qualifications.[45]

Even this case points to the ambiguities in the notion of politicization and the difficulties in drawing a line between what political leaders should and should not do when they disagree with estimates.[46] Intelligence said that "we consider it highly unlikely [that the Soviets] will attempt within the period of this estimate to achieve a first-strike capability."[47] This prediction was reasonable—and turned out to be correct—but it rested in part on judgments of the Soviet system and the objectives of the Soviet leaders, and these are the kind of questions that the top political leadership is entitled to answer for itself. On the other hand, to demand that intelligence keep silent on adversary intentions would be bizarre, and indeed, when the hardliners forced an outside estimate at the end of the Ford administration, the group of selected hawks who formed "Team B" strongly criticized the IC for concentrating on capabilities and ignoring intentions.

So it is not surprising that arguments about whether politicization occurred are rarely easy to settle.[48] In some cases the only people with firsthand

---

Struggles for Social Justice in the Age of Globalization (New Haven: Yale University Press, 2005), p. 127.

45 Stansfield Turner, *Burn Before Reading*, 130–32; also see John Prados, *The Soviet Estimate: U.S. Intelligence Analysis and Russian Military Strength* (New York: Dial Press, 1982), pp. 218–24, and Helms, A Look over My Shoulder, 386–88. For the (plausible) claim that political consideration led to the withholding of information on the status of Iran's "moderates" during the period when the Reagan White House was trading arms for hostages, see the memorandum from an Iranian analyst to the deputy Director of Intelligence, December 2, 1986, printed in Gentry, *Lost Promise*, 276–81.

46 For an attempt to draw such lines, see the speech that Robert Gates gave to analysts when he became DCI after deeply contentious confirmation hearings pivoting on whether he had politicized intelligence when he was deputy to William Casey: Gates, "Guarding against Politicization," *Studies in Intelligence* 36, no. 5 (1992): 5–13. Also see Jack Davis, "Intelligence Analysts and Policy-Makers: Benefits and Dangers of Tensions in the Relationship," *Intelligence and National Security* 21 (December 2006): 999–1021, and Richard Betts, *Enemies of Intelligence* (New York: Columbia University Press, 2007), ch. 4.

47 Turner, *Burn Before Reading*, 132.

48 When intelligence is most thoroughly politicized, evidence for this no longer appears. In an application of the familiar dynamic that power is most effective when it does not need to be applied openly, if an intelligence agency is filled with people who know and share the leader's views, intelligence will be supportive without leaving any fingerprints. Richard Russell, *Sharpening Strategic Intelligence: Why the CIA Gets It Wrong and What Needs to Be Done to Get It Right*

knowledge will have major stakes in the dispute, and in others even a video-tape of the meeting might not tell us what happened. Was the office chief be-moaning the fact that an estimate would cause him grief with policymakers, or was he suggesting that it be changed? Was the DCI's assistant just doing his job when he strongly criticized a draft paper, arguing that the evidence was thin, alternatives were not considered, and the conclusion went beyond the evidence, or was he exerting pressure to get a different answer? When people in the vice president's office and the office of the secretary of defense told the IC analysts to look again—and again—at the evidence for links between Sad-dam and al Qaeda and repeatedly pressed them on why they were discount-ing sources that reported such links, were they just doing due diligence?[49] Are analysts being oversensitive, or are leaders and managers being overasser-tive? Winks and nods, praise and blame, promotions and their absence are subject to multiple causes and multiple interpretations. In many of these cases I suspect that one's judgment will depend on which side of the substantive debate one is on, because commentators as well as the participants will bring with them their own biases and reasons to see or reject claims of pressure.

Ironically, while many of the critics of the IC's performance on Iraqi WMD highlighted the dangers of politicization, some of the proposed reforms (ones that appear after every failure) show how hard it is to distinguish a good intel-ligence process from one that is driven by illegitimate political concerns. It is conventional wisdom that good analysis questions its own assumptions, looks for alternative explanations, examines low-probability interpretations as well as ones that seem more likely to be correct, scrutinizes sources with great care, and avoids excessive conformity. The problem in this context is that an-alysts faced with the probing questions that these prescriptions imply may believe that they are being pressured into producing a different answer. The obvious reply is that consumers and managers must apply these techniques to all important cases, not just when they object to the initial answers. There is something to this, and it would make sense to look back at previous cases in which politicization has been charged and see whether only those estimates that produced the "wrong" answers were sent back for further scrutiny.

But even this test is not infallible. If I am correct that political leaders and top intelligence managers are entitled to their own broad political views, then they are right to scrutinize especially carefully what they think are incorrect judgments.[50] Thus the political leaders insisted that the IC continually reassess

---

(New York: Cambridge University Press, 2007), p. 121; John Diamond, *The CIA and the Culture of Failure* (Stanford: Stanford University Press, 2008), p. 43.

49 For a discussion of the latter case by the national intelligence officer in charge, see Paul Pillar, "Intelligence, Policy, and the War in Iraq," *Foreign Affairs* 85 (March/April 2006): 15–28.

50 It is the job of top IC officials to shield their subordinates from political pressures. But if there is any chance that intelligence will be listened to, they must also scrutinize unpopular as-

its conclusion that there were no significant links between Saddam and al Qaeda not only because they wanted a different answer but also because their feeling for how the world worked led them to expect such a connection, and they thought that the IC's assessment to the contrary was based less on the detailed evidence than on the misguided political sensibility that was dominant in the IC.[51] It is not entirely wrong for policymakers to require a higher level of proof from intelligence when the evidence cuts against their desired policy. This means that the greater probing of the grounds for judgments and the possible alternatives that are the objectives of good intelligence procedures may increase the likelihood both of politicization and of analysts' incorrectly levying such a charge.

Conclusion

Decision-makers need information and analysis, and intelligence gets its significance and mission from influencing those who will make policy. But this does not mean that relations between the two groups will be smooth. The grievances of the IC are less consequential because it has much less power than the intelligence consumers. Members of the IC often feel that policymakers shun complicated analysis, cannot cope with uncertainty, will not read beyond the first page, forget what they have been told, and are quick to blame intelligence when policy fails. In response, members of the IC grumble a great deal among themselves and, when sufficiently provoked, leak their versions to the media.

For their part, policymakers not only overestimate the subversive activities of the IC but also often find it less than helpful. This is true in two senses. First, they find that only on a few occasions can intelligence light a clear path. The evidence that can be gathered by other than supernatural methods is limited and ambiguous, and in many significant cases other states may not even know what they will do until the last minute. Even when intentions are longstanding, they and the associated capabilities often can be disguised, and the knowledge that deception is possible further degrades the available information. Even without this problem, it is difficult for intelligence officials to see the world as others see it and to penetrate minds that think quite differently than they do. This is especially true when the other side has beliefs and plans that, even when they become known later, make very little sense.

---

sessments with great care, trying to see that all objections have been met and that excessive claims have been avoided. To subordinates, this scrutiny may appear as illegitimate political pressure, and indeed in one sense it is.

51 Douglas Feith, *War and Decision: Inside the Pentagon at the Dawn of the War on Terrorism* (New York: HarperCollins, 2008).

Leaders find intelligence less than completely helpful in another sense as well. Leaders want to understand the world in which they are operating, but above all need to act and sustain themselves psychologically and politically. These requirements often conflict with the sort of analysis that intelligence is likely to provide. Leaders need confidence and political support, and all too often intelligence undermines both. In many cases, intelligence will increase rather than reduce uncertainty as it notes ambiguities and alternative possibilities. Even worse, intelligence can report that the policy to which the leader is committed is likely to entail high costs with dubious prospects for success. Occasionally intelligence can point to opportunities that the country can seize or to signs that the difficulties confronting a policy are only temporary. But more often it will indicate that the preferred path is not smooth, and may be a dead end.

No leader could have risen to the top without having frequently taken risks that others would shun and finding success where others expected failure. Experience will have taught them to place faith in their own judgments. But they will still seek sources of reassurance. Psychologically, they will not want to face the full costs and risks of their policies lest they become fearful, inconsistent, and hesitant. The political problems are even greater, as they need to rally others at home and abroad. The exposure of the gaps in the information, the ambiguities in its interpretation, and the multiple problems the policy is likely to confront will not be politically helpful.

The frictions between particular American presidents and the IC are often attributed to special circumstances or the personality quirks of the former and the intellectual failures of the latter. These all do abound, but the problem goes much deeper. The needs and missions of leaders and intelligence officials are very different, and the two groups are doomed to both work together and to come into conflict.

8

Identity and the Cold War

A central question for psychology and the Cold War is how Soviet and American national identities were shaped by the conflict. Defining identity is not easy, however.[1] Is it the same as self-image or self-perception? How does it relate to ideology and political culture?[2] Can we treat national identity as singular in the face of internal differences? What evidence can establish the content or even the existence of identities, and how do we go about determining their causes and effects?

Although in the end perhaps we have to settle for Supreme Court Justice Porter Stewart's definition of knowing it when we see it, more formally, national identity can be seen as the set of values, attributes, and practices that

1 For a good review, which also includes a discussion of methods for determining the substance of identities, see Rawi Abdelal, Yoshiko Herrera, Alastair Iain Johnston, and Rose McDermott, "Identity as a Variable," *Perspectives on Politics* 6 (December 2006): 695–712. For identity and political conflict, see, for example, Alexander Wendt, *Social Theory of International Politics* (New York: Cambridge University Press, 1999), and Consuelo Cruz, *Political Culture and Institutional Development in Costa Rica and Nicaragua: World-Making in the Tropics* (New York: Cambridge University Press, 2005). The role of the emotional nature of identity in influencing perceptions and thinking is developed in Richard Herrmann, "How Attachments to the Nation Shape Beliefs about the World: A Theory of Motivated Reasoning," *International Organization* 71 (Winter 2017).

2 The literature on ideology and the Cold War is extensive: for good recent statements, see Mark Kramer, "Ideology and the Cold War," *Review of International Studies* 25 (October 1999): 539–76; Nigel Gould-Daviesa, "Rethinking the Role of Ideology in International Politics during the Cold War," *Journal of Cold War Studies* 1 (Winter 1999): 90–109. Important older treatments include Samuel Huntington and Zbigniew Brzezinski, *Political Power: USA/USSR* (Westport, Conn.: Greenwood Press, 1982), ch. 9; Carew Hunt, "The Importance of Doctrine," in Alexander Dallin, ed., *Soviet Conduct in World Affairs* (New York: Columbia University Press, 1960), pp. 37–46.

members believe characterize the country and set it off from others. Identity is the (shared) answer to central if vague questions: Who are we? What are we like? Who are we similar to and different from? Identity is at work when people say, "We must act in a way that is true to what we are," as Jimmy Carter did in his 1978 State of the Union address when he declared that "the very heart of our identity as a nation is our firm commitment to human rights."[3] Identities then are states' conceptions or images of themselves and so call for analysis in terms of political psychology. They also carry heavy affective weight, and this helps explain why scholarly arguments about the Cold War are often very bitter because the stakes included what the Soviet Union and the United States were like or should be like.

Soviet and American Identities

As the preceding paragraph indicates, identities are like stereotypes in being over-generalizations. With this in mind, I think it is fair to say that the characteristics of the American identity during the Cold War included democracy; individualism and voluntarism as contrasted to acceptance of strong direction—let alone compulsion—from the government; opposition to concentrated power, especially when wielded by the government; the belief in a supreme being that supplies the meaning to life; and a faith that this model "way of life" can, should, and eventually will be adopted by the others. To say that the United States saw its model as potentially universal is not to say that it was viewed by Americans as yet widely shared. Quite the contrary: the idea of American exceptionalism is not merely an academic construct but has deep roots in American society. The United States was founded to be different from the rest of the world (meaning Europe), and it would or at least could remain uncorrupted. As Thomas Paine explained, "We have it in our power to begin the world over again."[4] Much of this can be traced back to the fact that the thirteen colonies were dominated by a middle-class fragment, which, as Louis Hartz argued, meant that unlike Europe the United States never had a bourgeois revolution or a strong socialist movement, and this in turn helps explain why the United States feared and failed to understand the revolutions and radicalism abroad.[5]

The Soviet identity also held out its system as one that would eventually spread throughout the world, but its content, of course, was very different in being built around the proletariat, the centrality of class conflict, and the trans-

3 See www.let.rug.nl~usa/P/jc39/speeches/su78jec.htm, 8.
4 Thomas Paine, *Basic Writings of Thomas Paine* (New York: Willey, 1942), p. 65.
5 Louis Hartz, *The Liberal Tradition in America* (New York: Harcourt, Brace and World, 1955).

formation of individuals and societies. As Stephen Kotkin puts it, "From its inception, the Soviet Union had claimed to be an experiment in socialism, a superior alternative to capitalism, for the entire world. If socialism was not superior to capitalism, its existence could not be justified."[6]

An additional aspect of Soviet identity, one about which Soviet leaders were ambivalent, came from interaction with the United States. That was the role of the Soviet Union as a superpower, equal in status to its rival. The ambivalence stemmed from the fact that at least some Soviets associated being a great power with behaving like a "normal" state—that is, seeking narrow advantage and exploiting others rather than behaving in accord with socialist principles. But as Soviet power grew and a global reach became possible, the sense of the Soviet Union as being an equal of the United States became much more important. It increasingly rankled the Soviet leaders that the United States consistently upheld a double standard and denied them the right to do things that the United States did routinely—for example, intervene in the Third World, establish bases all over the globe, and play a central role in the Middle East. The Soviets then bent their efforts less to restricting American activities than to establishing the right for them to behave in the same way. Leonid Brezhnev and his colleagues placed great store in the Basic Principles Agreement of 1972 because it seemed to ratify their equality (Richard Nixon and Henry Kissinger did not take the agreement seriously and signed it just to humor the Soviets); détente broke down in part because of disagreements over whether the Soviets could emulate American behavior in the Third World. Status as well as specific privileges were involved. As Kissinger put it in a memo to prepare Nixon for a possible meeting with Aleksei Kosygin, "It has always been one of the paradoxes of Bolshevik behavior that their leaders have yearned to be treated as equals by the people they consider doomed."[7]

Symmetries and Asymmetries in Soviet and American Identities

Soviet and American identities had four major similarities or parallelisms, but they heightened rather than dampened the conflict. First, each implied a form of universalism in that there was nothing unique about the country that meant its values could not spread. Some countries do have identities that are

6 Stephen Kotkin, *Armageddon Averted: The Soviet Collapse, 1970–2000* (New York: Oxford University Press, 2001), p. 19. Melvyn Leffler sees the Cold War as a struggle in these terms: *For the Soul of Mankind* (New York: Hill and Wang, 2007).

7 "Memorandum from the president's Assistant for National Security Affairs (Kissinger) to President Nixon," (undated), in U.S. Department of State, *Foreign Relations of the United States, 1969–1976*, vol. 11, *Soviet Union, January 1969–October 1970* (Washington, D.C.: Government Printing Office, 2006), p. 603 (hereafter *FRUS*, with year and volume number).

bounded in this way. Thus, while the British believe they have a distinctive and highly valued way of life that has much to offer others, they do not expect the world ever to be entirely British. But for somewhat different reasons, neither the United States nor the Soviet Union felt this way: both were founded not on nationality or myths of blood and common heritage, but on ideas. The United States is famously a country of immigrants, one in which it was possible to be "un-American" by believing incorrect ideas. For the Soviets, universalism was built into the ideology from the start. There was nothing particularly Russian about Marxism, and indeed the triumph of this doctrine in a backward country was regarded as a fluke. Indeed, for the Soviets, and to a lesser extent the Americans, the validity of the founding principles would be upheld only if they triumphed elsewhere.

Second and relatedly, both the United States and the Soviet Union saw themselves as the standard-bearers of progress and modernity. It was taken for granted that historical advancement is real and that while there might be setbacks, other peoples would eventually follow the same path that they did. Furthermore, within the world and within each country, there were progressive and regressive forces, and the former deserved encouragement, if not active support.

Third, in a break from traditional European thinking about international politics, both the Soviet and the American ideologies implied that states' foreign policies were deeply influenced by their domestic systems. In the framework of Kenneth Waltz, they were "second-image" thinkers.[8] A balance of power might temporarily yield peace and security, but because of the primary role of the nature of the domestic regime, the world could be made safe for democracy (for the United States) or for communism (for the Soviet Union) only if it became dominant if not universal throughout the world.

Finally, perhaps because the United States and the Soviet Union emerged as the result of revolutions, each was prone to expect and seek transformations of politics. For the USSR, the nature of the class struggle meant that gradual change was unlikely. Politics was not about small advantages and adjustments of interests, but about the basic question of *Kto-Kogo*—who-whom, who is going to dominate and who is going to be dominated. Transformationism was not as prominent an element in the American worldview, but President George W. Bush did not have to conjure up from nowhere the argument that the invasion of Iraq would lead to the remaking of the Middle East. As Steven Sestanovich has argued, during the Cold War the United States often reacted to setbacks not by limiting its goals or adjusting its tactics, but by seeking major changes, and this approach had deep roots in American history.[9]

8 Kenneth Waltz, *Man, the State, and War* (New York: Columbia University Press, 1959).
9 Stephen Sestanovich, "American Maximalism," *The National Interest* 79 (Spring 2005): 13–23.

These similarities created a malign environment. Most fundamentally, they meant that while temporary agreements were possible, especially to minimize the danger of war, deep and long-run cooperation was not. A second-image view of international politics implies that the international conflict can end only when the other's fundamental beliefs and domestic arrangements change.[10]

One shared belief restrained conflict, however, and indeed may have saved the world from war. Each side believed that time was on its side, and that if war could be avoided, the long term would bring not only survival but also victory. The most dangerous combination of beliefs is short-run optimism coupled with long-run pessimism, which gives great impetus to preventive wars; fortunately, most of the Cold War was characterized by long-term optimism even as predictions about the short term oscillated.

Equally as important as these similarities are four asymmetries between Soviet and American identities. First, Soviet identity came from the top down, and it remains unclear exactly how much of it was adopted by the population at large. This made Soviet leaders wary of permitting contact between their citizens and outsiders, and indeed their worries proved to be well founded. Second, the American identity was much less self-conscious than the Soviet self-image, and the lack of American awareness gave a certain flexibility to policy and resilience to its sense of self. Third, Soviet identity pivoted not on what Soviet society was, but what it could be, and, relatedly, on what it should lead the world to be. American identity, although also looking to the future, was based on a view of what American society actually was (of course this self-perception was an idealized one). Because the Soviet identity represented beliefs about what would develop, it could lead to grave disappointments. Fourth, Soviet identity grew out of an explicit ideology, one that both predated the Soviet state and was formed in explicit opposition to capitalism, the main force it would confront during the Cold War. American identity developed more slowly and, although it could readily be pressed into service against the Soviet Union, originated in differentiation from Europe, and especially Britain, which was seen as tyrannical.

Perhaps the most important implication of the asymmetries was that domestic reverses and the failure of the world to move in desired directions would be corrosive to the Soviet regime and identity. This also helps explain what I think is the fact that the American identity was left relatively unscathed by the Cold War. This conflict left its mark on U.S. domestic society, politics, and economy, but the nation's sense of self was altered relatively little. Hartz

10 This is why I think the Cold War can be described as a "deep security dilemma" in which each side was an inherent threat to the other's security: Robert Jervis, "Was the Cold War a Security Dilemma?" *Journal of Cold War Studies* 3 (Winter 2001): 36–60.

hoped that its encounter with the world in the Cold War would lead the United States to better understand itself and the range of social processes operating in the world. This turned out not to be the case, however.

The Theoretical Context

The disputes over the importance of identity as a cause of Soviet or American foreign policy would seem to be a classic example of what international relations (IR) scholars call the level of analysis question and what historians talk of as "Primat der Innerpolitik" versus "Primat der Aussenpolitik." Much of traditional IR and diplomatic history argues that the main determinant of states' foreign policies is their external environments. This means not only the general context of international anarchy (i.e., the lack of sovereign power above national governments), but also the particular landscape of adversaries and allies through which the state must navigate. The fundamental contrast is to arguments asserting that international characteristics and domestic politics are crucial, that different states will behave differently despite similarities in their external situation, and that foreign policies are guided by domestic factors and often aimed at producing domestic change in others.[11]

How Identities Operate

While identity is internal, in two crucial ways it operates differently, however, from the factors discussed in the previous paragraph. By its very nature, an identity cannot be completely internal because it forms in response to others. To hold an identity is to set a boundary, to separate Self from Others, to exclude as well as include. Furthermore, the very act of separating people into groups, even without any rational basis, leads to an in-group bias. Conversely, conflict usually leads the actor to see the adversary in a way that maximizes the contrast with it.[12] Thus, differences between the United States and the Soviet Union, great as they were, were often exaggerated in the United States at the start of the Cold War when differentiation was most necessary. Although the totalitarian model of the USSR had significant validity and was readily accessible because of the previous experience with Nazi Germany, its widespread acceptance owned at least something to the contrast it provided to American individualism, freedom, and lack of state control.

---

11 For more discussions of the empirical implications of theories at different levels of analysis, see Robert Jervis, *Perceptions and Misperceptions in International Politics* (Princeton: Princeton University Press, 1976), ch. 1.

12 The classic account is Henri Tajfel and J. Turner, "An Integrative Theory of Intergroup Conflict," pp. 33–47 in William Austin and Stephen Worchel, eds., *The Social Psychology of Intergroup Relations* (Monterey, Calif.: Brooks/Cole, 1979).

The links between seeing others as different and having a hostile relationship with them are reciprocal. To paraphrase Charles Tilly, "identity makes conflict, and conflict makes identity." Although more attention has been paid to the influence of identity on conflict, the reverse is at least as strong. Thus, while the feeling of racial superiority may underlie much imperialism, the perception of racial differences and their central importance often follows rather than precedes conflict and domination. For the United States in much of the nineteenth and twentieth centuries, when leaders or countries became targets of enmity or acquisition, they developed darker skins.[13] Similarly, conflicts can magnify, or even create a collective sense of self. Catholics and Protestants in Northern Ireland deepened their communal ties and identity when they were attacked for being Catholic or Protestant; Bosnians had little sense of this as a meaningful category and held a held a relaxed view of Islam until they were driven from their homes for being Bosnian and Muslim. Identity can then come from how others define you.

In the modern era when states must claim and believe to be fighting for more than simple material advantage, the need to differentiate will entail both real and perceived changes. Thus, with the violent breakup of Yugoslavia, Serb and Croats tried to develop distinct languages from what had been a shared Serbo-Croatian. They claimed to be purging "their" language of words introduced by the other and to be returning to the ancient and pure version, but in fact they achieved much of the differentiation by developing new words. In the Cold War, each side shunned anything that smacked of the other. In the mid-1950s, in addition to adding the phrase "under God" to the Pledge of Allegiance, Congress replaced "E pluribus Unum" as the official national motto with "in God we trust," which was also put on paper money. Arguments against increased federal spending for education received added power from the association of central control of education with Soviet indoctrination, and communitarian measures that smacked of compulsion rather than voluntarism had to be avoided. Along with actual changes came perceptual changes and exaggerations. The degree to which American society was in fact individualistic was exaggerated and episodes and areas that were communal or communitarian were downplayed. The role of government, including state governments, in American economic development was slighted and the quality of American democracy was exaggerated.

The conception of democracy was also at least marginally influenced by the Cold War, just as American ideas on this topic had been shaped by previous encounters with enemies. For scholars in the 1930s influenced by the

---

13 This is clear from the illustrations in Michael Hunt, *Ideology and U.S. Foreign Policy* (New Haven: Yale University Press, 1987), although he stresses the causation flowing in the opposite direction.

Great Depression, democracy had a significant economic dimension, and substantive outcomes were included. But as the Cold War developed, scholars came to define democracy solely in terms of procedures such as competitive elections and a free press. There are good intellectual reasons for this formulation and it might have been adopted in any event, but it was no accident that it provided a sharper contract between the United States and the Soviet Union than did the older one.[14]

Tension, Détentes, and Identities: The Limits of Sustainable Claims

If identities can be shaped by conflict, perhaps one of the root causes of conflict is the need of one or both sides to establish and maintain them, which is difficult to do in a relaxed international system. This need could be conscious or unconscious and could arise either from popular pressures or elite manipulation. We should then expect the Cold War to be at its most bitter when identity is under most pressure and, conversely, cooperative policies to be pursued when identities are more secure. The argument is not without some plausibility, and we could see the early Cold War years as ones in which each side, having been challenged by world war and domestic upheavals, felt a loss of self and turned to a foreign enemy for confirmation and consolidation. But it is difficult to see later periods of détente as arising from secure identities,[15] and counterfactuals illustrate how the supposed connections between posited identity considerations and foreign-policy behavior can all too easily be fitted to any history that unfolded. Had the United States and the Soviet Union reached out to each other in the early period, one could attribute this behavior to the social and psychological security that came from winning the world war, and if the Cold War had coincided with extensive immigration into the United States, this line of thinking would lead us to conclude that American elites conjured up a foreign threat in order to Americanize the newcomers.

If the argument that conflicts are created to differentiate between populations and produce unity within them is too Machiavellian, the less extreme claim that conflict induces homogeneity is worth more consideration. This claim implies that conformity will rise and fall with international tensions. There is something to this, especially on the Soviet side. At the start of the Cold War, Joseph Stalin launched a campaign to denigrate the West and en-

14 Ido Oren, *Our Enemies and Us: America's Rivalries and the Making of Political Science* (Ithaca: Cornell University Press, 2003).

15 Indeed, it can be argued that it was domestic unrest that forced the leaders into détente: Jeremi Suri, *Power and Protest: Global Revolution and the Rise of Détente* (Cambridge: Harvard University Press, 2003).

sure that Soviet citizens had no contact with it. But we should not be too quick to accept the common claims for a parallel process in the United States. Although the stereotype of the late 1940s and 1950s is indeed one of conformity, it is far from clear that this is accurate. Abstract Expressionism, often held up as an example of the way in which the United States differentiated itself from the Soviet Union and sought to win over the Europeans by showing them that it had a significant culture, was transgressive and met with fierce resistance, not least from conservatives who strenuously objected to government-sponsored exhibits of it abroad.[16] While McCarthyism policed the liberal flank of acceptable views, its success was less attributable to widespread domestic sentiment than to calculations and maneuvers by the mainstream Republican leaders.[17] The foundations for the later success of the civil rights movement were also laid down in the early Cold War years, and Cold War concerns were largely responsible for the limited support for racial equality that was provided by the Dwight D. Eisenhower administration. International tension did not consistently solidify a narrow identity or slow social change in the United States.

The early Cold War years also saw heightened homophobia, justified in part by the claim that homosexuals were security risks, which was a self-fulfilling prophesy because as long as being gay was stigmatized, homosexuals were vulnerable to blackmail. But the subsequent changing course of American attitudes toward homosexuality does not track with increases and decreases in international tensions. Here as elsewhere, the influences on American culture were numerous and the Cold War was not the most potent one. Even more strikingly, the economic policies not only of Harry Truman but even of Eisenhower did not maximize the differentiation from socialism. Although the onset of the Cold War may have diminished liberal impulses, the role of the government in the economy in the 1940s and 1950s looks very large from today's perspective, with vigorous antitrust measures, a degree of economic planning, the consolidation of the welfare state, and high taxes on upper-income brackets. Many of the measures undertaken to meet the perceived Soviet threat increased federal direction of the society, most obviously the increased role of Washington in education, and an interstate highways project that literally reshaped the American landscape. Two general conclusions follow. First, international competition can lead to measures that do not easily fit with identity or can undermine it. Second, the fact that the United

16 Taylor Littleton and Maltby Sykes, *Advancing American Art: Painting, Politics, and Cultural Confrontation at Mid-Century* (Tuscaloosa: University of Alabama Press, 1989).

17 Michael Rogin, *The Intellectuals and McCarthy: The Radical Specter* (Cambridge: MIT Press, 1967).

States, unlike the Soviet Union, has a relatively strong society and a relatively weak state means that many of the forces acting on it came internally, and, while not unaffected by the course of the Cold War, had much autonomy from it.

Identity and the Standard View of the Cold War

Arguments for the importance of identity come through most clearly by contrast with what is the standard account, at least in IR, which is that the United States and the Soviet Union were "enemies by position," to use the felicitous phrase by Raymond Aron.[18] They emerged from World War II as the only superpowers; no other state could menace them and each by its capabilities menaced the other. The normal frictions of international politics, the desire by each country to ensure its own security, and—perhaps—expansionism by one or both sides then made the latent Cold War manifest.

This story is not all wrong, but it is incomplete. First, although both the United States and the Soviet Union were potential superpowers by dint of their size, they were able to play this role only when they mobilized significant domestic resources and placed themselves at the head of their respective blocs, something that only followed their clashes. Second and relatedly, bipolarity may tell us that each superpower would view the other warily, but structure and even specific instances of friction do not automatically produce the degree of hostility and fear that characterized the Cold War. Would hostility have grown as it did if the two superpowers had had compatible identities? Third, while it is true that each side thought that the other was menacing its interests, only to some extent can we explain how each conceived of its interests by reference to uniform and unchanging factors of international politics. Identity and interest can shape each other or even merge.[19] Each side's interest in many questions was defined in part by its identity, and the interactions of the contending interests in turn affected each side's sense of self. While the competition for Western Europe can perhaps be understood in terms of the need for countries to contend for the potential centers of power, the conflict over the Third World is not explicable in this framework, and it is to this topic that we will now turn.

18 Raymond Aron, *Peace and War: A Theory of International Relations,* trans. by Richard Howard and Annette Baker Fox (Garden City, N.Y.: Doubleday, 1966), p. 138; see also p. 544. I am indebted to Marc Trachtenberg for noting that this phrase does not fully reflect Aron's views of the conflict, which is less deterministic than this.

19 R. Brian Ferguson, "Introduction: Violent Conflict and Control of the State," pp. 1–58 in Ferguson, ed., *The State, Identity and Violence: Political Disintegration in the Post–Cold War World* (New York: Routledge, 2003).

Conflict in the Third World

At first glance, it might seem that Soviet-American competition in the Third World can be readily explained by traditional IR theories.[20] These tell us, after all, that major states struggle for power and advantage, that each will try to match what the other does, and that clients will be sought. Just as the European powers divided Africa and much of Asia during the period of imperialism, so the United States and the Soviet Union sought to spread their influence around the globe. But in fact the competitive logic of international politics does not lead to this conclusion. The most prominent IR theory, Waltz's neorealism, argues that because the superpowers were so much stronger than everyone else and able to balance against the adversary by mobilizing their internal resources, they did not need to pay much attention to the Third World.[21]

The power of identities and the related fact that each side understood the Cold War as a clash of social systems explains much here. With Europe and China having chosen one way of life or the other, the Third World represented the uncommitted states and peoples. What was at stake was nothing less than each side's view of the rightness of its cause, the universalism of its values, and the answer to the question of whose side history was on. Kissinger's reaction to Salvador Allende's election in Chile was particularly telling: "I don't see why we have to let a country go Marxist just because its people are irresponsible."[22] The idea that an educated and sophisticated country would choose a different path was deeply upsetting for reasons that go beyond standard interstate power competition.

The Soviets felt that supporting revolutionary forces was not only good international politics because it weakened the adversary, but also a revolutionary duty. The whole purpose of the Bolshevik Revolution was to lead others to the same path. One of the great surprises in Soviet archives was that the elites spoke the same way in private as they did in public. Politburo stationery bore the heading "Proletariats of the world unite!" and while this did not mean that Soviet security was to be risked to help foreign comrades, this mission was a central part of Soviet identity. Class conflict was the driver of politics,

20 For the best survey, see Odd Arne Westad, *The Global Cold War* (New York: Cambridge University Press, 2006). See also Robert McMahon, *The Cold War on the Periphery: The United States, India, and Pakistan* (New York: Columbia University Press, 1994); Jerry Hough, *The Struggle for the Third World: Soviet Debates and American Options* (Washington, D.C.: Brookings Institution, 1986).

21 Kenneth Waltz, *Theory of International Politics* (Reading, Mass.: Addison-Wesley, 1979); for a critique, see Jervis, *System Effects: Complexity in Political and Social Life* (Princeton: Princeton University Press, 1997), p. 118–22.

22 Quoted in Walter Isaacson, *Kissinger* (New York: Simon and Schuster, 1992), p. 290.

and without its revolutionary mission the Soviet Union would have no convincing self-justification.

The sense of being on the right side of historical forces and the duty to help them along come out nicely in the Kennedy-Khrushchev discussions—a mild word for the exchange—at Vienna in 1961. To the president's plea that events in the Third World had to be managed so that they were not unduly upsetting to either side,

> Mr. Khrushchev said that the West and the U.S. as its leader must recognize one fact: Communism exists and has won its right to develop.... The Soviet Union is for change. It believes that it is now in the political arena and it is challenging the capitalist system just as that system had challenged feudalism in the past. Mr. Khrushchev ... wondered whether the United States wanted to build a dam preventing the development of human mind and conscience. To do such a thing is not in man's power. The Spanish Inquisition burned people who disagreed with it but ideas did not burn and eventually come out as victors. Thus if we start struggling against ideas, conflicts and clashes between the two countries will be inevitable. Once an idea is born it cannot be chained or burned. History should be the judge in the argument between ideas.... Did the President want to say that Communism should exist only in those countries that are already Communist and that if Communist ideas should develop in the U. S. would be in conflict with the USSR? Such understandings of the situation is incorrect, and if there really is such an understanding, conflicts will be inevitable. Ideas do not belong to any one nation and they cannot be retracted.[23]

Although Khrushchev may have enjoyed tweaking his younger and less experienced counterpart, there is no reason to doubt his sincerity, just as there is no reason to doubt that he shared the sentiment that Anastas Mikoyan expressed to him that meeting Fidel Castro made him feel young again.[24]

Since the Third World started out as noncommunist, if not necessarily friendly to the United States, the main American objective was to keep it that way. Although it always hoped for the spread of democracy and American values, the primacy of blocking the Soviet Union meant that it was relatively open-eyed in its support of tyrannies when this proved necessary, as it often did. As President Kennedy explained in the aftermath of the assassination of Rafael Trujillo in the Dominican Republic, "There are three possibilities in

---

23 *FRUS, 1961–63*, vol. 5, pp. 174–76: for an interesting discussion of this conversation, see Vladislav Zubok and Constantine Pleshakov, *Inside the Kremlin's Cold War* (Cambridge: Harvard University Press. 1996), pp. 243–48.

24 Aleksandr Fursenko and Timothy Naftah, *"One Hell of a Gamble": Khrushchev, Castro, and Kennedy, 1958–1964* (New York: Norton. 1997), p. 39.

descending order of preference: a decent democratic regime, a continuation of the Trujillo regime, or a Castro regime. We ought to aim at the first, but we really can't renounce the second until we are sure that we can avoid the third."[25] The Soviets were also willing to be pragmatic and often supported friendly Third World countries that repressed the local communist parties, such as in Egypt. But on those occasions they had to tell themselves that these regimes, as bourgeois nationalists, were historically progressive and would eventually lead to socialism. This helps explain their continuing faith in the Third World despite the almost unbroken record of disappointment.

Of course neither side reacted to the Third World as it actually was, but to what they perceived, and each saw events and possibilities through the lens of their own experience, hopes, and fears. For both sides, modernization was crucial, but in quite different ways. The United States believed that revolutions and communism grew out of poverty and despair. If countries could be launched on the path of economic development, and if the difficult years of destabilizing transition could be weathered, then they would begin to resemble the West. Walt Rostow's *The Stages of Economic Growth* was the clearest statement of this outlook, but it was only one of a whole shelf of related volumes. The Soviet Union also placed great faith in modernization, which it was undergoing itself. The model of how it was leading its Asian populations to modernity was particularly important to it. This produced optimism, the sense that many Third World regimes were or soon would be ripe for revolution, and the perception that many Third World leaders had the skill and will to lead their countries to socialism at home and into alignment with the USSR. If the United States suffered from exaggerated fears, the Soviet Union held exaggerated hopes. Both saw the Third World in terms of their understanding of their own history.

Khrushchev, the Thaw, and the Third World

Both Soviet identity and the USSR's response to the Third World changed more than those on the American side, and this was not a coincidence. Khrushchev's de-Stalinization and the relaxation of domestic tensions ("the thaw," as it was called) were built on a less rigid view of the role of class and class conflict, just as reciprocally the earlier perception of a great threat from the capitalists made it seem dangerous to permit domestic relaxation. As Ted Hopf explains, acknowledging difference at home made the acceptance of differences abroad less threatening. When the distinction between workers and members of the bourgeoisie was taken to be either-or, with no mixtures

25 Quoted in Arthur Schlesinger, Jr., *A Thousand Days: John F. Kennedy in the White House* (Boston: Houghton Mifflin. 1995), p. 769.

or complex combinations possible, compromise was difficult at home and abroad; by making class only one of many possible identities for another state, the Soviet Union multiplied its possible relationships in the world.[26] The wider scope for what it meant to be a good Soviet citizen made it much easier for Khrushchev to see the bourgeois nationalist regimes as potential allies, as countries that were moving in the right direction rather than being irretrievably noncommunist. Indeed, local communist parties could be sacrificed because the local regime was acceptable and a more progressive outcome would come in due course. There was more than a dose of hypocrisy and traditional international political calculation in this thinking, but we may wonder whether it would have been possible without a change in the sense of what the USSR was.

The relations among the thaw, modifications of Soviet identity, and external relations bring us back to interactions. Identities are shaped by existing and desired relations as well as shaping them. The realization that the Third World was the best ground on which to compete with the West and that this would be possible only if the USSR courted regimes that were constituted differently was conducive to constructing a less rigid Soviet identity. What the Soviet *New Times* said in its retrospective survey of 1955 also characterized the changes in domestic attitudes: "The desire to find what unites countries, not disunites them, became a universally accepted slogan."[27] Similarly, the pressing need for relaxing tension with the West in order to decrease the danger of war and gain access to Western economic resources and technology not only provided a strong impetus to peaceful coexistence, but also made it more likely that Soviet leaders would adjust their self-image to be consistent with the new policy. People want to think of themselves as principled and consistent, and so their beliefs about many things, including themselves, will be modified to justify their behavior.

Détente, Identity, and the End of the Cold War

The relations between identity and foreign policy are brought out well by the 1969–75 détente and the end of the Cold War, and to compare them brings us back to the asymmetry between the Soviets and American identities. What is most important for my analysis is the decline of détente, but this cannot be examined without some discussion of its origins and course. As usual, we know more about the American side, for which Vietnam was central, Nixon inherited a bloody and unpopular war and like Lyndon Johnson before him,

---

26 Ted Hopf, *Social Construction of International Politics: Identities and Foreign Policies, Moscow 1953 and 1999* (Ithaca: Cornell University Press. 2002), p. 41, 92

27 Quoted in ibid., 94.

could neither win it nor afford a defeat. For Johnson and Nixon, what was at stake was the credibility of American commitments around the world, and the importance of credibility was greatly enhanced by a nuclear strategy that stressed the role of resolve and signals in producing deterrence in an era when total war meant total destruction.[28] This also meant that it was not so much defeat that was unacceptable as it was defeat of a type that would produce these unfortunate effects. Thus, if the communists won not by pushing out American troops, but only after a "decent interval" following an American withdrawal, the harm to the United States would be less and the domino effects could be greatly attenuated. Furthermore, if the Soviet Union could be pressured into helping end the war, it might not take the American actions as indications of weakness.

Such a "soft landing" was also needed for reasons more closely related to identity, as an open defeat in Vietnam could undermine the self-confidence of the American public, and perhaps of the U.S. leaders. From the start of the Cold War, the U.S. elite worried that the public lacked the steady nerves that the struggle required and was prone to vacillate between defeatism and excess fear on the one hand and unwise bellicosity on the other.[29] Defeats were particularly dangerous because they could lead to an overreaction in either direction, and if the United States was to keep on track, the war had to be ended in a way that minimized its adverse consequences. If American leaders worried about domino effects,[30] they knew the big domino was American public opinion. Nixon new that public support for the war was weak and declining but even if it ended badly, as long as the public believed that the peace came with a modicum of honor, the American self-image as a country willing to stand up for its allies and to its principles could be preserved.

Soviet motives for détente both overlapped and differed, and also were partly related to identity. For them, Vietnam was both a danger and an opportunity. The danger was that the war could spread. Chinese influence could grow, and chances for economic relations with the West would decline. (In fact, Soviet-American relations entered such a deep freeze that President Johnson and Soviet Ambassador Dobrynin were reduced to discussing whether the Broadway musical *Hello Dolly* would be permitted to travel to the USSR.) The benefits of the war were equally obvious: the United States was wasting its efforts, dividing its alliances, and alienating much of the Third World. Furthermore, for the Soviets, Vietnam had intrinsic value as a revolutionary

28 For further discussion, see Jervis, "Domino Beliefs," in this volume.

29 Gabriel Almond, *The American People and Foreign Policy* (New York: Harcourt Brace, 1950); the excellent rebuttal twenty years later does not change the fact that this was widely believed: see William Caspary, "'The Mood Theory': A Study of Public Opinion and Foreign Policy, *American Political Science Review* 64 (June 1970): 536–47.

30 See Jervis, "Domino Beliefs," in this volume.

movement, and they had the duty to support it as this was the raison d'être for Soviet existence. Even had it not been for competition with the People's Republic of China (PRC), it would have been very difficult for the Soviets to cooperate with the United States in a way that kept South Vietnam non-communist.[31]

For them, as for the Americans, the Third World was also important, but in a quite different way. As Brezhnev explained in 1976, détente did "not abolish or alter the laws of class struggle."[32] The Soviets hoped that by stabilizing the central issues of arms and Europe, détente would allow them to proceed with competition in the Third World from a position of equality. Being treated as an equal was both a necessary part of a robust policy in the Third World and a valued end in itself. The Revolution had truly arrived: Moscow was recognized as a power equal to Washington; the capitalists finally realized that communism was permanent; this would now set the stage for its eventual triumph. For the Soviets, détente offered a great opportunity to confirm what they were.

The Decline of Détente

At bottom, détente failed because the two sides had incompatible expectations.[33] The United States saw the easing of tensions as a way to maintain the status quo in the face of its weakness; the Soviets saw it as a way to attain equal status and gains in the Third World. Although a variety of calculations, miscalculations, and accidents were at work, even under the best circumstances détente could not have brought the Cold War to an end, because the United States and the Soviet Union, being founded on such different principles, were inherently a threat to each other as long as they were what they were. For the Soviets, there were then real limits beyond which détente could progress if it meant restraining itself in the Third World; the policies that were dictated by the Soviet conception of its interests and duties meant that it would be hard to maintain good relations for long in the face of U.S. resistance.

It remains unclear whether Nixon and Kissinger pursued détente in truly cooperative terms and thought that it might be semi-permanent. This is the view expounded by Kissinger in the first two volumes of his memoirs and

31 The best discussion of the challenge posed for the United States in Vietnam and the rest of Asia by the Sino-Soviet split is Thomas Christensen, *Worse than a Monolith: Alliance Politics and Problems of Coercive Diplomacy in Asia* (Princeton: Princeton University Press, 2011).

32 Quoted in John Soars, Jr., "Strategy, Ideology, and Human Rights: Jimmy Carter Confronts the Left in Central America, 1979–1981," *Journal of Cold War Studies* 8 (Fall 2006): 59.

33 For an exaggerated but interesting argument along these lines, see Eric Grynaviski, *Constructive Illusions: Misperceiving the Origins of International Cooperation* (Ithaca: Cornell University Press, 2014).

vigorously attacked by Raymond Garthoff, who argues that the administration never ceased pursuing unilateral advantage.[34] In the aftermath of the fall of the Soviet Union, however, Kissinger dropped his earlier stance and endorsed Garthoff's, using the third volume of his memoirs to argue that he saw détente as a way of gaining breathing space until the public would support a harder line, and claiming that the United States made no concessions in the hopes of establishing long-term cooperation. For our purposes, what is crucial is that Kissinger's second view implies that the USSR remained a revolutionary power, driven by its ideology and identity. Whether or not this view was correct, to the extent that American policymakers believed it, détente could not have been permanent.

From the start, détente was opposed by neoconservatives who argued not only that the United States was getting the worse end of the bargain, but that the very notion of détente was flawed because it abandoned America's deepest ideals of supporting the forces of freedom throughout the world. Although some of the critics were opportunistic in seeking domestic political advantage, their stance was effective because it represented a strong reaffirmation of American identity and the parallel claim that the Soviets were driven by theirs. A détente that accepted a communist Soviet Union was a betrayal of American values and would at most buy a temporary respite since it could not tame the expansionist Soviet policy that stemmed from its identity. Furthermore, such a policy would sacrifice domestic support because even if Kissinger, Nixon, and Gerald Ford were realists, the bulk of the American population remained truer to traditional American values.

Jimmy Carter's presidency embodied and magnified the contradictions in Kissinger's view. On the one hand, Carter and some of his advisers thought the United States had exaggerated the Soviet threat and believed that there was a great deal of common interest that could be realized through diplomacy— the United States and Soviet Union were, after all, normal states. On the other hand, he and others in his administration believed that the Soviet Union would press the United States wherever possible throughout the world yet was itself vulnerable because its domestic system, which drove its foreign policy, was increasingly recognized as a failure. Carter, who viewed human rights as a matter of principle, also saw that Soviet failings here were an additional Soviet weakness.

But even had Carter ignored human rights, détente probably would have failed. The Soviets saw a number of opportunities to support movements and states in Africa that they believed to be progressive, if not revolutionary. The United States was being forced to grudgingly acknowledge Soviet equality,

---

34 Raymond Garthoff, *Détente and Confrontation: American-Soviet Relations from Nixon to Reagan* (Washington, D.C.: Brookings Institution, 1994).

and even if the Soviet moves harmed relations with the United States, this was a price worth paying. Some of the gains came in traditional power-political terms, but at least as important was the Soviet feeling that they could not be true Soviets if they abandoned the progressive cause. This played a role in the dispatch of troops to Afghanistan that gave the coup de grâce to détente. Not only would the USSR lose a client on its borders, but a potentially socialist state would revert to the forces of reaction.

Conclusion

The Cold War ended when Soviet identity shifted, and Reagan refused to reciprocate Soviet concessions until he believed that this was occurring. This provides a fundamental contrast with the earlier détente. The change in Soviet policy and identity, furthermore, grew out of comparisons and interactions with the West.

Mikhail Gorbachev and his colleagues realized that the Soviet system was failing. But this failure was relative, not absolute. The economy was not collapsing, indeed it was growing a bit. There was no starvation or privation, and despite the concern of Soviet military leaders, the large and secure nuclear arsenal was adequate to deter an American attack. The inadequacies of the Soviet performance appeared only when compared to the capitalist world. This had always been true, but in the past Soviet leaders could tell themselves that they were catching up. The contrast between East and West Germany was particularly striking since many of the other excuses of the weak socialist performance were implausible there. Furthermore, increased travel and contacts with the West meant that more members of the Soviet elite understood the situation, which undermined their confidence in their system and the beliefs that had produced it. The prospects for competition in the Third World by military activities, foreign aid, or serving as a model of development all appeared to have dimmed. Since the Third World represented the future, impending failure there cast doubt on Soviet prospects. Even more centrally, the knowledge that socialism had failed to out-compete capitalism struck at the core of Soviet beliefs about themselves and the world.

To reform the Soviet economy, Gorbachev needed better relations with the West to reduce military spending and gain access to Western investment and technology. Thus, he began a series of initiatives and concessions, mostly dealing with arms control. These were accompanied by a basic shift in outlook toward world politics, summarized in the phrase "new thinking." Whether these ideas were largely rationalizations for policies forced on him by pressing circumstances or whether they were autonomous and more freely adopted is heatedly debated but is of less importance here than the fact that the new thinking implicitly if not explicitly contradicted key elements of Soviet identity. Not only was lowering international tensions given priority over supporting progressive movements, but also the sources of tension were located in the traditional dynamics of international conflict, especially misperceptions and spirals of unnecessary hostility and fears, In arguing that Soviet isolation and Western belligerence were largely brought on by ill-advised Soviet actions, Gorbachev adopted what IR scholars call security dilemma analysis. Although not new to Western observers, this line of thought not only was innovative in the Soviet context but also constituted a denial of the crucial idea that politics pivots around class conflict. Thus, at the 27th Party Congress in 1986, for the first time there was no mention of the "world revolutionary process," and by December 1988 Gorbachev abandoned talk of defending the "Socialist Commonwealth," of supporting progressive revolutions, and of the dangers from "American imperialism."[35]

Once Gorbachev and his colleagues concluded that they needed a deep rapprochement with the West, it was hard for them to maintain that the difference between the Soviet and American social systems had to be central to their relationship. So it is no accident that Yegor Ligachev, who opposed Gorbachev's policies, claimed, "We proceed from the class nature of international relations. [Any other approach] only confuses the Soviet people and our friends abroad."[36] Once class conflict was dropped, little remained of the unique Soviet identity and mission in the world. Even if the Soviets thought that their system was more humane and progressive than capitalism, there was no reason to believe that Soviet security required keeping the West on the defensive, resisting concessions on arms control, or maintaining Soviet clients in the Third World. As Marx and Engels had said, the revolutionizing power of capitalism was so great that under its influence "all that is solid melts into air."[37]

Gorbachev famously declared that he was going to do something terrible to the United States—he was going to deprive it of an old enemy. In fact, what is striking is how little the United States actually changed after the Cold War. While Soviet identity was formed in opposition to a capitalist world, American identity did not need communism, and the United States came out of the Cold War with little more knowledge of itself or others then it had at the start. Whether the American identity would have withstood prolonged reversals

35 Jon Jacobson, *When the Soviet Union Entered World Politics* (Berkeley: University of California Press, 1994), p. 30; minutes of the Politburo, December 27–28, 1988, in *Cold War on International History Project Bulletin* 12/13 (Fall/Winter 2001): 24–29.

36 Quoted in Robert English, *Russia and the Idea of the West* (New York: Columbia University Press, 2000), p. 25.

37 Karl Marx and Friedrich Engels, *The Communist Manifesto* (New York: Monthly Review Press, 1968), p. 7. Of course, Marx and Engels were referring to the displacement of precapitalist systems by the rise of the bourgeoisie, but the point to have more general validity.

abroad or falling behind the USSR in economic and technological competition is an interesting question. Certainly American self-confidence was shaken at a number of points, especially in the late 1950s and early 1960s. But having deep roots in its own society and history, the American identity had a resilience that the Soviet one did not. Although American society changed markedly during the Cold War, it is far from clear that it would have been much different had those years been peaceful or characterized by conflict with a different adversary. Furthermore, to the extent that American identity did change during the Cold War, there was a broadening of sense of self, a greater tolerance for diversity, and, at least until the late 1970s, the acceptance or a greater role for government in many spheres of life,[38] just the opposite what we would expect if-the Cold War had led to an exaggeration of those features that separated the United States from the USSR.

It is not hindsight that leads to the conclusion that the asymmetries outlined earlier were crucial. Maintaining Soviet identity depended on the future unfolding according to plan: a cooperative worker's society was to be put in place, the Soviet Union was to modernize, class conflict would dominate until the workers prevailed, and the superiority of communism would be demonstrated by overtaking the West and by the triumph of revolutions abroad. Until these hopes were dashed only limited détentes were possible, and these would be undermined by the refusal of the other side to give up the competition. Conversely, when the hopes faded and politics was not seen as dominated by class conflict, there was no reason for the Soviet Union to either menace or fear the United States, and once American leaders concluded that the Soviet domestic system was changing, issues that had bedeviled the relationship for so long were easily resolved. The Cold War ended only when one side's identity did; it could not have ended peacefully otherwise.

38 Jacob Hacker and Paul Pierson, *American Amnesia: How the War on Government Led Us to Forget What Made America Prosper* (New York: Simon and Schuster, 2016).

PART IV

Psychology and National Security

9

Deterrence and Perception

In the most elemental sense, deterrence depends on perceptions. But unless people are totally blind, we need not be concerned with the logical point that if one actor's behavior is to influence another it must be perceived. Rather, what is important is that actors' perceptions often diverge both from "objective reality" (or later scholars' perceptions of it, which is as good a measure as we can have) and from the perceptions of other actors. These differences, furthermore, both randomly and systematically influence deterrence. Unless leaders understand the ways in which their opposite numbers see the world, their deterrence policies are likely to misfire; unless scholars understand the patterns of perceptions involved, they will misinterpret the behavior.

An example both shows that the problem extends to perceptions of third parties, as well as to those of main adversaries, and underlines the way in which attempts at deterrence could not only fail but also backfire if the assumptions about others' perceptions are incorrect. To mobilize British assistance in the American-Japanese political conflict of 1907–8, President Theodore Roosevelt sought to portray the situation as quite tense. He expected that Britain would then aid him by restraining Japan. Unfortunately, and contrary to the president's assumption, the British perceptions of both him and the Japanese differed from those that Roosevelt held: "The British felt it was Washington, not Tokyo, which stood in need of a warning." As Sir Charles Hardinge, the permanent undersecretary of the foreign office, put it, "[T]he President is playing a very dangerous game, and it is fortunate that he has such cool-headed people as the Japanese to deal with."[1] Thus, rather than

---

1 Charles Neu, *An Uncertain Friendship* (Cambridge: Harvard University Press, 1967), p. 199.

moving Britain closer to the United States, as Roosevelt expected, his actions made that country less willing to cooperate in opposing Japan.

In light of the dangers inherent in misperceptions, one might expect that statesmen would pay careful attention to how others perceive them. In fact, this is usually not the case. While they are aware that determining others' intentions and predicting others' behavior is difficult, they generally believe that their own intentions are clear, especially when they are not expansionist. As a result, they rarely try to see the world and their own actions through their adversary's eyes,[2] although doing so would be to their advantage. If a policy is to have the desired impact on its target, it must be perceived as it is intended;[3] if the other' behavior is to be anticipated and the state' policy is a major influence on it, then the state must try to determine how its actions are being perceived. One would think, therefore, that every government would establish an office responsible for reconstructing the other's view of the world and that every policy paper would have a section that analyzed how the alternative policies would be seen by significant audiences. One theme of this essay is that the failure to undertake this task—and I do not mean to imply that it would be easy to accomplish—explains many cases of policy failure. It is hard to find cases of even mild international conflict in which both sides fully grasp the other's views. Yet all too often statesmen assume that their counterparts see the world as they see it, fail to devote sufficient resources to determining whether this is actually true, and have much more confidence in their beliefs about the other's perceptions than the evidence warrants.

Misperception and the Failure of Deterrence

It is a simplification but serviceable to say that one actor deters another by convincing him that the expected value of a certain action is outweighed by the expected punishment. (This puts aside the other's perceived costs and benefits on not taking the action.) The latter is composed of two elements: the perceived cost of the punishments that the actor can inflict and the perceived probabilities that he will in fact inflict them. Deterrence can misfire if the two sides have different beliefs about either factor.

---

2 The British tried to do this, with some success, during World War II: see Donald McLachlan, *Room 39* (New York: Atheneum, 1968), pp. 252–58.

3 Of course accidents can lead to desired ends in ways decision-makers had not intended, but I do not think this is common. One example may be the U.S. Navy's unauthorized harassment of Soviet submarines in the Cuban missile crisis, which probably helped convince the Soviet leaders that the confrontation was too dangerous to be permitted to continue. See Alexander George, David Hall, and William Simons, *The Limits of Coercive Diplomacy* (Boston: Little, Brown, 1971), pp. 112–14.

(MIS)PERCEPTIONS OF VALUE

Judging what constitutes harm is generally easier than estimating whether threats will be carried out, but even here there is room for differences that can undermine deterrence. On occasion, what one person thinks is a punishment another may consider a reward. The model is Br'er Rabbit. Only rarely do states in international politics want to be thrown into a briar patch; but Teddy Roosevelt's threat to intervene in the Cuban internal conflict of 1903 comes close. He declared that, if American property were raided in the course of the fighting, he would have to send in troops. Unfortunately, both factions believed that American intervention would work in their favor and busily set to work harassing Americans and their property.[4]

One could not have coerced Pol Pot by threatening to destroy his cities and a similar, if less extreme, point lies behind some of American strategic policy in the 1970s and 1980s. As former Secretary of Defense Harold Brown argued, the United States must "take full account of the fact [sic] that the things highly valued by the Soviet leadership appear to include not only the lives and prosperity of the peoples of the Soviet Union, but the military, industrial and political sources of power of the regime itself."[5] This required targeting the army, internal security forces, and the Communist Party. A related argument was that the Soviet leaders were ethnic Russians who cared about maintaining the dominance of Great Russia and who would be deterred by the threat to attack it but spare the other areas of the USSR, thereby enabling the other nationalities to rise up and either gain their independence or dominate the postwar state. Without endorsing the answers he provided, one can agree with Brown's argument that "our strategy has to be aimed at what the Soviets think is important to them, not just what we might think would

---

4 Allan Millet, *The Politics of Intervention* (Columbus: Ohio State University Press, 1968). The point is nicely made in an anecdote about a British General made by B. H. Liddell Hart: "Jack Dill was a delightful man for any enthusiast to meet or serve. But he was quite unable to understand that the average officer did not share his burning ardour for professional study and tactical exercises. An illuminating example of that incomprehension occurred in his way of dealing with the major commanding a battery attached to his brigade who had failed to show the keenness Dill expected. To emphasize his dissatisfaction Dill told this officer that he would not be allowed to take part in the remaining exercises—a punishment, drastic in Dill's view, which was a great relief to the delinquent, who had been counting the days until he could get away to join a grouse-shooting party in Scotland": *The Liddell Hart Memoirs, 1895–1938* (New York: Putnam, 1965), p. 72.

5 Harold Brown, *Department of Defense Annual Report Fiscal Year 1981* (Washington, D.C.: U.S. Government Printing Office, 1980), p. 67. It should also be noted that if these arguments are correct, the threat to carry out these attacks would be no more credible than the threat to attack Soviet cities, because there would be no reason for the Soviet response of retaliating against American cities to be different.

be important to them."[6] But this kind of analysis must be carried to its logical conclusion, not stopped at a point that is convenient to the analyst's political predilections. To argue that the Soviets could be deterred by threatening to destroy the party and internal security forces implies not only that these instruments were needed to maintain communist rule, but also that the Soviet leaders realized this. This may be correct, but if they believed what they said, they would have thought that the regime enjoyed the support of the population and so concluded that the party would regenerate after the war.

As we have seen, threats of coercive war can misfire if the state does not understand what the opponent values. Threats to use brute force, on the other hand, do not involve this pitfall, but they do require the state to determine how its adversary evaluates the military balance and estimates who would win a war. This issue arose in the 1930s as the British leaders debated how to deter Hitler. Some felt that "economic stability," which required that military spending be kept relatively low, contributed to this goal:

> The maintenance of our economic stability ... [could] be described as an essential element in our defense system ... without which purely military effort would be of no avail.... Nothing operates more strongly to deter a potential aggressor from attacking this country than our stability.... This reputation stands us in good stead, and causes other countries to rate our power of resistance at something far more formidable than is implied merely by the number of men of war, airplanes and battalions which we should have at our disposal immediately on the outbreak of war. But were other countries to detect in us signs of strain, this deterrent would at once be lost.[7]

On the other hand, Churchill stressed the need for larger military forces: "an immense British army cast into the scales" was a great deterrent "and one of the surest bulwarks of peace."[8] Neither side in the argument, however, tried to learn how Hitler saw the world and what sort of configuration of forces might have deterred him.

Deterrence can also be undercut if the aggressor does not understand the kind of war that the state is threatening to wage in response to an attack. The Japanese had no doubt that the United States would fight if they attacked Pearl Harbor. But many of Japan's leaders thought that the stakes for the United States were not sufficiently high to justify an all-out effort and that the Americans would instead fight a limited war, and, being unable to prevail at that

6 U.S., Congress, Senate, Committee on Foreign Relations, *Hearings on Nuclear War Strategy* (Washington, D.C.: U.S. Government Printing Office, 1981), p. 10.

7 Sir Thomas Inskip, Minister for Coordination of Defense, quoted in Martin Gilbert, *Winston S. Churchill,* vol. 5, *1922–1939* (London: Heinemann, 1976), p. 891.

8 Quoted in ibid., 945.

level of violence, would agree to a settlement that would give Japan control of East Asia. Similarly, Hitler expected Britain and France to fight in September 1939 but doubted that they would continue to do so after Poland was defeated. Britain especially, he believed, had sufficient common interest with Germany to conclude a peace treaty after limited hostilities. In neither case did either side understand the other's beliefs or values. Indeed, the German and Japanese perceptions of their opponents would have seemed to the latter so out of touch with reality as to hardly deserve consideration. British and American leaders knew their own outlooks so well that they thought it obvious that others knew them also. To have recognized that alternative views were possible would have implied that their self-images were not unambiguously correct and that their past behavior might be interpreted as indicating a willingness to sacrifice friends and agree to less than honorable settlements.

Because Britain, France, and the United States did not understand the other side's expectations, their deterrence strategies could not be effective. Their task was not only to convince their adversaries they would fight if pushed too far, but also that they would continue to fight even after initial reverses.[9] Doing this would have been extremely difficult since it would have involved presenting evidence and making commitments about how they would behave a few years later under grave circumstances. But had the statesmen been aware of the German and Japanese perceptions, they might have at least made some efforts. For example, President Franklin Roosevelt could have stressed the American tradition of vacillating between isolation and extreme involvement in international politics, of seeing the world in Manichean terms, of fighting only *unlimited* wars. Prime Minister Chamberlain might have done better explaining why he had abandoned appeasement, why Britain could not allow any power to dominate the continent, and why it would have no choice but to resist even if the military situation was bleak. Similarly, throughout the 1960s, the United States misjudged how much North Vietnam valued reunification and believed that an American threat to fight a prolonged war and inflict very heavy punishment on the North[10] could dissuade the North from continuing its struggle. American decision-makers paid a great

9 Churchill had a better understanding of the problem. In 1938 he stressed to a German diplomat that "a war, once started, would be fought out like the last to the bitter end, and one must consider not what might happen in the first few months, but where we should all be at the end of the fourth year." Quoted in ibid., 964. For a related argument, see Alan Alexandroff and Richard Rosecrance, "Deterrence in 1939," *World Politics* 29 (April 1977): 404–24.

10 As Walt Rostow put it, "Ho has an industrial complex to protect; he is no longer a guerilla fighter with nothing to lose." Quoted in Department of Defense, *Pentagon Papers*, edited by Sen. Mike Gravel (Boston: Beacon Press, 1971), vol. 3, p. 153. That North Vietnam absorbed almost unprecedented punishment is shown by John Mueller, "The Search for the Single 'Breaking Point' in Vietnam: The Statistics of a Deadly Quarrel," *International Studies Quarterly* 24 (December 1980): 497–519.

deal of attention to how to make their threats credible, but their misjudgment led them to ignore what was actually the crucial problem—that the North was willing to fight the sort of war the United States was threatening rather than concede.[11] The Americans might not have been able to solve the problem even had they been aware of it, but, as it was, they never even came to grips with it.

(MIS)PERCEPTIONS OF CREDIBILITY

Misperceptions of what the target state values and fears probably are less important causes of deterrence failure than misperceptions of credibility. Conclusions are difficult to draw in this area, however. Although many arguments about deterrence turn on questions involving credibility, scholars know remarkably little about how these judgments are formed and altered. For example, how context-bound are these estimates? Obviously the credibility of a threat is strongly influenced by the specific situation in which it is issued. The threat to go to war in response to a major provocation could be credible, when the threat to respond in this way to a minor insult would not. But there also is a component of credibility that inheres in the threatener, not the situation. In the same circumstance, one country's threat can be credible where another's would not be. Part of this difference of course comes from the country's strength, its ability to carry out the threat, and its ability to defend against the other's response. But there's more to it than this. Some states have reputations for being bolder, more resolute, and more reckless than others. That is, states are seen to differ in the price they are willing to pay to achieve a given goal. But it is not clear how these reputations are established and maintained or how important they are compared to the other influences on credibility. We cannot predict with great assurance how a given behavior (e.g., refusing to change one's position on an issue) will influence others' expectations of how the state will act in the future.[12]

To start with, does reputation attach to the decision-maker, the regime, or the country? If one president acts boldly, will other states' leaders draw inferences only about him or will they expect his successors to display similar resolve? After a revolution, do others think the slate has been wiped clean or does the reputation of the earlier regime retain some life? If one kind of regime (e.g., a capitalist democracy) displays willingness to run high risks, do

---

11 For what we now know about the North's perspectives and values, see Pierre Asselin, *A Bitter Peace: Washington, Hanoi, and the Making of the Paris Agreement* (Chapel Hill: University of North Carolina Press, 2002); Lien-Hang Nguyen, *Hanoi's War: An International History of the War for Peace in Vietnam* (Chapel Hill: University of North Carolina Press, 2012).

12 In the years since this essay was written, in 1982, the literature on reputation has greatly increased, spurred by Jonathan Mercer's *Reputation and International Politics* (Ithaca: Cornell University Press, 1996). I do not think I need to change what is said here, however.

others draw any inferences about the resolve of similar regimes? How fast do reputations decay?

On these points we have neither theoretically grounded expectations nor solid evidence. In another area, we at least can be guided by a good theory. One of the basic findings of cognitive psychology is that images change only slowly and are maintained in the face of discrepant information. This implies that trying to change a reputation for low resolve will be especially costly because statements and symbolic actions are not likely to be taken seriously. Only the running of what is obviously a high risk or engaging in a costly conflict will suffice. On the other hand, a state with a reputation for standing firm not only will be able to win disputes by threatening to fight, but has the freedom to avoid confrontations without damaging its image. But these propositions, although plausible, still lack empirical evidence. The question of the relative importance of beliefs about the state's general resolve as compared to the role of other factors is also impossible to answer with any precision. How often do states make overall judgments about the prices others are willing to pay as opposed to looking primarily at the specific situation the other is in? In other words, how context-bound are estimates of how others will behave?[13] The debate over the validity of the domino theory reminds us both of the importance of this topic and the difficulty of coming to grips with it. If others were more impressed by America's eventual defeat in Vietnam than by the fact that it was willing to fight for years for a country of little intrinsic value, they would adjust downward their estimate of American resolve. But did they, and if so by how much? When the new situation closely resembles a previous one in which the actor displayed low resolve, others are likely to expect similar retreat.[14] But when the situation is different, it is not clear whether a judgment of the state's overall resolve has much impact on others' predictions of its behavior. It is easy to attribute any behavior contrary to American wishes to the lack of resolve which some observers think the United States displayed in Indochina. But it is much harder to establish that this is a better explanation of U.S. behavior than local conditions or general trends such as the increase of Soviet power.[15]

---

13 This question can be linked to the "levels of analysis" problem in international politics—i.e., the question of whether the main causes of a state's behavior are to be found in its internal characteristics or its external environment—but a full discussion would take us far afield.

14 For a paradoxical exception to this generalization, see discussion of the *Mayaguez* incident below.

15 The best study, Ted Hopf, *Peripheral Visions: Deterrence Theory and American Foreign Policy in the Third World, 1965–1990* (Ann Arbor: University of Michigan Press, 1994), shows that the Soviets doubted that the United States would resist their moves in the Third World, but the reason was not that they thought that the loss in Vietnam revealed that the United States had little resolve, but that the effort had exhausted the United States and changed its resolve. For

We can turn this example around and ask about the impact of the U.S. attempt to rescue the hostages in Iran in 1978. Others probably raised their estimates of the likelihood that the United States would respond similarly in other cases in which American citizens were taken prisoner. But were perceptions of American resolve to run risks in other kinds of situations altered? One of the main arguments in favor of using force was that such perceptions would indeed be changed, that U.S. promises and threats would be more credible. But scant evidence supports this view. The cost that the United States foresaw in this case was not Soviet intervention, but adverse Third World reaction; would others have expected the United States to act strongly in later situations when the costs to be incurred were of a very different kind? Others would draw such an inference if they employed the concept of "willingness to incur costs" or "propensity to act with boldness" as a homogeneous category. They might, of course, be correct to do so. The willingness to act in the face of Third World opinion might be linked to a willingness to defy the threat of a Soviet military response. But we know little about whether broad characterizations hold true or whether leaders think that they do.

One can also ask whether the inference would have been different had the rescue mission succeeded, or had it resulted in the death of the hostages. Ironically, this same logic dictates that the impact on U.S. credibility would have been greater in the latter case than in the former. Had the hostages been killed, observers would probably have thought that the American leaders knew the operation was terribly risky. If they projected this pattern of risk taking onto later events, they would conclude that the United States would act even when it might not succeed. By contrast, if force had succeeded and others assumed that the Americans had been confident that this was going to be the result, they would not see the act as so bold. I admit this argument is strained, and indeed I doubt that observers would follow the train of reasoning I have presented. But this uncertainty underscores the difficulty of determining the inferences people do draw in these situations.

The crucial question is the degree to which observers make general judgments about others' credibility rather than basing their predictions largely on the nature of the specific situation and, if the situation is a continuing one, on the history of the other's behavior concerning it.[16] To a significant extent, deterrence theory rests on the assumption that such general judgments are important. It is this which makes it both possible and necessary for a state to credibly threaten to react to an attack on an unimportant third country by a

---

further discussion of actions that can change rather than reveal actors' types and the problems this creates for standard approaches, see Jervis, "Signaling and Perception," in this volume.

16 I put aside here the possibility that the behavior will change the actor's willingness to run risks: see "Signaling and Perception," in this volume.

response that will involve greater costs than the intrinsic value at stake. Such a threat can be credible because what the state will lose by not responding is not just the third country, but also its reputation for protecting its interests, a reputation that is more valuable than the costs of fighting. By the same logic, this response is necessary, because to fail to rise to the challenge is to lead others to doubt the state's willingness to pay costs to defend the rest of the status quo. Both prongs of this reasoning depend on actors making relatively context-free judgments of credibility.

Even if they do, the way in which these judgments are made can defeat significant aspects of the theory and practice of deterrence. When an actor either carries out or reneges on a threat, observers can make either or both of two kinds of inferences that will influence her future credibility. First, they may alter their estimate of what I have elsewhere called his "signaling reputation"— that is, her reputation for doing what she says she will do.[17] The bargaining tactic of commitment, so well-known in deterrence literature, is supposed to be effective because the state increases its cost of retreating by staking its reputation on standing firm. But this tactic will work (and this explanation of actors' behavior will be appropriate) only if actors try to determine how likely it is that others will live up to their promises and threats rather than predicting their behavior solely on the basis of estimates of what they value and the prices they are willing to pay to reach various objectives. This is the second kind of inference that actors draw from others' past behavior. It ignores statements and other signals that can be easily manipulated and looks only at whether the other stood firm, compromised, or retreated in the past, irrespective of what she said she would do. If this kind of inference is dominant, then signals of commitment have little impact.

To use Schelling's terms, actors would be able to issue warnings, but not threats.[18] This would mean that an actor could not deter others by symbolically committing himself to a course of action and staking his reputation on living up to his pledges.

Finally, an ironic possibility should be noted. A concern for reputation can lead states to act and draw inferences in a pattern opposite from the one that we and most other analysts imply. This is not to dispute the common starting point; states often refuse to back down not because of the immediate and direct costs of doing so, but because of the belief that a retreat will be seen as an indication of general weakness and so lead others to expect retreats

17 Robert Jervis, *The Logic of Images in International Relations* (Princeton: Princeton University Press, 1970; 2nd ed, New York: Columbia University Press, 1989), pp. 20–26, 66–112; Jervis, "Signaling and Perception," in this volume; Anne Sartori, *Deterrence by Diplomacy* (Princeton: Princeton University Press, 2005).

18 Thomas Schelling, *The Strategy of Conflict* (Cambridge: Harvard University Press, 1960), pp. 123–24.

in the future. But the desire to counteract such undesired consequences may lead a state that has retreated on one issue to pay especially high costs to avoid defeat on the next one. Thus the United States was not only willing but anxious to use force to free the *Mayaguez* because it wanted to show others that its withdrawal from Indochina did not mean that it would not defend its other interests—the very consequence that it had predicted would follow from a defeat in Vietnam and that justified its participation in the war. If others understand this logic and expect states to behave in this way and to follow retreats with displays of firmness, then reputations for carrying out threats do not influence estimates of credibility because, to compound the paradox, reputations are so important that states must rebuild them when they are damaged. If you have been caught bluffing in poker, are others likely to call you in the next round in the belief that you bluff a lot or are they unlikely to do so because they think that you know it is no longer safe to bluff? To the extent that the latter is the case, perceptions of credibility are influenced by the state's recent behavior, but in a way that produces equilibrating negative feedback rather than the positive feedback of the domino dynamics.[19]

JUDGING THE ADVERSARY'S ALTERNATIVES

Deterrence may fail and defenders be taken by surprise not only if their threats are insufficiently credible or directed at the wrong values, but also if they fail to grasp the expansionist's dismal evaluation of the alternatives to fighting. Although the deterring state realizes that its adversary has strong incentives to take action—or else deterrence would not be necessary—it usually thinks that the latter has a wide range of choice. Furthermore, the deterring state almost always believes that the adversary is tempted to act because of the positive attraction of the gains he hopes to make. In fact, however, the other state often feels that it has little choice but to act because, if it does not, it will not merely forgo gains, but will also suffer grave losses.[20] Status quo powers often underestimate the pressure that is pushing the other to act and therefore underestimate the magnitude of threat and/or the degree of credibility that will be required to make the other refrain from moving. The pressures

19 It is possible, of course, that under some circumstances a retreat leads statesmen to expect other retreats and that under other conditions they draw the opposite inference, but we do not know enough to specify the conditions. I have discussed this deterrence theory paradox at greater length in *System Effects: Complexity in Political and Social Life* (Princeton: Princeton University Press, 1997), pp. 271–75.

20 Ole Holsti, "The 1914 Case," *American Political Science Review* 59 (June 1965): 365–78; Richard Ned Lebow, *Between Peace and War: The Nature of International Conflict* (Baltimore: Johns Hopkins University Press, 1981); Jervis, "Prospect Theory: The Political Implications of Loss Aversion," in this volume.

felt by Japan in the fall of 1941 and by China in the fall of 1950 illustrate why the target state can feel it must act even though it knows some sort of war will result. China and Japan perceived the alternative to fighting not as maintaining the status quo—which was tolerable—but as permitting a drastic erosion of the positions they had established. Because the United States did not understand this, it did not grasp the difficulty of the job of deterrence that it was undertaking. This is one reason why it thought that its superior power was sufficient to keep the adversary at bay.

The case of the Chinese entry into the Korean War is especially striking since the United States did not even grasp the Chinese fear that, if the U.S. conquered North Korea, it would threaten China. Deterrence failed; but more than this, the deterrence strategy could not be adequately crafted since it was not based on a correct assessment of what the other side valued and feared. Similarly, the basic question of whether deterrence was possible was not adequately faced. In neither instance did the United States consider that even a well-developed deterrence policy might fail and therefore that it should balance the costs of war against the costs of making concessions; since deterrence seemed likely to succeed, the painful alternative of sacrificing some values and abandoning some foreign policy goals was not to be taken seriously.

Self-Deterrence

The previous sections provided some reasons why inaccurate or conflicting perceptions can lead to failures of deterrence. Most treatments of this subject deal with cases like surprise attacks in which statesmen incorrectly believe that they have deterred others. While this problem is fascinating and important, we should not neglect the less dramatic other side of this coin: states can successfully deter others unintentionally or unknowingly. Because actors can perceive things that are not there, they can be deterred by figments of their own imagination—"self-deterrence," if you will. An example is the British fear throughout the 1930s that Germany would wipe out London at the start of a world war.[21] Although the Germans fed this fear by exaggerating their air strength, the enormity of the gap between the British beliefs and the German activities indicates that most of the explanation must lie with the former's perceptual predispositions. Ingenious deception schemes rarely work unless they fit with what the target already believes.

The British made two notable errors. First, they greatly overestimated the damage that would be caused by each ton of bombs dropped. Perhaps even more startling than the fact that their estimate was off by a factor of twenty-five

21 The most thorough treatment is Uri Bialer, *The Shadow of the Bomber: The Fear of Air Attack and British Politics, 1932–1939* (London: Royal Historical Society, 1980).

is the low level of effort that they put into developing the estimate.[22] Since British policy rested in significant measure on the belief that war would entail what would later be called "unacceptable damage," one would think that great care would have been devoted to estimating how much damage aerial bombardment would cause. In fact, almost all British analyses rested on a simple and badly biased extrapolation from the few raids on London during World War I. No competing studies were generated; no alternative sources of data or methods were used.

This error was compounded by a fundamental misreading of German air policy and air strength. The British belief that Hitler had the intent and the capability to make British cities his prime target was incorrect on both counts. The German air force was predominantly designed to support ground troops. Doctrine, plans, and aircraft for strategic bombardment did not exist.[23] The effort Germany mounted in the summer of 1940 in circumstances that neither side anticipated was an improvised one.

Part of the explanation for these errors is that the German bombing raids in World War I left a strong imprint on the decision-makers. The public had demanded greater protection and panic had been a significant problem. But I do not think that purely cognitive or unmotivated factors were of primary importance. That is to say, the misperceptions and miscalculations cannot be accounted for by innocent intellectual and information-processing errors, such as mislearning from history, which would have been corrected had they been pointed out to the decision-makers. Rather, the errors served important functions and purposes for those who were making them. To a significant extent, the errors were motivated ones, in the sense of being useful to the actors, of facilitating valued actions, positions, or attitudes. We usually adduce perceptions and calculations as proximate explanations of decisions. But in this case the main causation runs the other way: the pessimistic assessments of German bombing were as much the product of policies as they were a cause of them.

This seems a particularly odd argument in this context, because the decision-makers were conjuring up mythical threats that restricted their country's freedom of action and eventually undermined its security. Nevertheless,

---

22 For a good discussion, see Paul Bracken, "The Unintended Consequences of Strategic Gaming," *Simulation and Games* 8 (September 1977): 300–315.

23 Even during the first years of the war, Hitler did not pay careful attention to the bombing campaign against Britain. See R. J. Overy, "Hitler and Air Strategy," *Journal of Contemporary History* 15 (July 1980): 410–12. Later Hitler placed great faith in the new terror weapons, the V-1 and the V-2, but he never analyzed the probable effect of these weapons with any care. For an argument that takes partial exception to the view expressed here, see Williamson Murray, "The Luftwaffe before the Second World War: A Mission, a Strategy?" *Journal of Strategic Studies* 4 (September 1981): 261–70.

different sectors of the British elite had different reasons for finding the fear of bombardment congenial. The Royal Air Force (RAF), which produced and analyzed much of the intelligence on which the estimates were based, was predisposed to believe in a potent German bombing threat because its identity as a separate service rested on the efficacy of strategic bombardment. To have recognized that the German air force's main mission was ground support would have introduced the question of whether Britain's air force should not be similarly employed. For the same reason, the RAF resisted the idea that defense against bombers might be possible and insisted that counter-bombardment was the only effective peacetime deterrent and wartime strategy. It was the civilian leaders, especially the Minister for Co-ordination of Defense, Sir Thomas Inskip, who saw that changing technology allowed fighters to destroy a sufficient proportion of bombers to make defense against prolonged bombing feasible.

Proponents of appeasement and anti-appeasement also had reasons to accept the pessimistic air estimates. For the appeasers, the estimates were useful by showing that the costs of war would be terribly high, thus reinforcing the need for international conciliation. The British could contemplate opposing Germany only if they were sure that their vital interests were at stake. If the issue were only the British abhorrence of the German domestic regime and its uncouth behavior, or the mere possibility that German aims were unreasonable, confrontations were too costly to be justified. Furthermore, if the threat were from the air, the British response had to be in the same realm. Little money could be spared for the other services, especially the army. This fit the appeasement policy nicely because a defense posture based on air power would limit spending and facilitate a foreign policy that would remain within British control rather than requiring close cooperation with allies. Before 1914 the cabinet had become partly committed to France through joint naval planning and when it decided for war found that the only war plan available subordinated the British army to the French. In the 1930s, such cooperation would imply prewar ties that could interfere with appeasement and drag England into a dangerous anti-German stance. This danger could be avoided by a military policy that shunned a large army.

Ironically, the anti-appeasers also had reasons to overestimate German air strength. They thought Hitler was highly aggressive and therefore expected him to build what they believed would be a maximally effective air force. Failing to see the German weaknesses and inefficiencies, they expected the air fleet would be larger than it was. Being preoccupied with their own fears—they vastly underestimated the staying power of the working class—they were sure that Germany was planning to rely on weapons of terror. A month after Hitler came to power, Robert Vansittart, the permanent undersecretary of the foreign office, argued that the Germans were "likely to rely for their military power ... on the mechanical weapons of the future ... and above all [on] military aircraft.... Aviation in particular offers Germany the quickest and easiest way of making their power effective."[24] "It must ... be remembered," Churchill said in 1936, "that Germany has specialized in long-distance bombing airplanes."[25] This misreading also fit nicely with the attempts to mobilize the British public. The greater the German air force, the greater the British air force should be. Furthermore, the high estimates implied that Germany was aggressive, since it was building more than its defense required.

The British, then, did much of Hitler's work for him. While he did seek to deter Britain, the British perceptions cannot be completely explained by the German behavior. British fantasies, developed by different groups for different reasons, inhibited accurate analysis of the German air threat and led decision-makers to accept pessimistic views. As a result, the fact of deterrence far outran the German policy of deterrence.

In parallel, American hawks in the Cold War who argued that the Soviets were gaining usable nuclear superiority in the 1970s and 1980s may have produced a degree of self-deterrence by imputing to the Soviets (incorrectly, it turns out)[26] the belief that they had the upper hand and so could stand firm in crises with the United States, in which case the only rational American response would be to back down.

Limits to Rationality

Most arguments about deterrence, including those made above, assume that both sides are fairly rational. Some of the general problems raised by this claim have been treated elsewhere.[27] Here I want to focus on four barriers to accurate perception that reduce actors' sensitivity to new information and limit their ability to respond to unexpected situations.

24 Quoted in D. C. Watt, "British Intelligence and the Coming of the Second World War in Europe," in Ernest May, ed., *Knowing One's Enemies: Intelligence Assessment Before the Two World Wars* (Cambridge: Harvard University Press, 1984), p. 268.

25 Quoted in Gilbert, *Winston S. Churchill*, 797.

26 John Hines et al., *Soviet Intentions 1965–1985*, vols. 1 and 2, (Washington, D.C.: BDM, September 22, 1995), available at http://nsarchive.gwu.edu/nukevault/ebb285/. Also see Pavel Podvig, "The Window of Vulnerability That Wasn't: Soviet Military Buildup in the 1970s," *International Security* 33 (Summer 2008): 118–38.

27 See, for example, Philip Green, *Deadly Logic* (Columbus: Ohio State University Press, 1966); Patrick Morgan, *Deterrence* (Beverly Hills: Sage, 1977); Robert Jervis, "Deterrence Theory Revisited," *World Politics* 31 (January 1979): 299–301, 310–12.

OVERCONFIDENCE

First, there is solid evidence from laboratory experiments and much weaker, but still suggestive, evidence from case studies that people overestimate their cognitive abilities. For example, people's estimates of facts usually are less accurate than they think. When asked to give a spread of figures such that they are 90 percent certain that the correct answer lies somewhere between them, most people bracket the true figure only 75 percent of the time.[28] Similarly, people generally overestimate the complexity of the way they use evidence. They think they are tapping more sources of information than they are, overestimate the degree to which they combine evidence in complex ways, and flatter themselves by thinking that they search for subtle and elusive clues to others' behavior. Acting on this misleading self-portrait, people are quick to overreach by trying mental operations they cannot successfully perform. Thus, when people are given a little clinical training in judging others' psychological states, they make more errors than they did previously because they incorrectly think they can now detect all sorts of peculiar conditions.[29] Overconfidence is also exhibited in the common rejection of the well-established finding that simple computer programs are superior to experts in tasks like graduate student admissions and medical diagnoses which involve the combination of kinds of information amenable to fairly objective scoring.[30] People believe that, unlike a simple computer program, they can accurately detect intricate, interactive configurations of explanatory or predictive value. In fact, their abilities to do so are very limited.

Although a full explanation of this phenomenon is beyond the scope of this chapter, overconfidence is probably fed by three factors. First, many of our cognitive processes are inaccessible to us. People do not know what information they use or how they use it. They think some information is crucial when it is not and report that they are not influenced at all by some data on

---

28 Baruch Fischhoff, Paul Slovic, and Sara Lichtenstein, "Knowing with Certainty: The Appropriateness of Extreme Confidence," *Journal of Experimental Psychology: Human Perception and Performance* 3 (1977): 552–564. Good applications to international politics are Dominic Johnson, *Overconfidence and War: The Havoc and Glory of Positive Illusions* (Cambridge: Harvard University Press, 2004), and Johnson and Dominic Tierney, "The Rubicon Theory of War," *International Security* 36 (Summer 2011): 7–40. Robert A. Burton, *On Being Certain: Believing You Are Right Even When You're Not* (New York: St. Martin's, 2008) examines when and why we feel certain.

29 Stuart Oskamp, "Overconfidence in Case-Study Judgments," *Journal of Consulting Psychology* 29 (1965): 261–65.

30 For a review of this literature, see Lewis Goldberg, "Simple Models or Simple Processes? Some Research on Clinical Judgments," *American Psychologist* 23 (July 1968): 483–96.

which in fact they rely.[31] This makes it easier for them to overestimate the sophistication of their thought processes. Second, a specific aspect of this lack of awareness is that people often rely more than they realize on analogies with past events, especially recent events that they or their country have experienced firsthand.[32] Since these events seem clear in retrospect, much of this certainty is transferred to the current situation. A third cause of overconfidence, also linked to lack of self-awareness, is that people not only assimilate incoming information into their preexisting beliefs, a point to which we will return, but do not know they are doing so. Instead, they incorrectly attribute their interpretations of events to the events themselves; they do not realize that their beliefs and expectations play a dominant role. Thus, people see evidence as less ambiguous than it is, think that their views are steadily being confirmed, and so feel justified in holding to them ever more firmly.

Some of the consequences of overconfidence for deterrence strategies are best seen in light of the two other perceptual handicaps, and so the discussion of them should be postponed. But some effects can be noted here. First, statesmen are likely to treat opposing views quite cavalierly since they are often quite sure that their own beliefs are correct. Cognitive dissonance theory asserts that this intolerance arises only after the person has made a firm decision and has become committed to a policy, but our argument is that it occurs earlier, when even a tentative conclusion has been reached. Second, decision-makers tend to overestimate their ability to detect subtle clues to the other's intentions. They think it is fairly easy to determine whether the other is hostile and what sorts of threats will be effective. They are not sufficiently sensitive either to the possibility that their conclusions are based on a cruder reading of the evidence or to the likelihood that highly complex explanations are beyond their diagnostic abilities. Third, because decision-makers fail to realize the degree to which factors other than the specific events they are facing influence their interpretations, their consideration of the evidence will be less rational than they think it is and less rational than some deterrence strategies require. For example, while people realize that it makes no sense to believe that another country is likely to be an aggressor just because a state they recently faced was one, in fact the previous experience will greatly increase the chance that the state currently under consideration will be seen as very dangerous. Similarly, beliefs about the kinds of deterrence strategies that will be effective are also excessively affected by recent successes and failures.

31 Richard Nisbett and Timothy Wilson, "Telling More Than We Can Know: Verbal Reports on Mental Processes," *Psychological Review* 84 (1977): 231–57. Later research is summarized in Wilson, *Strangers to Ourselves* (Cambridge: Harvard University Press, 2002).

32 Robert Jervis, *Perception and Misperception in International Politics* (Princeton: Princeton University Press, 1976; 2nd ed. 2017), ch. 6.

ASSIMILATION OF NEW INFORMATION
TO PREEXISTING BELIEFS

The most pervasive and significant cognitive process is the tendency for people to assimilate new information into their preexisting beliefs, to see what they expect to be present. As I have discussed at length elsewhere,[33] ambiguous or even discrepant information is ignored, misperceived, or reinterpreted so that it does minimum damage to what the person already believes. Although this tendency is not always irrational and does not always decrease the accuracy of perception, it creates a variety of problems for deterrence strategies. First, images of other states are difficult to alter. Perceptions do not quickly respond to new information about the other side; once a statesman thinks he knows whether the other needs to be deterred and what kind of strategy is appropriate, only the most dramatic events will shake him.[34] Those who see the other side as an aggressor usually argue that if this image is incorrect, the other can easily demonstrate that its bad reputation is not warranted. In fact, the ambiguity of most evidence coupled with the absorptive power of most beliefs means that an inaccurate image may not be corrected at a point when the situation can still be controlled.

An important analytical question that arises in many cases of deterrence failure and other situations in which one country is surprised by what another does, even though surprise was not intended, is whether the failure was one of signaling or of perception. That is, did one state fail to make its intentions clear and credible or did the target miss what it should have picked up? Of course both are possible, judgments are difficult, and we do not have enough studies to support a generalization. But it is clear that expectations can screen out threats that observers who held different preconceptions would have found credible. Perhaps the most important case is the German failure to anticipate that Britain would fight in 1914 if a continental war developed. The historiography is large and contested, but I believe that conversations between the British Foreign Secretary, Sir Edward Grey, and the German ambassador, while not without ambiguity, should have led a reasonable listener to see that British entry into the war was likely. The fact that when Britain did join, the ambassador did not share the sense of betrayal felt by his superiors in Berlin indicates that the latter were not perceptually ready to hear the message (in part because they had lost their faith in the ambassador).[35]

33 Jervis, *Perception and Misperception* (1976), 143–72, and "Understanding Beliefs," in this volume.

34 Glenn Snyder and Paul Diesing, *Conflict Among Nations* (Princeton: Princeton University Press, 1977), pp. 389–404.

35 For a good summary of the latest thinking, see the special issue of *International History Review* on "Sir Edward Grey and the Outbreak of the First World War," vol. 38 (April 2016).

Expectations that Britain would stay out were strong and supplemented by the motivated biases discussed in the next sections because it would have been painful for German leaders to see that Britain would fight.

Related, cognitive impediments place sharp limits on the degree to which deterrence strategies can be fine-tuned, limits that are more severe than statesmen generally realize. For example, states commonly try to develop policies that exert just the right amount of pressure on the other—that is, enough to show the other that the state is very serious, but not enough to provoke desperate behavior. At the tactical level, intricate bargaining maneuvers are planned and subtle messages are dispatched. For example, in the discussions within the U.S. government in early 1965 about what sort of troops to send to Vietnam, Assistant Secretary of Defense John McNaughton dissented from the view that the initial deployment should be the Marines. The problem, he argued, was that the Marines would bring with them "high profile" materiel such as tanks, which would indicate to the North that the United States was in Vietnam to stay. It would be better to send the 173rd Airborne Brigade, which lacked heavy equipment; this would signal to Hanoi that the United States would withdraw if a political settlement could be reached.[36] But even if the actions are carried out as the decision-maker wants them to,[37] precision is often defeated by the screen of the other side's perceptual predispositions. As a result, while subtlety and sophistication in a policy are qualities that observers usually praise and statesmen seek, these attributes may lead the policy to fail because they increase the chance that it will not be perceived as it is intended. It is hard enough to communicate straightforward and gross threats; it will often be impossible to successfully apply complex bargaining tactics that involve detailed and abstruse messages. Furthermore, because it is very hard to tell what others have perceived, statesmen often fail to see that they have failed to communicate.

Finally, since discrepant information is likely to be misinterpreted, deterrence strategies must be tailored to the other's preexisting beliefs and images, thus limiting the range of strategies that can succeed. Because the inferences which the other draws are largely determined by its initial beliefs, acts which will deter one decision-maker will be ignored or interpreted differently by another. If the perceiver thinks that the state is deeply concerned about the issue and has high resolve, deterrence will be relatively easy. If he has the opposite view, it will take great efforts to make a credible threat. But unless the state's leaders know what the other side thinks, they will neither know

36 *Pentagon Papers*, 421.

37 Most studies of policy implementation reveal that this rarely happens. For a nice analysis that combines bureaucratic and perceptual factors that complicate attempts at coercion, see Wallace Theis, *When Governments Collide* (Berkeley: University of California Press, 1980).

what they have to do to deter it nor be able to judge the chances of success. A frequent cause of deterrence failure is the state's misdesign of its actions growing out of incorrect beliefs about its adversary's perspective. For example, American leaders were taken by surprise in October 1962 because they thought it was clear to the Soviet Union that placing missiles in Cuba would not be tolerated. Since the Americans believed that the Soviets were not likely to run high risks, they found it hard to imagine that the USSR would try to establish a missile base abroad. U.S. leaders did not think that great efforts at deterrence were necessary because they did not realize that the move would not look risky to the Soviets.[38]

Leaders sometimes think that disagreements about how to proceed can be clarified if not resolved by a fresh look. But often the best the person's initial beliefs will tell us more about what she will see than will the new evidence. In a classic case, President Kennedy put off a decision on Vietnam pending the return a "fact-finding" mission staffed by a State Department official and a representative of the Department of Defense. When they came back and delivered starkly different assessments, "Kennedy looked quizzically from one to the other: You two did visit the same country, didn't you?'"[39] In effect, they didn't because they really visited their own minds. In the same way, one can often make better predictions about how a state will interpret others' behavior by knowing the former's predispositions than by knowing what the latter actually did. Unfortunately, statesmen rarely appreciate this and, to compound the problem, usually have a much better idea of what they think they are doing and what messages they want to convey than they do of what the others' perceptual predispositions are. The difficulty is two-fold and two-sided. The fact that perceptions are strongly influenced by predispositions means that it is very difficult to convey messages that are inconsistent with what the other already believes. And the fact that statesmen do not understand this influence reduces their ability to predict how others will react. Even if decision-makers understood the problem, prediction would be difficult because it is so hard for them to grasp the way in which others see the world. But in this case they would at least realize that many of their messages would not be received as they were sent. Since this understanding is often lacking, decision-makers' messages not only convey different meanings to each side, but each is usually unaware of the discrepancy. Statesmen are then likely to err both in their estimates of what the other side intends by its behavior and in their beliefs

38 Klaus Knorr, "Failures in National Intelligence Estimates: The Case of the Cuban Missiles," *World Politics* 16 (April 1964): 455–67. For an alternative argument, see Richard Ned Lebow, "The Cuban Missile Crisis: Reading the Lessons Correctly," *Political Science Quarterly* 98 (Autumn 1983): 431–58.

39 Roger Hilsman, *To Move a Nation: The Politics of Foreign Policy in the Administration of John F. Kennedy* (Garden City, N.Y.: Doubleday, 1967), p. 502.

about how the other is reading their behavior. Severe limits are thus placed on the statesman's ability to determine whether and what kind of deterrence strategy is called for and to influence the other's perceptions in a way which will allow this strategy to succeed. A failure to understand these limitations imposed by the way people think will make it more difficult for scholars to explain state behavior and, more importantly, will lead a statesman to attempt overly ambitious policies that are likely to bring his country to grief.

NOT SEEING VALUE TRADE-OFFS

The third important mental process that influences deterrence is the motivated propensity for people to avoid seeing value trade-offs.[40] That is, to minimize psychological discomfort people often believe that the policy they favor is better than the alternatives on several logically independent value dimensions. For example, those who favored a ban on nuclear testing believed that the health hazards from testing were high, that continued testing would yield few military benefits, and that a treaty would open the door to further arms control agreements. Opponents disagreed on all three counts. This kind of cognitive consistency is irrational because there is no reason to expect the world to be arranged so neatly and helpfully that a policy will be superior on all value dimensions. I am not arguing that people never realize that a policy that gains some important values does so at the price of others, but only that these trade-offs are not perceived as frequently and as severely as they actually occur.

This impediment has several implications for deterrence. First, it complicates the task of balancing the dangers entailed by issuing threats with the costs of making concessions. Rather than looking carefully at this trade-off, statesmen are likely to be swayed by one set of risks and then evaluate the other costs in a way that reinforces their initial inclinations. For example, a decision-maker who is preoccupied with what she and her state will sacrifice if she compromises on an issue is likely to convince herself that the danger of war if she stands firm is slight; the statesman who concludes that this danger is intolerably high is likely to come to see the costs of retreating as low. As long as the risk on which she focuses is in fact the greater one, and as long as the situation remains unchanging, this minimization of the trade-off is not likely to lead the decision-maker to choose a policy that differs from the ones she would have adopted had she been more rational. But if either of these two conditions is not met, then the quality of the policy will suffer. Thus, if the decision-maker focuses first on the risks of war and finds that it looms large,

---

40 For a further discussion of this, see Jervis, *Perception and Misperception* (1976), pp. 128–42, and "Understanding Beliefs," in this volume.

she may incorrectly judge the costs of retreating as less. She could then abandon a policy of deterrence when rationality would dictate maintaining it.

In other cases, a decision-maker who has decided to stand firm may minimize the value trade-off by failing to take full account of the costs of her position. For example, she may come to believe that, while conciliatory measures would lower the short-run risk, they would increase the danger over a longer period by leading the adversary to think that it was safe to trifle with the state's interests. In this arrangement of perceptions and evaluations, standing firm appears preferable to being conciliatory on both the dimension of prevailing on the issue in dispute and the dimension of avoiding war.[41]

The failure to face trade-offs also helps explain the tendency for states to become overextended, to refuse to keep ends and means in balance, and to create more enemies than they can afford. For example, in the years preceding World War I, Germany added Russia and Britain to its list of enemies. On top of the conflict with France, this burden was too great even for a state as strong as Germany. Although both international and domestic factors were also at work, the psychological difficulty of making trade-offs should not be overlooked. When the German leaders decided to drop the Reinsurance Treaty with Russia in 1890, they perceived minimum costs because they expected that ideological conflict would prevent Russia from joining forces with Germany's prime enemy, France. Similarly, the decision to build a large navy and pursue a belligerent policy toward England was based on the assumption that England's conflicts with France and Russia were so deep that eventually British leaders would have to seek an understanding with the Triple Alliance. German statesmen did not see that their policy involved a greater risk of turning Russia and Britain into active enemies than was entailed by the rejected alternative policy of conciliation and compromise.

This failing was not peculiar to Germany. French policy between 1882 and 1898 sought both to rebuild a position of strength against Germany and to contest English dominance of Egypt. To pursue either objective meant risking war with one of these countries. This might have been within the bounds of French resources; war with both was not. So an effective policy required France to set its priorities and decide whether it cared more about its position in Europe or about colonial issues. For over ten years, however, French leaders refused to choose, instead thinking that the same policy could maximize the chances of gaining both goals. It took the shock of England's willingness

---

41 Jack Snyder, "Rationality at the Brink," *World Politics* 30 (April 1978): 345–65. But for the phenomenon to fit the analysis here, the value dimensions must be logically independent. This will not be true if both the perceptions of the need to stand firm and evaluations of the costs of not doing so are produced by a coherent image of the adversary.

to go to war in the Fashoda crisis for French statesmen to realize that they could not afford too many enemies and had to make a hard choice.

President Jimmy Carter's foreign policy provides a final example. To most of the goals of the preceding Ford Administration, the president added an increased concern with preventing proliferation and protecting human rights. He and his advisers did not seem to appreciate that pushing states on one front might diminish their ability to push them on others. Only when crises arose to clarify the mind did they decide to relax the human rights pressures in order to increase the chance of enlisting support for what were taken to be the more important national security goals. But by this time, a large price had been paid in terms of antagonizing others and appearing hypocritical; the overly ambitious initial policy jeopardized America's ability to achieve more limited goals.

Defensive Avoidance

A related impediment to accurate perception that can complicate or defeat deterrence is also affective rather than purely cognitive. In a process known as defensive avoidance, in which the pressures of political and psychological needs cripples people's ability to perceive and understand threatening stimuli.[42] Thus Paul Schroeder has argued that the British images of Russia in the period leading up to the Crimean War cannot be explained either by Russian behavior or by long-standing and deeply imbedded cognitive predisposition but rather were caused by shifting British needs to see Russia as threatening or accommodating.[43] Whether England tried to deter Russia or conciliate with it depended on internal factors that were neither rationally related to foreign policy goals nor susceptible to Russian influence. Similarly, states may come to think that it is relatively safe to challenge the adversary's deterrent commitments when a modicum of rational analysis would indicate that the risks far outweigh the slight chances of success if domestic or foreign needs for a challenge are very strong.

This is not to deny that the costs of yielding can be so high as to rationally justify a challenge that the statesman knows is likely to fail; this may be unfortunate for the state but is not troublesome in terms of perceptions. Rather my point here is that the knowledge of the high costs of accepting the status quo can lead statesmen to ignore or distort information about the costs of challenging it. Thus, Lebow shows that the reason why India in 1962, the United

42 The fullest discussion is in Irving Janis and Leon Mann, *Decision Making* (New York: Free Press, 1977).

43 Paul Schroeder, *Austria, Great Britain, and the Crimean War* (Ithaca: Cornell University Press, 1972).

States in the fall of 1950, and the Soviet Union before the Cuban missile crisis were not able to see that their adversaries would inflict painful rebukes if they persisted was that they were preoccupied with the costs they would pay if they did not.[44] The failure of the American attempts to deter Japan mentioned earlier provides another example. The feeling that acquiescing to the American demands was intolerable led the Japanese to adopt an unrealistically favorable view of the alternative because the only way they could avoid facing the need to sacrifice very deeply held values was to believe that the United States would fight a limited war. That their conclusion was driven by this need rather than by objective analysis is indicated by the quality of their deliberations: "Instead of examining carefully the likelihood that the war would in fact be a short, decisive war, fought under optimum conditions for Japan, contingency plans increasingly took on a strangely irrational, desperate quality, in which the central issue, 'Can we win?' was shunted aside. Rather, it was as if Japan had painted itself into a corner."[45] The result is that deterrence can be difficult if not impossible. Threats that should be credible and effective, even when the cognitive impediments discussed above are not operating, may be missed or misread. It usually will be hard for the deterrer to realize that it is facing this danger, and even an understanding of the situation will not easily yield an effective policy since the other's perceptual screens are often opaque.

Conclusion

It is obvious but sometimes forgotten that deterrence only works—or fails to work—through perceptions. Threats may not be noticed, capabilities that the actor has (or believes that he has) may be dismissed by perceivers, and potential punishments that the actor believes to be powerful may be ones the perceiver finds tolerable. In other cases, of course, deterrence may work when the actor and disinterested observers think that it should not. The United States inadvertently coerced Iran when the latter mistakenly interpreted the American accidental shooting down of its airliner over the Persian Gulf in

44 Lebow, *Between Peace and War*. Also see Richard Cottam, *Foreign Policy Motivation* (Pittsburgh: University of Pittsburgh Press, 1977); Alexander George and Richard Smoke, *Deterrence in American Foreign Policy* (New York: Columbia University Press, 1974); and Jack Snyder, *The Ideology of the Offensive: Military Decision Making and the Disasters of 1914* (Ithaca: Cornell University Press, 1984), which does a particularly fine job of separating motivated from unmotivated errors. Sharp-eyed readers will note a shift from some of my earlier views on this point. For further discussion, see Robert Jervis, "Political Decision Making: Recent Contributions," *Political Psychology* 2 (Summer 1980): 89–96. For later views, see Jervis, Lebow, and Janice Stein, *Psychology and Deterrence* (Baltimore: Johns Hopkins University Press, 1985).

45 Robert Scalapino, introduction to James Morley, ed., *The Fateful Choice: Japan's Advance into Southeast Asia, 1939–1941* (New York: Columbia University Press, 1980), p. 119. Also see Gordon Prange, *At Dawn We Slept* (New York: McGraw-Hill, 1981), pp. 16, 21.

1988 as an indication that the United States would openly intervene on Iraq's side unless Iran settled the war with its neighbor. In parallel, the cyber-attack on the Iranian uranium enrichment facility with the Stuxnet virus in 2010 may have increased the credibility of the implicit American threats to use force if Iran came close to producing nuclear weapons, although this presumably was not the American purpose. In many ways it disadvantages the United States that other countries are prone to exaggerate the ability of the CIA to harass if not over throw them, but on some occasions this undoubtedly produces behavior that the United States desires.

Beliefs about deterrence may also generate self-fulfilling and self-denying prophecies. Although the empirical verification supporting the common American deterrence arguments lucidly articulated by Schelling is thin at best, these ideas have proved so intellectually powerful that they may have influenced American behavior. If other countries have similarly absorbed these ideas, or if they understand that the United States has, deterrence through tactics like commitment may now be more efficacious than they once were. The other side of this coin is that an appreciation of forms of deterrence can lead others to counter or design around these behaviors.[46]

In a related way, an understanding of the biases I have discussed can perhaps lead analysts and policymakers to both reduce the extent to which they cloud their own thinking and allow them to better understand the way adversaries are likely to perceive their behavior. Both parts of this are tall orders, however. Nevertheless, it is not out of the question that deterrence policies could be designed with at least one eye out for how they will be perceived. Indeed, American intelligence is often tasked with predicting how others are likely to react to alternative courses of action that the nation could adopt. Unfortunately, as far as I know, no one has ever looked back at these predictions to assess how accurate they were, and even in principle this would be possible only for ones that concerned actions the United States did take. But policymaking might be improved if every paper included a section explicating the underlying beliefs about how others would perceive and react to the actions being advocated. Policies might also be designed with a greater understanding of the uncertainties involving others' perceptions involved. A policy that will work only if it is understood by the adversary exactly as the state intends is fragile at best. Excessive precision and subtlety, while attractive in theory, may give too many hostages to fortune through noise in the signaling system and the difficulties in correctly estimating the other's needs and expectations.[47]

46 For a related discussion of the problems with theories that are both descriptive and prescriptive, see Jervis, "Political Psychology Research and Theory: Bridges and Barriers," in this volume.

47 For further discussion of these two major influences on perceptions, see Jervis, "Understanding Beliefs," in this volume.

If it is impossible to know exactly how the other will perceive your actions and policies, it may still be possible to monitor how the other is reacting and make mid-course corrections. Even this is very difficult, of course, because in a hostile relationship the other is not likely to oblige by providing comments or responses that will better enable it to be coerced. The understanding that you may misperceive your adversary and that it may misperceive you at least sensitizes actors to what can go wrong. It also may facilitate the designing of policies that are less sensitive to aspects of the other's perceptual screens. It is dangerous for leaders to develop policies that will fail very badly if the other does not act exactly as expected. When possible, a large margin of error should be built in. Policies that are premised on the assumption that they will be perceived as intended are likely to have unintended consequences.

10

Psychology and Crisis Stability

Preemption was always one way that wars could start in the past; it is the only way an all-out nuclear war could start. Although this danger came to the fore in the Cold War and so has received less attention recently, it remains a risk in American relations with North Korea, Russia, and China and, even more, between India and Pakistan.[1] It could not occur without the belief that imminent war was inevitable and that, as terrible as striking first would be, receiving the first blow would be even worse. These twin beliefs are not required for the use of lower levels of violence, even the limited use of nuclear weapons. Indeed, they would make such exercises self-defeating. But as long as total war would be more disastrous than even the loss of limited war or a crushing political defeat, a statesman would initiate a full-scale attack only if he or she thought that the other side was about to do so. If war is seen as inevitable, neither deterrence nor surrender is possible. Deterrence implies not only the threat to retaliate if the other attacks, but also the promise not to attack if the other is similarly restrained.[2] By definition, such promises will not be believed by a state that has concluded that war is certain. The belief that war

---

1 See, for example, Avery Goldstein, "First Things First: The Pressing Danger of Crisis Instability in U.S.-China Relation," *International Security* 37 (Spring 2003): 49–89; Keir Lieber and Daryl Press, "The Next Korean War," *Foreign Affairs Online*, April 1, 2013, https://www.foreign affairs.com/articles/north-korea/2013-04-01/next-korean-war; Jennifer Lind, "Geography and the Security Dilemma in Asia," pp. 719–736 in Saadia Pekkanen, John Ravenhill, and Rosemary Foote, eds., *The Oxford Handbook of the International Relations of Asia* (New York: Oxford University Press, 2014).

2 Thomas Schelling, *The Strategy of Conflict* (Cambridge: Harvard University Press, 1960), p. 120.

cannot be avoided also implies that surrender is impossible. Peace cannot be bought, even at the cost of enormous concessions.

A decision-maker with even a modicum of sanity will prefer even a very unsatisfactory peace to war, but this might not be the choice facing him. In a crisis of unprecedented severity, he might come to believe that the choice was between war immediately and war in the near future; between a war his state started and a war the other side initiated. If the former was preferable to the latter, war could result even though both sides want to avoid it. This chapter will argue that this problem, known as "crisis instability," is, in part, a psychological one. Psychological aspects have not, however, been sufficiently appreciated. This discussion focuses the psychological dimension and says relatively little about other facets of the problem.

More than fifty years ago, Thomas Schelling built on the argument of Albert Wohlstetter that the balance of terror was delicate (i.e., that a first strike would have major advantages) and developed the now-familiar claim that one of the greatest dangers of war was "the reciprocal fear of surprise attack."[3] Since each side fears being taken by surprise, each must remain on the alert. But being alert means not only carefully monitoring the other side's military activities (although, as we will note below, even this passive and seemingly harmless stance can be troublesome), but also preparing one's forces to act. It is pointless to have a warning system if there are no ameliorative actions one would take on the basis of information received.

These reactions, however, can lead the other side to conclude that the state may be going to attack. The other side would then move to an increased state of readiness, thus confirming the state's suspicions that an attack was likely and causing it to move to an even higher level of alert. The result would be an awful self-fulfilling prophesy in which the actions each side takes, out of the fear that it may be the victim of surprise, fuel the fears of the other side, producing a war neither side sought.

Under the conditions of crisis instability, because the actions a state would take to defend itself against possible aggression closely correspond to those it would take if it were going to attack, the danger of all-out war would increase as decision-makers became increasingly concerned that war might break out. This is a particularly dangerous example of the security dilemma that characterizes so much of international politics. This term is often used loosely to

---

3 Ibid., ch. 9, and Thomas Schelling, "The Dynamics of Mutual Alarm," ch. 6 in Schelling, *Arms and Influence* (New Haven: Yale University Press, 1966). This concern grew out of the famous RAND study of how the Strategic Air Command's bombers should be deployed. A sanitized version was printed as Albert Wohlstetter, "The Delicate Balance of Terror," *Foreign Affairs* 37 (January 1959): 211–34, and a summary of the original study is now available as E. S. Quade, "The Selection and Use of Strategic Air Bases; A Case History," pp. 24–63 in Quade, *Analysis for Military Decisions* (Chicago: Rand McNally, 1966).

refer to the difficulties states have in gaining security. The precise definition is more useful: the means by which states try to make themselves more secure often have the undesired and unintended consequences of making others less secure.[4] Thus mutual security, even if desired by both sides, may be beyond reach. The security dilemma is not, however, a constant; it can operate to a greater or lesser extent depending on geography, technology, and human insight. Thus in any crisis in which neither side is bent on war or unacceptable political concessions, we need to ask whether the states can protect themselves without greatly increasing their ability to menace the adversary.

The security dilemma could easily operate in a nuclear crisis because most of what a state would do if it feared an imminent attack would be very similar to what it would do to prepare a first strike of its own (with the important exception that it would try to keep its preparations secret in the latter case whereas in the former it might want them observed). Thus, to increase its security, the state would go on alert (what is known as "generating" its forces), which would not only increase the number of weapons that would survive an attack, but would also at least marginally increase the number that would be available for a first strike.[5] It would be safer if countries would take actions that would have only the former, but not the latter, effect. This would be true of measures that would decrease the vulnerability of the forces without increasing their capability for getting the first blow in. Sending submarines that were in port out to sea or dispersing land-mobile missiles would fit this description.

But even such seemingly innocuous measures entail significant dangers. First, the other side might see them as indicating that the state's leaders had decided to go to war or would be unable to maintain political control of their forces. Secondly, because striking first is more effective against an adversary who has not yet put his forces on alert, the other side might attack in anticipation of the forces being generated. In a situation that is becoming tense, the knowledge that the advantage of a first strike would shortly be diminished would therefore create crisis instability. Secretary of Defense McNamara recognized this dynamic in this Draft Presidential Memoranda on tactical nuclear weapons in the late 1960s, noting that in a crisis "the temptation would

4 The idea is as old as Thucydides. In the modern era, it was first discussed by Herbert Butterfield, *History and Human Relations* (London: Collins, 1951), pp. 19–20; John Herz, "Idealist Internationalism and the Security Dilemma," *World Politics* 2 (January 1950): 157–80; and Arnold Wolfers, *Discord and Collaboration* (Baltimore: Johns Hopkins University Press, 1962), p. 84. I have developed the implications and resulting problems in *Perception and Misperception in International Politics* (Princeton: Princeton University Press, 1976; 2nd ed. 2017), ch. 3, and in "Cooperation under the Security Dilemma," *World Politics* 30 (January 1978): 16–214.

5 At least this is what the United States probably would do, as it has done in the past. The Soviet Union, however, seems never to have put its nuclear forces on alert.

be high ... to attack the enemy's nuclear delivery systems before they could be used or to destroy his massed ground forces before they could disperse."[6] Throughout the Cold War and even today the vulnerability of command and control systems, compounded by the propensity for states to combine or collate the systems used for nuclear and for conventional forces, remains high.

Psychology and Crisis Stability

But if the nuclear balance during the Cold War was never as delicate as Wohlstetter and his colleagues believed, the danger of crisis stability has simultaneously been misunderstood by ignoring psychological factors, which usually increase the danger. First, the quality of decision making usually suffers because of a number of general psychological biases, which are compounded by the stress of a crisis. Second, the way people process information is likely to lead them to overestimate the likelihood that the other is about to attack during a crisis. Third, related processes can lead them to fail to see the extent to which their actions are leading the adversary to believe that war is inevitable. Fourth, psychological factors can lead decision-makers to overestimate the advantages of striking first. Finally, psychology can also produce restraint. These topics will be considered in turn.

GENERAL CONSIDERATIONS

Statesmen at the brink of war would be subject to enormous psychological pressures and the quality of the decision-making process therefore would be likely to suffer. Although it is difficult to predict the substance of the decisions that would result, it seems likely that blunders would occur that would increase the chance of war.

Most research indicates a curvilinear relationship between stress and the quality of decision making.[7] People do not use their full resources when the matters they are dealing with are inconsequential and do best when they are

6 Quoted in Joshua Epstein, *Strategy and Force Planning* (Washington, D.C.: Brookings Institution, 1987), p. 19; also see p. 20

7 Ole Holsti and Alexander George, "The Effects of Stress on the Performance of Foreign Policy-Makers," pp. 255–319 in Cornelius Cotter, ed., *Political Science Annual*, vol. 6, (Indianapolis: Bobbs-Merrill, 1976); Ole Holsti, "Theories of Crisis Decision-Making," in Paul Gordon Lauren, ed., *Diplomacy* (New York: Free Press, 1979), pp. 99–136; Alexander George, "The Impact of Crisis-Induced Stress on Decision Making," pp. 529–52 in *The Medical Implications of Nuclear War* (Washington, D.C.: National Academy Press, 1986); Ole Holsti, "Crisis Decision Making," pp. 8–84 in Philip Tetlock, Jo Husbands, Robert Jervis, Paul Stern, and Charles Tilly, eds., *Behavior Society, and Nuclear War*, vol. 1 (New York: Oxford University Press, 1989). The psychological literature is summarized in Richard Lazarus, *Psychological Stress and Coping Process* (New York: McGraw-Hill, 1966).

under some pressure. But past a certain point of stress, several factors con-
spire to decrease people's ability to think clearly. First, information is likely to
be abundant but ambiguous. In the modern age, sensors and bureaucracies
will produce much more information than can be assimilated. Thus, during
the Iranian hostage crisis, the National Security Council (NSC) staff member
in charge of Iran found himself confronted with over one thousand pages of
reports a day.[8] Second, time-pressures will be very great. Decisions will have
to be reached quickly, often without permitting the solicitation of a wide
range of opinions or the discussion of more than a few choices. Third, people
will have to work long hours and soon will be functioning without adequate
rest or energy. Fourth, the awareness that millions of people could die as a
result of the actions being ordered will produce incredible strain. In these
circumstances, it is not surprising that some decision-makers literally collapse.
This was true of Prime Minister Anthony Eden during the Suez crisis and of
Chief of Staff Yitzhak Rabin during the Six Day's war. Robert Kennedy and
Theodore Sorensen have hinted at these problems obtaining during the Cuban
missile crisis and one high official told Alexander George that "two important
members of the President's advisory group ... had been unable to cope with
the stress, becoming quite passive and unable to fulfill their responsibilities."[9]

Furthermore, crises are likely to exacerbate several psychological processes that, even under more benign circumstances, reduce the quality of
decision making. Three factors are of particular importance to crisis stability: the tendency to avoid facing hard value trade-offs, the paucity of empathy
with which statesmen view adversaries, and the difficulties in correctly understanding the messages others are trying to convey.

There are two imperatives in a crisis: to avoid war and to avoid political
defeat, if not gain victory. To stand firm serves the latter value but, if the other
also refuses to back down, may lead to war. Thus it is crucial that statesmen
carefully judge what their adversary is likely to do and balance the competing
values that they seek. The problem is that people often resist facing painful
value trade-offs,[10] which means that if they come to believe that standing firm
is necessary to avoid defeat, they are likely to conclude that the policy can
succeed. Instead of weighing the risks in a clear and unbiased manner, they are
likely to come to believe that this policy will maximize the chances of pre-
serving peace as well as avoid defeat.[11] This perceptual tendency will make it

8 Gary Sick, *All Fall Down* (New York: Random House, 1985), p. 280.

9 Robert Kennedy, *Thirteen Days* (New York: Norton, 1969), p. 22; Theodore Sorensen,
Decision-Making in the White House (New York: Columbia University Press, 1964), p. 76; Alexander George, "Impact of Crisis-Induced Stress," 541.

10 See Jervis, *Perception and Misperception* (1976), 128–42, and the literature cited there.

11 For further discussion, see Jack Snyder, "Rationality at the Brink," *World Politics* 30 (April
1978): 345–65. Although I believe Snyder's conclusions are valid, his discussion does not fully

harder for decision-makers to manage the tension between the competitive tactics of crisis bargaining and the more cooperative approach of crisis management. The danger with stressing the former is undesired war; with the latter the danger is excessive concessions that give the impression of weakness and invite further hostility. It is rarely easy to determine the proper balance and the chance for error is always present, but it is even greater when statesmen are likely to convince themselves that the tactics they adopt will simultaneously reduce both dangers. What will actually be reduced will be their ability to comprehend and cope with the crisis.

The propensity for people to assimilate incoming information into their preexisting beliefs also affects behavior in a crisis because expectations about how the adversary will act will change only slowly and in response to unambiguous information. As Glenn Snyder and Paul Diesing have documented, incorrect beliefs are as likely to be compounded as corrected during the course of a confrontation.[12] Although the other's behavior will be carefully scanned for evidence about what it will do next, the perceiver's predispositions will strongly influence the inferences that are drawn. As a result, messages and signals are often interpreted very differently from the way they were intended. States often try to send carefully crafted and subtle messages by their diplomatic statements and military maneuvers, but the noise in the system, fear of deception (which is often warranted) and the power of the perceiver's beliefs and images mean that what is received is likely to be very different. Complexity and balance are apt to get filtered out. It is difficult for states to signal both that they are planning to stand firm on the issue at stake and simultaneously that they will keep their military forces restrained—that they will not readily retreat but neither will they strike first, at least not yet.[13]

A final, general complicating psychological factor is the difficulty statesmen have in empathizing with the other side.[14] Especially when relations are deeply hostile, people rarely attempt to put themselves in the other's shoes

---

come to grips with the possibility that some of the links among the beliefs he is examining can be explained by logic.

12 Glenn Snyder and Paul Diesing, *Conflict Among Nations* (Princeton: Princeton University Press, 1977), pp. 389–405.

13 For an exemplary analysis of the cognitive and organizational impediments to the sending and receiving of complex, balanced, and subtle signals, see Wallace Theis, *When Governments Collide* (Berkeley: University of California Press, 1980).

14 This was not true, however, for the Israelis in 1973. Because they viewed the previous war as an unavoidable war, they were focused on the danger of the reciprocal fear of surprise attack and so were very restrained. See Janice Stein, "Calculation, Miscalculation, and Conventional Deterrence II: The View from Jerusalem," pp. 60–88 in Robert Jervis, Richard Ned Lebow, and Janice Stein, eds., *Psychology and Deterrence* (Baltimore: Johns Hopkins University Press, 1985). Richard Betts argues that similar fears could mitigate against NATO's mobilizing, in *Surprise Attack* (Washington, D.C.: Brookings Institution, 1982).

and try to see how the situation could appear from another vantage point. Of course, the other side may be very different from the perceiver, and Chamberlain and his colleagues erred in seeing Hitler as too much like themselves. But more often, statesmen see other states as very different from their own. As a cause and an effect of this view, they tend to attribute other's undesired behavior to their hostile predispositions rather than to situational factors and, when they are planning a forceful response, fail to ask how they would act if they were confronted by such a stance. In a crisis, the result can be that decision-makers will both be too quick to infer that the other side's preparations indicate that it is about to go to war and too slow in considering that their actions may produce this impression on the part of the other.

War as Inevitable: Psychological Factors

Crisis instability is driven by the twin beliefs that war is inevitable and that striking first would yield some advantage. To begin with the former, we should explore how the ways people process information and draw inferences could lead them to overestimate the likelihood that the other side was about to strike. During a crisis, the heightened fear of attack leads people to gather more evidence and examine it more closely than they do in calmer times. Although this makes perfect sense, it also creates problems, especially because in any nuclear crisis each side would see a great deal of unfamiliar military activity on the other side. Making sense of unusual events would be particularly difficult even in the best of circumstances. But in a crisis, what is unusual is likely to seem threatening. Of course, conveying a threat is one reason why a state would go on alert, but the inference may be not that it will attack if the conflict cannot be resolved but that it is about to attack no matter what happens.

Furthermore, the conclusion that the adversary is engaging in unprecedented preparations for war may be a product of the increased perceptual sensitivity that accompanies a crisis. Even if the other's behavior has not in fact changed, looking at it closely will usually lead the person to see things not previously noticed. Intelligence officers and decision-makers may detect details of troop movements that, although routine, are not recognized as such because they have never before been examined so carefully. The activities will then be seen as new and, given the context provided by the alert, as threatening. Ironically, the fact that today Russia is less of a menace than the Soviet Union was means that the United States lacks some of the fine-grained knowledge it had in the earlier period that could minimize the problem.

IGNORING NEGATIVE EVIDENCE

Statesmen and analysts, like people in their everyday lives, usually fail to treat their expectations as hypotheses. The "scientific method" implies that we should ask ourselves, "If this proposition (e.g., that the other is going to attack) is correct, what evidence should I be able to detect?" The investigator should note not only the behaviors that are consistent with the proposition, but also those that are inconsistent, including actions that should have occurred were the hypothesis correct, but which in fact were not taken. As we know from Sherlock Holmes, dogs that do not bark in the night can provide crucial evidence. But as we also know from the story, explained in an earlier chapter, most people are slow to realize this. Things that have not happened do not attract attention and are easy to overlook.[15] The intelligence community has attempted to correct for this bias by its system of "indications and warning," which is designed to keep track of what the other is—and is not—doing with its forces, but it is not clear that this degree of systematization, useful as it is, can entirely overcome the natural tendency to miss evidence whose significance lies in its being absent. The result could easily be that the evidence that the other side would strike would seem more overwhelming than it was. Although the invasion of Iraq was preventive rather than preemptive, it is worth noting that one of the causes of the WMD intelligence failure was the lack of sensitivity to what should have been seen if Iraq had had active WMD programs.[16]

PERCEPTION AND THE SECURITY DILEMMA

As we noted, the actions that states take to increase their security often have the effect of making others less secure. In a nuclear crisis, furthermore, the security dilemma itself is apt to be quite severe, in that the actions the state will take to prepare to retaliate are likely closely to resemble those it would take if it were going to attack. The resulting problems are compounded because decision-makers fail to realize this and so, when the other's actions appear to menace the state, they are likely to infer that this was the other's intentions. It is alarming to have one's security decreased, but it is even more alarming if it is believed that this was the other side's goal. Of course in many instances this inference is warranted, but statesmen usually fail to consider the possible alternative that this was the only way the other could protect

15 I have analyzed some of the implications of this in "Cooperation under the Security Dilemma," and, in this volume, "The Drunkard's Search."

16 Robert Jervis, *Why Intelligence Fails: Lessons from the Iranian Revolution and the Iraq War* (Ithaca: Cornell University Press, 2013), pp. 151–55.

itself. Acts that the other is taking to put itself in a better position, should war start, are likely to be taken as showing that the other believes that war is certain and, indeed, is about to start it. Thus if the objective dangers created by the security dilemma are not understood, they can be compounded by leading decision-makers to see war as inevitable.

Equally important is the other side of this coin: in a crisis decision-makers are likely to underestimate the extent to which their actions menace others.[17] In the autumn of 1950, the United States did not think that moving its troops to the Yalu would threaten China's security, and in a nuclear crisis statesmen who are preoccupied with their own fears could easily forget that the adversary's fears would be increased by measures motivated by the desire to ensure that the state's forces would survive an attack. On both sides, decisions to put forces on alert could be taken simply on the basis of consideration of how the move might directly affect its own security. To the extent that the other side was considered, the only question likely to receive attention would be whether the adversary would be deterred.

Even measures that do not directly menace the other side can lead that state to infer that war can no longer be avoided. This might be the effect, for example, of an American decision to reduce its vulnerability by moving the president to a secret location. Although this would not increase the American ability to launch a first strike, can one be sure that the adversary would not read it as indicating that the United States believed that war was almost certain? Sensing the other's fears requires a knowledge of how the other sees the world, an appreciation of the fact that one's restraint may not be apparent to the other side, and an ability to empathize with the adversary. But empathy is likely to be in short supply when tensions and hostility are at their highest.

COGNITIVE PREDISPOSITIONS

The effects discussed so far are magnified by the propensity of people to assimilate new information into their preexisting beliefs. Expectations and cognitive predispositions strongly influence the way evidence is interpreted. Ambiguous information that during calm times would not be seen as menacing will be taken very differently in a crisis. This effect is compounded because

---

17 Of course, the most important factors are not entirely psychological. Given current and foreseeable technology, it is extremely difficult for states to take measures that decrease the vulnerability of their forces without simultaneously increasing their ability, if not to strike first, then at least to undertake provocative actions. Indeed, if the state is not willing to back down, it must take actions that convince the other of the need to retreat, or at least to seek a compromise. But the objective problems are compounded by the tendency for decision-makers to believe that the other side knows that they are reasonable and not to feel unduly threatened by the measures they are taking in their own self-defense.

people are unaware of it. They usually believe that their inferences are driven exclusively by the evidence before them rather than by the beliefs and expectations they already hold. As a result, people grow increasingly confident as they are presented with additional information that is, in fact, highly ambiguous because they incorrectly believe that each new bit of information provides independent confirmation of their views.[18] Thus the expectation that the other was likely to strike could become consolidated by the receipt of a stream of information that, while not totally inconsistent with this belief, does not point only in this direction.

PERCEPTIONS OF COORDINATION, PLANNING, AND CENTRALIZATION

States tend to see the behavior of others as more planned, coordinated, and centralized than it is. Actions that are in fact accidental, or the result of different parts of the bureaucracy following their own policies, are likely to be perceived as part of a coherent, and often devious, plan.[19] In the case of a nuclear crisis, the propensity to see all the other side's behavior as part of a plan is especially likely to yield incorrect and dangerous conclusions. As each side goes on alert, military units will not only carry out the prescribed instructions (which may send undesired messages) but also to some extent will act on their own discretion. After the USSR erected the Berlin Wall in 1961, General Lucius Clay, sent back to the city to reassure Berliners and take charge of the American forces, practiced using specially equipped tanks to tear down the barrier.[20] Not only was this not ordered by Washington, but officials there did not even know it was happening. The Soviets, of course, did and almost surely attributed it to high-level policy. It is almost unavoidable that during a superpower confrontation many of each side's acts would spring from confusion and lack of coordination and that the other side would tend to see these as fulfilling the orders of the leaders, and so provocative actions taken by local commanders may be seen as evidence that the other side has decided to go to war. While these might not be the result of the policy of central decisionmakers, the other side is likely to infer the existence of a threatening plan.

18 For further discussion, see Jervis, *Perception and Misperception* (1976), 181–87. Experimental confirmation is provided in Charles Lord, Lee Ross, and Mark Lepper, "Biases Assimilation and Attitude Polarization: The Effects of Prior Theories on Subsequently Considered Evidence," *Journal of Personality and Social Psychology* 37 (November 1979): 2098–109.

19 For further discussion and evidence, see Jervis, *Perception and Misperception* (1976, 2017), ch. 8.

20 Raymond Garthoff, "Berlin, 1961: The Record Corrected," *Foreign Policy*, no. 84 (Fall 1991): 142–56.

RESISTANCE TO SEEING TRADE-OFFS

There are logical links between the belief that striking first yields significant advantages and the perception that war is inevitable because the larger the gap between striking first and striking second, the more likely a state is to attack. Similarly, if a state thinks the adversary has concluded that there are significant advantages in striking first, then it will expect the adversary to attack in a crisis. But some of the links between the two elements are psychological. A statesman who is convinced that striking first is better than striking second (but still is much worse than maintaining the peace) will be under increasing psychological pressure as a confrontation develops. To strike first would be to sacrifice the chance of peace; to hold back would be to run the risk of the worst possible outcome. To escape from this painful choice, the statesman may distort some of the information and make his decision seem less costly. This can help lead to peace if he reduces his estimates of the likelihood of war, thereby justifying his inclination to preserve the possibility of avoiding war. But if the advantages of striking first (and the costs of allowing the adversary to do so) are uppermost in his mind, he may come to exaggerate the probability of war in order to bolster the decision to attack.

It is difficult to determine which of these distortions is more likely or, more importantly, the conditions that are likely to trigger off one or the other. But the controlling value is likely to be the one that first becomes most firmly planted in the decision-maker's mind.[21] In this way crisis stability may be enhanced by the fact that most of the time decision-makers pay little attention to the possible advantages of striking first and are always deeply aware of the need to try to preserve peace.

CIRCULAR NATURE OF BELIEFS

One important, if vague, factor that would influence whether war was seen as inevitable during a crisis is the general sense of optimism or pessimism that prevailed in a country before the crisis arose. Gloom produced by belief that the tide of events was running against the country has been important in the past, most clearly in 1914. But because of the stability of the nuclear balance, what might be more important in our age are general feelings about whether war can be avoided indefinitely. Obviously, this is not a question with an objective answer, and so it is susceptible to swings in moods. If people become convinced that nuclear weapons cannot be held at bay forever, the chances are greater that a severe crisis will lead to war. Although optimism cannot cure all ills, the belief that nuclear deterrence has made our world quite safe

21 See Jervis, preface to second edition of *Perception and Misperception* (2017).

and the prediction that this stability can be maintained may themselves noticeably contribute to crisis stability.

Finally, we should remember the self-fulfilling nature of beliefs about the inevitability of war. Given a perceived advantage to striking first, war will become inevitable if one or both sides believes it is. Thus war becomes more likely as one or both sides think that the other believes that war is likely. And this, in turn, depends on the state's judgment of the other side's estimate of how likely it is that the state will strike first. It is hard to know how such estimates of estimates are formed; indeed, we cannot be sure how far statesmen's thinking would progress along the road to infinite regress. But the other problem is an odd and peculiarly psychological one.

TENDENCY TO NEGLECT THE NEED FOR PROMISES

In a crisis, leaders usually see their task as convincing the other side that their resolve is high and to neglect the need to give the reassurance that they will accept a reasonable solution rather than go to war. Combining threats and promises is rendered even more difficult because both academics and decision-makers have paid little attention to the latter.[22] The frequently discussed "credibility problem" refers to threats; there is no such literature on promises. The implication is that aggressors might doubt that the defender would use force, but not that it prefers to remain at peace.[23]

This problem has received some attention. In his original discussion of the reciprocal fear of surprise attack, Schelling notes the value of "positive inspection."[24] During a crisis, a state that wanted to show its adversary that it was not about to attack could invite the other to observe its military facilities to determine that this was indeed the case. One historical precedent was the tour taken by the British military attaché in Germany in May 1938, which revealed that, contrary to the reports from Czechoslovakia, the German army was not about to march. That the delayed effects of this incident were unfortunate—the British mistrust of the Czechs increased and Hitler, feeling humiliated, became more committed to smashing his enemies—does not detract from the

22 The importance of rewards is argued in David Baldwin, "The Power of Positive Sanctions," *World Politics* 24 (October 1971): 19–38. The need to combine threats and rewards is discussed in Alexander George, David Hall, and William Simons, *Coercive Diplomacy* (Boston: Little Brown, 1971), pp. 100–103; Snyder and Diesing, *Conflict Among Nations*, 489–93; Jervis, *Perception and Misperception* (1976), 111–13; Jervis, "Deterrence Theory Revisited," *World Politics* 31 (January 1979): 304–5; and Richard Ned Lebow, "The Deterrence Deadlock: Is there a Way Out?" pp. 180–202 in Jervis, Lebow, and Stein, eds., *Psychology and Deterrence*.

23 Of course the other's fear of a first strike brings pressure on him to terminate the crisis quickly, and so reassurance should not be unconditional.

24 Schelling, *Strategy of Conflict*, 250.

virtues of the technique. The problem arises when states want to generate their forces, both to demonstrate resolve and to safeguard their second-strike capability, but also need to show that they want to maintain the peace. The agreements on confidence-building measures reached at the end of the Cold War that were designed to prevent unwarranted fears caused by military maneuvers in Europe perhaps were most important for making statesmen sensitive to the need to reassure as well as to threaten the other side.[25]

Psychological Factors in First Strike Advantage

Even if war is believed to be inevitable, crisis instability will arise only if one or both sides believe that it is better to strike first than to permit the other side to do so. Psychological biases play a role here too.

MILITARY BIASES TOWARD THE OFFENSIVE

Both because they are attracted to the notion of counterforce and because they seek to maintain control of the war, military organizations tend to prefer taking the offensive to standing ready to receive the first blow.[26] During the Cold War, counter-city attacks, which were not much more difficult on a second strike than on a first, were not attractive to either the American or the Soviet military, who resisted the notion that their purpose was to be prepared to incinerate millions of civilians rather than to fight the other's military. Furthermore, both sides' military leaders are fully aware that a counterforce war would be easier to wage with a first than with a second strike, even if the former could not promise to disarm the other side. They also knew that taking the initiative is one way of controlling the uncertainty that accompanies any battle and that doing so usually reduces civilian interference in the military's task of conducting the fighting. There is every reason to believe that this outlook still characterizes the militaries of the nuclear powers.

None of this is to say that military leaders are belligerent or ignorant of the costs of a war. But the task of being ready to fight if need be and the awareness of the overwhelming difficulties of fighting a war with a force that has been badly damaged by an enemy first strike predisposes them to conclude that if there is going to be a war, the chances of a favorable outcome are greatly increased if they can strike first. How much influence the military would have

---

25 In order to reduce dangerous misinterpretations, the United States had taken the Soviet fears into account in its conduct on routine airborne intelligence operations. See Seymour Hersh, *The Target Is Destroyed* (New York: Random House, 1986), pp. 38–43.

26 This paragraph draws heavily on Barry Posen, *The Sources of Military Doctrine: Britain, France, and Germany between the Two Wars* (Ithaca: Cornell University Press, 1984).

during a crisis cannot be determined and presumably would depend on many aspects of the situation. But the potential for such influence, linked to the belief in the advantages of striking first, is significant.[27]

MINIMIZING THE COSTS OF STRIKING FIRST

Earlier, we noted that states might inadvertently provoke others by foreclosing on the acceptable alternatives to war. More directly, a decision-maker who believes that the alternative to fighting is the sacrifice of core values may avoid the painful value trade-off that confronts him by underestimating the costs of war and overestimating the chances of victory. This is part of the explanation for the behavior of Japan in 1941, Pakistan in 1965, and Egypt in 1973. In these cases, states attacked much stronger adversaries. Seeing the prospects for diplomacy as bleak, they came to believe that attacking might achieve their goals. The unpalatable characteristics of remaining at peace led decision-makers to underestimate the unattractiveness of going to war.

In parallel, a leader who felt that his country's position was deteriorating badly and that concessions during the crisis would further weaken it would feel psychological pressure to seize on the hope that a first strike could offer a way out of the dilemma. If he believed that a concession would provide only a short respite, he might conclude that if his country is not to surrender, it will have to fight sooner or later. This set of beliefs would not be as dangerous as it was in the past because the costs of any conceivable first strike are so high, but the horror of decline and surrender could still lead to a degree of unjustified optimism about the military alternative.

PROSPECT THEORY: RISK ACCEPTANCE FOR LOSSES

It is commonly accepted that no sane decision-maker would wager the fate of his country on the cosmic throw of the dice; and indeed, under most circumstances people do seem to be risk-averse. As numerous experiments have shown, people will choose a certainty of winning $10 over a 20 percent chance of winning $51. This caution would contribute to crisis stability because it would inhibit people from pushing hard to make gains. But what could prove to be disturbing is that people seem to be risk-acceptant if the alternative to a gamble is a sure loss. In order to increase the chances of avoiding any loss at all, people are willing to accept the danger of an even greater sacrifice.[28]

27 Bruce Blair, *The Logic of Accidental Nuclear War* (Washington, D.C.: Brookings Institution, 1993).

28 For further discussion, see Jervis, "Prospect Theory: The Political Implications of Loss Aversion," in this volume.

The implications of this psychology of choice for crisis stability are several. First, because the status quo forms people's reference point, they are willing to take unusual risk to recoup recent losses. In a crisis, then, a decision-maker might risk world war if it held out the possibility of avoiding or reversing a defeat. Where fully rational analysis would lead a person to cut his losses, the use of the status quo as the benchmark against which other results are measured could lead him to persevere. As in so many areas, politics pulls in the same direction. Public opinion is likely to be intolerant of defeats; the leader who accepts one will probably suffer in domestic politics. Indeed, persisting in a losing cause in the hope of reversing the course of events may be a gamble that is bad for the national interest but justified in terms of the politician's personal power.[29]

Reference to the status quo could also render dangerous the strategy of the *fait accompli*. George and Smoke note that deterrence can be defeated if an expansion can alter the status quo before the defender has time to react. But unless the latter quickly adjusts to the new situation, she may be willing to run unusually high risks to regain her previous position. Such situations are particularly dangerous because each side is likely to see itself as defending the status quo. The chance of war, already significant, will be increased if each side is driven by a strong aversion to accept what it sees as an unfavorable change.

A second consequence of loss-aversion is that if the decision-maker thinks that war (and therefore enormous losses) is almost certain if he does not strike, and that attacking provides a small chance of escaping unscathed, he may decide to strike even if the standard probability-utility calculus were to call for restraint. Similarly, in less severe crises, with his attention riveted on the deterioration that will occur unless he acts strongly to reverse the situation, the decision-maker might take actions that entail an irrationally high chance of major escalation.

Finally, the response can be influenced by how the decision is framed. The powerful aversion to losses could lead the decision-maker to hold back if she thought that striking first would lead to certain retaliation while holding back would gain some chance—even if small—of keeping the peace. On the other hand, if the decision-maker takes as her base-line not the existing situation, but the causalities that would be suffered in a war, her choice between the same alternatives might be different. She would then judge the policies according to lives that might be saved, not lost, with the results that she would choose a course of action that she believed would certainly save some lives rather than another that might save more, but might not save any. The obvi-

29 George Downs and David Rocke, "Gambling for Resurrection," ch. 3 in Downs and Rocke, eds., *Optimal Imperfection* (Princeton: Princeton University Press, 1995).

ous danger is that a first strike that would significantly reduce the other side's strategic forces would meet the former criterion while restraint could not provide the certainly of saving any lives and so would not seem as attractive as standard utility maximization theory implies.

Conclusion

Crisis stability and its twin, crisis instability, may be as much the product of the way people think during a crisis as it is a consequence of the objective incentives to strike first. Throughout this chapter I have noted the psychological mechanisms that make the world more or less dangerous. Crisis instability was a major concern during the Cold War and drove much of the arms control effort. With the demise of this conflict the phenomenon may seem of merely academic interest. But it is not. Although the conflicts that the United States has with Russia, China, and North Korea are much less than those that characterized the Cold War, they are significant nevertheless. Of course, the United States has much larger and more capable military forces than those of these adversaries, but this may not alleviate the danger. The United States could see a real possibility of coming out unscathed if it attacked first, and the adversaries could believe that attacking first is the only possible way to limit damage to themselves.

The fact that we are alive shows that no Cold War crises got completely out of hand or set off the self-fulfilling fears that theorists worry about. Part of the reason is that decision-makers in both the United States and USSR came to understand the dangers and to make their retaliatory forces as invulnerable as possible. Some of the measures contemplated might have made things worse. The Soviets, who it is now clear were always weaker than the United States, moved toward the doctrine of launching their missiles on receipt of warning that an American strike was on its way, a posture that in fact was beyond the capabilities of their warning systems. This was based on the fear that Soviet missiles were vulnerable, not on the more symmetrical understanding of Schelling's reciprocal fear of surprise attack. The Americans—or at least some Americans—worried about the vulnerability of Soviet as well as American systems, but there is no evidence that any Soviet officials reciprocated. This is partly because while American leaders and analysts worried that war might come about through accidents, misunderstanding, and the kind of dynamics discussed in this chapter, their Soviet counterparts saw war much more as the product of intractable political disputes.

Nevertheless, although Khrushchev famously ridiculed the idea of accidental war during the 1961 Vienna summit meeting with Kennedy (strategy may have played a role here as he correctly saw Kennedy's warnings about the dangers of accidents as a way of seeking to deter him from pressing the Soviet case on Berlin), he clearly recognized the danger during the Cuban missile crisis. As he put it with moving eloquence in a letter to Kennedy:

> Mr. President we and you ought not now to pull on the end of the rope in which you have tied the knot of war, because the more the two of us pull, the tighter the knot will be tied. And a moment may come when that knot will be tied so tight that even he who tied it will not have the strength to untie it. And then it will be necessary to cut that knot, and what that would mean is not for me to explain to you, because you yourself understand perfectly well of what terrible forces our countries dispose.[30]

In one of the many ironies that characterized the impact of nuclear weapons on world politics, leaders' awareness of the possibility that they could stumble into war played a large role in keeping them further from the brink. They were generally very cautious when the danger of nuclear war arose. Standard theories of bargaining would lead us to expect states to have been bolder and more assertive than they were, and partly because of their caution they never saw situations as hopeless.

Soviet-American crises were rare after the Soviet development of robust second-strike capability in the wake of Cuban missile crisis,[31] and so evidence becomes thin, but it seems that especially, if not only, on the American side, understanding of the possible self-fulfilling dynamics grew. During the missile crisis Kennedy referred to Barbara Tuchman's *The Guns of August* as a cautionary tale and while neither he nor his successors read any of the psychology I have drawn upon here, they did seem to understand that excessive pessimism was dangerous. Here they were undoubtedly reinforced by the propensity common among leaders to think that they retain a significant influence over how events will unfold.

Of course with the end of the Cold War the world is less dangerous, at least for the United States. Despite difficult relations with Russia, China, and North Korea, the post–Cold War era has not seen a crisis that held out a significant possibility of ending in nuclear war. The notion of crisis instability may then be of antiquary and interest only. We cannot be sure of this, however. Tensions among the nuclear powers persist, and the very paucity of crises may render theses states less able to handle them if they occur. Furthermore, relations are most tense between India and Pakistan. Without engaging in the debate between those who think that nuclear weapons stabilize a con-

---

30 U.S. Department of State, *Kennedy-Khrushchev Exchanges* (Washington, D.C.: Government Printing Office, 1996), p. 177.

31 For further discussion, see Robert Jervis. *The Meaning of the Nuclear Revolution: Statecraft and the Politics of Armageddon* (Ithaca: Cornell University Press, 1989), ch. 1.

flicting pair and those who fear it makes war significantly more likely,[32] it is hard to dismiss the possibility that war could develop through each side's fear that the other was about the attack. The weapons deployed and the geographic proximity that radically limits warning time, perhaps compounded by inadequate intelligence, probably makes this conflict more dangerous than the Cold War. The United States, of course, has an interest in avoiding a nuclear exchange and has worked to walk the countries back from the brink of war when they approached it. But whether the leaders on the subcontinent are aware of the ways in which their thinking might increase the chance of the outbreak of a war that neither one wants is far from clear. The problem of crisis instability then unfortunately remains with us.

32 See, for example, Kenneth Waltz and Scot Sagan, *The Spread of Nuclear Weapons: An Enduring Debate* 3rd ed. (New York: Norton, 2013); Šumit Ganguly and S. Paul Kapur, eds., *India, Pakistan, and the Bomb: Debating Nuclear Stability in South Asia* (New York: Columbia University Press, 2010).

11

Domino Beliefs

The first and greatest dangers [to Spain in 1635] are those that threaten Lombardy, the Netherlands and Germany. A defeat in any of these three is fatal for this Monarchy, so much so that if the defeat in those parts is a great one, the rest of the monarchy will collapse; for Germany will be followed by Italy and the Netherlands, and the Netherlands will be followed by America; and Lombardy will be followed by Naples and Sicily, without the possibility of being able to defend either.
—ADVISER TO KING PHILIP IV

Our retreat from Berlin would be tantamount to an acknowledgement of lack of courage to resist Soviet pressure short of war and would amount to a public confession of weakness under pressure. It would be the Munich of 1948 ... [and] would raise justifiable doubts in the mind of Europeans as to the firmness of our European policy and our ability to resist the spread of communism.
—ROBERT MURPHY, AMERICAN POLITICAL ADVISOR TO GERMANY

If we let Korea down, the Soviets will keep right on going and swallow up one piece of Asia after another ... if we were to let Asia go, the Near East would collapse [and there is] no telling what would happen in Europe.
—PRESIDENT HARRY S. TRUMAN BRIEFING MEMBERS OF CONGRESS, JUNE 27, 1950

We begin to see light. Germany is playing for the highest stakes. If her demands are acceded to either on the Congo or in Morocco, ... it will mean definitely the subjection of France. The conditions demanded are not such as a country

having an independent foreign policy can possibly accept. The details of the terms are not so very important now. This is a trial of strength, if anything. Concession means not loss of interests or loss of prestige. It means defeat, with all its inevitable consequences.
—SIR EYRE CROWE, JULY 18, 1911

It is a most critical moment in European politics. If Russia is not checked [in her demands against Turkey], the Holy Alliance will be revived in aggravated form and force. Germany will have Holland and France, Belgium and England will be in a position I trust I shall never have to live to witness. If we act in the manner I have generally indicated, we shall probably in conclusion obtain some commanding stronghold in Turkey from which we need never recede.
—PRIME MINISTER BENJAMIN DISRAELI DURING THE EASTERN CRISIS OF 1877-78

[A friend told me] "that Russia was in Armenia, that Armenia is the key to Syria, that Syria is the key to Egypt, and that anyone advancing into Egypt has the key to Africa." That is characteristic of the apprehensions I hear around me. It has generally been acknowledged to be madness to go to war for an idea, but if anything is more unsatisfactory, it is to go to war against a nightmare.
—LORD SALISBURY ON THE EASTERN CRISIS OF 1877-78

Is this the end of an old adventure or is it the beginning of a new? Is this the last attack upon a small State, or is it to be followed by others? Is this, in fact, a step in the direction of an attempt to dominate the world by force?
—PRIME MINISTER NEVILLE CHAMBERLAIN, SPEECH IN BIRMINGHAM AFTER THE GERMAN TAKEOVER OF CZECHOSLOVAKIA

Because most scholars regard domino beliefs[1] as misguided and the proximate cause of destructive American meddling throughout the world and the disastrous war in Vietnam, they are arguments rarely taken seriously, instead being seen as rationalizations for economic motives, domestic competition

1 King Philip IV's adviser is quoted in Paul Kennedy, *The Rise and Fall of the Great Powers* (New York: Random House, 1988), p. 51; Murphy's quotation comes from U.S. Department of State, *Foreign Relations of the U.S., 1948*, vol. 2, *Germany and Austria* (Washington, D.C.: U.S. Government Printing Office, 1973), p. 920; Truman is quoted in Lloyd Gardner, "Truman Era Foreign Policy: Recent Historical Trends," in Richard Kirkendall, ed., *The Truman Period as a Research Field, a Reappraisal, 1972* (Columbia: University of Missouri Press, 1974), p. 63; Sir Eyre Crowe's statement can be found in G. P. Gooch and Harold Temperley, *British Documents on the Origins of the War*, vol. 7 (London: His Majesty's Stationery Office, 1932), p. 372; Disraeli is quoted in R. W. Seton-Watson, *Disraeli, Gladstone, and the Eastern Question* (New York: Norton, 1972), p. 109; Salisbury is quoted in ibid., 222; and Chamberlain's quotation is from his work *The Struggle for Peace* (London: Hutchinson, 1940), p. 418.

for power, or personal character flaws.[2] This is a mistake. The revulsion against American policy in the Third World does not provide a good platform from which to understand why people behaved as they did, and while the fact that the fall of Vietnam did not topple many other dominoes should lead us to ask why many people expected this outcome, it does not necessarily mean that the beliefs were insincere or happened to be rationalizations. Instead of, or at least before, condemning domino beliefs we should try to understand them.

They are central because many foreign policy disagreements turn on different evaluations of the consequences of concessions and limited defeats.[3] States often stand firm in a confrontation, not because the issue is important when taken in isolation, but because they believe that how it is resolved will strongly influence the course of other events, often far removed in time, substance, and geography. Although President Eisenhower is credited with inventing the metaphor of falling dominoes, the phenomena and beliefs are ancient. Here we will examine the internal structures, logics, and implications of these beliefs and then briefly analyze their validity.

By domino beliefs I mean the expectation that a defeat or retreat on one issue or in one area of the world is likely to produce, through a variety of mechanisms discussed later, further demands on the state by its adversaries and defections from its allies. Two aspects of these beliefs are unusual. First, we often expect that decision-makers will focus on the short run. But here they are looking well into the future. In criticizing the British attempt to overthrow Nasser in 1956 because of their concerns about what might happen years later if they did not, Eisenhower said that he had "insisted long and earnestly that you cannot resort to force in international relationships because of your fear of what might happen in the future."[4] The British policy

2 Cold War revisionists stress economic motives, although how these would explain the costly involvement in a country with no economic value is left unexplored. For the importance of domestic competition, see Craig Campbell and Fredrik Logevall, *America's Cold War: The Politics of Insecurity* (Cambridge: Harvard University Press, 2009); for accounts that attribute Johnson's Vietnam decisions to his fear of humiliation see Blema Steinberg. *Shame and Humiliation: Presidential Decision-Making on Vietnam* (Pittsburg: University of Pittsburg Press, 1996), and Fredrik Logevall, *Choosing War: The Lost Chance for Peace and the Escalation of War in Vietnam* (Berkeley: University of California Press, 1999).

3 See, for example, the alternative predictions of the effect of the fell of Vietnam made by members of the NSC staff and representatives of the Joint Chiefs of Staff in *The Pentagon Papers* (Senator Gravel edition), vol. 3 (Boston Press, 1972), pp. 625–28.

4 Quoted in Stephen Ambrose. *Eisenhower*, vol. 2, *The President* (New York: Simon and Schuster, 1984), p. 365. Similarly, when German Chancellor Konrad Adenauer told Eisenhower that the communists were responsible for the Algerian rebellion and that if it succeeded, Morocco, Tunisia, and the Middle East would also fall to communism, Eisenhower responded that he could not "foresee such a chain of disaster," ibid., 538.

certainly was unwise, but few statesmen, even Eisenhower himself, would be willing to adopt his standard all the time.

That the immediate issue is not a vital one is beside the point. As Lord Palmerston noted, "Any nation which were to act upon the principle of yielding to every demand made upon it, if each separate demand could be shown not to involve directly and immediately a vital interest, would at no distant period find itself progressively stripped of the means of defending its vital interests, when those interests came at last to be attacked."[5] Social scientists discovered this principle—Reinhard Selten's "chain store paradox"[6]—almost a century and a half later. A large department store that has a monopoly in a small town is faced by the opening of a smaller store that is providing effective competition. It would be less costly to accommodate the newcomer at the sacrifice of some profit than to engage in a price war. But to follow this course of action might be to encourage others to open additional stores, further eating into the department store's profits and power. If the store can succeed not only in driving its competitor out of business, but also in convincing would-be entrants into the market that they will suffer the same fate, then the cost of a price war is a good investment.

The second point is more familiar but easy to forget when we focus on domino dynamics: as Kenneth Waltz and Stephen Walt have stressed, states usually oppose rather than join the most menacing state in the system. Power balancing is the rule, band-wagoning the exception.[7] This dichotomy goes under other terms as well, such as negative versus positive feedback or instability versus stability. The question is whether the change of a variable will

5 Quoted in Roger Bullen, *Palmerston, Guizot and the Collapse of the Entente Cordiale* (London: Athlone Press, 1974), p. 56.

6 Reinhart Selten, "The Chain Store Paradox," *Theory and Decision* 9 (April 1978): 127–59. For a discussion of how that actors' understanding of these dynamics can alter them, see Robert Jervis, *System Effects: Complexity in Political and Social Life* (Princeton: Princeton University Press, 1997), pp. 266–71.

7 Kenneth Waltz, *Theory of International Politics* (Reading, Mass.: Addison-Wesley, 1979); Stephen Walt, "Alliance Formation and the Balance of World Power," *International Security* 9 (Spring 1985): 3–43; Walt, *The Origins of Alliances* (Ithaca: Cornell University Press, 1987). Also see Arnold Wolfers. "The Balance of Power in Theory and Practice," pp. 122–24 in Wolfers, *Discord and Collaboration* (Baltimore: Johns Hopkins University Press, 1962). For other analyses of domino effect, see Jerome Slater, "Dominos in Central America: Will They Fall? Does it Matter?" *International Security* 12 (Fall 1987): 105–34; Betty Glad and Charles Taber, "The Domino Theory," in Betty Glad, ed., *War: The Psychological Dimension* (Syracuse, N.Y.: Syracuse University Press, 1988); Ross Gregory, "The Domino Theory," pp. 275–80 in Alexander DeConde, ed., *Encyclopedia of America Foreign Policy*, vol.1 (New York: Scribner's 1978); and Lars Schoultz, *National Security and United States Policy Toward Latin America* (Princeton: Princeton University Press, 1987). For the analogy, not to dominoes, but to ten-pins, see Stewart Alsop quoted in Kennedy, *Rise and Fall of the Great Powers*, 382. For a general discussion of feedbacks, see Jervis, *System Effects*, ch. 4.

call up forces that tend to return that variable to its previous value or whether the changes will lead to further movement in the same direction, thus leading to a reinforcing cycle of change. As we will discuss later, domino dynamics can operate through a number of quite different mechanisms. But those who hold the domino beliefs rarely acknowledge that their expectations run contrary to the most widely accepted generalization held by both theorists and practitioners of international politics alike. Instead, they usually imply that positive feedback is the "natural order" in international politics.[8]

What Is at Stake?

As long as the particular issue is relatively unimportant, the costs of resisting a strongly motivated adversary are likely to be greater than the costs of conceding. But a decision-maker who believes that the failure to resist will undercut his state's general position may conclude that he must stand firm. Those who seek to persuade the state to follow a conciliatory path argue that, on the contrary, the issue is in fact isolated from others. "No war for Danzig" makes sense when the issue is put that way. As Chamberlain said in his speech during the Munich crisis the year before, "However much we may sympathize with a small nation confronted by a big and powerful neighbor, we cannot in all circumstances undertake to involve the whole British Empire in a war simply on her account. If we have to fight it must be on larger issues than that."[9] The classic generic counterargument was made by Pericles in the crucial debate at the start of the Peloponnesian War:

> Let none of you think ... that we should be going to war for a trifle if we refuse to revoke the Megarian decree. It is a point they make much of, and say that war need not take place if we revoke this decree; but if we do go to war, let there be no kind suspicion in your hearts that the war was over a small matter. For you this trifle is both the assurance and the proof of your determination.[10]

Similar beliefs underpinned the American resistance to Soviet demands in Berlin. During the 1948 Berlin blockade, the American military governor in Germany, General Lucius Clay, stressed to his superiors, "Please remem-

8 For the concept of natural order, see Stephen Toulmin, *Foresight and Understanding* (New York: Harper and Row, 1963).

9 Quoted in Telford Taylor, *Munich* (Garden City, N.Y.: Doubleday, 1979), p. 885. Some in the cabinet endorsed the appeasement on the quiet different grounds that Hitler already dominated the continent and so what happened to Czechoslovakia did not matter: ibid., 750–51.

10 Thucydides, *The Peloponnesian War*, trans. Rex Warner (Harmondsworth, England: Penguin Books, 1954), p. 92.

ber, emphasize and never stop repeating that currency in Berlin is not the issue—the issue is our position in Europe and plans for western Germany."[11] In the crisis over the access routes thirteen years later, most American statesmen agreed with Dean Acheson that, in Arthur Schlesinger's paraphrase, "West Berlin was not a problem but a pretext. Khrushchev's ... object ... was not to rectify a local situation but to test the general American will to resist.... Since there was nothing to negotiate, willingness on our part to go to the conference table would be taken in Moscow as evidence of weakness and make the crisis so much worse." Those who disagreed did so because they did not see the issue in such general terms. "Some who knew the Soviet Union best, like Ambassadors Thompson and Harriman, believed that, on the contrary, Khrushchev's objectives might well be limited. Thompson argued ... that the predominant Soviet motive was the desire to improve the communist position in Eastern Europe rather than to achieve world-wide political humiliation of the United States."[12] Nikita Khrushchev described the issue in terms that mirror Acheson's:

> The question of access to West Berlin and the whole question of the peace treaty is for [the Western Powers] only a pretext. If we abandoned our intention of concluding a peace treaty, they would take this as a strategic breakthrough and would in no time broaden the range of their demands. They would demand the abolition of the socialist system in the German Democratic Republic. If they achieved this too, they would, of course, undertake to wrest from Poland and Czechoslovakia the lands that were restored to them under the Potsdam Agreement—and these are Polish and Czechoslovak lands. And if the Western powers achieved all this, they would come forward with their principal demand—that the socialist system be abolished in all the countries of the socialist camp.[13]

In none of the conflicts of the Cold War in which the United States fought was the country being defended important enough to justify heavy loss of American life. Thus in the words of one presidential adviser, "The real basis of the Korean decision had almost nothing to do with Korea. It had to do with aggression."[14] The central justification for fighting in Vietnam was identical,

11 Quoted Avi Shlaim, *The United States and the Berlin Blockade, 1943–1949* (Berkeley: University of California Press, 1983), p. 188. The Soviets clearly agreed. For them, the major objective in all the Berlin crises has been to influence Western policy on wider German issues. Berlin was a pressure point, not an issue of great instinct importance.

12 Arthur Schlesinger, Jr, *A Thousand Days* (Boston: Houghton Mifflin, 1965), pp. 381–83.

13 Quoted in Robert Slusser, *The Berlin Crises of 1961* (Baltimore: Johns Hopkins University Press, 1973), p. 112.

14 Quoted in Glenn Paige, *The Korean Decision* (New York: Free Press, 1968), p. 298.

and in Angola Kissinger argued that "the question is whether America still maintains the resolve to act responsibly as a great power—prepared to face a challenge when it arises."[15] In other words, it is the expectation of future interactions that creates, or at least magnifies, the conflict. Contrary to the well-known cases in which states cooperate in one instance because they think that doing so will encourage cooperation over the long run, when competitiveness is higher, the knowledge that the game will continue makes actors less willing to be conciliatory.

Taken to its limit, this way of looking at the future not only expands but homogenizes the state's interests. Thus Secretary of Defense Casper Weinberger could argue, "In every corner of the globe, America's vital interests are threatened by an ever-growing Soviet military threat."[16] Without a belief in domino dynamics, it is hard to see how even the most important country in the world could have literally vital interests in all parts of the globe. As Douglas Macdonald has noted, this perspective makes it impossible to separate central from peripheral interests, as demonstrated when President Kennedy admitted, "I don't know where the non-essential areas are."[17] Indeed, often what makes an interest or a geographical area essential is the fact that it is threatened by the adversary. Because the two states are in a struggle for influence, each must take the opposite side from the other. It would otherwise be hard to explain why the United States supported Jonas Savimbi in Angola. The French prime minister reasoned similarly about the rivalry with Britain in the mid-nineteenth century: his country had to weigh in strongly on behalf of one faction in the dispute over royal marriages in Spain because "Palmerston wishes to deny the Duchess her natural rights, we must therefore support them."[18]

Four consequences follow from the inflation of the importance of local disputes caused by the expectation of domino dynamics. First, the adversary can create a crisis at the time and place of its choosing. This is unfortunate, but inevitable: "Unlike those sociable games it takes two to play, with chicken it takes two *not* to play. If you are publicly invited to play chicken and say you would rather not, you have just played."[19] Second, cooperative adjustments

15 *Department of State Bulletin* 74 (February 16, 1976): 175.

16 Annual Report to the Congress for Fiscal Year 1988 (Washington, D.C.: US. Government Printing Office, 1987), p. 4.

17 Douglas Macdonald, "The Truman Administration and Global Responsibilities: The Birth of the Falling Domino Principle," in Jack Snyder and Robert Jervis, eds., *Dominos and Bandwagons: Strategic Beliefs and Great Power Competition in the Eurasian Rimland* (New York: Oxford University Press, 1991), ch. 5; the quotation from Kennedy can be found on p. 133 and comes from Herbert Parmet, *JFK. The Presidency of John F. Kennedy* (New York: Dial Press, 1983), p. 328.

18 Roger Bullen, *Collapse of the Entente Cordial*, 268.

19 Thomas Schelling, *Arms and Influence* (New Haven: Yale University Press, 1966), p. 188, emphasis in the original.

of local disputes will be difficult because one obvious mechanism for conflict resolution is nullified. States are often willing to make concessions when they believe that the other's interests are more deeply involved than their own. But if what is at stake is a reputation that will strongly influence future disputes, conflicts have a zero-sum cast. Third, there is at least an element of self-fulfilling prophecy here. The small issue really is vital because it is treated as such. The logic of the defender rests at least in part on the belief that the challenger believes that the defender believes that what is at stake is the future relationship between them. Fourth, as Walt argues, to the extent that the state expects domino dynamics, it cedes great power to its local allies. The threat to abandon them will lack credibility if the client state realizes that the patron believes that a local defeat will endanger its own vital interests.[20]

Threats, Promises, and Credibility

While scholars and decision-makers have stressed that failing to live up to threats undermines the state's position, almost nothing has been said about the value of a reputation for living up to promises.[21] Reneging on one promise would seem to produce a sort of domino effect in that other promises, at least of a similar nature, would not be believed. But most current discussions apply this argument only in cases where the promise is the obverse side of a threat, such as the American promise to protect a country against communist predation.[22] Only occasionally is the issue raised in other contexts. For example, during World War II President Roosevelt argued that "the only reason we stand so well with the Russians is that up to date we have kept our promises."[23] Similarly, in 1962 the Russians resisted Chinese pressures to violate their commitment to the United States and supply arms to the Pathet Lao by saying that to do so "would put in the hands of our enemies a great political trump; enabling them to say in their propaganda that socialist countries do not meet their obligations. For example, how would socialist proposals to guarantee a free city status for West Berlin look if socialist countries began to violate

20 Stephen Walt, *Origins of Alliances* (Ithaca: Cornell University Press, 1987), pp. 21, 45.

21 This error was not made by Schelling. See Thomas Schelling, *The Strategy of Conflict* (Cambridge: Harvard University Press, 1960), pp. 43–46, 131–37.

22 Kissinger's claim for the importance of living up to our promises to Pakistan in the 1971 war was partly based on this consideration: *White House Years* (Boston: Little Brown, 1979), pp. 895–913.

23 Quoted in Deborah Larson, "The Non-Strategy of Containment," unpublished ms. (Columbia University), p. 7. See Churchill's similar statement of the importance of convincing the Russians that the West would respect its promises in Martin Gilbert, *Winston S. Churchill: Road to Victory*, vol. 7 (Boston: Houghton Mifflin, 1986), p. 639.

the only recently signed Geneva agreement?"[24] But such concerns seem to be exceptional. More typically, few people raised the question of whether the American withdrawal from the ABM treaty has reduced the value of its other commitments. More recently, Obama's decision to overthrow Qaddafi despite the agreement to normalize relations with him in return for his giving up his nuclear and chemical weapons will probably reduce the efficacy of future promises of this kind.

Although states seem preoccupied with the credibility of their threats and uninterested in the credibility of their promises, the reverse appears to be the case when they examine others' past behavior. If another state, especially an adversary, fails to live up to a promise, this is sharply noted and taken as evidence that other pledges are worth little. Thus, those who claimed that the Soviet Union violated its arms control agreements argued that this behavior showed that other treaties would not be likely to restrain a Soviet arms buildup. The belief that the Soviets broke the Basic Principles Agreement of 1972 when it failed to notify the United States that Egypt and Syria were about to attack Israel in October 1973 led many to conclude that the Soviets would not abide by promises to respect the "rules of the game." Similarly, when in late 1988 it seemed that the Soviets might not withdraw from Afghanistan by the promised date, a Western diplomat said: "if they're not out by February 15 [1989], the cost will be tremendous."[25]

But while seizing on occasions when the adversary appears not to live up to its promises, states seem to pay little attention when others fail to carry out their threats to harm them. The evidence here is particularly impressionistic, but the point is important because it contradicts one of the central premises of the domino theory. Thus, for example, it is not clear that Soviet credibility greatly suffered from the fact that its leaders failed to respond vigorously to the NATO deployment of INF, returned to the bargaining table after saying they would not do so, and eventually making major concessions. Similarly, the failure of the USSR to carry out its threats over Berlin in the first decade of the Cold War did not seem to have convinced the United States that Russia was prone to bluff. Neither did the Soviet retreat from Afghanistan lead the United States to draw inferences parallel to those it thought others would draw after it withdrew from Vietnam.

24 Quoted in David Hall. "The Laos Neutralization Agreement, 1962," in Alexander George, Philip Farley, and Alexander Dallin, eds., *U.S.-Soviet Secretary Cooperation* (New York: Oxford University Press, 1988), p. 457. For another example, see Glen Seaborg with Benjamin Loeb, *Stemming the Tide: Arms Control in the Johnson Years* (Lexington, Mass.: Lexington Books, 1987), p. 328.

25 Philip Taubman. "Moscow Suspends Pullout of Its Afghan Forces: Charges Violations of Pact," *New York Times*, November 5, 1988.

INTERCONNECTIONS

Seemingly small issues are seen as highly consequential because the world is believed to be tightly interconnected.[26] It is one world; behavior cannot be separated into rigid compartments; "we cannot abandon friends in one part of the world without jeopardizing the security of friends everywhere."[27] Thus Oliver Harvey, principal private secretary of the British foreign secretary in the late 1930s, reminded his boss that "foreign policy must be regarded as a whole. It is not possible to take a strong line in one quarter and a weak one in another indefinitely." As he put it in his diary, "We are weak with Franco and as a direct consequence Japan is now bullying us. If we are weak again with Japan, we shall have Hitler and Mussolini beating us up. And, above all, if we are weak in helping China, who is fighting our battle, we shall find our own little allies ratting on us. Why shouldn't they?"[28] So it is not surprising that one common axis of disagreement on American policy is between those who focus on the specific situation and the particular nations involved (often State Department officials are area experts), and those who take a global geopolitical perspective (often in the White House or outside foreign policy generalists). The former usually believe that states in a region are strongly driven by domestic concerns and local rivalries; the latter are predisposed to think that these states look to the major powers for their cues and have only little control over their fate.[29]

26 For a discussion in these terms of American decision-makers' belief systems during the Berlin blockade, see Alexander George and Richard Smoke, *Deterrence in American Foreign Policy* (New York: Columbia University Press, 1974), pp. 109–17 and Avi Shlaim, *The U.S. and the Berlin Blockade 1948–1949: A Study in Crisis Decision-Making* (Berkeley: University of California University, 1983), pp. 68–69. For arguments that American statesmen have generally overestimated the extent to which events all over the world are tightly coupled, see Max Singer and Aaron Wildavsky, "A Third World Averaging Strategy," pp. 13–35 in Paul Seabury and Aaron Wildavsky, eds., *US Foreign Policy: Perspectives and Proposals for the 1970s* (New York: McGraw-Hill, 1969); Robert Johnson, "Exaggerating America's Stakes in Third World Conflicts," *International Security* 10 (Winter 1985/86): 32–68; Patrick Morgan. "Saving Face for the Sake of Deterrence," pp. 125–52 in Robert Jervis, Richard Ned Lebow, and Janice Stein, eds, *Psychology and Deterrence* (Baltimore: Johns Hopkins Press, 1985); Charles Kupchan. "American Globalism and the Middle East," *Political Science Quarterly* 103 (Winter 1988/89): 585–611.

27 Henry Kissinger, in *Department of State Bulletin* 72 (April 14, 1975): 461–62. Secretary of State Cordell Hull made a similar point in 1937 when he told the Japanese ambassador, "There can be serious hostilities anywhere in the world which will not one way or another affect interests or rights or obligations of this country." Quoted in Jonathan Utley, *Going to War with Japan, 1937–1941* (Knoxville: University of Tennessee Press, 1985), p. 5.

28 John Harvey, ed., *The Diplomatic Diaries of Oliver Harvey, 1937–1940* (New York: St. Martin's, 1970), pp. 229, 425.

29 Of course there are many exceptions. Thus Susan Purcell, a Latin America expert, attributes Central American countries' willingness to sign the Arias plan even though they had

Kinds of Interests

In many cases, the interconnections of domino dynamics work through the kind of national interest that is believed to be involved.[30] We can distinguish between intrinsic interests and what can be called image or reputational interest. As Glenn Snyder explains,

> Intrinsic values are "end values"; they are valued for their own sake rather than for what they contribute to the power relations between the protagonists. They include such things as the value we place upon our own independence ... , the value we attach to the independence (or nonCommunization) of other countries with which we feel a cultural or psychic affinity (apart from what their independence contributes to our security), the economic values which we find in trading with other free countries (to the extent that these values would be lost should these countries fall under communist control), and moral values such as self-respect [and] honor.[31]

If the world is not tightly interconnected, behavior will be driven by the intrinsic value of the issue. But if statesmen believe that others are drawing important inferences from their behavior, reputational interests will be crucial. The latter represent the influence the state's behavior will have on other events because of the changes in the expectations about how the state will behave in the future. When others think that the state has defaulted on a pledge, they may be less likely to believe its other promises and threats; when the state has displayed boldness or weakness in one case, they may expect similar behavior in other cases.

When observers believe intrinsic interests to be primary, they will expect the state's behavior to vary greatly depending on the situation. But if reputa-

---

previously objected to some of its key provisions to "the decline in the power and prestige of the United States in general and of President Regan in particular in the wake of the Iran-Contra Affair." See Purcell, "The Choice in in Central America," *Foreign Affairs* 66 (Fall 1987): 177.

30 Of course, domino dynamics are not the only ways in which events can be tightly coupled. For example, military leaders often are preoccupied by the danger that increasing military forces in one area will make it harder for the state to live up to other obligations elsewhere by decreasing the resources that remain available. The perspective characterized the American military establishment from the onset of the Cold War to the vast increases in the military budget that occurred in the wake of the Korean conflict. For an example of similar thinking on the part of British military officials in the earlier twentieth century, see Keith Jeffery, "The Eastern Arc of Empire: A Strategic View, 1850–1950," *Journal of Strategic Studies* 5 (June 1982): 531–45.

31 Glenn Snyder, *Deterrence and Defense* (Princeton: Princeton University Press, 1961), p. 31. Also see Franklin Weinstein, "The Concept of Commitment in International Relations," *International Studies Quarterly* 12 (March 1969): 39–56; George and Smoke, *Deterrence in American Foreign Policy*, 552–61; Schelling's distinction between threats and warnings in *Strategy of Conflict*, 123–24; and Samuel Huntington, "Patterns of Intervention," *National Interest* 7 (Spring 1987): 39.

tional interests are seen to dominate, similar behavior will be expected over a wide range of situations, because observers will attribute the state's behavior to its relatively unchanging characteristics. Thus the argument for why Britain had to suppress the Irish Rebellion in 1917 even though doing so detracted from the war effort: "[I]f you tell your empire in India, in Egypt and all over the world that you have not got the men, the money, the pluck, the inclination, and that backing to resolve order in a country within twenty miles of your own shore, you may as well begin to abandon the attempt to make British rule prevail throughout the empire at all."[32]

At first glance arguments like these make perfect sense, and indeed are often correct. But the alternative should be explicated. If a country retreats rather than pays an enormous price for an object of little intrinsic value, it is not clear that others should or will expect it to back down on issues that matter more to it. Thus at the start of the Korean War the State Department intelligence office made a statement that seems self-evident, but in fact is not: "Japanese reaction to the invasion will depend almost entirely upon the course of action pursued by the United States since they will regard the position taken by the United States as presaging U.S. action should Japan be threatened with invasion."[33] But if the Japanese reasoned that their country was much more important to the United States than was South Korea, they would have no reason to expect that U.S. unwillingness to fight for the latter meant that they would not be protected.

What is largely at issue, then, is how others see the world and the kind of interest they believe predicts the state's behavior. This was explicitly recognized by Kissinger in a response to a reporter's question a month before Saigon fell: "With respect to Indo-China, we are not equating the intrinsic importance of each part of the world, and we are not saying that every part of the world is strategically as important to the United States as any other part of the world.... [But whether or not we give economic and military aid to Vietnam] is a fundamental question of how we are viewed by all other people."[34] Kissinger's prediction of the dire consequences of not opposing the Soviet Union in Angola ten months later rested on a similar analysis of others' beliefs:

> When one great power tips the balance of forces decisively in a conflict through its military intervention—and meets no resistance—an ominous precedent is set, of grave consequences even if the intervention occurs

32 Quoted in Brian Bond. *British Military Policy Between in Two World Wars* (Oxford: Clarendon Press, 1980), p. 18.

33 Department of State. *Foreign Relations of the United States, 1950*, vol. 7, *Korea* (Washington, D.C.: U.S. Government Printing Office, 1976) (hereafter *FRUS*, with year and volume number), p. 151.

34 *Department of State Bulletin* 72 (April 14, 1975): 462.

in a seemingly remote area.... To claim that Angola is not an important country, or that the United States has no important interests there, begs the principal question. If the United States is seen to waver in the face of massive Soviet and Cuban intervention, what will be the perception of leaders around the world as they make decisions concerning their future security? And what conclusion will an unopposed superpower draw when the next opportunity for intervention beckons?[35]

George Kennan's argument reveals both the obvious line of rebuttal and its difficulty: "It is important to recognize that not all places ... are of equal importance.... There are some, such as Korea and Cuba, that are of high strategic importance in the sense that they affect the interest of this country and other great powers in an intimate and sensitive way. There are others ... [that] are of minor significance from the standpoint of the world balance of power. The two must not be equated."[36] But the criteria by which Cuba had "high strategic importance" are far from clear. Indeed, Walter Lippmann's central criticism of Kennan's original article on containment was that this doctrine did not permit discrimination between vital and less central interests.[37] Yet, as Kennan himself sometimes recognized, defeats in the periphery could demoralize elites and the publics in areas of high intrinsic importance. Psychological connections must either be altered or accommodated.[38]

The belief in the centrality of reputational interests makes extended deterrence (i.e., the deterrence of attacks on allies) both possible and necessary. Extended deterrence is possible because if potential aggressors believe that the defenders see events as interconnected they will conclude that the latter will be willing to pay more to resist than the area's intrinsic value would merit.[39] For the same reason, extended deterrence is necessary because a failure to act at the periphery menaces areas of greater intrinsic value. To put this another way, much of the discussion of the importance of enforcing certain "rules of conduct" during the Cold War, especially the prohibition against either superpower using force to change the status quo, rested on the importance of reputational interests. If the Soviets were allowed to use force in Af-

---

35 Henry Kissinger. "Containment of Kremlin," *Washington Post*, February 16, 1976, p. A15.

36 George Kennan. "Containment of Kremlin," *Washington Post*, February 16, 1976, p. A15

37 *The Cold War* (New York: Harper and Brothers, 1947).

38 See John Lewis Gaddis, "Introduction: The Evolution of Containment," in Jerry Deibel and Gaddis, eds., *Containment: Concept and Policy*, vol. 1 (Washington, D.C.: National Defense University Press, 1982), pp. 85, 88.

39 Sometimes even the core values being protected do not seem to justify the effort at resisting the initial predation period. The possibility is raised by Margaret Thatcher's jurisdiction of using force to reclaim the Falklands: "We can't let this go. Otherwise, what would happen to Gibraltar, Belize and to other similar places?" Quoted in William Borders, "'Iron Lady' Displays Grit at Reception," *New York Times,* April 22, 1982.

ghanistan, they and others would believe that they, and perhaps other countries as well, would be permitted to use force elsewhere. Because people expect a high degree of consistency, undesired behavior on one issue or in one area of the world must be resisted to prevent it from becoming accepted as normal.

It was often argued that the United States (and presumably the USSR) needed to display high resolve in limited conflicts to deter the other superpower from challenging it in places and ways that could produce an all-out war. But "scaling up" from small issues and wars to nuclear confrontations is problematical because the costs and the stakes of the latter are incomparably greater than those of the former. It seems unreasonable that anyone should have drawn inferences about how the United States might have behaved at the brink of nuclear war from how it acted in Vietnam. Indeed, if fighting a small war would markedly increase the American ability to deter the Soviets from menacing its vital interests, then the war in Vietnam would have been a cheap way to protect the United States. This example shows that inferences about resolve can undermine rather than support themselves: if the United States felt that fighting a small war for a country of little intrinsic value would have led others to conclude that it would display high resolve in a dangerous confrontation, then this action actually would not provide reliable evidence because the United States would fight this war in order to create a favorable impression irrespective of whether or not it would run high risks in a nuclear challenge.[40] In many instances, then, for a state to admit that it is behaving as it is in order to bolster its reputation should be self-defeating; there would be no reason for others to see the behavior as typical of what the state will do in the future.

EARLY RESISTANCE CAN BE EFFECTIVE

If small gains and losses lead to larger ones, it is obviously important to stop the bandwagon before it gathers momentum. Thus in the spring of 1985, the U.S. National Intelligence Officer for the Near East argued that both the United States and the Soviet Union "lack ... preferred access to Iran. Whoever gets there first is in a strong position to work towards the exclusion of the other."[41] But claims like this imply that the target state will remain passive or that the

40 Reputation remains understudied but has received more attention following the publication of Jonathan Mercer's path-breaking *Reputation and International Politics* (Ithaca: Cornell University Press, 1996). For a discussion of the cultural influences on honor, which leads to a concern for reputation, see Allan Dafoe and Devin Caughey, "Honor and War: Southern U.S. Presidents and the Effects of Concern for Reputation," *World Politics* 26 (April 2016): 341–81.

41 Quoted in the *President's Report of the Special Review Board* (Tower Commission) (Washington, D.C.: U.S. Government Printing Office, 1987), p. B-6.

dynamics of its internal politics will work to the advantage of whichever out-side state first recruits important political allies. In faction-ridden countries, this is quite questionable. Shifting the focus to international struggles, propo-nents of the domino theory often also believe what Jack Snyder has called the Thermopylae Corollary—the claim that it is easier to resist the adversary at the point of the initial challenge than to fend off later attacks on more central values.[42] Thus, in 1950 the State Department working group advocating mili-tary aid for the French in Indochina argued that "[t]he choice confronting the United States is to support the French in Indochina or face the extension of Communism over the remainder of the continental area of Southeast Asia and, possibly, farther westward. We then would be obliged to make stagger-ing investments in those areas.... It would seem a case of 'Penny wise, Pound foolish' to deny support to the French in Indochina."[43] When the other side is seen as currently weak, the resulting paper-tiger image strongly supports immediate resistance.[44] This kind of claim is implicit in Kissinger's arguments about Angola quoted earlier. A firm American response to the Soviet and Cuban intervention would have been met not by matching escalation but by a retreat, because the other side lacked the physical capability and the resolve to carry the struggle to a higher level of violence.

Why can it be believed—or rationalized—that resistance is cheaper and safer when it comes early? First, and most obviously, conquests can add to the aggressor's physical strength. Thus Hitler found it easier to wage World War II once he had absorbed Czechoslovakia's resources. A second reason is that the adversary's initial probes may be tentative because of uncertainty about the defender's reactions. But if the latter retreats once or twice, the former, expecting similar behavior in the future, will become bolder and can be stopped only by stronger resistance. The belief that the other's move is a probe implies both that it must be and that it can be resisted. One reason why the United States thought it was relatively safe to fight in Korea was the belief that if the Russians had been willing to engage in all-out war, they would have launched a full attack rather than move in the periphery.[45] Furthermore, probes can be turned to the defender's advantage. The Moscow embassy ca-bled this message to Washington the day after the outbreak of the Korean War: "Kremlin's Korean adventure ... offers us opportunity to show that we mean what we say by talking of firmness, and at the same time, to unmask present

---

42 See Jack Snyder, *Myths of Empire: Domestic Politics and International Ambition* (Ithaca: Cornell University, 1991).

43 *FRUS, 1950*, vol. 6, p. 714.

44 Snyder, *Myths of Empire.*

45 For an analysis of the American interpretations, see Alexander George, "American Policy-Making and the North Korean Aggression," *World Politics* 7 (January 1955): 209–32.

important Soviet weaknesses before eyes [of the] world and particularly Asia where popular concept [of] Soviet power [is] grossly exaggerated as result [of] recent Soviet political and propaganda successes."[46]

MUNICH

Thermopylae and paper-tiger beliefs, like the domino theory itself, were made more salient by the experience of the 1930s. The secret discussions at the time hit all the notes that are now familiar. During the Munich crisis French Prime Minister Edouard Daladier argued the following to Chamberlain:

> Germany's real aim was the disintegration of Czechoslovakia [rather than the incorporation of the Sudeten Germans] and the realization of pan-German ideals through a march to the East.... The result would be that in a very short time Germany would be master of Europe, and, in particular, of the wheat and petrol of South-Eastern Europe. Within one year we might expect her to turn back against France and Great Britain, who would then have to meet her in much more difficult circumstances than those existing today.[47]

The British analysis differed: "Chamberlain did not accept this view and mentioned that the absorption of Austria had not proved easy and had in any event stirred world opinion."[48] A parallel difference emerged a bit later in a conversation between the British foreign secretary and the French ambassador. According to the former, the latter

> said that if it was only a question of Czechoslovakia, it might be possible to judge the issue differently. The French Government, however, felt that if this contemplated aggression were allowed to pass unrested, their turn would come next. I said that this really was an argument in favor of a certain war now, against the possibility of war, perhaps in more unfavorable conditions, later. With that argument I had never been able to feel any sympathy: nor did I think that the conclusion of it could be justified.[49]

46 *FRUS, 1950* vol. 7, p. 139.

47 E. L. Woodward, Rohan Butler, and Margaret Lambert, eds., *Document on British Foreign Policy-1939, Third Series*, vol. 2, *European Affairs, July-September 1938* (London: His Majesty's Stationery Office, 1949), p. 384.

48 Ibid., 213. Although this remark was made two weeks before Daladier's and not in direct response to it, the nature of the dialogue remains clear.

49 Ibid., 277. As noted above, Chamberlain implicitly gave a different answer to this question six months later when Germany invaded the non-German portions of Czechoslovakia.

Although the experience of the 1930s has provided the matrix for later arguments for the need to stop aggressors early, in fact there was no way to deter Hitler—some sort of war was unavoidable. (The only plausible line of rebuttal is to argue that if the Allies had stood firm at Munich, the German generals would have overthrown Hitler. Obviously, a definitive conclusion is hard to draw, but I remain skeptical.) Indeed, Hitler's appetite did not grow with the eating because it was enormous from the beginning. This is not to deny that British and French weakness produced significant band-wagoning— Belgium returned to neutrality, Hungary, Bulgaria, and Rumania supported Germany, and even as major a power as the Soviet Union finally did so, although whether or not in response to Western policy is hotly debated.[50] Furthermore, forcibly resisting Hitler in the first years would have been easier than fighting in 1939. We should not lose sight of three points, however. First, even a war fought as early as the 1936 Rhineland crisis would not have been quick or easy.[51] Second, it is not clear whether the year that intervened between Munich and the start of World War II benefited the Germans or the Allies.[52] Third, an earlier war would have left large segments of the Allied countries—let alone Germany—unconvinced that the war was necessary, thereby creating an uneasy postwar world.

DOMINO MECHANISMS

Critics of the domino theory note that it is vague on how a local defeat will be transformed into a far-reaching one. Part of the reason for this is that there are many channels by which these effects can be produced. Indeed, the validity of domino arguments may vary not only according to the circumstances, but also according to the particular mechanism that is supposed to be at work.

The most obvious possibility was mentioned earlier: the conquest or dominance of one area of the world can significantly increase the state's physical resources. Thus in reply to Treasury Secretary George Humphrey's claim that the United States did not have a major stake in areas of the Third World outside of the Western Hemisphere, President Eisenhower "pointed out that India contained a population of 350 million, among which was a lot of very

50 On Belgium, see David Kieft, *Belgium's Return to Neutrality* (Oxford: Clarendon Press, 1972); on Russia compare, for example, Jiri Hochman, *The Soviet Union and the Failure of Collective Security, 1934–38* (Ithaca: Cornell University Press, 1984); and Jonathan Halsam, *The Soviet Union and the Search for Collective Security* (New York.: St. Martin's, 1984)

51 See Stephen Schuker, "France and the Remilitarization of the Rhineland, 1936," *French Historical Studies* 14 (Autumn 1986): 299–338.

52 See Williamson Murray, *The Change in the European Balance of Power, 1938–1939* (Princeton: Princeton University Press, 1984), chs. 7–8, including the literature cited there; and Milan Hauner, "Czechoslovakia as a Military Factor in British Considerations of 1938," *Journal of Strategic Studies* 1 (September 1978): 194–222.

good military material."[53] At Munich and in the first years of World War II the Allies failed to appreciate the magnitude of this effect. In other cases, what can be more important is the increased vulnerability of the status quo power, rather than a positive accretion to the resources of the expansionist state. Thus, if the Soviet Union could have denied the West access to oil from the Persian Gulf, the West would have been greatly weakened.

Geography provides a related form of domino dynamics: the fall of one area of the world can give an aggressor access to surrounding areas. In the nineteenth century, British statesmen argued that Russian influence had to be kept out of Afghanistan lest neighboring India be menaced. President Reagan made a similar claim about Central America: "Using Nicaragua as a base, the Soviets and Cubans can become the dominant power in the crucial corridor between North and South America. Established there, they will be in a position to threaten the Panama Canal, interdict our vital Caribbean Sea lanes, and ultimately move against Mexico."[54] Indeed, the United States has so many interests that it is easy to argue for the geographical importance of any country, especially if the effects of its falling to communism are seen as spreading from one neighbor to the next. Thus, although Henry Kissinger initially rebuffed those who were alarmed by the Allende regime with the quip that "Chile is a dagger pointed at the heart of Antarctica," he soon came around to arguing that its geography did indeed endow it with special importance.

More often, especially in the Cold War era, the mechanisms are seen as less direct and more psychological, being mediated by the predictions about the inferences actors will draw from the state's behavior, as I have discussed in earlier sections of this chapter. The state will be especially likely to expect others to draw wide-ranging inferences if it believes that the local conflict is a probe designed to determinate the resolve and character of the defender.

The state is also likely to be especially concerned if it thinks that the instruments being used in the local conflict are under the aggressor's control. In addition to the direct use of threats or force, revolutions stimulated from abroad fit this category. Thus, one difference between those who accepted and those who rejected domino theories in the late 1970s and 1980s is that the former tended to see conflicts and insurgencies as sponsored by the Soviet Union, whereas the latter argued that indigenous actors play the dominant role.[55] Similarly, one reason why Kissinger was adamant that the United States

---

53 *FRUS, 1952–1954*, vol. 2, *National Security Affairs, Part I*, p. 838.

54 Barnard Weinraub, "Regan Condemns Nicaragua in Plea for Aid to Rebels," *New York Times*, March 17, 1986.

55 Note Adenauer's view of the Algerian rebellion cited above in note 3, and also Prime Minister Disraeli's description of the Balkan unrest in the late 1870s: "The so-called insurgencies are not natives of any Turkish province, but are simply an invasion of revolutionary bands, whose strength lay in the support afforded to them by Serbia and Montenegro, acting on the instigation

support Pakistan in the 1971 crisis was his belief that "the Soviets encouraged India to exploit Pakistan's travail in part to deliver a blow to our system of alliances, in even greater measure to demonstrate Chinese importance."[56] This is not to say that the belief that the adversary is responsible for the conflict is a necessary condition for believing that it will draw broad inferences from the state's behavior. Some argued that it was important for the United States to protect Kuwaiti shipping against Iranian attacks in order to impress the Soviet Union even though that country was not behind the conflict and indeed may have had as much to lose from Iranian victory as the United States did. But if the adversary is seen as directly involved, the conclusion that it will expect any weakness to be repeated almost always follows.

States need to impress allies as well as adversaries. American statesmen often said they needed to stand firm in a conflict in the Third World in order to show the NATO countries that we would protect them. But the expected inference could be less direct. Thus Nixon's explanations of the "tilt" toward Pakistan in the 1971 contest with India: "If we failed to help Pakistan, then Iran or any other country within the reach of Soviet influence might begin to question the dependability of American support."[57] Particularly important was the fact that this conflict occurred just as the United States was developing its opening to China, an effort in which Pakistan played an important role. One of Kissinger's assistants argued that "we had to show China that we respect a mutual friend and opposed the crossing of international borders. So it was not so much a 'thanks, Yahya, for helping us with China' as demonstrating to China we were a reliable country to deal with."[58]

A country that fails to stand up for one ally is presumed to be unwilling to stand by others as well. One reason why Kissinger was so vexed at Congress for cutting off aid to Southern Vietnam in that country's dying moments was that just as this was happening, the United States was in the midst of trying to broker peace between Egypt and Israel. Later Kissinger attributed the breakdown of these negotiations in part to the congressional limits in Vietnam because "one of our problems was to substitute American assurance for some physical terrain features."[59]

---

of foreign agents and foreign committees," quoted in R. W. Seton-Watson, *Disraeli, Gladstone, and the Eastern Question* (New York: Norton, 1972), p. 44.

56 Kissinger, *White House Years*, 886; also see 767, 913.

57 Richard Nixon, *RN: The Memories of Richard Nixon* (New York: Grosset and Dunlap, 1978), p. 527.

58 Quoted in Seymour Hersh, *The Price of Power: Kissinger in the Nixon White House* (New York: Summit Books, 19830), p. 458.

59 "Secretary Kissinger's news conference of March 26, *Department of State Bulletin* 72 (April 14, 1975): 463. It should be noted, however, that Kissinger went on to say that "the major reason for the breakdown of the negotiations was intrinsic to the negotiations themselves."

In other cases, the third countries of concern may be neutrals, or at least countries without formal alliances to the status quo power. During the Cold War, those states were more likely to fear internal unrest than direct Soviet pressure, let alone invasion. What many feared might lead them to join the Soviet bandwagon was not the belief that an American army would not be coming, but rather the vaguer feeling that communism represented "the wave of the future." For this reason, the views of political elites and mobilizable masses may be as important as the inferences of the top decision-makers. This was the dynamic that most worried George Kennan in 1947:

> One of the vital facts to be borne in mind about international communist movement in the parts of Europe which are not yet under Soviet military and police control is the pronounced "bandwagon" character which that movement bears. By that I mean the fact that a given proportion of the adherents to the movement are drawn to it by no ideological enthusiasm ... but primarily by the belief that it is the coming thing, the movement of the future ... and that those who hope to survive—let alone to thrive—in the coming days will be those who had the foresight to climb on the bandwagon when it was still the movement of the future.[60]

PRESTIGE, CREDIBILITY, AND INFERENCES

When an earlier contest affected either side's physical power, the arguments for why domains should fall are obvious, although not uncontroversial. But when the claim is that the contest has undermined the defender's prestige or credibility, the reasoning needs to be explicated. In many cases, statesmen and analysts stress the importance of precedent, as Kissinger did when he argued that Soviet intervention in Angola was dangerous because it set "an ominous precedent."[61] Similarly, the reason why the United States strongly resisted New Zealand's demand that the United States declare that American warship entering its harbors were not carrying nuclear weapons was the fear that Australia, Japan, and other countries would be primed to make the same demand.[62] The way in which the precedent is supposed to influence future behavior is

60 Quoted in Larson, "The Non-Strategy of Containment," 33–34.

61 Kissinger. "Containment of the Kremlin," 15. Kissinger referred to "the unacceptable precedent of massive Soviet and Cuban military intervention in conflict thousands of miles from their shores [that had] broad implications for the rest of America and, indeed, many other regions of the world." Also see Henry Kissinger, "Foreign Policy and National Security," *International Security* 1 (Summer 1976): 189; and Kissinger, *American Foreign Policy*, 3rd ed. (New York: Norton, 1977), pp. 317–21.

62 For similar American fears about the effects of renegotiating American military rights in Spain, see Paul Delaney, "U.S. and Spain Still Far Apart in Talks on Bases," *New York Times,* October 4, 1987.

not entirely clear, however. It can be argued that behavior sets exceptions, if not rules, that will guide how it and others can act later. Thus, Abram Chayes notes that the American justification for quarantining Cuba in October 1962 was carefully crafted to avoid legitimizing justification that could be used against the West.[63] While those claims make sense within a framework of shared norms and international law, most of the proponents of this view are realists who ordinarily stress power and narrow national interest. Doing less violence to the framework they ordinarily use, realists can employ a second argument: precedents are important because statesmen expect consistency in national behavior.

A third line of reasoning is a bit more complex. Rather than simply projecting behavior forward in time, observers draw inferences according to their explanations of the state's behavior. Other actors try to determine not only *what* a state did, but also *why* it did so. The underlying assumption is that state motivation is fairly stable, and so the reasons why a state took certain actions will be reflected in later behavior. For example, in his speech announcing the American incursion into Cambodia in April 1970, Nixon argued that it is "our will and character that is being tested," and that "if we fail to meet this challenge, all other nations will be on notice that despite its overwhelming power the United States, when a real crisis comes, will be found wanting."[64] To act under duress therefore is likely to produce domino effects. This is one reason why states resist accepting unequal bargains even if the issue at stake is unimportant. It also explains why during the Cuban missile crisis the United States was willing to inform the Soviet Union that it would soon carry out its decision to withdraw intermediate-range ballistic missiles (IRBMs) from Turkey, but resisted openly trading them for the Soviet missiles in Cuba.[65]

If cooperation is viewed not as the product of a laudatory impulse to reach a reasonable solution, but rather as the course of action forced on the state by its inability to protect its interests, the result is likely to be increased pressure for further concessions. Russian statesmen believed that they had inadvertently set this process in motion in the decade before World War I. According

63 Abram Chayes, *The Cuban Missile Crisis* (New York: Oxford University Press, 1974). For a general discussion of precedents, see Elizabeth Kier and Jonathan Mercer, "Setting Precedents in Anarchy: Intervention and Weapons of Mass Destruction," *International Security* 20 (Spring 1996): 77–106.

64 *New York Times*, May 1, 1970. Some of the rationale for building the Peacekeeper missile was similar—the United States had to go ahead in part because the Soviets opposed it and American domestic resistance had led many at home and abroad to conclude that deployment was beyond the country's abilities.

65 For further discussion, see Robert Jervis, "The Cuban Missile Crisis: What Can We Know, Why Did It Start, and How Did It End?" pp. 1–39 in Len Scott and R. Gerald Hughes, eds., *The Cuban Missile Crisis: A Critical Reappraisal* (New York: Routledge, 2015).

to the Russian foreign minister, "Germany had looked upon our concessions as so many proofs of our weakness and far from having prevented our neighbors from using aggressive methods, we had encouraged them."[66] As is so often the case, the basic point can be found in Thucydides. Pericles argues against acceding to the demand to withdraw the Megarian decree in terms that were probably familiar even then: "If you give in, you will immediately be confronted with some greater demand, since they will think that you only gave way on this point through fear."[67] Similarly, if the state refrains from opposing the adversary when it has both an interest in doing so and the necessary capabilities, others will see fear as the explanation. Thus the argument by John Foster Dulles and Dean Rusk in the spring of 1950 that the United States had to protect Formosa:

> If the United States were to announce that it would neutralize Formosa, not permitting it either to be taken by Communists or to be used as a base of military operations against the mainland, that is a decision which we could certainly maintain, short of open war by the Soviet Union. Everyone knows that is the case. If we do not act, it will be everywhere interpreted that we are making another retreat because we do not dare risk war.[68]

This reasoning can be carried a step further. There is no reason why only international actions should be used to infer the character of the state and its leaders. That is, if observers are interested in the state's—and the decision-maker's[69]—willingness to pay a significant price to reach valued objectives, then domestic behavior can also be highly diagnostic. Jonathan Schell may be correct to argue that one reason why Nixon was so disturbed by the domestic protests against the Vietnam war was that he believed that foreign adversaries would infer that an unwillingness to suppress them indicated "softness" that would also be reflected in foreign policy.[70] In the same way, it is possible that Ronald Reagan's firing of the air controllers did more to impress the Russians than did his increase in the defense budget or the liberation of Grenada.[71]

66 Quoted in D. C.B. Lieven, *Russia and the Origins of the First World War* (London: Macmillan, 1983), pp. 141–42.

67 Thucydides, *Peloponnesian War*, 92

68 Identical memoranda were submitted by Dulles and Rusk and can be found in *FRUS, 1950*, vol. 1, pp. 314–16 (Dulles), and *FRUS, 1950*, vol. 6, pp. 349–51 (Rusk).

69 I have explored the question of whether the characteristics of interests are believed to reside in the individual leader, the state, or the type of state in "Deterrence and Perception," in this volume.

70 Jonathan Schell, *The Time of Illusion* (New York: Vintage, 1976), pp. 132–34.

71 I am grateful to George Quester for this point, which is also made by Governor Scott Walker of Wisconsin: see Philip Rucker, "At Donor Summit, 2016 GOP Hopefuls Talk Foreign Policy and Fiscal Issues," *Washington Post*, February 28, 2016. Similar calculations may have

Effect or Effort?

The reasoning processes described in the previous section help explain the puzzling fact that statesmen often argue that the damage to their state's reputation comes, not from being unable to prevent a local defeat, but from refusing to make a major effort to do so. This leads to what Assistant Secretary of Defense John McNaughton called the "good doctor" approach to Vietnam. To impress "other nations regarding U.S.... resolve and competence," the United States had to "be tough, take risks, get bloodied, and hurt the enemy badly" even if it did not win.[72] Perhaps the strongest version of this argument was made by a White House assistant who justified continued American support for what was clearly a losing cause in Iran in 1979 in these terms: "The goal now is to bend over backward to reassure a lot of jittery allies that we are prepared, if necessary, to go up in flames with the Shah."[73] In the same vein, at the outbreak of the Korean War, Secretary of State Acheson argued that "it was important for us to do something even if the effort were not successful." Secretary of Defense Johnson agreed: "Even if we lose Korea [providing aid] would save the situation."[74] A few years later President Eisenhower put a positive cast on a similar argument for the importance of strong resistance if the Chinese communists were to attack the offshore islands of Quemoy and Matsu:

> While it is true under the system one or more of the forward positions might eventually be lost, such loss would occur only after the defending forces had exacted a fearful toll from the attackers, and Chiang's prestige and standing in Southeast Asia would be increased rather than decreased as a result of a gallant, prolonged and bitter defense conducted under these circumstances.[75]

This line of thought is not unique to the Cold War era or to the United States. After Pearl Harbor, Eisenhower argued that even though the United States was outnumbered, it had to defend the Philippines because the people

---

influenced President Bush's behavior during the Eastern Airline strike. Bernard Weinraub, "Airline Dispute: Rite of Passage for Bush," *New York Times*, March 3, 1989.

72 *Pentagon Papers*, vol. 3, p. 604; also see William Gibbons, *U.S. Government and the Vietnam War*, pt. 2 (Princeton, Princeton University Press, 1986), p. 367.

73 Quoted in Richard Burt, "U.S. Reprises Persian Gulf Policies," *New York Times*, January 1, 1979. Also see Scott Armstrong, "Vance Was Preoccupied with SALT as Shah's Rule Disintegrated," *Interactional Herald Tribune*, October 31, 1980.

74 *FRUS, 1950*, vol. 7, p. 182. The quotations are from detailed minutes of the meetings and may not be the actual words that were used.

75 Dwight D. Eisenhower, "Memorandum for the Secretary of State," April 5, 1955; *FRUS, 1954–56*, vol. 2, p. 450. For other examples, see Kissinger, *White House Years*, 898–99; Zbigniew Brzezinski, *Power and Principle* (New York: Farrar, Straus and Giroux, 1983), pp. 182–83.

of Asia "may excuse failure but they will not excuse abandonment."[76] Earlier that year, British Foreign Minister Eden urged support for Greece against the overwhelming German attack on similar grounds: "No doubt our prestige will suffer if we are ignominiously ejected, but in any event to have fought and suffered in Greece would be less damaging to us than to have left Greece to her fate."[77]

The claim is not that audiences will be impressed by empty gestures. It is rather that the effort indicates that the state will incur high costs to help its allies. Thus in early 1975 Secretary of Defense Schlesinger urged continued American aid to South Vietnam because it was crucial that the fall of Indochina "should clearly be marked as the result of the ineptitude of the [Cambodian and South Vietnamese] governments rather than due to a cut-off of American aid."[78] The skill, dedication, and capabilities of regimes under communist pressures would vary from one instance to another, and American aid might not always be able to prevent defeat. But if countries believed that the United States would stand behind them, the fall of Vietnam would not convince them that resistance was hopeless.

This line of argument must be qualified, however, and several implicit assumptions brought to the surface. First, sometimes it is the effect rather than the effort that is believed to be primary. If others believe that even though their patron will support them, this support will not be sufficient to deter or defeat the adversary, they may bandwagon. Thus, at the outbreak of the Korean War the State Department Office of Intelligence Research disagreed with the claims of Acheson and Johnson quoted above, and argued, "If the United States abandons South Korea, whether or not token military assistance has been provided, the Southeast Asian leaders will lose whatever confidence they may have had in the effectiveness of U.S. aid to combat communism." The reasoning is not obscure: "Should U.S. support prove insufficient to prevent defeat of [South Korea], the question of the value to Japan of similar support

76 Quoted in Stephen Ambrose, *The Supreme Commander: The War Years of General Dwight D. Eisenhower* (Garden City, N.Y.: Doubleday, 1970), p. 6.

77 Quoted in Martin Gilbert, *Winston S. Churchill: Finest Hour, 1939–41*, vol. 6 (London: Heinemann, 1983), p. 1029.

78 Quoted in John Finney, "Schlesinger Terms Cambodian Situation Grim, Not Hopeless," *New York Times*, February 24, 1975. When the NSC working group considered "fall-back objectives" for Vietnam in 1964, it stressed the importance of making "clear to the world ... that failure in South Viet Nam, if it comes, was due to special local factors that do not apply to other nations we are committed to defend—that, in short, our will and ability to help those nations defend themselves is not impaired." The representatives of the Joint Chiefs of Staff were not impressed, calling this plan "a slight paraphrase of Aesop's fox and grapes story. No matter how we talk amongst ourselves, (defeat) could only be completely transparent to intelligent outside observers." *Pentagon Papers*, vol. 3, p. 624; also see p. 657.

... will inevitably be raised."[79] Second, the effort to help an ally, whether successful or not, will not make the desired impression if others believe that it has so drained the defender's power or resolve that it will not repeat the exercise. Thus even had North Vietnam conceded defeat in the early 1970s, it is far from clear that anyone would have expected the United States to send troops abroad under similar circumstances in the near future.[80] Third, results, not the level of effort, will be primary if the country under attack owes its importance to its resources or geographical location.

Finally, the obvious drawback of making a major effort, aside from the direct costs involved, is that if the effort does not succeed, the price the state will pay in terms of its reputation will be greater. That is, after all, the way in which the tactic of commitment is supposed to work. Thus, Secretary of State Cyrus Vance was unpersuaded by National Security Advisor Zbigniew Brzezinski's argument that the United States should move an aircraft carrier task force off the coast of Ethiopia to deter that country from following its defeat of the Somalian forces in the Ogaden with an invasion of its neighbor. If Brzezinski's advice were taken but Somalia was nonetheless invaded, "it would be viewed as a failure of the U.S. task force to do its job, and that failure would impair the credibility of such task forces in future crises elsewhere."[81]

Conclusion

The debacle of Vietnam led to widespread rejection of the domino theory in the academic world and, for a period, among the general public. But it never lost its hold on leaders and the national security bureaucracy. This is not surprising because domino beliefs were not an American invention, have a long pedigree, and are still relevant. The validity of the theory (or really theories, because this chapter has indicated that it comes in a number of variants) can be debated, and elsewhere I have provided some criticisms.[82] When we look at the behavior of a powerful state, the theory can be hard to test because if it is believed, the state will undertake strenuous efforts to avoid limited defeats and only in a few cases, such as Vietnam, will we be able to observe what follows from them. Critics may argue that these fears were overblown and led the state to engage in unnecessary confrontations and conflicts, but these claims rest on unverifiable counterfactuals. It is easier, but of course still not

79 *FRUS 1950*, vol. 7, pp. 151, 153–54.

80 For a critical analysis of this assumption in relation to theories of signaling, see Jervis, "Signaling and Perception," in this volume.

81 Brzezinski, *Power and Principle*, 183.

82 Jervis, "Domino Beliefs and Strategic Behavior," pp. 39–43 in Snyder and Jervis, eds., *Dominos and Bandwagons*.

easy, to gather at least superficial evidence on the proposition that states often act on the domino theory in contesting and even fighting over issues of little intrinsic value. It is then easier to verify that the domino theory is widely held and that it is valid.

Valid or not, we still lack a thorough explanation for why the theory is held. My previous discussion is much more an explication than an explanation. As is the case for many beliefs, the causes are elusive, varied, and complex. It is unlikely that there is one account that will fit all cases. Rather, I suspect both that the causes vary across cases and that most individual instances involve several strands. In the post–World War II era the hold of the Munich analogy was very strong. Perhaps America's inexperience with world politics played a role as well. Without long involvement with great power politics, American leaders may have been attracted to a theory that gave clear and simple guidelines for policy. Revisionists would see darker motives at work, portraying belief in the domino theory as a rationalization for an expansionist policy rooted in the needs of the capitalist economy. The reply, of course, is that the theory was believed because it had a large measure of plausibility and supporting evidence. Reality appraisal more than functional needs was the main driver.[83] The fact that domino beliefs have been held by decision-makers in many countries over quite different periods of time casts doubt on explanations stemming from uniquely American or uniquely capitalist factors.

Although leaders rarely talk about falling dominos today, the question of how interconnected areas and events are remains a central one. Part of the division between analysts who favor a more assertive American policy and those who urge restraint is that the former see multiple interconnections throughout the world such that problems and reductions in American influence in areas or on issues of little intrinsic importance will have significant ramifications. The latter, by contrast, either are skeptical of this and see the world as full of more fire-breaks or believe that local or regional dynamics will produce an equilibrium even (or especially) in the absence of strenuous American efforts. As some of the analysis behind the call for American restraint indicates, dense interconnections can lead to negative as well as to positive feedbacks, and dominos are not the only way in which one event can influence subsequent ones. Nevertheless, in a world in which the United States remains the only superpower, it is not surprising that domino-type reasoning remains.

This does not tell us whether these beliefs are a cause or an effect of policy preferences, or if both can be traced to a third factor. Nor does it tell us why some people see positive feedback, other expect negative feedback, and still

83 For the distinction, see Jervis, "Understanding Beliefs," in this volume.

others see the main determinants of the outcome of the individual disputes as stemming from the particular situation. So I make no pretense to have unraveled all the puzzles here. It seems clear, however, that beliefs about domino dynamics play a large role in a state's foreign policy and are worthy of further analysis.

12

Perception, Misperception, and the End of the Cold War

> We have discovered how much mistrust there was and how many misjudgments there were, and I think this is one of the basic lessons for the future leaders and for the present leaders: Please check two or three times before you make a decision, because the information you have may be wrong, the inclinations may be erroneous, and the advice you receive may not be perfect.
> —ALEXANDER BESSMERTNYKH, SOVIET FOREIGN MINISTER

Even colleagues much younger than I will spend their lifetimes thinking about the origins, course, and end of the Cold War.[1] There is so much to learn that much of what we say now is likely to be quite wrong. In this way, the situation of scholars resembles that of statesmen as described by Alexander Bessertnykh. Our conclusions are not likely to do as much good or as much harm for the world as did those of the decision-makers we are studying, but it is not entirely self-importance that leads us to think that the lessons we learn from the prolonged conflict will influence what is done in the future. In seeking this understanding, our closeness to the events is both a handicap and an advantage. A handicap because we lack the perspective and the still-secret information that our successors will have, and advantage in that we can draw on our own experiences, and more importantly, on the still-vivid memories of the participants.

---

1 Alexander Bessmertnykh is quoted in William Wohlforth, ed., *Witnesses to the End of the Cold War* (Baltimore: Johns Hopkins University Press, 1996), p. 186.

These reports and the recently declassified documents that accompany them say much about the patterns of perception and misperception that characterized the Cold War. Before discussing them, however, I want to note that while this fascinating information can shed at least some light on other fundamental questions, it cannot fully answer them. Most obvious is the issue of the origins of and responsibility for the conflict. Put most crudely, was the United States an expansionist power or was it largely reacting to a perceived Soviet menace? Were its perceptions accurate? Were its responses prudent? If it overperceived the threat and overreacted, is this to be explained by normal genitive biases or was it the product of the need to justify expansionistic impulses by the apparent perception of external menaces? Of course, one can ask the same question of the Soviet Union.

New information will certainly be of value here. For example, learning that Stalin sanctioned the North Korean attack on South Korea makes it hard to see Soviet policy as simply defensive.[2] But multiple interpretations will remain. We are still unsure about the origins of World War I even though all of the archives have been open for years.[3] Arguments about the sources and the motives for American policy at the start of the Cold War are driven not primarily by new documents but by broader intellectual and political trends and perspectives. Of course, we know much more about how American statesmen saw the world and what they were trying to achieve in the late 1940s now that the records are open, but the fact that we can still debate the reasoning behind the American policy implies that even when we have read the Kremlin archives we will not agree on the answers—and perhaps we will not even agree on the questions.

A second and related question of whether the Cold War can be best explained by structure of the international system or by the nature of the states involved is also partly beyond the reach of documents and memories. Proponents of traditional realism argue that foreign policy is a product of the state's external environment. More rigorously and single-mindedly, structural realism argues that in a bipolar system the two dominant states will be adversaries and the resulting configuration will be stable.[4] The United States and the

2 Kathryn Weathersby, "Soviet Aims in Korea and the Origins of the Korean War, 1945–1950; New Evidence from Russian Archives," working paper no. 8, Woodrow Wilson International Center for Scholars, Cold War International History Project, Nov. 1993; Weathersby, "New Findings on the Korean War," *Cold War International History Project Bulletin*, no. 3 (Fall 1993): 1, 14–16; Weathersby, "Korea, 1949–50: To Attack or Not to Attack? Stalin, Kim Sung, and Prelude to War," *Cold War International History Project Bulletin*, no. 5 (Spring 1995): 1–9.

3 Some German documents, presumably incriminating ones, have been destroyed, however: Holger Herwig, "Clio Deceived: Patriotic Self-Censorship in Germany after the Great War," *International Security* 12 (Fall 1987): 1–44.

4 The classic statement is Kenneth Waltz, *Theory of International Politics* (Reading, Mass.: Addison-Wesley, 1979).

Soviet Union were the enemies by position.[5] With only two dominant powers in the system, each could only menace the other. The word "only" has two complementary meanings here: no other state could menace either of them, and each had no choice but to menace the other, because the threat posed by the other was generated not by specific policy but by its very existence as a state that had the capability to challenge if not destroy its rival.

Those who see the basic source of foreign policies as coming from within the state reject this explanation. For them, the Cold War was a clash not of two abstract states but of two differing social systems. Right at the start, after all, Stalin had accurately predicted, "This war is not as in the past; whoever occupies a territory also imposes on it his own social system."[6] The other side of the coin is revealed toward the end of the Cold War, when Gorbachev declared that the West could have faith in the sincerity and the permanence of the changes in Soviet foreign policy because they were accompanied by enormous domestic changes. This argument comes in two main variants, one attributing responsibility for the Cold War to the United States and the other attributing responsibility to the Soviet Union. The latter stems from the Kantian and Wilsonian tradition that argues that democracies are peaceful, or at least do not fight each other. The Soviet Union, by contrast was expansionist because it was a dictatorship, and a country that cannot live at peace with its own people cannot live at peace with the world. Parallel in form but quite different in content is the attribution of the Cold War to American expansionism growing out of the U.S. economic system, on the grounds that a system that is exploitative if not oppressive at home has to be exploitative and repressive abroad if the domestic order is to be maintained. Of course, each of these arguments does not exclude the other—both the United States and the Soviet Union could have been driven to challenge the other because of domestic impulses. Alternatively, the clash could have come about not from the nature of either regime but from the fact that they were very different from one another. Because their governments were based on different forms of legitimacy, the very existence of each challenged the other's right to exist.[7]

Both the way the Cold War ended and the comments by the Soviet participants at the Princeton Conference[8] lend credence to the importance of

5 Raymond Aron, *Peace and War: A Theory of International Relations*, trans. by Richard Howard and Annette Baker Fox (Garden City, N.Y.: Doubleday, 1966), p. 138.

6 Milovan Djilas, *Conversations with Stalin,* trans. Michel B. Petrovich (New York: Harcourt, Brace, and World, 1962), p. 114.

7 For a related argument, see Stanley Hoffmann, "International Systems and International Law," in Klaus Knorr and Sidney Verba, eds., *The International System* (Princeton: Princeton University Press, 1961), pp. 210–15, 223–33.

8 This paper was originally written in response to a conference of Soviet and American officials discussing the end of the Cold War held at Princeton University in 1993. The transcript and

domestic sources of the Cold War, especially those within the Soviet Union. Bessmertnykh argued that the decision to intervene in Afghanistan had been based on ideological rather than strategic considerations and that Gorbachev's "first step" toward ending the Cold War had been to remove "ideology from foreign policy."[9] As Soviet leaders came to place less weight on socialist values, both the importance and the possibility of building socialism in Afghanistan diminished. If socialism was not that different from capitalism—and certainly not much better than it—why spend blood and treasure to establish it? If socialist countries did not necessarily follow the foreign policies different from those of countries with different economic systems, why would establishing socialism abroad aid the Soviet Union? This train of thought was highly subversive. Soviet foreign policy had been underpinned by the assumptions that socialism was morally and economically superior and that the dominant sources of foreign policy were domestic. If international politics was no longer to be seen as a reflection of the class struggle, the basic postulates of Soviet foreign policy had to be called into question. Thus, rather than quibbling over the words, Gorbachev and his domestic critics were engaging in a fundamental dispute when the former argued that national and international interests had primacy over class ones and the latter reasserted the traditional Soviet view.[10]

Evidence from the last years of the Cold War, although not yet definitive, parallels the emphasis placed on ideological changes by the Princeton Conference participants. On the Soviet side, the decline in faith in Marxism-Leninism preceded and produced changes in Soviet foreign policy. The case of Afghanistan has already been noted. More drastic, of course, was the freeing of Eastern Europe. As I will discuss later, Gorbachev does not seem to have expected the results to be as dramatic as they were. But even a willingness to allow a diversity of regimes in those countries would not have been possible without the sense that no one social system was best for all countries and that domestic changes were compatible with a pro-Soviet foreign policy. Furthermore, the basic reorientation of the Soviet policy toward the West was premised on the twin beliefs that countries with different social systems did not

---

subsequent papers can be found in William Wohlforth, ed., *Witnesses to the End of the Cold War* (Baltimore; Johns Hopkins University Press, 1996).

9 For Bessmertnykh's remarks on removing ideology from foreign policy, see ibid., chap. 1; for Afghanistan, see chap. 5. Also see John Mueller, "What Was the Cold War About? Evidence From its Ending," *Political Science Quarterly* 119 (Winter 2004/05): 609–31.

10 Mikhail Sergeevich Gorbachev, *Perestroika: New Thinking for Our Country and the World* (New York: Harper and Row, 1987), pp. 144–48; and idem, speech to the United Nations, December 7, 1988, *Pravda*, December 8, 1988, I-2, reprinted and translated in *Current Digest of the Soviet Press* 40 (January 4, 1989): I-7. Ligachev's views are quoted in Bill Keller, "Gorbachev Deputy Criticizes Soviet Policy Trend," *New York Times*, August 7, 1988.

need to be enemies and that the American hostility toward the Soviet Union was the product not of the capitalist regimes' need to control the world or their fear that socialist states, by their very existence and example, menaced them, but rather stemmed from ill-conceived Soviet policies. The profound shift involved in the adoption of a view that saw the Cold War as unnecessary and mutual security as feasible, epitomized by Gorbachev's December 1988 speech to the United Nations, was made possible by the belief that the problem was Marxism-Leninism, not Western, American or capitalist ideology.

Those who stress the importance of the international structure and a state's external environment are not without replies, however. They could start by noting that whereas Gorbachev saw his predecessors' misguided ideology as much the source of international conflict and argued that a democratized Soviet Union would be peaceful, his UN speech focused on the systemic level. Even more than did Robert McNamara in his speech in San Francisco decrying the arms race a generation earlier, Gorbachev in New York accepted the centrality of the security dilemma. If the attempt by one state to increase its security has the unintended consequence of making others less secure, then understanding this dynamic can lead not only to a fruitful arms control treaty but also to unilateral moves such as the withdrawal of large numbers of Soviet troops from Eastern Europe, which by making the other side more secure can in turn increase the state's own security.[11] Thus, Gorbachev recognized that structural sources of rivalry are hard to overcome even if all of the major states have social systems that are conducive to peace and cooperation.

More fundamentally, those who stress the importance of the state's external environment can argue that the domestic and ideological changes were, if not mere superstructure, at least produced in large measure by external pressures. That is, Gorbachev did not renounce communism as the result of careful intellectual study, nor did the domestic changes occur in a vacuum. Rather, the extent of the domestic failure, the need for drastic change, and Gorbachev's recognition that he had to change Soviet foreign policy in order to carry out internal reforms grew out of the pressures of the external environment. Indeed, Waltz's neorealist argument catches the essence of what happened quite well: the Soviet Union lagged badly behind in the competition with its rival, was in grave danger of "falling by the wayside," and therefore had to emulate the policies, including the domestic policies, of its more successful competitors.[12] To return to the example of Afghanistan, had the West not supported the mujahedeen in a way that allowed those fighters to deprive

11 Indeed, an understanding of these dynamics may have been crucial not only for Gorbachev and his civilian colleagues but also for Soviet military authorities, who, being charged with safeguarding the Soviet Union, had to be convinced that military cuts could decrease rather than increase the chance of war.

12 Waltz, *Theory of International Politics*, pp. 74–77, 127–28.

the Soviet leaders of an easy victory, the imperative to rethink the Soviet position would have been much less.

More broadly, the perception of domestic failure was vivid only because it could be contrasted to what was happening abroad: if the capitalist countries had not been growing as fast as they were, the state of the Soviet economy would not have been seen as so deplorable and few would have argued that liberalization would improve it. Of course, the West was not only a standard against which the success of socialism could be judged but also a rival whose successes compelled matching efforts. As the Princeton Conference participants noted, even when Strategic Defense Initiative (SDI) no longer was seen as a potential grave menace to Soviet security, the kind of technology it embodied epitomized the Soviet Union's inability to compete in areas that were likely to be vital in the future. It was also clear that it would be dangerous if not impossible for Gorbachev to embark on wide-ranging domestic reforms in the absence of much better relations with the West. Trade and technical assistance, if not aid, were necessary, and the domestic groups that opposed perestroika would be greatly strengthened by international tension. Thus the Soviet Union had to end the Cold War not only because it was unable to stay in the competition but also because maintaining hostility toward the West would have prevented those domestic changes that held out some promise of eventually rebuilding Soviet strength.

In this view, while it is true that the end of the Cold War coincided with the change of the Soviet domestic system, the major sources of change were external. The sort of removal of ideology from Soviet foreign policy that the conference participants described was real, but was itself the product of the failure of Cold War policies. Many of the changes in thinking were then rationalizations for change rather than reasons. The decision-makers were not fully aware of this process, and so even the most perceptive memories are less than fully revealing. Motivated biases—the impact that powerful needs have on perceptions and beliefs—were at work, and the sources of the pressures that drove the changes were external.[13] But whether as a cause, an effect, or

13 For discussion of motivated biases, see Jervis, "Understanding Beliefs," in this volume; Irving Janis and Leon Mann, *Decision Making* (New York: Free Press, 1977); Richard Cottam, *Foreign Policy Motivation* (Pittsburgh: University of Pittsburgh Press, 1977); Richard Ned Lebow, *Between Peace and War: The Nature of International Crises* (Baltimore: Johns Hopkins University Press, 1981); Robert Jervis, Richard Ned Lebow, and Janice Stein, *Psychology and Deterrence* (Baltimore: Johns Hopkins University Press, 1985). The latter two books see most sources of motivated bias as stemming from domestic politics, but the basic processes are independent of the source of the needs that drive perceptions. In the Soviet case, Sarah Mendelson stresses the importance of domestic politics, Douglas Blum sees beliefs as more autonomous, and Jeff Checkel takes a position in between: Mendelson, "International Battles and External Wars: Politics, Learning, and the Soviet Withdrawal from Afghanistan," *World Politics* 45 (April 1993): 327–60; Blum, "The Soviet Foreign Policy Belief System: Beliefs, Politics, and Foreign Policy Outcomes,"

both, the reduced ideological distance between the two superpowers was associated with reduced hostility between them as well.

The pattern of changing Western perceptions of threat provides other clues about the degree to which the Cold War was driven by differences in social systems, as contrasted with either bipolar rivalry or specific menacing actions taken by the adversary. From what former Secretary of State George Shultz said, it appears that the United States was more impressed by the renunciation of ideology in Gorbachev's UN speech than by the concrete promises to reduce troop levels in Eastern Europe.[14] But since the introduction of domestic reform in the Soviet Union, changes in foreign policy positions and reductions in military strength all proceeded in fairly close order, separating the impact of each element is difficult. Those who stress material factors could stress the importance of freeing of Eastern Europe in 1989, which eliminated the Soviet threat to Western Europe and the danger of war growing out of a conflict on the continent. The Soviet withdrawals would have ended the Cold War even if it had not been accompanied by significant changes in the Soviet domestic system. Indeed, those who feared Soviet power rather than Soviet ideology should not have been impressed by the latter changes in the absence of the former. But many people were impressed, which provides evidence for the importance of belief about states' domestic systems. Thus, when Ronald Reagan went to Moscow in 1988 Soviet power appeared unchanged, and although the INF Treaty had been signed and the Soviets had begun withdrawing from Afghanistan, Soviet foreign policy behavior had not yet been radically altered. But Reagan's beliefs about the USSR had been. When asked how he could be so friendly toward the "evil empire" he replied, "I was talking about another time, another era."[15]

In at least two other respects, a realist would have trouble understanding Reagan and Gorbachev. Put simply, these two statesmen were not realists.

International Studies Quarterly 37 (December 1993): 373–94; Checkel, "Ideas, Institutions, and the Gorbachev Foreign Policy Revolution," *World Politics* 45 (January 1993): 271–300.

14 See Wohlforth, *Witnesses*, ch. 3.

15 Quoted in Don Oberdorfer, *The Turn: From the Cold War to a New Era* (New York: Poseidon Press, 1991), p. 299. Two aspects of Regan's outlook, documented by Keith Shimko in *Images and Arms Control: Perception of the Soviet Union in the Regan Administration* (Ann Arbor: University of Michigan Press, 1991), esp. pp. 142, 217, 236–38, may have facilitated his openness toward the Soviet Union. First, he was much less pessimistic than many of those in his administration. Although he felt that the United States needed to increase its defense capabilities, he neither believed that the desired goals were out of reach nor shared the belief of many hardliners that negotiation, especially over arms control, would undermine domestic support for his foreign policy. Second—again unlike many other hardliners—he attributed the Soviet-American rivalry not only to the ambitions of the Soviet Union but also to mutual suspicion and incompatible security requirements. Thus, he was more open to the possibility of agreements and better relations than one might think from reading some of his strikingly anti-Soviet pronouncements.

Realists are supposed to seek to ameliorate problems, not solve them. Tally-rand said that a diplomat's motto should be *"pas de zèle,"* and when Dean Rusk was appointed secretary of state he reported to have said that he could be pleased if he finished his term with the world in no worse shape than it was in when he took office. The attitude of Regan and Gorbachev was very different. They thought that they could fundamentally change Soviet-American rela-tions. Reagan initially believed that the main instruments would be strength and firmness; Gorbachev used concessions and accommodation. But more striking than the difference in means was that both sought drastic change. More specifically, the two leaders were not realists in their rejection of nu-clear weapons. All respectable experts believed that such weapons were here to stay; indeed, many—myself included—argued that mutual second-strike ca-pability helped maintain U.S-Soviet peace. Furthermore, the experts thought that it would be foolish to seek to eliminate these weapons or even to limit stockpiles to a very low number. If such an effort were successful, the result would be great instability because the side that cheated just a bit could obtain first-strike capability. The knowledge that this was the case would encourage cheating, even on the part of a country that wanted only to be secure. Rea-gan, and apparently Gorbachev, would have none of this. Thus, Reagan not only yearned for SDI but really did mean to share it with the Soviet Union if it were developed. For Reagan and probably for Gorbachev as well, the desire to abolish nuclear weapons did not stem from prolonged analysis. Rather, it came from the instinctive feeling that, as Reagan told a press conference in 1983, "To look down an endless future with both of us sitting here with these horrible missiles aimed at each other, and the only thing preventing a holo-caust is just so long as no one pulls this trigger—this is unthinkable."[16] The conclusion, of course, may be correct. But realists are supposed to rely on rationality, not feelings.

Living in Different Worlds

The sharing of documents and memories from the Cold War makes it increas-ingly clear that each side lived in its own world. Each thought that its percep-tions were universally valid and failed to realize that others saw a very different world. This is not unusual: it is hard to find any case of international conflict, or even of sustained international interaction, in which each participant was able to fully grasp the other's perceptions.

Of course in the Cold War, as in previous conflicts, each side believed that the other held different values and sought different goals than it did. It is only

16 "Transcript of Press Interview of President at White House," *New York Times*, March 30, 1983.

a slight exaggeration to say that each side saw itself as good and the other as evil; itself as protecting and furthering the best values of mankind and the other as destroying them; itself as honest and moral and the other as deceptive and hypocritical; itself as seeking security and the other as aggressive. But the sense of these deep differences did not make it easier for either side to understand how the other saw the world; indeed, each acted a though the other's deviant values did not prevent the other from sharing some of its rival's basic perceptions. Thus it is not surprising that the Cold War was filled with cases in which once side or the other was taken by surprise. I suspect that only rarely could one side's statesmen write a position paper as the other side would have written it.

The reasons lie in three interrelated perceptual process that characterize international politics. First, *Rashomon* effects are common: different states see the same situation very differently.[17] Because leaders proceed on their own understanding of situations, they will often be in their own perceptual and conceptual worlds. Furthermore, leaders are not likely to understand this and will assume that others see the world the way they do. Second, perceptions by leaders of how their nation is viewed by others are also important.[18] Does the state think that the other side believes that the state is aggressive? That it will retreat in the face of demonstrations of strength? That it is acting on the basis of long-range plans? These perceptions are likely to be major influence on the other's behavior, and so the state needs to grasp them if it is to understand and affect what the other does. These can be called second-order perceptions. Third, behavior is influenced by leaders' perceptions and beliefs about their own nation (self-perceptions).[19] A state that sees itself in decline is likely to see others and to behave very differently from one that conceives of itself as continuing to be strong, if not dominant. Self-images thus often became the battleground for policy. Furthermore, appreciating others' perceptions

17 This also can be true within a state as well. For a striking example, see the account by Greenstein and Immerman of the January 19, 1961, meeting between President Eisenhower and President-elect Kennedy in which three of the participants concluded that Eisenhower was recommending American military intervention in Indochina, one concluded that he was recommending against intervention, and two concluded that he was recommending no recommendation but simply stating contingencies. Fred Greenstein and Richard Immerman, "What Did Eisenhower Tell Kennedy about Indochina? The Politics of Misperception," *Journal of American History* 79 (September 1992): 568–87.

18 Work in marriage counseling has developed protocols to see how accurately each spouse is able to estimate how the other sees him or her. R. D. Laing H. Phillipson, and A. R. Lee, *Interpersonal Perception: A Theory and Method of Research* (New York: Harper and Row, 1976).

19 For an account of debates within a nation's foreign policy establishment about what the nation's self-image should be, see Aaron Friedberg, *The Weary Titan: Britain and the Experience of Relative Decline, 1895–1905* (Princeton: Princeton University Press, 1988).

of the state is especially difficult and painful when this view contradicts the state's self-image.

It is rarely easy for a leader to see that others view her country and the acts she undertakes on its behalf very differently than she sees them. Part of the difficultly is cognitive: adopting a perspective different from one's own calls for mental agility and the ability to interpret information from alternative perspectives, often employing alien concepts. This is one reason why scientific breakthroughs are so difficult.[20] Where self-images are concerned, additional barriers are in place as well. To realize that others see you in a different, and presumably an unflattering light, is to acknowledge the possibility that they are right, or at least that you did something that could have given rise to this impression. Thus, most American leaders and member of the general public have difficulty understanding how sensible and well-motivated people abroad might see the United States as overbearing if not aggressive. It is clear to most Americans that when their country supported foreign dictators there were overriding considerations of national security at stake and the alternative was a violent left-wing regime that would have been worse for the people of the country. To see an alternative interpretation would be to call into question many deeply held beliefs about American life and society, as well as the wisdom of specific policies. It is thus no accident that the citizens of a country who are most critical of its foreign policy usually hold very different beliefs about the government, if not the country as a whole, than do most other citizens, and that Gorbachev and his colleagues changed their views of Soviet society as they carried out radical changes in foreign policy.

Even in the absence of extreme ideological differences, the *Rashomon* effect and related processes can defeat a state's policy, as is shown by two important cases in which American policymakers were taken by surprise: the Japanese attack on Pearl Harbor and the Iranian Revolution. The Japanese and American leaders lived in very different perceptual worlds. Each side interpreted the unfolding events of that year very differently and, to the extent that it paid any attention to the other's interpretations, it saw them as deceptive or as rationalizations. This is part of the reason why neither side was able to predict how its behavior would affect the other. Although American leaders realized that the oil embargo was pushing Japan into a corner and that Japan was therefore likely to strike at its enemies, they could hardly imagine an attack against Pearl Harbor because this would mean total war with the United States, which Japan could not possibly win. The alternative course of action of attacking the Dutch East Indies and Malaya, coupled, if necessary, by a move against the Philippines, made much more sense. But Japanese leaders

20 The classic study is Thomas Kuhn, *The Structure of Scientific Revolutions* (Chicago: University of Chicago Press, 1962).

believed, on the one hand, that a move southward would automatically lead to an American attack against their supply lines from the Philippines, and on the other hand, that faced with immediate defeats, the United States would be willing to lose a limited war. The former belief did not make much sense to the Americans because they knew that it would be difficult for them to attack Japanese forces if the United States itself has not been struck. The latter prediction was, from the American perspective, even more bizarre: the idea that the United States would fight a limited war hardly crossed anyone's mind because it was so discrepant with the American self-image.

Some of the reasons why the United States failed to understand the unrest in Iran in 1978 are to be found in similar cognitive processes. Despite the fact that relations between the United States and the Shah's regime were close and the level of communication was high, neither understood the other and its perceptions. The Carter administration called for both liberalization and stability in Iran but failed to see that its double message was interpreted as confusing, contradictory, and even menacing. To American analysts, the fact that the Shah had not used all the forces at his disposal indicated that he thought he had the situation under control; to the Shah, the fact that America was urging continued liberalization in face of unrest indicated that it was sympathetic to the opposition and perhaps had turned against him. The Americans believed the Shah was strong and decisive; the Shah and his advisors knew that this was not the case, assumed that the Americans knew this, and therefore read strange and disturbing meanings into the American refusal to urge him on. To Iranians, whose history predisposed them to see plots and disguised external interference, a conspiracy among the Shah's enemies—which to an increasing number appeared to include the United States—seemed the best explanation for the unfolding events; American officials were less prone to perceive conspiracies and so could not believe that the Iranians truly were concerned about them.[21]

Indeed, almost every intelligence failure is a mutual and second-order failure. One reason that American analysts did not expect the Soviets to put missiles in Cuba is that they believed that the Soviets knew that the United States would respond very strongly if they did; American leaders did not think that it was necessary to issue explicit deterrent threats to protect Kuwait because, even without carefully considering the situation, they knew that the United States could not permit a successful invasion; in 1967–68 American officials in Vietnam knew that a Viet Cong uprising would lead to a military

21 For further discussion, see Robert Jervis, *Why Intelligence Fails: Lessons from the Iranian Revolution and the Iraq War* (Ithaca: Cornell University Press, 2013), ch. 2; Charles Kurzman, *The Unthinkable Revolution in Iran* (Cambridge: Harvard University Press, 2004); Andrew Cooper, *The Fall of Heaven: The Pahlavis and the Final Days of Imperial Iran* (New York: Henry Holt, 2016).

defeat and so they were taken by surprise by the Tet offensive.[22] In each case the United States made an error because the other side made an error, and that error was at least in part a misjudgment of the United States.

The propensity for people to live in different perceptual worlds is not limited to relations between adversaries. Even under the most propitious circumstances actors may misperceive each other and fail to understand the other's perceptions of them. Thus Richard Neustadt has shown that the two most serious Anglo-American crises of the postwar era (the Suez crisis and Kennedy's cancellation of the Skybolt missile program) were occasioned by a failure of each side to understand the other's interests and perspectives and, even more strikingly, the second-order failure to understand the extent to which the other failed to understand them.[23] Indeed, even people in the same society may reveal the same pattern of perceptual differences: after all, *Rashomon* was not about international politics.[24]

Further evidence of the pervasiveness of these problems, and the propensity for statesmen to underestimate them, is revealed when two countries' records of the same conversation are laid side by side. In the most extreme cases, which are not infrequent, it is hard to believe that the two accounts are reporting the same conversation. In other cases, each participant records more of what he said than of his counterpart's remark, loses crucial nuances, and confidently tells his superiors that his message was received as intended.[25]

As the Cold War came to an end, perceptions converged and statesmen realized that others could see them differently than they saw themselves. As usual, the strong adjusted much less than did the weak; indeed, to a considerable extent, many of the standard American beliefs about the origins and sources of the Cold War were confirmed by what the Soviet leaders said at the end of the conflict. [26] But we should not be too quick to assert the accuracy of various perceptions. Finding and explaining divergences and convergences may be the more appropriate task, at least at this stage.

Most obviously, we want to know whether the two states saw the military balance in the same way.[27] Although more research is needed for a complete

22 James Wirtz, *The Tet Offensive* (Ithaca: Cornell University Press, 1991).

23 Richard Neustadt, *Alliance Politics* (New York: Columbia University Press, 1970).

24 For example, see Greenstein and Immerman, "What Did Eisenhower Tell Kennedy about Indochina?"

25 This conclusion rests on preliminary research I have done on parallel reports on conversations between European diplomats.

26 Much scholarship has similarly moved toward a more orthodox interpretation of the Cold War.

27 For discussion how the Soviets conceptualized some of those questions, see William Wohlforth, *The Elusive Balance: Power and Perceptions during the Cold War* (Ithaca: Cornell University Press, 1993).

picture, it seems clear that in at least some instances both sides tended to engage in "worst case" analysis. The result was that each feared that the other was superior to it in strength, that trends were running against it, and that the other would be likely to exploit this imbalance. In the early 1980s, for example, both the United States and the Soviet Union saw the situation as dangerous and deteriorating. As Bessmertnykh put it,

> In a certain way I was happy to hear the CIA's appraisal of our efforts, because almost the same story was reported to the Soviet government by our own intelligence services.... As for prevailing in a nuclear war, which the United States suspected the Soviet Union believed it might do, I think that in the minds of the Soviet leaders it was completely an opposite picture.... We thought the American idea of "prevailing" in the Cold War might include the possibility of a first strike. So you see the two mirrors, the two reflective situations, which were caused by a tremendous suspicion of each other.[28]

It will be very interesting to learn whether earlier periods in which American leaders felt insecure were also characterized by Soviet perceptions of falling behind or whether there was greater agreement on the state and the meaning of military balance. In 1949–50, for example, American leaders were extremely disturbed about what they saw as growing Soviet strength that would permit aggression. This view, epitomized by NSC-68, was seemingly confirmed by the Korean War. But we now know that while some of the American perceptions of the war were accurate, others were not. It seems clear that the war was started by the North with Stalin's approval, but that the initiative was Kim Il Sung's, with Stalin acceding to his wishes somewhat grudgingly. Furthermore, contrary to what the Americans believed at the time, he did not view this as a test of American resolve and indeed did not think that the United States would respond.[29] Of course, this does not answer the important counterfactual questions of whether Stalin would have seen the United States as weak if it had not fought, and would he have been more adventuresome if the United States had behaved as he expected?[30] The strength

28 See Wolforth, *Witnesses*, ch. 2. The American estimates of Soviet military strength can be found in National Intelligence Estimate 11-3/8-82, excerpted in ibid., 290–309. For later evaluations, see John Hines et al., *Soviet Intentions 1965–1985*, vols. 1 and 2, (Washington D.C.: BDM, September 22, 1995), available at http://nsarchive.gwu.edu/nukevault/ebb285/ and Pavel Podvig, "The Window of Vulnerability That Wasn't: Soviet Military Buildup in the 1970s," *International Security* 33 (Summer 2008): 118–38.

29 The American perceptions at the time are analyzed in Alexander George, "American Policy-Making and the North Korean Aggression," *World Politics* 7 (January 1955): 209–32.

30 The Europeans feared this inference as much as the Americans.

the United States attributed to the Soviet Union was probably not felt by its leaders, however, who I suspect saw the American military posture as stronger and more threatening than the Americans did.

Many Americans were also deeply pessimistic in the late 1950s and early 1960s. Although fears of a "missile gap" were in large part a product of lack of access to highly classified intelligence data (reinforced by Democrats' desires to attack the incumbent Eisenhower administration), the general sense of unease was fueled by more than missile estimates.[31] American domestic institutions seemed weak, American education ineffective, economic growth slow, and American ideals decaying and lacking in appeal abroad. The Soviet Union, by contrast, was seen as growing stronger. The arrival of Soviet second-strike capability would undermine the credibility of the American threat to protect Europe, and the Soviet appeal to the decolonialized states in Africa and Asia seemed great and menacing. Kissinger's stark opening of *The Necessity of Choice* embodies much of the mood of the times: "The United States cannot afford another decline like that which has characterized the past decade and a half. Fifteen years more of a deterioration of our position in the world such as we have experienced since World War II would find us reduced to Fortress America in a world in which we had become largely irrelevant."[32]

Khrushchev hoped to benefit from this American mood, but it is not clear that he thought that it was any more accurate than the American fears of inflated Soviet missile strength, which he deliberately reinforced. His pressures on the West, especially in Berlin, were real, but it has yet to be shown whether they were driven by optimism and feelings of strength or by pessimism and fear of weakness. He needed victories abroad partly to hold together his domestic coalition, and this generated pressures on him to believe that he could wring concessions from the West.[33] It still is not clear that he thought that the world was moving in a desirable direction, however; his frantic efforts indicate a fear that it was not.

Despite the fact that the Cuban missile crisis has been more thoroughly studied than any other episode in the Cold War, much about it remains in dispute. The declassified documents and discussions among the participants reveal the *Rashomon* effect. The symmetry between American deployment of IRBMs in Europe, felt by Americans as clearly defensive and necessary to maintain deterrence and reassure the Europeans, and a Soviet deployment in Cuba seemed obvious to Khrushchev but escaped the attention of most Amer-

---

31 The general question of the causes of moods of optimism and pessimism is a fascinating one that I cannot even begin to answer.

32 Henry Kissinger, *The Necessity for Choice* (New York: Harper and Brothers, 1960), p. 1.

33 Jack Snyder, *Myths of Empire* (Ithaca: Cornell University Press, 1991), ch. 6.

icans.[34] That pressures on the Soviet Union would be increased by the Kennedy administration's defense buildup also seemed implausible to Americans.

The Soviets called these events the Caribbean Crisis. The name is not arbitrary: it argues that the confrontation was caused not by the Soviets placing the missiles in Cuba but by the American threats to Castro. Whether Khrushchev's desire to protect Castro was a major motivation behind the deployment remains unclear, but there is little reason to doubt that the Soviets did believe that Cuba was in danger. This the Americans failed to understand because they did not intend to invade,[35] and they assumed that the Soviets realized this. The result was not only that they overlooked an impulse that might reinforce the Soviet desire to deploy missiles to Cuba, but also that during the crisis they were slow to realize that a pledge not to invade could be a significant inducement to the Soviet Union to withdraw.

Statesmen often fail to understand that they live in their own worlds because they assume that the other has the same information that they do. Most obviously, the leaders of a state that does not seek to threaten others generally does not expect the security dilemma to operate because they believe that their benign intentions are clear to others, who therefore will not feel threatened by the state's security measures. As John Foster Dulles put it, "Khrushchev does not need to be convinced of our good intentions. He knows we are not aggressors and do not threaten the security of the Soviet Union."[36] Similarly, after the Chinese entered the Korean War, Dean Acheson argued that "no possible shred of evidence could have existed in the minds of the Chinese communist authorities about the open [peaceful] intentions of the forces of the United Nations."[37] The United States may be particularly prone to self-righteousness, but it is not unique in assuming that its knowledge and understanding of its own behavior and intentions are both valid and clear to others. Eyre Crowe's famous "Balance of Power" of 1907, which laid out the evidence for German aggressiveness, was built on the premise that Germany understood that England did not threaten legitimate German interests.[38] To take an

---

34 Eisenhower anticipated this response, however, if only in passing: see his remarks quoted in Marc Trachtenberg, *History and Strategy* (Princeton: Princeton University Press, 1990), p. 203.

35 I believe that this is the case despite the fact that covert action and invasion plans were well under way: James Hershberg, "Before 'The Missiles of October': Did Kennedy Plan a Military Strike against Cuba?" *Diplomatic History* 14 (Spring 1990): 163–98.

36 Quoted in Richard Nixon, *Six Crises* (Garden City, N.Y.: Doubleday, 1962), p. 62.

37 Quoted in John Spanier, *The Truman-MacArthur Controversy and the Korean War* (New York: Norton, 1965), p. 97.

38 Eyre Crowe, "Memorandum on the Present State of British Relations with France and Germany," pp. 397–431 in G. P. Gooch and Harold Temperley, eds., *British Documents on the Origins of the War, 1898–1914*, vol. 3, *The Testing of the Entente, 1904–6* (London: His Majesty's Stationery Office, 1928).

earlier case, the skirmishing between France and England in North America developed into the Seven Years' War partly because each side incorrectly thought that the other knew that its aims were sharply limited.[39]

In these cases, self-image was one of the causes of the informational discrepancies. But strong and incorrect assumptions about what the other side must know can operate in the absence of this factor. A good example is provided by one reason why the United States was taken by surprise in the Tet offensive. We usually think that states are taken by surprise because they lack information. In a sense, of course, this must be true. But in this case the United States had information that was too accurate for its own good. That is, the United States was sufficiently well informed about conditions in South Vietnam to know that an enemy offensive would not trigger a mass uprising. The problem came in the next step in the American reasoning: because the Viet Cong and the North Vietnamese had extensive intelligence networks, they too would realize that the offensive could not bring about a revolution. We now know, however, that the latter parties did expect a general uprising; contrary to what the United States assumed, they were quite ill-informed about conditions in the South.[40] While the U.S. failure was not driven by self-image, North Vietnam's may have been: North Vietnam's rulers deeply believed in the justice and popularity of their cause; it would have been not only cognitively difficult but also emotionally painful for them to realize that their support in the South was less than overwhelming and that a "people's war" could not bring victory.[41] The fact that the North's information was in part distorted by motivated bias made it more difficult for the United States to realize that the information it had would not be available to the other side. Even when statesmen can intellectually grasp the fact that the other's perceptions are driven by impulses that they do not share and that they find alien, it is next to impossible for them to get a sense of the emotional power of these biases.

The Princeton Conference reveals two cases in which statesmen were misled by the assumption of informational symmetry. Both sides report that the start of a meeting between Shultz and Gorbachev was very stormy because the latter complained vociferously about a hostile speech that Ronald

39 Practice Higonnet, "The Origins of the Seven Years' War," *Journal of Modern History* 40 (March 1968): 57–90.

40 Wirtz, *Tet Offensive*. Contrary to common belief, the North Vietnamese did not launch their attack in the hope of altering American public opinion, which is in fact what happened. For general discussions of how the North saw the war, see Pierre Asselin, *A Bitter Peace: Washington, Hanoi, and the Making of the Paris Agreement* (Chapel Hill: University of North Carolina Press, 2002) and Lien-Hang Nguyen, *Hanoi's War: An International History of the War for Peace in Vietnam* (Chapel Hill: University of North Carolina Press, 2012).

41 The failure of the North to win the kind of victory that it had sought is perceptively discussed in Timothy Lomperis, *The War Everyone Lost—and Won: America's Intervention in Vietnam Twin Struggles* (Baton Rouge: Louisiana State University Press, 1984).

Reagan had just given. Shultz's response was vague and less than completely satisfying, in part because he and his assistants did not understand what Gorbachev was talking about. Policy had not changed; no major speech by the president had been given. It turned out that in a routine address to Massachusetts Republicans in order to rouse the faithful, Reagan had repeated the old Cold War themes. Presumably he gave it little thought; he certainly had no expectation that it would reach Soviet ears. But modern communications techniques did him in. "The full texts of this and other Reagan speeches, most of which were reported at modest length or less in the U.S. press, were routinely obtained by the Soviet Embassy in Washington and propelled by the latest electronic means to the desks of Polituro members only a few hours after they were made."[42]

The difficulty was that Gorbachev assumed that the speech had a foreign policy purpose.[43] It showed, he said, that "the U.S. administration is not abandoning stereotypes, not abandoning reliance on force, not taking account of the political realities and the interests of others, the balance of interests."[44] Gorbachev further assumed that he and the secretary of state lived in the same informational world: Shultz would know all about the speech and would understand Gorbachev's concerns and react accordingly. Shultz could not, as he explains: "I didn't know what Gorbachev was talking about. I looked over at Colin Powell, the national security advisor ... and said, 'What's he talking about, Colin?' He didn't know about it either."[45]

This incident did not have major effects. The shooting down of a Korean airliner in 1983, and the Soviet defense of that action, did. Later reports confirm what seemed apparent from the public record: American leaders' outrage at the destruction of the airliner was compounded by the Soviet reaction. Far from apologizing, or even claiming that they had made an understandable if unfortunate error, the Soviets went beyond the argument that they were within their rights to shoot down a plane violating their air space and claimed that the aircraft had acted as though it were on a spying mission by taking evasive actions, keeping the running lights extinguished, showing no lights from inside what purported to be a passenger compartment, and failing to respond to tracer fire. The Americans not only knew that these claims were preposterous, they knew that the Soviets knew this, because they were able to read the conversations of the Soviet air defense network. They assumed, as I expect even the most sophisticated observers would have done, that the facts that were known to the local officials had been accurately transmitted

42 Oberdorfer, *The Turn*, 284.

43 This sort of error is quiet common: see Robert Jervis, *Perception and Misperception in International Politics* (Princeton: Princeton University Press, 1976, 2nd ed. 2017), chs. 8–9.

44 Quoted in Oberdofer, *The Turn*, 284.

45 See Wohlforth, *Witnesses*, chap. 4.

up the chain of command to the Politburo. In fact, the report that Ustinov, the defense minister, had given to the Politburo was incorrect on all these points.[46] Whether he meant to mislead his colleagues or whether he himself was being misled by his subordinates is not clear. But in either case, the Soviet behavior is now more comprehensible. Had Ustinov's report been true, there would have been reason to believe that the flight was a provocation if not a security threat. The American claims of outrage would have been hypocritical, if not part of a plot to paint the Soviet Union as evil.

Coming into the Same World

It would be too extreme to say that the end of the Cold War was caused by perceptual convergence. But it does seem that cases of the *Rashomon* effect became fewer in the late 1980s. Three aspects of this that I think were causal as well as symptomatic were discussed by the conference participants. First was the seemingly minor matter of switching from consecutive to simultaneous translation. As Shultz notes about the first meeting with Foreign Minister Eduard Shevardnadze in which this was done, "We got eight hours' work done in four hours. But more important, it allowed there to be conversation. It may be a small point."[47] Small but perhaps not insignificant. It not only allowed listeners to match the speaker's gestures and facial expressions with his words, and so to gain a deeper understanding of what was being said, but also permitted a more natural exchange of views. Informational asymmetries and incorrect assumptions about what the other knows and believes were a bit less likely to survive this environment.

More broadly, the Americans (particularly Shultz) were able to convince their counterparts (especially Gorbachev) that in the modern era information and knowledge were power, that a freer flow of information between East and West would benefit both sides, and that the Soviet Union could not thrive internally unless it utilized more and more honest information. Many Soviet policymakers were aware that the information they received from the bureaucracy was suspect. Thus Shevardnadze's assistant, Sergei Tarasenko,

---

46 See ibid., ch. 3. The report of the Politburo can be found in ibid., 295–303. Similarly, Pavel Palazchenko noted that "in some U.S. statements there was an implication that the plane was shot down knowingly; that they knew that it was a passenger plane, not just deliberately but knowingly. I don't think that there was enough information for the United States to make that statement or even a statement with that implication. And that further aggravated the overall mutual suspicion" (see ibid., 66).

47 Shultz made this observation in his opening remarks at the Princeton Conference. Also see Shultz, *Turmoil and Triumph: My Years as Secretary of State* (New York: Scribner's, 1993), p. 573. For further commentary on the effects of simultaneous translation, see Wohlforth, *Witnesses*, ch. 1.

notes his habit, upon arriving at his office, "of listening to a BBC broadcast ... just to hear the world news."[48] The Chernobyl catastrophe had great impact not only because the damage was a vivid reminder of what a nuclear war would do, but also because it proved extremely difficult for the Soviet leaders to learn what had happened from their own bureaucracies: the West often provided faster and more accurate information. This must have alerted Gorbachev and his colleagues to the possibility that in other instances as well the internal information he was receiving about both the West and his own country was not accurate.

Most generally, of course, the end of the Cold War coincided with democratization and glasnost. Although this was not a central topic of the Princeton Conference, it is clear that foreign policy change and the desire for better information went hand in hand. An attitude of openness, of testing one's ideas against evidence, of considering alternatives, and of developing conflicting sources of information was perhaps a necessary condition for seeing that previous Soviet policies were self-defeating, in part because they were based on inadequate perspectives. A willingness not only to try to understand Western points of view but also to consider their validity both supported and was supported by glasnost. Without these efforts to see the world differently, Gorbachev could not have thought it possible to end the Cold War or developed strategies for doing so.

This is not to say that all his beliefs proved to be accurate. Indeed, many of his crucial decisions were based on incorrect premises. Although he saw how deep the domestic problems ran, he underestimated the difficulties of reform from above and believed that the Soviet system not only required but also could survive radical reforms. Similarly, Gorbachev did not understand that pushing the Eastern European countries to liberalize would result not in their putting into place the kind of system he was seeking in the Soviet Union, but in the end of communism in those countries. Most Western observers knew that the East European regimes remained in place only because of fear and the threat of force, and so were confused by what Gorbachev was doing, but Bessmertnykh explains that Gorbachev expected the Eastern Europeans to "change their systems, but ... not necessarily ... that there would be a very deep breakdown in the Soviet-East European relationship. He believed that the reform would unite us more than any other kind of ties."[49] But Tarasenko argues that by the time the Solidarity government took office in Poland in August 1989 he and his colleagues foresaw not only the revolutions but the partial breakup of the Soviet Union as well.[50] I suspect that we will never have

48 Wohlforth, *Witnesses*, ch. 3.
49 Ibid., ch. 3.
50 Ibid., ch. 4.

a definitive answer to this question, in part because different people had different expectations and the same person may have believed one thing on a cognitive level and another on a more instinctive or emotional one. Nevertheless, there is much to the statement by Bessmertnykh with which I began this chapter. Decision-makers often assume that the information they receive is correct and think that their way of seeing the world is the only possible one. They are likely to live in a world that is quite different from that of their counterparts. Often the first step toward dealing with serious conflicts is to understand this. But there is a tension if not a paradox here. The realization that information may be incorrect and that *Rashomon* effects are possible may reduce a statesman's confidence in his ability to chart a new course. Fortunately, the leaders at the end of the Cold War were both confident and willing to try to live in a common world.

INDEX

Hun Sen, 119
Hungary, 97, 250

ICBM (intercontinental ballistic missile), 58
    Atlas missiles, 44
    Minuteman missiles, 44
IDF (Isareli Defense Force), 80. *See also*
    Israel
Iklé, Fred, 90
imperialism, 65, 66, 175, 187
India, 10, 93, 122, 212, 216, 232, 245, 251, 252
Indonesia, 110
intelligence community (IC), 43, 138, 152,
    223
intermediate-range ballistic missiles
    (IRBM), 254, 274
intermediate-range nuclear forces (INF),
    242, 267
Iran, 18, 27, 37, 83, 159, 160, 161, 198, 213,
    214, 220, 247, 252, 256, 271
    Iranian Nuclear Weapons, 31, 214
    Iranian Revolution, 9, 270
Iran-Iraq war, 161
Iraq, 16, 18, 24–26, 28, 31, 33, 136, 137,
    138–42, 151–53, 155–58, 160, 164, 166,
    172, 214, 223
Islam, 16, 175
Israel, 27, 91, 94, 95, 101, 152, 242, 252
    Israeli intelligence, 80
    Israeli Air Force, 69

Japan, 6, 18, 23, 24, 27, 32, 51, 79, 80, 94, 117,
    159, 191, 192, 194, 195, 201, 213, 229, 243,
    245, 253, 257, 270, 271
Johnson, Lyndon, 45, 148, 154, 156, 164, 182,
    183
Joll, James, 19
Jones, Paula, 112

Kahn, Herman, 52
Kahneman, Daniel, 8, 63, 67, 69, 72, 76, 80,
    81, 85
Kantian tradition, 263
Kaplan, Morton, 36, 129
Katyn massacre, 117
Kennan, George, 246, 253
Kennedy, John, 44, 87, 131, 153, 158, 180,
    209, 220, 231, 232, 240, 272
Keynes, John Maynard, 148
Khrushchev, Nikita, 103, 117, 158, 163, 180,
    181, 182, 231, 239, 274, 275
Kissinger, Henry, 19, 56, 93, 149, 150, 157,
    161, 164, 171, 184, 185, 240, 245, 248,
    251–53, 274

Korea, 93, 117, 119, 234, 239, 246, 248, 256,
    277
    Korean airliner, 117, 277
    Korean War, 93, 133, 201, 245, 248,
        256, 257, 273, 275
Kosovo, 114, 154, 155
Kosygin, Aleksei, 171
Kotkin, Stephen, 171
Kurds, 27
Kuwait, 143, 252, 271

Larson, Deborah, 34, 35
Lebanon, 28
Lebow, Richard Ned, 31, 122, 212
LeMay, Curtis, 95
Ligachev, Yegor, 187
Lippmann, Walter, 33, 246
Ludendorff, Erich, 90

Macdonald, Douglas, 240
Machiavelli, 42, 130, 176; Machiavelli's
    Fortuna, 69
Mannheim, Karl, 36
March, James, 50
Market Garden, Operation, 160
Marshall Plan, 130
Marx, Karl, 36, 125, 187
    Marxism, 20, 33, 115, 129, 172, 179,
        264, 265
Massachusetts, 277
Matsu, 256
Mayaguez, 70, 200
McCain, John, 155
McCone, John, 163,
McNamara, Robert, 159, 218, 265
McNaughton, John, 208, 256
Mearsheimer, John, 127
Middle East, 16, 24, 28, 95, 152, 160, 171,
    172
Milosevic, Slobodan, 37, 154, 155
Montgomery, Bernard, 160
Morgenthau, Hans, 126, 127
Moscow, 184, 239, 248, 267
Munich analogy, 11, 259
Murrow, Edward R., 16
Mussolini, Benito, 243

National Security Council (NSC), 150, 162,
    220, 273
NATO, 44, 52, 59, 242, 252
Nazi Germany, 117, 120, 121, 163, 174. *See also*
    Germany; Hitler
Nehru, Jawaharlal, 122
neorealism, 179

GPSR Authorized Representative: Easy Access System Europe - Mustamäe tee 50, 10621 Tallinn, Estonia, gpsr.requests@easproject.com